A Social History of Tennis in Britain

From its advent in the mid to late nineteenth century as a garden-party pastime to its development into a highly commercialised and professionalised high-performance sport, the history of tennis in Britain reflects important themes in Britain's social history. In the first comprehensive and critical account of the history of tennis in Britain, Robert J. Lake explains how the game's historical roots have shaped its contemporary structure, and how the history of tennis can tell us much about the history of wider British society.

Since its emergence as a spare-time diversion for landed elites, the dominant culture in British tennis has been one of amateurism and exclusion, with tennis sitting alongside cricket and golf as a vehicle for the reproduction of middle-class values throughout wider British society in the twentieth and twenty-first centuries. Consequently, the Lawn Tennis Association has been accused of a failure to promote inclusion or widen participation, despite steadfast efforts to develop talent and improve coaching practices and structures. Robert J. Lake examines these themes in the context of the global development of tennis and important processes of commercialisation and professional and social development that have shaped both tennis and wider society.

The social history of tennis in Britain is a microcosm of late-nineteenth and twentieth-century British social history: sustained class power and class conflict; struggles for female emancipation and racial integration; the decline of empire; and Britain's shifting relationship with America, continental Europe and the Commonwealth nations. This book is important and fascinating reading for anybody with an interest in the history of sport or British social history.

Robert J. Lake is a faculty member in the Department of Sport Science at Douglas College, Canada. His research centres on the history and sociology of tennis, particularly related to social class, gender, nationalism, social exclusion, coaching and talent development.

Routledge Research in Sports History

The *Routledge Research in Sports History* series presents leading research in the development and historical significance of modern sport through a collection of historiographical, regional and thematic studies which span a variety of periods, sports and geographical areas. Showcasing ground-breaking, cross-disciplinary work from established and emerging sport historians, the series provides a crucial contribution to the wider study of sport and society.

Available in this series:

1 *Representing the Sporting Past in Museums and Halls of Fame*
Edited by Murray G. Phillips

2 *Physical Culture and Sport in Soviet Society Propaganda, Acculturation, and Transformation in the 1920s and 1930s*
Susan Grant

3 *A Contemporary History of Women's Sport, Part One Sporting Women, 1850–1960*
Jean Williams

4 *Making Sport History Disciplines, Identities and the Historiography of Sport*
Edited by Pascal Delheye

5 *A Social History of Tennis in Britain*
Robert J. Lake

A Social History of Tennis in Britain

Robert J. Lake

LONDON AND NEW YORK

First published 2015
by Routledge

2 Park Square, Milton Park, Abingdon, Oxon OX14 4RN
711 Third Avenue, New York, NY 10017, USA

Routledge is an imprint of the Taylor & Francis Group, an informa business

First issued in paperback 2016

Copyright © 2015 Robert J. Lake

The right of Robert J. Lake to be identified as author of this work has been asserted by him in accordance with sections 77 and 78 of the Copyright, Designs and Patents Act 1988.

All rights reserved. No part of this book may be reprinted or reproduced or utilised in any form or by any electronic, mechanical, or other means, now known or hereafter invented, including photocopying and recording, or in any information storage or retrieval system, without permission in writing from the publishers.

Notice:
Product or corporate names may be trademarks or registered trademarks, and are used only for identification and explanation without intent to infringe.

British Library Cataloguing in Publication data
A catalogue record for this book is available from the British Library

Library of Congress Cataloging-in-Publication Data
Lake, Robert (Assistant Professor of Kinesiology and Physical Education)
  A social history of tennis in Britain / Robert J. Lake.
    pages   cm. – (Routledge Research in Sports History)
  Includes bibliographical references and index.
  1. Tennis–Great Britain–History. 2. Tennis–Social aspects–Great Britain.
  I. Title.
  GV1002.95.G7L35 2015
  796.3420941–dc23
  2014016816

ISBN 978-0-415-68430-9 (hbk)
ISBN 978-1-138-69531-3 (pbk)

Typeset in Sabon
by Out of House Publishing

For Shuv

Contents

Acknowledgements ix
List of abbreviations xi

Introduction 1

1 'A highly Christian and beneficent pastime': the emergence of lawn tennis in late nineteenth century Britain 7

2 Pat-ball and petticoats: representations of social class and gender in early lawn tennis playing styles, etiquette and fashions 24

3 Social aspiration, social exclusion and socialites: clubs, tournaments and "pot-hunting" in pre-war lawn tennis 41

4 The LTA's struggle for legitimacy: early efforts in talent development, coaching and the retention of amateurism 57

5 British tennis as an imperial tool: international competitions, racial stereotypes and shifting British authority 69

6 Reconciliation and consolidation: early struggles for British lawn tennis in the aftermath of war 92

7 'New people' and 'new energy': advances for women and children amidst British decline 106

8 'Demand for the game was insatiable': interwar developments in club/recreational tennis 122

Contents

9 "The Goddess" and "the Monarch": Lenglen, Tilden and the "Amateur Problem" in lawn tennis 134

10 Developments for professional coaches and the early (failed) push for "open" tournaments 150

11 New British success and renewed issues of amateurism in the 1930s 162

12 'We must face the hard facts that confront us': early post-war recovery efforts in British tennis 177

13 Shifting attitudes toward talent development, coaching, commercialism and behavioural etiquette in post-war British tennis 191

14 The enduring amateur–professional dichotomy and the new struggle for authority in world tennis 213

15 "All whites" at Wimbledon? The achievements of Gibson, Ashe and Buxton amidst shifting race relations in Britain 237

16 'Particularly concentrated upon the boys': persistent struggles for women in post-war tennis 247

17 'A sporting event as much as a social phenomenon': nationalism, commercialism and cultural change at Wimbledon 265

Conclusion: Continuity and change in the social history of tennis in Britain and future directives for the LTA 288

Index 298

Acknowledgements

At the elite level, tennis is essentially a team sport. It is played by individuals, more often than not one-on-one, but, like boxing, in every corner are handfuls of people working alongside a competitor to ensure he or she has all the resources necessary to do their best. In many ways, this has been my experience writing this book, which, naturally, would not have progressed so smoothly or been such a wonderful experience had it not been for the dozens of individuals assisting me at key moments along the way, whether that be for material, intellectual, or moral support.

I must first acknowledge the staff at the Sir Kenneth Ritchie Library at the All England Lawn Tennis Club, and in particular Audrey Snell, Alan Little and Kay Crooks, who supported me throughout the ongoing data-collection phase. I have some wonderful memories of my time spent trawling through the extensive library, putting you each to work at various stages. Thank you again for your kindness, generosity and willingness to assist.

Throughout the writing process, Andy Lusis became my go-to-guy for historical information on tennis clubs. His excellent book on the history of tennis in Nottinghamshire demonstrated good local tennis history and I am indebted to his consistent help in many areas where he was able to provide statistics and other information for my use.

My reviewers, Martin Polley and Marcus Hunt, provided excellent support and guidance in the final stages, and I have been particularly blessed to have worked with Simon Whitmore, the Commissioning Editor from Routledge, who from our very first conversation over five years ago offered sound advice and encouragement that has culminated in the completion of this book.

I would also like to acknowledge the following people for their assistance, providing documents, insight or other tangible and intangible forms of guidance that I benefitted from over the course of researching and writing this book: Malcolm Maclean, Stephen Wenn, Richard Holt, Catherine Budd, Bill McTeer, David Dee, Erik Jensen, Martin Roderick, Mike Courey, Sam Clark, Tim Elcombe, Chris and Sue Elks, Jonathan Blunt, Richard Jones, Ian Wellard, Dion Georgiou, Fiona Skillen, Carol Osborne, Mark Falcous, Kevin Jefferys, Frank Galligan, Janice Forsyth, Matt Llewellyn, Dominic Bliss, Ben

Swann, Thomas Turner, Neil Carter, David Gilbert, Wray Vamplew, Alex Channon, Mark Eys, Adam Metzler, Jaime Schultz, and Laura Misener.

Lastly, but certainly mostly, I would like to thank my close friends and family, and in particular my wife Siobhan and two daughters Aoife and Carys for their unending love and support throughout this project.

Abbreviations

AELTC	All England Lawn Tennis Club
AELTCC	All England Lawn Tennis & Croquet Club
AIS	Australian Institute of Sport
ALT	*American Lawn Tennis* (magazine)
ASI	*Amateur Sport Illustrated* (magazine)
ATA	American Tennis Association
ATP	Association of Tennis Professionals
BOA	British Olympic Association
CCPR	Central Council for Physical Recreation
CPC	Coaching Professional Committee
FA	Football Association
FFT	Fédération Française du Tennis
FIFA	Fédération Internationale de Football Association
GAA	Gaelic Athletic Association
ILTF	International Lawn Tennis Federation
IMG	International Management Group
IOC	International Olympic Committee
ITF	International Tennis Federation
LT&B	*Lawn Tennis & Badminton* (magazine)
LT&C	*Lawn Tennis & Croquet* (magazine)
LTA	Lawn Tennis Association
LTAA	Lawn Tennis Association of Australia
LTF	Lawn Tennis Foundation
MIPTC	Men's International Professional Tennis Council
NTL	National Tennis League
PCC	Professional Contact Committee
SI	*Sports Illustrated* (magazine)
TPI	*Tennis Pictorial International* (magazine)
USLTA	United States Lawn Tennis Association
USNLTA	United States National Lawn Tennis Association
VS	Virginia Slims

WCT	World Championship Tennis
WITF	Women's International Tennis Foundation
WT	*World Tennis* (magazine)
WTA	Women's Tennis Association
WTT	World Team Tennis

Introduction

At 5.24pm on the 7th of July 2013, as the world's number-one tennis player Novak Djokovic watched his forehand crash into the net, the Scotsman Andy Murray and millions around the world celebrated. Commentators, journalists and fans alike were unable to restrain themselves from noting the historic importance of this moment; the ghost of Fred Perry had been laid, as Murray became the first British male to win the Wimbledon singles title since 1936. Oliver Holt from the *Daily Mirror*, in a Special Champion Souvenir entitled *Magnificent Murray: History Maker* perhaps captured it best:

> When Murray brought closure to the 77-year quest ... it was a time for farewells. Farewell to those agonised cries of 'C'mon Tim' that were the shrill accompaniment to Tim Henman's quartet of near misses. Farewell to the doomed annual lionisation of also-rans like Jeremy Bates, Buster Mottram and John Lloyd. Farewell to the memories of Roger Taylor's three semi-final defeats in the late 60s and early 70s and Mike Sangster's in 1961. Farewell to the sensation of hearing the name Perry, who won the men's title three times between 1934 and 1936, and feeling its stinging reproach. And, best of all, farewell to the idea that British tennis is for losers and spoiled little rich kids.
>
> (Holt 2013:9)

The BBC reported record-setting figures that attested to the great significance of Murray's victory: an estimated 17.3 million viewers in Britain watched the televised final; in the match's closing stages, eight out of ten UK top trending topics on Twitter were Murray-related, which equated to 120,000 "tweets" per minute. Congratulatory messages from Ewan McGregor, Gary Lineker, Boris Johnson, Kenny Dalglish, Jessica Ennis and Lennox Lewis, among countless other celebrities, attested to the national significance of his achievement. Throughout the Championship fortnight, Murray's popularity had soared; during the second week alone, more than 230,000 new Facebook fans were added to Murray's page. By the end of the year, he was able to add BBC's coveted Sports Personality of the Year award to his 2012 US Open and 2013 Wimbledon trophies and 2012 London Olympic Gold medal, garnering 56 per cent of the nation's vote.

The huge amount of attention his achievement received was evidence enough of how far Murray himself had progressed throughout his career. In 2005, the esteemed Wimbledon referee, Alan Mills, mentioned Murray alongside another talented upstart, Miles Kasiri, as two young British players to watch for the future. Like seemingly so many of his contemporaries, however, Kasiri's early successes, which included reaching the 2004 Junior Wimbledon final, were not repeated on the senior tour. Murray, conversely, proved any cynics wrong by building on his 2004 Junior US Open title by climbing into the world's top 100 within just 15 months, and into the world's top 20 by August 2006. His successes at the highest competitive levels in 2012 and 13 were a reminder of just how many home-grown players had succeeded in disappointing British tennis fans, who were arguably some of the most expectant of home success in the world. For many, Murray's victory spelled redemption, satisfying that crippling and perhaps unrealistic but nonetheless ever-pervasive belief of entitlement. The immutable thought is: 'Tennis was created in Britain and we should lead the world at it'.

It is an indisputable fact that tennis matters to the British public, and the Wimbledon Championships provide an annual reminder. The fascination with tennis, and Wimbledon most specifically, is not so much about the possibility of witnessing home success as about relishing the occasion itself. Wimbledon is a quintessential British institution, and as a sporting venue, the All England Lawn Tennis Club (AELTC) ranks alongside Lords, Wembley and Twickenham as a bastion of British historical sporting significance. Through the stylish design of its physical environment and deep-rooted cultural connection to the Victorian-era garden party, it has managed to sustain public interest and its privileged social position in Britain for decades. Wimbledon's cachet stretches right back to the first men's Championships in 1877, and though the event and club itself has changed markedly to the point of it being almost unrecognisable from its embryonic form – indeed, the actual site of Wimbledon was relocated in 1922 – key aspects of its culture, which have also shaped British tennis as a whole, have been retained.

Within the various contexts of social change and continuity, one can read the social history of tennis in Britain as a historical case-study analysis of the rise and fall of British sporting prowess. In this respect, tennis shares a history with countless other sports played extensively in Britain, particularly those with a broadly middle-class following, like cricket, rugby union, athletics and golf. Periods of British success in tennis have often corresponded to eras of dominance in other sports, and at times they have also reflected British supremacy on a global-political scale. At times, the reverse was also true. The late Edwardian era and after, for example, witnessed a transfer of sporting dominance from Britain to the United States, which also corresponded with trends in athletics and rowing. Interwar austerity and melancholy transferred to sporting mediocrity, yet challenges to the British-inspired amateur ethos were evident in new playing styles and the increasing seriousness afforded to playing practices and overall success. Cricket's "bodyline bowling" incident in 1932–33 highlighted controversial advances in British training methods and tactics, while professionalising developments in tennis arrived at that time in the form of Fred Perry, who benefitted undoubtedly from the new opportunities for general participation and advancement that arrived as tennis underwent a process of democratisation after the war. The decline of Britain's fortunes in the post-war period, for both male and female players, was matched also by challenges to English supremacy in football. Moreover, it appears the historic 1966 World Cup win helped inspire British tennis administrators to "go it alone" and defy international sanctions by staging an "open" Wimbledon in 1968, accessible to both amateurs and professionals for the first time. Concurrent global developments in civil rights for ethnic minorities and equal rights for women around this time were also brought to bear upon tennis in Britain, as Wimbledon remained a key site for the manifestation of such power struggles in sport, and numerous British players were implicated to various extents in the proceedings. The largest demonstration of any kind occurred in 1973 as a consequence of a conflict between the embryonic players union and the beleaguered international governing body, which resulted in an almost comprehensive boycott by the biggest male stars. The strength of Wimbledon's aura and cultural significance as an institution in itself was revealed by the huge crowds and vast profits that were experienced nevertheless.

Global socio-political movements were also brought to bear upon developments throughout the 1970s, 80s and 90s, which transformed tennis into a hugely popular, revenue-generating business, where jet-setting, globetrotting players became millionaires alongside the swelling host of "partners" that influenced the sport during this period, including corporate sponsors, television networks, players' agencies and management groups. The numerous power struggles that emerged between various factions each competing for profits or administrative control suggests the great significance that such power wielded. Quite simply, if the rewards had not been so great, the sport's administrative and financial structures would have remained far more rudimentary. In a British context, the 1990s and 2000s represented a sharp turnaround in terms of overall administrative objectives. The outcomes of the mass-participation movement, though it would have contributed notably to the strength of club tennis and to the general population's health and well-being, had produced little of ostensible returnable value to the elite level. Growing Wimbledon profits throughout this period afforded the undertaking of increasingly comprehensive talent-development initiatives, which also included the construction of an impressively grand and expensive national training centre, which was finally opened in 2007.

This book concerns itself with the social history of tennis in Britain, which stretches far beyond Wimbledon and into the clubs and tournaments that constitute and have always constituted the "bread and butter" of British tennis, and the millions of people who play, teach, watch, administrate, invest in, write about, study or simply follow the sport. A key objective is to attempt to articulate how this history can be read as a social history of Britain more generally from around the 1870s to the present day. It seeks to investigate what makes events and developments in British tennis a matter of importance around the world, what makes the sport globally important to people in Britain, and why achieving success at it has become a (sometimes painful) national obsession. In what areas and to what extent have developments in the social history of tennis in Britain played a significant, though likely surreptitious, hidden or taken-for-granted, role in broader social movements or historical processes? What key socio-cultural aspects of tennis that characterised its earliest forms have remained today? At first glance, one can point to its middle or upper-middle-class following; its ostensible gender parity, but with masked deeper-lying inequalities between the sexes; its predominant white British playing demographic; its superficial connections with British nobility and royalty; its development driven by the manpower of the voluntary sector, manifested through clubs; its cultural connections with imperialism and nationalism, and ostensible links with cultural ideals of "Britishness" or "Englishness"; and its rule structure that presupposes the voluntary adherence to sportsmanship ideals, "fair play" and behavioural etiquette.[1]

The social history of tennis in Britain represents more than a story of the leading players or key events that made newspaper headlines, but also what went on behind the scenes. Outside of the AELTC's gates, in the thousands of clubs where tennis is less an industry or a commercial enterprise and more a summer recreation, a means to develop business contacts, maintain fitness levels, spend time with friends, find a suitable marriage partner, or simply while away an afternoon in the sunshine, the story of its historical development is equally compelling. Moreover, the challenges and opportunities ordinary people faced with regard to access, education and talent development in the sport, alongside seemingly mundane but telling considerations like how to dress for an afternoon's play; how to join a local club; how to adjust performance according to an opponents' age or ability to ensure everyone's enjoyment; or how to converse with and impress established club members, did often reveal deep-rooted structures of social class, gender, sexuality, race/ethnicity, religion or national identity. Understanding these complex connections and demonstrating an ability to critically analyse rather than merely celebrate the subject is arguably the key to writing good social history and remains the underlying objective of this text. While tennis is honoured and praised, it is also challenged and criticued, and so too are the people who have run and played the sport throughout its existence and their overall attitudes, beliefs, values and actions.

The early period of tennis history, in the mid to late Victorian era, has often been written as though the security and future prosperity of the game itself was assured, in the sense that it was bound to "take on" and "take off" like we know it eventually did. One might also assume the sport's historical development was a simple one-directional narrative of fairly *constant* progress: from its humble beginning, its rules were standardised, players were recruited, clubs were formed, tournaments were organised, and the sport spread to all corners of the globe. The reality, however, was that tennis developed unsteadily and moved through a number of key phases where its progress was threatened. Until the early 1900s, the conflicting newspaper and magazine reports from leading lawn tennis literary commentators demonstrated how precarious the sport's position was among a discerning and ruthless upper-middle class, who could choose to indulge in a growing plethora of other leisure activities.

Tennis progressed through several other dark phases, including the first and second world wars, the economic crisis of the early 1930s, post-war austerity in the late-1940s/early-1950s era, the social, cultural and political unrest of the 1960s and 70s, and the subsequent economic downturn into the 1980s. Throughout such phases of societal instability, the sports' administrators fought to sustain a positive image despite the fairly constant emergence of issues related to or reflected by these broader social developments, such as gender inequity, racial intolerance, corruption and hypocrisy, and economic insolvency. Throughout history, for the millions of people that played tennis recreationally, millions more were denied these opportunities; for the handfuls of top British players fulfilling their dreams of playing at Wimbledon, countless others never had the chance to develop their talents. For the thousands of clubs that opened their doors with renewed enthusiasm each spring, some of them with improved facilities or more members than the previous one, many others were forced to keep theirs closed because their land was usurped by the council or an unforgiving landlord, they were forced to sell up because of falling membership numbers, or they moved or merged with another club or changed their emphasis away from tennis, perhaps as a distant outcome of some wider societal development.

For sure, the endless possibilities of play, stroke production and tactics, alongside the seemingly interminable production of interesting on-court "personalities" in the major tournaments, meant tennis from its humble beginnings seemed to attract considerable attention wherever and whenever it was played. With the advent of new media in the interwar years, its social position was cemented as a quick and exciting sport that demanded a high level of skill mastery and tactical acumen, while simultaneously providing for even the most advanced players limitless opportunities for improvement. Into the twenty-first century, players and their coaches continue to experiment with new strokes, shots and tactics, with outcomes assisted in part by technological developments in racket production alongside racket-string, tennis ball and playing surface composition. Thus, the sports' dynamic practical features have ensured its survival over the years but, undeniably and very importantly, often to a fairly narrow demographic. In this book, key themes of gender, social class, race/ethnicity and national identity are investigated, to present the changing social composition of tennis players, administrators and fans over time and to explore changes to key features of its play, rule structure, behavioural etiquette, and overall approaches toward coaching, talent identification and development, commercialism, amateurism/professionalism and political involvement.

Note

1. Where appropriate, reasonable efforts have been made to use the correct terms, either England/English or Britain/British, but it was evident that in many cases where the terms were used in published materials, particularly prior to WWII, the term England/English was taken to mean Britain/British.

Bibliography

Holt, O. (2013). How Andy Finally Brought British Tennis Home. In C. M. Alen Jewell, *Magnifi ent Murray: History Maker* (pp. 6–10). London: Trinity Mirror.

1 'A highly Christian and beneficent pastime'

The emergence of lawn tennis in late nineteenth century Britain

The Victorian and Edwardian eras in Britain represented a period regarded commonly as a tumultuous turning point in class relations. The deep-rooted, secure and widely accepted political and social dominance of the aristocracy gave way to increasing status competition between themselves and the insurgent middle classes (Huggins 2008). The Great Reform Act of 1832 and the Corn Laws repeal of 1846 set in motion the decline in aristocratic authority and brought what many believed was the 'zenith of middle-class political power' throughout the mid-Victorian period, ushering in a period of relative peace, stable class relations and political consensus during the third quarter of the nineteenth century (Cannadine 1999:121). Further Parliamentary Reform Acts in 1867 and 1884/5, which expanded the electorate from 1.3 to 5.6 million men, however, forced the landed aristocracy, and the Conservatives, to loosen their unequivocal grip on political power. Particularly from around 1885 onwards, peerages were offered in far greater numbers to the bourgeoisie; 'some people looked on their arrival as new blood; others maintained that it was a prostitution of honours', argued Bédarida (1979:129). The House of Lords nevertheless remained chiefly hereditarily empowered and Tory-dominated, while the House of Commons underwent a far quicker and more notable change. After the 1906 General Election loss to the Liberals and, with 29 seats, the insurgence of Labour as the 'second party in the state' (Cannadine 1999:131), aristocratic power was weakened still further to the extent that by 1910, they constituted just one in seven Members of Parliament (Bédarida 1979). Moreover, the 1911 Parliament Act facilitated the transfer of decision-making power away from the House of Lords to the House of Commons, and removed the power of veto from the former.

These developments that represented the decline in traditional hierarchies of political power were the culmination of decades of shifting class relations, which began toward the end of the Industrial Revolution, when urbanisation and the damaging effects of an agricultural depression left land ownership, once the basis of aristocratic wealth and 'the prime source of authority, prestige and influence', now increasingly a mere status symbol (Bédarida 1979:25). The potential for wealth to be accrued through white-collar jobs in business, commerce and industry had become more lucrative and dynamic and those who exploited it best, the expanding and socially aspirational upper-middle class of bankers, city merchants, successful industrialists, factory, railway and public works owners and magnates, alongside some of the most successful professionals in law and medicine, had the keys to become Britain's new ruling class. This position they assumed with enthusiasm, confidence, assertiveness and a fresh sense of entitlement, yet their quest for supreme authority remained incomplete, because they often deferred to the established aristocracy in matters of lifestyle, tastes and cultural values. Bédarida (1979:46) elaborated:

> Grand or not, the nobility constituted the natural elite in the eyes of the vast majority. Everything encouraged this reverence – social pressure, education, institutions and the many networks that encouraged a sense of dependence among both the humblest and most sophisticated. This applies as much to the spontaneous respect shown by servants … to the vanity of bourgeois parvenus who were proud to consort with titled people.

While the middle class grew to dominate in key political and economic institutions, the upper class remained invariably the cultural reference group against which the former measured themselves.

> The more [the old landed society] lost on the political plane, the more it sought to shine on the social plane. … Its gift for display continued unrivalled, and its splendour, supported by its ancient lineage, easily excelled the vulgar luxury of the new-rich.
> (Bédarida 1979:131)

Undoubtedly, some distinctions between the classes had blurred. The prosperous upper-middle class were invariably welcomed into "society" life. Despite lacking the foundations of aristocratic heritage, familial inheritance or a public school or Oxbridge education of their own, many were able to gain peerages, purchase country estates with servants, send their sons to public school and marry their daughters into the aristocracy (Bédarida 1979). The upper class also adopted middle-class employment; some aristocrats departed their idle lifestyles and became successful businessmen and company directors or trustees (Holt 1989). In time, the parameters of what constituted being a "gentleman" were redefined 'more in terms of conduct than heredity' (Bailey 1978:86), wherein the adoption of behaviour demanding greater self-restraint and discipline as well as leadership, intellectual foresight and chivalry toward women was recognised alongside more inveterate, hereditary determinants of class (Baker 2004; Dunning and Sheard 2000). The public schools, celebrated in the literary work of Thomas Hughes' *Tom Brown's School Days* and recognised as principal breeding grounds for the education of 'Muscular Christians' and future elites in government, economics, law, business and diplomatic matters of empire, became key locations where sons of aristocracy mixed openly and with increasing frequency with boys of less noble means (Bédarida 1979). As they grew into adulthood, argued Eisenberg (1990:268), 'gentlemen of right saw themselves continually accompanied by gentlemen of honour or of education, by so-called merchants and gentlemen, by officers and gentlemen, by Christian gentlemen'. What resulted gradually from the "gentlemen" of public schools was what became known as the 'Mid-Victorian compromise': a fusion of value systems necessitating the mutual accommodation of interests of, and the sharing of power between, the middle and upper classes. Bédarida (1979:79) described it as 'an alliance between the aristocracy of land and birth and the aristocracy of money and ability'.

Team sports like cricket and rugby, as they came to develop in the public schools, were charged with instilling values of this new social elite: toughness, self-reliance, intellectual ability, gentlemanly conduct, morality, diligence, discipline, a sense of British superiority, an expectation of servility from lower social orders, and a competitive spirit as the engine for Britain's global economic expansion (Collins 2009). Over time, the boys came to establish a set of beliefs for how *all* sports should be played, moulded on middle-class ideas of Protestant self-help (Gruneau 2006) and stressing fundamental "Corinthian" amateur principles: strict behavioural constraints; sportsmanship and the values of honesty, fair play, integrity and playing the game 'as an end in itself'; distinct codes of deferential conduct and rituals of status distinction to differentiate amateurs from professionals; a deeply rooted abhorrence to physical training, preparation and specialisation; and the concomitant celebration of natural aptitude, the display of effortless style and grace, and celebration of the 'all-rounder' (Allison 1980; Holt 1989; Williams 2006). These characteristics marked the quintessential British gentleman-amateur sportsman, whose sporting mastery ably demonstrated and promoted ideas of innate national and racial superiority (Mangan 1981, 1992; Polley 2011). Such inveterate and widely held ideas were reinforced by numerous factors, argued Bédarida (1979:93–4), most notably: 'the quiet conviction of being the centre of the world'; the fact that Britain embodied the 'three great forces of the age', industrialism, Protestantism and liberalism; and the 'striking demonstration of naval and diplomatic supremacy'. The *Illustrated London News* claimed: 'We are a rich people, powerful, intelligent, religious. ... Our spirit governs the universe' (22 July 1848); later, they were celebrated as 'the harbingers of civilization' before claiming: 'All the regions of the globe feel our physical, moral and intellectual presence. ... They could not live without us' (13 October 1849). Their sporting practices as they developed throughout the nineteenth century were a direct reflection of this.

F.B. Malim (1917:152), headmaster of five public schools throughout his career, wrote in 1917:

As we desire our games to foster the spirit that faces danger, so we shall wish them to foster the spirit that faces hardship, the spirit of endurance. That is why I think that golf and lawn tennis are not fit school games; they are not painful enough.

Indeed, lawn tennis was excluded from Eton, Harrow and other elite public schools until well into the interwar years, mostly because of its public perception of effeteness and lack of potential to develop mental and physical toughness. This did not stop the sport being infused with public-school values, however; such was the power and pervasiveness of this code generally that even sports not played in public schools were conditioned by its behavioural norms, ethics and values. Many early enthusiasts of tennis were old boys from the leading schools and universities, particularly Harrow and Cambridge, respectively. The first three Wimbledon champions, Spencer Gore, Frank Hadow and Rev. John Hartley, were old Harrovians. The Renshaw brothers, William and Ernest, who dominated in the 1880s, both attended Westminster and later Cambridge University. They and the host of other young men similarly socially positioned took to lawn tennis with a clear sense of how and according to what values and rules it should be played; blending the upper-class ostentatious want to display elegance, luxury and artistic refinement with the middle-class spirit of enterprise, competition and individualism. Thus, the exclusion of tennis from the public schools did not necessarily prevent the inculcation of amateur values or the need for its male players to behave as "gentlemen" should; it merely defined a particular type of gentleman for participation and ensured the game began and remained for a long time principally a sport for adults. This was crucial.

While the fact of its omission from the leading schools might have hindered Britain's long-term ambitions to develop talent, given that most males did not seriously take up the game until early adulthood, it likely had little effect on the sport's popularity among the status-conscious upper-middle classes. In fact, it is suggested that its initial exclusivity, for the most part, ensured that the comfortable and relaxed air that characterised occasions for play in country-house gardens and clubs remained a central feature. Moreover, sports like lawn tennis would have played a significant role in separating the various middle-class factions from one another, at a time when, in Hobsbawm's (1983:291) words, 'the fluidity of [class] borders made clear criteria of social distinction unusually difficult'. The problem was, according to him, 'how to define and separate the genuine national elite of an upper-middle class once the relatively firm criteria … [of] descent, kinship, intermarriage, the local networks of business, private sociability and politics no longer provided firm guidance'. The key lay in the preservation of "hierarchy" as a notion and an ideal, which, according to Cannadine (1999:125), was successfully accomplished by the middle classes, who 'refurbished, reconstructed and reinvented' it.

The various factions of the middle class had two things in common: they each sought to distinguish themselves from social inferiors, while also simultaneously aspiring upwards and seeking pathways toward social mobility for themselves. Certainly, differences in employment, income, standards of living, land ownership, culture and even religion and politics belied claims to a common middle-class identity. Crudely speaking, below the upper-middle class were the "middle-middle" class, which included owners of industrial firms and large businesses, professionals like civil engineers, professors, doctors, barristers and solicitors, alongside wealthy merchants, accountants and most government civil servants (Bédarida 1979). Their lives were not entirely uncomfortable, and despite adopting a defensive position on matters of materialism, as evident in their "conspicuous consumption" (Veblen 1899/1994), they continued to denigrate those whose prime objective in work was making money, namely the lower-middle class, who were thought collectively 'contaminated ... by direct contact with merchandise and cash ... [and] sick with ambition' (Bédarida 1979:52). This latter group consisted of small employers, shopkeepers, salesmen, office workers, bank clerks, low-ranked civil servants and teachers, who as a collective group were concerned to 'show one's respectability and distinguish oneself from the common herd, to the point of aping without discrimination the life and habits of the superior classes' (Bédarida 1979:52).

Alongside institutions of employment and other areas of society, class rivalry and competition was played out culturally and within seemingly innocuous social institutions like tennis clubs. At a time when class barriers were eroding and education, line of work and the conspicuous consumption of expensive goods were failing to demarcate the classes as categorically and effectively as they once had, tennis clubs allowed unashamedly hierarchical constructions of social interaction to manifest under the guise of polite civility. Where, when, how and by whom the game was played had a strong impact on its associated values and general "social character".

The aims of this chapter are to describe the earliest versions of lawn tennis played in Britain and discuss the various men responsible for "reinventing" them and bringing them to prominence. Majors Harry Gem and Walter Clopton Wingfield, in particular, have been credited with playing key but independent roles in this process and a critical assessment of their relative inputs in the context of the game's growth is conducted. This is not in any way intended to clear up "once and for all" who the actual inventor of lawn tennis was, as the answer to this question is and likely always will be not a question of facts about who made what impact, but rather more a question of defining what "reinvention" means and then making arbitrary assessments about whose relative input merits the title of being the most significant. Instead, the aim here is to consider the various aspects of the sport that each "inventor" had a hand in developing and then assessing the extents to which these aspects constituted something not only unique but enduring. Inevitably, the social aspects of the sport as they developed were initially the key features that drew participants in. The actual features of its play as defined by the rules, equipment and court layout defined by the "inventors" played a far less important role early on. Thus the question of "Who invented the sport?" is a moot one in any case.

From its conception, lawn tennis was a major feature of garden parties, which afforded its hosts, from old and new money alike, excellent opportunities to convey wealth. For the young adults in attendance, tennis garden parties invited possibilities for romance and ensured the enhancement of status. It was said that to avoid tennis garden parties wholly

> is impossible to any man of social pretensions. ... A man with no reputation to keep up, or with a reputation strong enough to stand alone, might even admit that he enjoyed them, but comparatively few players can afford to be thus candid.
> (*Pastime* 27 August 1890:162)

Garden parties sometimes lasted an entire weekend and combined lawn tennis with a host of other forms of entertainment, such as a "flower show" or "bazaar". In its earliest years, evidence suggests numerous royal and titled members of society were attracted to the sport, holding their own garden parties or attending others where lawn tennis was the chief attraction. *The Fifeshire Journal* from 1877 (27 September) reported a "tennis party" held at Balcarres House, home of Sir Coutts Lindsay, founder of the Grosvenor Art Gallery in London. Queen Victoria's youngest son, Prince Leopold, was in attendance with sixty or seventy other eminent invited guests, and it was recorded: 'The distinguished party remained for nearly two hours on the lawn engaged at tennis'. Elks (2004:20) suggested that tennis parties filled an important social role in helping to 'attract the eligible bachelors of the area' whereupon the young single ladies and gentlemen could frolic and flirt with one another in what was assumed a safe environment. Thus, tennis garden parties became part of the social "season". Alongside the private residences of local elites, vicarage gardens were also suitably respectable locations for tennis parties, with such relaxed, adult-centred and largely non-competitive social occasions run by the local clergy (Elks 2004). Such settings differed markedly from the more aggressive, male-dominated, competitive sporting environments associated with football, rugby and also, to a lesser extent, cricket. For a start, they would have attracted a different sort of "gentleman", and the partial inclusion of women in tennis settings was a key element of their unique characterisation.

From the earliest days, the presence of women was hugely significant. Garden parties were extensions of home life, so naturally women took charge of culinary efforts and refreshments, while men demanded the lion's share of court-time. Some clubs were known to have denied access to women but found very quickly the necessity of their inclusion, if only for economic reasons. The Northern LTA (Lawn Tennis Association) lifted its initial ban on female members in 1893, and Queen's Club waited until 1906 to follow suit, but McKelvie (1986:22) recalled that women were still 'not allowed to propose men candidates or book the covered courts [and were] ... barred from playing on the east court on Saturdays and Sundays and the west after 12.30 pm'. Often, clubs created certain conditions that privileged males, such as "men's only nights" or "gentlemen's rooms". Men ensured their authority by denying women any part in the formation of rules or decision-making processes, and the restrictive dress and strict behavioural conventions ensured that women's play was weak and featureless for many years. Nevertheless, their inclusion both on and off the court fulfilled an important social function, because women at this time were crying out for a game more physical and challenging than croquet that could be played in a similar private, outdoor setting. Before any of this could happen, however, someone needed to recognise the game's "social" potential and market it to the right audience. Enter Major Walter Clopton Wingfield.

There is a great degree of debate about precisely who should be credited with the (re)invention of lawn tennis, but one thing is certain: the societal preconditions into which the game fit were more important than any one person. Common myths surrounding the origins of both baseball and rugby, which have given primacy to Arben Doubleday and William Webb Ellis, respectively, have either ignored conflicting evidence in an effort to reinforce a particular glorified past, or have underestimated the importance of wider societal developments that played a part in facilitating the sport's emergence (Collins 2009; Guttmann 2004). Popular lawn tennis history has also tended to lean toward a particular inventor or reinventor without sufficient evidence, which has been to the neglect of a more critical analysis that uncovers a host of important individuals and wider societal developments that played a part in the sport's incipient creation, not to mention the earlier games from which the various individuals borrowed features and equipment.

Initially, badminton emerged around the mid-nineteenth century and, after some experimentation in England and India, had become recognised as a game suitable for ladies and gentleman, and more enjoyable than croquet (Hutchinson 1996). Throughout mid–late 1873, *The Field* published numerous articles to this effect, which player-turned-historian A.E. Crawley posited 'formed the seed that germinated the following month in Major Wingfield's brain' (*LT&B* 10 April 1913:176). What is popularly recorded is the fact that, after experimenting throughout the spring and summer of 1873, the retired army major Walter Clopton Wingfield formally introduced his outdoor ball game called 'Sphairistiké' to a fashionable audience at Nantclwyd Hall on 16th December, before returning to London to secure its patent in February of 1874. Sphairistiké (translated Greek for 'playing ball') was an outdoor game amalgamating several features of badminton with Real Tennis and racquets. Wingfield borrowed from badminton the six-foot-high drooping net and possibly the hourglass-shaped court, from Real Tennis the rackets with wooden handles and bent heads, and from racquets the scoring system with 15-point sets (Alexander 1986). It followed that Wingfield would market his game to the same clientele as these others and also adopt their social features, namely ritualised behavioural etiquette and high-class fashions (Lake 2009). Like its predecessors, the new game was also to be significant as a means of conspicuous consumption for the upper and upper-middle classes.

Wingfield's version of lawn tennis was, from its outset, imbued with the elite Victorian spirit of social aspiration. The price of his box-set alone determined its target audience. Five guineas – the cost of a net, two net-posts, four rackets, six balls and a set of instructions – was a price only reasonably affordable for the aristocracy or late-Victorian *nouveau riche*. Only the most prestigious magazines like *The Field*, *Vanity Fair*, *The Army and Navy Gazette* and the *Court Journal* carried notices and advertisements; readers of the latter, for example, were 'mostly members of the court, and those who strove to become members' (Alexander 1986:89). In his 5th edition of *Book of the Game*, published in 1875, he provided the full names of every titled aristocrat who purchased a set, which included: 11 princes and princesses, 7 dukes, 17 marquis and marchionesses, 54 earls, 12 countesses, 10 viscounts, 41 lords, 44 ladies, 46 honourables, 5 right honourables and 55 knights. The lucidity of his marketing campaign ensured its commercial success; he sold over a thousand box-sets between the summers of 1874 and 1875 alone, and more than a third of them to the aristocracy (Hutchinson 1996). The upper class not only comprised a large and significant proportion of the game's first players but an even larger proportion of club presidents or patrons.

In many respects, Wingfield did not actually invent anything new. The idea of playing tennis outdoors was not unique either. The memoirs of the London bank-merchant William Hickey from 1767 mentioned the outdoor game of 'field tennis' played during the summer in Battersea fields:

> This club consisted of some very respectable persons. … The game we played … afforded noble exercise. The situation of the house … rendered it as private as if it had been exclusively our own. … At four our sport commenced, continuing until dark; during the exercise we refreshed ourselves with draughts of cool tankard, and other pleasant beverages. The field, which was of sixteen acres in extent was kept in as high order and smooth as a bowling green.
>
> (Hickey 1767:72)

Nothing is known about how the game was played or with what equipment, but its clientele and the particular occasions on which it was played suggest a close affinity with other established racket games.

Other similar games were said to have been played in the century or so before Wingfield designed his version, but technological advances in the mid-nineteenth century proved crucial in sustaining interest. The lawnmower and garden-roller helped cultivate smooth grass courts, and the invention of vulcanised rubber in 1839 by Charles Goodyear was of even greater significance (Gillmeister 1997; Todd 1979).

Shortly after Wingfield's advertisements were published in *The Field*, a swathe of other gentleman wrote in to claim they had been playing similar games for years. From the basic descriptions offered, they all bore numerous similarities in rules, rackets, shape of court and the hollow rubber balls being propelled, but most strikingly, and most importantly, they were almost identical in their social features. These were upper-middle-class gentlemen playing outdoor versions of established aristocratic racket games on private lawns, among social equals and usually as part of grand social occasions. Like established Real Tennis and racquets players, it seems likely that for these men, their respective games served a similar conspicuous, status-enhancing social function.

This feature was particularly important to Harry Gem, another retired British army major, and his Spanish friend Juan Batista Augurio Perera, who claimed they had played a game called "pelota" in Edgbaston for 15 years prior to Wingfield's advertisement (*The Field* 21 November 1874). Unlike Wingfield, however, they kept their game secret, played exclusively among a select group of friends and, even after forming the world's first tennis club, Leamington LTC, in 1872, they made no efforts to expand the game or raise the club's profile (Holland 2011). Gem was modest and by all accounts indifferent to sharing Wingfield's fortune (Gibbons 1986), but still he and the Birmingham public sought recognition. *Edgbastonia* (December 1881) proclaimed as 'an unquestionable fact' in Gem's obituary in 1881, that he was 'the first to bring [lawn-tennis] before the public'. This was incorrect, of course, unless one classes a small and specially selected group of friends as "the public". Nevertheless, by the time Gem wrote in to *The Field*, the game had enjoyed nine months of publicity and correspondence, and players were experimenting with

> the shape and dimensions of the court, the height of the net, the position of the service line, the conditions of service, the mode of scoring and many other details, with the object of constituting and settling the game on the best possible basis.
> (*LT&B* 7 August 1913:690)

In an effort to clean up the mess brought about by the different rules and court dimensions that made play difficult between separate factions, the Marylebone Cricket Club (MCC) held a meeting on 8th March 1875 for the purpose of agreeing common rules. Several versions of lawn tennis were experimented with and votes were taken. Three weeks later, *The Field* published the "agreed-upon" rules that tended to favour Wingfield's features over others, but correspondence over the next two years, while respectful to the MCC's efforts, still exposed an unsatisfied public. When, in 1877, the All England Lawn Tennis & Croquet Club (AELTCC) sought to formulate rules for its first Championships, the sub-committee of Henry Jones, Julian Marshall and C.G. Heathcote agreed wisely to alter or scrap altogether several of Wingfield's most unpopular features. They dropped the racquets scoring method of 15-point games for the Real Tennis method of 15, 30, 40 and game; they introduced the double-fault; and they proposed a rectangular court instead of Wingfield's hourglass shape. Despite going against the MCC's rules, the AELTCC recognised the importance of their support, so joint authority over lawn tennis rested temporarily in the hands of both clubs.

The incipient development of lawn tennis was a long and complex process, drafting opinions and suggested alterations from many different men and amalgamating features of numerous games. Though the debate as to who invented the game is moot, futile and ultimately subjective, it can reasonably be claimed that the timing of Wingfield's public launch of Sphairistiké, within the specific socio-historical context of mid-Victorian Britain, was the most significant condition that determined its rise to fame. Thus, crucially, the sport's rapid growth owes more to Wingfield than anyone else, for he was alone in venturing to expand the game outside of an exclusive circle. For over a decade, Gem and Perera made no efforts toward greater inclusivity, and likely the game would have remained hidden from popular consciousness had Wingfield not seized its commercial potential through his clever and 'energetic campaign of publicity and promotion' (Barrett 1986:19). It was into an environment of upper-class status insecurity, middle-class social aspiration and within a broadened framework of appropriate gentlemanly conduct and budding female emancipation that lawn tennis emerged, developed, expanded and found its niche.

The success of rule standardisation that lawn tennis enjoyed demanded, first, a sufficiently large body of players motivated to experiment and discover the most favourable conditions for play, and, second, the means by which to communicate and debate openly such alterations. Thus, the influence of J.H. Walsh, the editor of *The Field* since 1857, should not be overlooked; given his enthusiasm for the game, he welcomed rather than restricted discussion about lawn tennis, despite the magazine's traditional emphasis on field sports. Walsh also played a pivotal role in the formation of the All England Croquet Club in 1868, chaired the inaugural meeting that took place in his office and donated the 25-guinea Silver Challenge Cup for the 1877 Championships. He was just one of the many gentlemen responsible for the sport's initial development.

The first Wimbledon Championships was a quiet affair. Spencer Gore won from a field of 22 gentlemen, all British, who each paid a guinea entrance fee. Descriptions of the playing styles suggest a form of "pat-ball", as most players adapted strokes and tactics specific to Real Tennis or racquets that incorporated massive amounts of cut and slice; the high net prevented them from hitting with pace (Barrett 1986; Birley 1993; Chalmers 2004). Not until the Renshaw brothers emerged four years later did the first "proper" lawn tennis style uncorrupted by other racket games reveal itself. Their arrival brought an increased popularity to Wimbledon, with challenge-rounds in the early 1880s engaging upwards of 3,500 spectators. This gave the AELTC added impetus to take matters into their own hands with regard the formulation of playing rules. The MCC gradually relinquished their authority throughout the early 1880s, but still for some time longer and even after the formation of the Lawn Tennis Association (LTA) in 1888, players continued to experiment with new types of scoring in an effort to find potentially more interesting alternatives; such was the creative spirit and resourcefulness of the Victorian elite.[1]

It was an amalgamation of aristocratic and bourgeois elites that formed the first generation of lawn tennis players who fostered the game's incipient creation. The dominance of the former, with which Wingfield had so successfully galvanised early support, lasted only a few years. The process of their desertion of lawn tennis began in the 1880s as they sought out more exclusive pursuits like golf and polo (Walker 1989). By the 1890s, this process was almost entirely complete, bar a scattering of noble patrons of clubs and associations and a handful of isolated clubs that sought seclusion from the growing number populated with ladies and gentlemen of "new money". Nevertheless, the cultural expressions of upper-class taste sought by the most aspirational upper-middle-class players had a lasting impression upon the sport. From its very beginnings, principally because of its noble heritage as a game derived from Real Tennis and racquets and also due to its earliest upper-class enthusiasts, lawn tennis attracted those seeking to improve their social positions. All the features that characterised the sport, including the general atmosphere and tone of its clubs and parties, its associated fashions and cultural accoutrements, its rules and etiquette and a sense of how lawn tennis should be played, reflected the general motivations of social mobility for the upper-middle classes.

Lieutenant-Colonel Robert Osborn (1881:11–12) described ideal conditions for lawn tennis:

> The scene should be laid on a well-kept garden lawn. There should be bright warm sun overhead, and just sufficient breeze whispering through the trees ... to prevent the day from being sultry. Near at hand, under the cool shadow of a tree, there should be strawberries and cream, and iced claret mug, and a few spectators who do not want to play, but are lovers of the game, intelligent and appreciative. If all these conditions are present, an afternoon spent at lawn tennis is a highly Christian and beneficent pastime.

This account reveals that even though the game had been formally organised less than a decade earlier and was still in its infancy, its clientele, associated settings, paraphernalia, and underlying values were already firmly set. Osborn could have easily been describing the ideal conditions for a host of other outdoor games, like croquet, polo or cricket. The 'well-kept' lawn suggests a private residence; the need for 'warm sun' and 'sufficient breeze' suggests a summer game; the addition of refreshments denotes sociability and emphasises the importance of the occasion itself; the inclusion of 'intelligent and appreciative' spectators implies some form of exclusivity; its 'Christian' ethos connotes "respectable" behaviour and restrained play. The omission of detail about the quality of play indicates its lack of importance at this time. It is precisely because the game's earliest players cared more about who they were with and in what social setting they played than who won or lost that class distinctions were considered so essential for the mid-Victorian elite.

Reports from matches and competitions from this early period reveal a strikingly similar emphasis on external features rather than on the actual play or results. The first two sentences from the Buxton tournament report from 1888 read:

> The wet season showed but little improvement last week, when the favourite Derbyshire tournament suffered, as most others have done, from the inclement weather. On the Monday play was impracticable, on Thursday a heavy thunder-shower marred an otherwise delightful day, and prevented play taking place on the grass during the afternoon, and on Saturday, after two of the finals had been decided – partly during the showers – rain fell in torrents, and rendered inevitable a postponement of the other events until Monday.
>
> (*Pastime* 8 August 1888:108)

Far from innocuous, such comments were subtle yet clever ways to convey affluence. Given that so few were able to experience outdoor leisure so abundantly, it was a mark of class distinction to complain that one's lawn tennis plans were spoiled by inclement weather. Thus, tournament secretaries made every effort, in writing their reports, to bring such matters to attention.

Before the turn of the century, particularly as a long-term outcome of the Enclosure movement that withdrew open spaces from public recreational use, the opportunity to pursue outdoor leisure activities in rural settings was a privilege for those with sufficient time and money (Baker 1979; Vamplew 1988b). The middle classes came to associate urban centres with working-class poverty and poor hygiene, but found excitement in outdoor recreational pursuits, born in earlier generations from the rise of fishing, hunting and field sports, developed through the increasing popularity of seaside excursions, fostered in the publicised exploits of adventure conquests by Alpine mountaineers, and cemented in the public schools (Baker 1979; Holt 1989; Hutchinson 1996). In addition, as a counter to the harmful effects of industrial, urban Victorian life, afternoons spent in the fresh country air, playing mildly strenuous games like lawn tennis or golf, were endorsed through medical discourse that stressed their physiological and psychological benefits (Holt 2006; Lowerson 1993; Polley 2011). Seaside resorts were particularly fond of allocating provisions for such sports, given their transient but affluent middle-class clientele that demanded 'gentle athleticism' and 'social exclusivity' (Durie and Huggins 2007:177). Giving its readers some ideas for pleasant sojourns, *Pastime* (25 July 1888:67) highlighted its five-week end-of-summer 'Western tour' as the 'most attractive', taking in tournaments at Exmouth, Teignmouth, Torquay, Bournemouth and Eastbourne. Outdoor features of lawn tennis appealed also to certain romanticised notions of "Old England", here depicted in *Pastime* (23 September 1885:210): 'The mere fact of a game being conducted in the open air enhances its enjoyment, to say nothing of the pleasure of a warm summer afternoon spent on a well-kept lawn in one of our old English gardens'. This testimony to the quintessential British love of "nature" and "the outdoors" is a product of the changing definitions of both concepts during the 1880s. From being defined in terms of the products of nature (i.e. leaves, trees, grass, fresh air, etc.), it took on social meaning and moral significance; in essence, "nature and the outdoors" changed from being something tangible to something cultural, which could be found, obtained and used for personal benefit, most likely as 'an antidote to the urban environment' (Bédarida 1979:26).

The outdoor social features of lawn tennis were popularised in large part thanks to the proliferation of artwork in the late-Victorian era. Belfast-born but Glasgow-bred, John Lavery, in particular, produced numerous paintings that glorified and celebrated the sport's traditional rural setting; *A Rally* (1885), *Played!!* (1885), *The Tennis Party* (1885) and *Paisley Lawn Tennis Club* (1889), in particular, reinforced culturally defined notions of the English garden-party pastime (McConkey 2011). Alongside similar impressions by other artists like George Kilburne, Mary Hayllar, Arthur Melville, James Guthrie and Charles March Gere, these prime occasions for upper-middle-class mixed-gender sociability were forever immortalised on canvas (Sumner 2011).

The extent to which tennis garden parties, and in particular games of mixed doubles, provided opportunities for men to make modest sexual advances toward women is clearly highlighted in several pieces; Charles March Gere's, *The Tennis Party* (1900) is perhaps the best example. In the mildly satirical *Love's Labor Lost* (1897) by George Du Maurier, three unmarried daughters are shown thanking their father for providing facilities for lawn tennis, where apparently the game is so enjoyable that the need to find husbands is negated; the accompanying description reads: 'Papa has taken this beautiful house and garden solely with the view of tempting eligible young men to come and play lawn-tennis, etc.' (McConkey 2011:59). Eligible bachelors are more lucky but nevertheless rebuffed by the female subjects of their respective attentions in Lavery's *The Tennis Match* (1885) and Edith Haylarr's *A Summer Shower* (1883). Still, the extent to which polite courtship pervaded artistic impressions of lawn tennis garden parties before the war suggests how central a feature it was.

Much like cricket and golf, lawn tennis fit perfectly within these burgeoning discourses of sociable sport in an outdoor, rural setting, and afforded numerous opportunities for those participating to convey status or enhance prestige. The re-creation of garden-party atmospheres, the centrality of "gentlemanly amateurism" as the fundamental ethos guiding how lawn tennis was played, and the structures according to which clubs and tournaments were formed and organised, clearly expressed elements of social exclusivity. Alongside the enjoyment of the game itself, the fact that it could be played in confined spaces away from the masses ensured its continued popularity and social significance, as did the game's perceived playing requirements of physical and emotional restraint and foresight in decision-making. Osborn (1881:44) stated that an ideal tennis player plays 'almost as much with his brain as with his hand'. Two decades later, the American J. Parmly Paret (1904:vi) likened lawn tennis to 'the mimic warfare of the chess-board', in its elements of 'attack and defence, of finesse and coupe' and in its required 'severe physical exertion, coupled with activity of mind in constantly thinking out the rapid problems that present themselves during the course of the play; it needs coolness of nerve and eye'. For Pembroke Vaile (1906:125), the game necessitated 'the highest qualities which a man should possess ... courage, stamina, strength tempered with restraint, equanimity under adverse circumstances, quickness of eye and mind to see and decide, and of body and limbs to execute'. These accounts suggest few perceived differences in the attributes of a fine gentleman from those of a good tennis player.

In general, the exhibition of behaviour that displayed self-restraint and foresight came to signify elite "gentlemanly" status during the late nineteenth century, when the ostensible advances in bourgeois power posed a continuous threat to aristocratic authority. As a way of explaining the central features of many sports of this period, Elias (1986:151) made a plausible connection between what he termed "sportisation" – the gradual process of nineteenth-century "games" coming to be governed by rules, order and routine to become "sports" – and the shifting behaviour of the upper classes more generally: '"Sportisation" had the character of a civilising spurt ... where the tightening of rules of etiquette played a significant part'. The fact that lawn tennis was patronised by the upper and upper-middle classes, who presided over its leading clubs and associations despite being numerically outnumbered, meant the sport was, from its inception, conditioned by a code of ethics and behavioural conduct that matched their class in tone and character. The middle class dominated the sport as players and administrators, but, broadly speaking, belonged to a heterogeneous and internally divided group. Their differences were reflected clearly in their attitudes toward socially inferior classes.

Late-nineteenth-century middle-class Liberals like Charles Booth and Seebohm Rowntree considered it a personal duty to help improve, or at least to seek to understand, the apparently poor living conditions of the working classes, who continued to be economically and socially exploited (Bédarida 1979; Cannadine 1999). This was despite the numerous government acts that prompted changes in their working hours and conditions (Ten Hours Act 1847; Factory Act 1878), extended educational rights to the poorest children (Education Act 1870), and enabled working men greater mobility in search of employment (Union Chargeability Act 1876). The combined sentiments of guilt and responsibility were also found among those who sought, through a combination of paternalism and preaching, to reform working-class leisure pursuits, which were considered morally offensive, socially subversive and an impediment to industrial progress due to their association with alcoholism, gambling, violence, animal brutality, foul language, blasphemy and Sabbath-breaking (Baker 1979; Holt 1989; Vamplew 1988a). While these middle-class reformers promoted new outdoor pursuits to improve working-class physical and moral health, others attempted to enact an opposite policy of exclusion, enacting strong opposition to trade influence within private clubs and promoting self-restraint, modesty and "respectable" behaviour as a means of social demarcation (Lowerson 1993).

Lawn tennis was one of the chief and most successful sports through which the upper-middle class was able to separate themselves from social inferiors and trade influence, in addition to it being played and organised to reflect the ideals of social aspiration. Thus, it is plausible to suggest, as Llewellyn (2011a) did, that a deep-rooted fear of the commercialisation and popularisation of sport during the Victorian era provided a chief impetus to promote the ideals of amateurism that cleverly blended social exclusivity with anti-commercial sentiment. As the next chapter discusses, the amateur ethos was as much about playing sport for love as demonstrating a virtuous playing style that served as a reference point to convey status, promote social aspiration and exclude outsiders who did not conform to these ideals.

Note

1. Houndiscombe's and Cricklewood's tournaments in the early 1890s experimented with a scoring method whereby the first player to score 100 points won each match, and in the Hamburg tournament of 1892, sets of 21 points, rather than six games, were tried.

Bibliography

Alexander, G. E. (1986). *Wingfield: Edwardian Gentleman*. Portsmouth: Peter E. Randall.
Allison, L. (1980). Batsman and Bowler: The Key Relation of Victorian England. *Journal of Sports History*, 7(2), 5–20.

Bailey, P. (1978). *Leisure and Class in Victorian England*. London: Routledge and Kegan Paul.

Baker, N. (2004). Whose Hegemony: The Origins of the Amateur Ethos in Nineteenth Century English Society. *Sport in History*, 24(1), 1–16.

Baker, W. (1979). The Leisure Revolution in Victorian England: A Review of Recent Literature. *Journal of Sport History*, 6(3), 76–87.

Barrett, J. (1986). *100 Wimbledon Championships: A Celebration*. London: Collins.

Bédarida, F. (1979). *A Social History of England 1851–1975*. London: Methuen.

Birley, D. (1993). *Sport and the Making of Britain*. Manchester: Manchester University Press.

Cannadine, D. (1999). *The Rise and Fall of Class in Britain*. New York: Columbia University Press.

Chalmers, A. (2004). *Tennis and How It Gave Birth to Lawn Tennis*. Retrieved 5 May 2006, from Tennis Book Shop: http://www.tennisbookshop.com/real.htm

Collins, T. (2009). *A Social History of English Rugby Union*. London: Routledge.

Dunning, E., and Sheard, K. (2000). *Barbarians, Gentlemen, Players: A Sociological Study of the Development of Rugby Football*. London: Routledge.

Durie, A., and Huggins, M. (2007). Sport, Social Tone and Seaside Resorts of Great Britain, c.1850–1914. *International Journal of the History of Sport*, 15(1), 173–187.

Eisenberg, C. (1990). The Middle Class and Competition: Some Considerations of the Beginnings of Modern Sport in England and Germany. *International Journal of the History of Sport*, 7(2), 265–282.

Elias, N. (1986). An Essay on Sport and Violence. In N. Elias and E. Dunning, *Quest for Excitement: Sport and Leisure in the Civilising Process* (pp. 150–174). Oxford: Blackwell.

Elks, S. J. (2004). *From Lycra to Whalebone: A Fashion Journey through Midlands Lawn Tennis History*. Birmingham: Susan J. Elks.

Gibbons, W. (1986). *Royal Leamington Spa: The Seeds of Lawn Tennis*. Coventry: Jones-Sands.

Gillmeister, H. (1997). *Tennis: A Cultural History*. Leicester: Leicester University Press.

Gruneau, R. (2006). 'Amateurism' as a Sociological Problem: Some Reflections Inspired by Eric Dunning. *Sport in Society*, 9(4), 559–582.

Guttmann, A. (2004). *Sports: The Five First Millennia*. Boston, MA: University of Massachusetts Press.

Hickey, W. (1767). *Memoirs of William Hickey*. London: Hurst & Blackett.

Hobsbawm, E. (1983). Mass-Producing Traditions: Europe 1870–1914. In E. Hobsbawm and T. Ranger, *The Invention of Tradition* (pp. 263–308). Cambridge: Cambridge University Press.

Holland, R. (2011). Edgbaston's Gem of a Game: The Origins of Lawn Tennis. In A. Sumner, *Court on Canvas: Tennis in Art* (pp. 35–46). London: Philip Wilson.

Holt, R. (1989). *Sport and the British*. Oxford: Clarendon.

Holt, R. (2006). The Amateur Body and the Middle-Class Man: Work, Health and Style in Victorian Britain. *Sport in History*, 26(3), 352–369.

Huggins, M. (2008). Sport and the Upper Classes: Introduction. *Sport in History*, 28(3), 351–363.

Hutchinson, R. (1996). *Empire Games: The British Invention of Twentieth-Century Sport*. London: Mainstream Publishing.

Lake, R. J. (2009). Real Tennis and the Civilising Process. *Sport in History*, 29(4), 553–576.
Llewellyn, M. P. (2011a). Prologue: An Indifferent Beginning. *International Journal of the History of Sport*, 28(5), 625–647.
Lowerson, J. (1993). *Sport and the English Middle Classes 1870–1914*. Manchester: Manchester University Press.
Malim, F. B. (1917). Athletics. In A. Benson, *Cambridge Essays in Education* (pp. 148–167). Cambridge: Cambridge University Press.
Mangan, J. (1981). *Athleticism in the Victorian and Edwardian Public School*. Cambridge: Cambridge University Press.
Mangan, J. (1992). *The Cultural Bond: Sport Empire and Society*. London: Frank Cass.
McConkey, K. (2011). Tennis Parties. In A. Sumner, *Court on Canvas: Tennis in Art* (pp. 47–82). London: Philip Wilson.
McKelvie, R. (1986). *The Queen's Club Story, 1886–1986*. London: Stanley Paul.
Osborn, R. (1881). *Lawn Tennis: Its Players and How to Play*. London: Strahan.
Paret, J. P. (1904). *Lawn Tennis: Its Past Present and Future*. London: Macmillan.
Polley, M. (2011). Sports Development in the Nineteenth-Century British Public Schools. In B. Houlihan and M. Green, *Routledge Handbook of Sports Development* (pp. 9–19). London: Routledge.
Sumner, A. (2011). *Court on Canvas: Tennis in Art*. London: Philip Wilson.
Todd, T. (1979). *The Tennis Players: From Pagan Rites to Strawberries and Cream*. Guernsey: Vallencey.
Vaile, P. (1906). *Lawn Tennis Guide or the Strokes and Science of Lawn Tennis*. London: British Sports Publishing Co.
Vamplew, W. (1988a). *Pay Up and Play the Game: Professional Sport in Britain, 1875–1914*. Cambridge: Cambridge University Press.
Vamplew, W. (1988b). Sport and Industrialisation: An Economic Interpretation of the Changes in Popular Sport in Nineteenth-Century England. In J. Mangan, *Pleasure, Profit, Proselytism: British Culture and Sport at Home and Abroad 1700–1914* (pp. 7–20). London: Frank Cass.
Veblen, T. (1899/1994). *The Theory of the Leisure Class*. Mineola, NY: Dover Publications.
Walker, H. (1989). Lawn Tennis. In T. Mason, *Sport in Britain: A Social History* (pp. 245–275). Cambridge: Cambridge University Press.
Williams, J. (2006). 'The Really Good Professional Captain Has Never Been Seen!': Perceptions of the Amateur/Professional Divide in County Cricket, 1900–39. *Sport in History*, 26(3), 429–449.

2 Pat-ball and petticoats

Representations of social class and gender in early lawn tennis playing styles, etiquette and fashions

Sport, according to the upper-middle classes, should be played according to the ethos of a "gentleman amateur". To be sure, an amateur was supposed to play for love, but also according to an unwritten code of behaviour that stressed sportsmanship, i.e. equality of game chances, voluntary and honest observance of rules and generous attitude towards opponents and umpires, and also prescribed particular pre-match preparations (Dunning and Sheard 2000). Baker (2004:1) argued: 'The amateur played the game vigorously and intensely but never took the outcome too seriously; his was a contained competitiveness'. The amateur rejected elaborate physical preparation, training or specialisation, given that such behaviours exhibited the moral, emotional and physical characteristics associated with the lower classes. Holt (2006:365–6) posited:

> sport was supposed to be a celebration of the natural, unforced qualities of the human body. ... Amateurs abhorred ... the corruption of the athletic body, wrenched out of its natural rhythm and forced into extreme patterns of eating, sleeping and exercise.

It was implied that true sporting success could be attained only if played with an appropriate "spirit", yet, as Wagg (2006:534) so brilliantly articulated, the unquantifiable qualities of gentlemen amateurs were 'pre-defined by their social position', meaning 'these values were only amateur when *expressed by them*' (emphasis in the original). It was chiefly a closed world, therefore, where the qualities that defined an amateur were self-defined by the amateurs themselves, and where the "spirit" with which someone played was often simply assumed based on their social class. That said, how did play according to an amateur ethos actually appear on court? What subtle dispositions highlighted class or defined a player's spirit? To be sure, the masking of enthusiasm in victory and disappointment in defeat were central features, underpinned by the necessity for self-restraint (Holt 2006), but this does not go far enough. What role did playing styles and behavioural etiquette play in the maintenance or erosion of class barriers? In what ways did they form part of the habitus of leading players? Also, in the light of shifting parameters of "gentlemanly" conduct that pressed for chivalry toward females, what role did playing style, etiquette and fashions of lawn tennis play in the emancipation of women or in shifting gender relations of this period? These are some of the questions addressed in this chapter.

It is perhaps unsurprising the extent that amateurism stretched to influence actual playing styles. Rugby and football players of the pre-professional era were known to have played with greater sportsmanship and respect for opponents and referees, and in a comparatively more restrained manner (Collins 2009). For Dunning and Sheard (2000), the behavioural code was distinguishable as it demanded a higher level of behavioural self-restraint and greater foresight, alongside greater refinement of manners and more elaborate taboos on behaviour. In lawn tennis, the amateur ethos defined appropriate behaviour toward opponents and (doubles) teammates and what types of shot were acceptable on court (Lake 2011a). For instance, the 'peculiar' practice of offering apologies began as a social necessity but became an expectation, as Paret describes:

> One partner in doubles always says [sorry] to the other when he misses a stroke, or if he makes a double fault, or if he calls a ball for out and it does not go out; while even opponents say it to each other, evidently with the hope of soothing over ruffled feelings, when a ball touches the net and rolls over, or when it bounds badly from the ground, and once I heard a player say, 'Sorry! Very sorry!' to his antagonist after he had smashed the ball out of his reach. ... He used the customary expression even when the cause of the other's misfortunes was his own good play.
> (*Lawn Tennis* 3 January 1900:453)

In this type of environment, one can appreciate the courage needed for a player to attempt a new stroke, particularly if it implied a more aggressive or purposeful approach. Spencer Gore, the first Wimbledon champion in 1877, provoked immediate criticism with his inclination to volley opponents' cuts and screws before they had taken effect (Baddeley 1895). The Earl of Cavan, who became LTA President in 1897, recalled that he had his 'character as a gentleman ... called into question by more than one man with whom I stood in otherwise friendly relationship' because of his early devotion to volleying (*Lawn Tennis* 19 May 1897:39). Its purpose was to kill rather than sustain a rally, so it reflected a deliberate and forthright intention to win a point. To those ignorant of its requisite skill and precision, it might have signalled an unwelcome shift toward the celebration of uncontrolled brute force; for some, the stroke was considered "unsporting" and vulgar.

Up until the early 1880s, the only approach permitted by the court conditions resembled badminton in its interminable "pat-ball" style, with weak, looping shots over the net imparted with spin. The decision taken by the AELTC over the course of several years to lower the net opened the floodgates for new playing styles.[1] Players could experiment with new strokes, hitting harder and lower, which was the most important change that brought about the creation of the unique "lawn tennis" style instead of one adapted from other racket games. The Renshaw brothers popularised this new style, particularly William, who 'took the ball early and hit it hard. He transformed the defensive cut and slice of the vicarage lawn into the modern style' (Barrett and Little 2006:7). More conservative players regretted this development; in 1890, *The Morning Post* observed: 'The standard of play has improved so much that a large class that once enjoyed the game have been thrust aside. ... The indifferent player has been driven from the lawn' (cited in *Pastime* 15 October 1890:279). Similarly, a correspondent in *The Times* lamented: lawn tennis 'has become altogether too paralysing for ordinary folk. Years ago ... the ball was gently spooned over the net'. Now, with the volley, 'it has drifted into the hands of trained athletes, whom moderate players hesitate to face, for their one object seems to be to kill the ball or, failing that, their opponent' (18 September 1891:10).

General opinion of the volley soon softened once it was demonstrated how to play it effectively *and* gracefully, but the lob was not adopted as wholeheartedly, demonstrating apparently a 'poverty of resource' (Ritchie 1910:59). Brownlee (1889:141) expressed vehement opposition: 'I have seen one or two players collapse when lobbing was introduced, alleging that they had come to play lawn tennis, not pitch and toss.' The lob emerged as a solution to the "problem" of the volleyer (Lake 2011a), but it was considered 'unattractive' to constantly lob an opponent, and unsporting if he/she was facing the sun (Baddeley 1895; Heathcote 1890). The Renshaw brothers exposed the lob's weakness by cultivating the overhead smash, which apparently, 'frightened the life out of opponents' (Haylett and Evans 1989:18), and etiquette demanded the control of force as a matter of self-regulation. 'Such violence is seldom necessary', argued Heathcote (1890:236), while Dwight (1886:35) considered smashing 'an amusement that should be strictly confined to exhibition matches'.

Originally, serving was a simple means of putting the ball in play and 'naturally of the under-hand species', and players experimenting with hard overhead serves were denounced as 'mean-spirited' (Baddeley 1895:14). Advice was given to limit its speed to just 30 mph; anything quicker 'is more than counterbalanced by the diminution of certainty' (*Pastime* 27 July 1883:134). Throughout the 1890s there were widespread calls for its temperance or even its complete abolition as it 'interferes with the real pleasure of a friendly game', makes long rallies 'impossible', 'drives women off the ground', and discourages 'many men who are not bad hands at the game' (*The Standard*, cited in *Pastime* 26 July 1893:50). Opinion was always divided on these subjects, and even some elite-level players pressed for rule changes that ensured longer rallies and a better balance between the server and receiver. The Scotsman H.S. Mahony proposed amendments to the foot-fault rule to ensure the serve-and-volley game did not continue to 'spoil' baseline play (*Pastime* 19 May 1897:38). Overall, there is a clear sense that aggressive play was something to be controlled closely, to avert the emergence of vulgar styles built on, as Gore (1890:290) described it, 'nothing but brute force and ignorance'.

Tactical, thoughtful and restrained play still commanded the greatest admiration, even if not necessarily the greatest success (Lake 2011a). Grace and effortlessness were equated with upper-class qualities, implying 'natural ability, and thus superiority over those who had to expend effort' (Collins 2009:34). This equation is noticeable when comparing casual descriptions of certain players. The 1887 Wimbledon singles champion, Herbert Lawford, played in a style that was

> effective in practice [but] theoretically incorrect. ... [His] strokes, though powerful, are without that grace and delicacy which are among the chief attractions of the game; and whose execution is diametrically opposed to that which is generally accepted as correct. ... [His] powerful hitting ... detracts much from the game as a spectacle.
> (*Pastime* 13 July 1887:126)

The Renshaw brothers, by comparison, played a "perfect" game, embodying refined athleticism and graceful aesthetic brilliance.

Descriptions of effortlessness stretched also to their off-court preparations. It was apparently 'well known' that William 'does not trouble about training' (Brownlee 1889:96), and similarly of Ernest, that he 'is supposed to do rather less [preparation], yet no one has exhibited more wonderful proofs of endurance' (Heathcote 1890:254). It was said similarly of Joshua Pim, arguably Ireland's greatest ever player: his game 'was executed with such ease and nonchalance as to give the impression that he was taking no interest in the proceedings' (Mahony; cited in Barrett and Little 2006:18). Such celebrations of effortlessness contradicted the calculated pre-match preparations that some of the best players were known to indulge in. Wilberforce (1889:55) advised living 'moderately' during tournament season: to be in bed by midnight, smoke no more than five cigarettes per day and abstain from alcohol. Baddeley (1895:78) added: 'refrain from eating pastry at lunch, avoid dancing until the early hours of the morning [and] drink iced-water with brandy as a refreshment'. Holt (1989:100) contextualised the idea of hard training as 'bad form': 'Practising too much undermined natural grace and talent. For amateurs were above all gentlemen, and gentlemen were not supposed to toil and sweat for their laurels.' Players gave the impression of effortlessness even if they "toiled" and "sweated" behind the scenes.

Dialogue in the leading lawn tennis magazines of the late nineteenth century focused predominantly on the men's singles game. Doubles was less popular at the elite level and commanded less attention, but there was also an assumption that playing styles, tactics and etiquette here naturally followed on from the singles game. Players often felt a personal responsibility to ensure their teammates and opponents enjoyed the experience; thus, the act of 'poaching' shots that were aimed at your partner was one particular practice that caused offence. Dwight (1886:61–2) advised:

> You may often see a ball which you feel sure that you can play better than your partner, although it is not on your side of the court. My advice would always be – 'don't touch such a ball'. ... It is a mistake to let [your partner] see that you do not trust him.

Similarly, Heathcote (1890:265) derided this 'selfish fellow' for 'entirely spoiling his partners play'; 'What a comfort it would be', he remarked, 'if he would only learn to play in a quiet and unostentatious way, and not take more than his share of the plums.'

Given their greater command of strokes, from a tactical perspective, men's doubles matches tended to be more exciting and interesting spectacles. The custom of both players attempting to approach the net together was quickly established, but of course demanded volleying skills. Women's doubles tended to garner less interest from spectators because the players often stayed at the baseline. In 1885, the AELTC rejected a proposal to introduce a ladies' doubles championship on the grounds that 'it would not represent serious competitive tennis', and most women agreed it would be 'no more than a boring and interminable form of pat-ball' (McCrone 1988:162). A review of the 1890 Brighton tournament brought the following analysis:

> Is it dreadfully ungallant to say that the least interesting contest at a lawn tennis tournament is the 'Ladies Doubles'? ... Such an opinion was frequently expressed last week. ... Many of the ties ... were tests of sheer endurance and patience rather than of skill.
> (*Pastime* 10 September 1890:195)

As an indirect consequence of falling spectator interest in these long matches of monotonous back-court play, the United States Lawn Tennis Association (USLTA) reduced the length of women's matches from best-of-five sets to best-of-three in 1902. The Irish Championships began in 1879 with best-of-five-set matches, but also soon reverted. In 1914, a British correspondent declared: 'We hope that no one will ever dream of proposing "five sets for women" in England. Just picture to yourselves a five-set match between four baseliners in a ladies' double!' (*LT&B* 8 January 1914:178).

Some suggested dropping women's events from tournaments altogether, but others with apparently greater foresight noted the importance of women's 'social charms' to a tournament's popularity (Myers 1903:166; Sterry 1903:122). Lowerson (1993:98) boldly asserted that women were 'the real arbitrating force' in tennis, responsible for setting standards of 'style, etiquette and petty nuances'. Their presence in sports in general, according to

Lady Greville (1894:iii–iv), was to raise its moral tone: to 'refine the coarser ways of men', 'contribute to the disuse of bad language' and 'lead the way in habits of courtesy and kindness'. The majority of clubs accepted females as regular members and in equal number to men, and chivalry demanded the accommodation of female involvement at least to some extent. It was in mixed doubles where the on-court impact of women was most clearly felt. Not only was it the game of choice in many garden parties and clubs, but it also offered a unique platform from which prevailing attitudes to appropriate uses of the body, on-court conduct between men and women, and the suitableness of female fashions could be judged (Lake 2012). Gender norms were reinforced on court, as men demonstrated a restrained form of physical prowess, combining strength, dexterity and agility, and women exhibited grace, delicacy and a carefree attitude to competition.

These characteristics of play were reinforced through the countless artistic impressions of mixed doubles in the late Victorian era. John Lavery, in particular, captured the physical restraints of women's play juxtaposed with male effortlessness in *A Rally* (1885), which showed a woman desperately stretching down for a ball wearing the most cumbersome of dresses, while her male opponent appears nonchalant across the net in a loose-fitting shirt and trousers. Similarly, George Kilburne in *A Game of Tennis* (1882) depicts two young ladies indulged in a game, clad in the tightest of corseted outfits; one is swinging gingerly toward the other, but discarded balls by their feet and their close proximity to the net illustrate the huge efforts required to sustain a rally. Such impressions provide testament to the determination, strength, flexibility and stamina needed for women to indulge in this pastime being seriously hampered not only through dress restraints but strict social conventions, which perhaps provides a rationale for why women dominated in artistic portrayals of lawn tennis up until the interwar years (Sumner 2011). Their involvement in physical activity of this nature was a novelty for others to observe; an image enhanced significantly by their tendency to be clad in their most attractive outfits.

Despite women being allowed and in some cases encouraged to play alongside men, their customary tight corsets, heavy dresses and hats ensured they were often hopeless partners (Elks 2004). Appeals were made in 1874 for gentlemen to 'serve easy balls' to ladies, play 'near to [them] as far as possible', and allow them to 'serve from [a] crease', five yards from the net (*The Field* 25 July 1874). It was recommended: 'a lady should be allowed to refuse as many services as she likes' (*The Field* 8 August 1874). Suggestions were made repeatedly for producing lighter-weight and/or smaller rackets for ladies, and in 1879, complaints were raised about 'the weight of the balls, the strain of the muscles of the hand, the danger of being hit in the eye'; special rules for women at garden parties were proposed to prevent injuries (Dod 1890:307). Given these social expectations, men in mixed doubles were expected to take most of the difficult shots, overhead smashes and volleys, and play on the more challenging backhand side (Lake 2012).

Given its less strenuous requirements, women typically preferred mixed or ladies' doubles ahead of singles. Cambridge University made an important statement in 1883 by introducing an inter-varsity Challenge Cup competition between the new women's colleges of Girton and Newnham, but only doubles was played (Birley 1995a). There was reportedly a widespread 'aversion to figuring as single combatants':

> No event in a programme is more difficult to fill than the Ladies Singles. There are sometimes at our great meetings only some two or three candidates for the valuable challenge cups or prizes, and one is fairly content if even a single match is seen.
> (*Pastime* 12 June 1889:378)

The doubles game more naturally suited the demand for restrained play, so perhaps women generally avoided singles because of their reduced mobility. Alternatively, perhaps they sought to avoid their appearance being marred by their efforts, as a *Daily Graphic* writer warned: 'In spite of the prettiest dress and daintiest hat ... a girl cannot help remembering that she is not looking her best when she is hot, flushed, dishevelled and thirsty after a well-contested game' (cited in *Pastime* 8 July 1891:22). Through behavioural practices in lawn tennis, the ideologies of female social docility and submissiveness, physiological frailty and emotional ineptitude were persistently reinforced, and combined to check their progress.

The "appropriate" social space for Victorian bourgeois women was in the home, where they were charged, according to the leading art critic and social commentator John Ruskin (1865), with securing 'order, comfort and loveliness'; women were venerated as 'the personification of innocence and purity ... the civilizing force of the universe ... the source of human warmth, tenderness [and] domestic peace' (Bédarida 1979:118). Young women especially were expected to appear as immaculate ornaments of beauty and respectability, as appearances reflected their respective fathers' or husbands' affluence and social standing more generally (Hargreaves 1985, 1994). Running, lunging and perspiring heavily on-court were certainly not activities "becoming" of a lady, thus women at garden parties tended to adopt roles that were merely an extension of home-life domestic duties, through the preparation and serving of refreshments. It was thought that rigorous physical activity was physiologically unsuitable for women, and that sporting participation would threaten established domestic conventions (Hargreaves 1994; Pfister 1990; Summers 2001; Vertinsky 1994). Similar ideas stretched across other sports, including golf (George 2010), cycling (Simpson 2001), swimming (Hargreaves 1985), hockey (Murray, cited in Dyhouse 1976) and rowing (Schweinbenz 2010). Shifting attitudes in the decades preceding WWI helped challenge these ideals, but developments in sport were part of a more comprehensive process of female emancipation that was never entirely completed. In some cases, women pushed the boundaries of female suitability, but, paradoxically, in others, their behaviour merely reinforced underlying assumptions about their physical subordination.

Throughout the late nineteenth century, middle-class women in growing numbers formed themselves into political movements, which campaigned, among other things, for greater economic freedom from husbands and fathers, and the rights to own property and vote. Feminists such as Elizabeth Stuart Phelps, who stressed the links between the body, physical emancipation, dress reform and wider goals of suffrage, were challenged by female writers such as the anonymous 'Young Widow' in 1892, who urged readers to 'remain womanly and womanish in every way' otherwise suffer 'unattractive spinsterhood' (cited in Summers 2001:147), and Social-Darwinists such as Arabella Kenealy, who declared that muscles acquired by girls through sport were 'stigmata of abnormal sex-transformation' (Fletcher 1985:149). Indeed, 'what made the struggle for feminists so hard ... in addition to the instincts of domination and the prejudices of men', argued Bédarida (1979:120), was that 'they had to cope with the passivity and resignation of their own sex'. Scientific arguments, religious exhortations and later eugenic theories opposed collectively the idea of women playing sport; taken-for-granted biological differences and social roles helped reinforce seemingly immutable female characteristics of nurturance, domesticity, passivity and intuitive morality (Mangan 1989). Hargreaves (1994:43–4) argued: 'Biological ideas were used specifically to construct social ideas about gender and to defend inequalities between men and women in sports. ... Scientific arguments [were used] to depict women as passive victims of their biology'.

The introduction of callisthenic activities in girls' public schools, the rampant spread of women's gymnastics in Madame Bergman Osterberg's colleges of physical training, and the growth of competitive sport among and between educational establishments, provided women with physical spaces to experiment with more vibrant and physically liberating exercise methods in the 1870s and 80s (Tranter 1998). Roedean, a private-residential school for girls that modelled its games structure on boys' public schools, provided lawn tennis facilities upon opening in 1885, as did Somerville Hall and Lady Margaret Hall of Oxford University (Holt 1989). Women excelled at hockey and, in the 1890s, they popularised cycling, which, although not universally approved, came to symbolise the increasing spatial freedom and familial independence that young women sought (Birley 1995a).

In the public domain, women's dress was a leading issue for first-wave feminists; it contributed to the justification of their subordinate social and political positions and inability to perform demanding physical movements (Hargreaves 1985; Park 1989). Warner (2006:46) remarked: the 'restrained and ladylike nature of the game was a blessing' for women urged to dress in the latest fashions, which in the 1880s demanded the 'tightest fit' of any decade since the seventeenth century. 'Corsets were considered a practical necessity if you wanted to be fashionable' (Elks 2004:12), and on the tennis court, it was evident that 'fashion should prevail over comfort' (Cunnington and Mansfield 1969:83). Moreover, elaborate clothing covering nearly the entire body sustained modesty for women and ensured protection from the potentially damaging (or tanning) effects of the sun (Elks 2011). White became the standard colour for lawn tennis, not only because of the game's associations with cricket and its ideals of modesty and amateur purity, but also, crucially for females, it kept players cool and hid perspiration patches (Elks 2004; Schultz 2014; Warren 1993).

When appeals were made for improved play throughout the 1880s and 90s, only modest recommendations for changing attire were accepted. The suggestion made in 1886 of a Moorish-styled outfit of loose silk trousers and bodice was opposed because it was considered 'hardly indicative of good taste'; the female correspondent was 'convinced' that, 'were any of the leading players to adopt the kind of dress advocated, it would deal a death-blow to lawn tennis in public' (*Pastime* 26 May 1886:351). Similarly, when the far more suitable "bloomer" outfit arrived as an apposite and earnest challenge to traditional corsetry, it was 'ridiculed and derided on both sides of the Atlantic' and widely regarded as risqué and unattractive (Summers 2001:145). For Schultz (2014:34), the bloomer was associated with 'dress reform, practicality, emancipation, personal preference and derision … publicly [challenging] gender norms [and] demonstrating clothing's powerful political symbolism'. At a deeper level, fears abounded that 'loose clothing meant loose morals'; thus, the issue was as much about gender and fears over sexual naivety as about class and the requirements of bourgeois respectability. For change to come, it had to be adopted by the social arbiters of good taste, both male and female, and had to be driven through avenues that did not directly challenge deeply rooted and widely held social norms.

Enter Lottie Dod. In 1887, the year of the first of her five Wimbledon singles Championships, she played in an uncorseted outfit, tolerable because she was just 15 years of age. Her free-flowing dress allowed movements that her older opponents wearing 'conventional English' costumes simply could not replicate (Schultz 2014). Moreover, she played with an attractive and exuberant style that was compelling for impressionable young girls. Her achievements coincided conveniently with growing medical opposition against corsetry; the 1888 British Medical Association conference featured a paper advocating 'moderate lacing' (Birley 1995a), though it was another decade at least until such opinions were majority-held by women. Nevertheless, Dod's opponents were forced to modify their own costumes to minimise her obvious advantage, a step that Dod (1890:312) fully advocated: 'How can they ever hope to play a sound game when their dresses impede the free movement of every limb?' Within 20 years, the 'great improvement … in the costumes worn by those who take part in tournaments' was noted by seven-time Wimbledon singles champion, Dorothea Lambert Chambers (1910:64), yet less experienced players were 'wont to appear in a "garden-party" trailing skirt, trimmed hat and dressy blouse – a most unbusiness-like costume for the game'. It seems the top players led the way in promoting more comfortable and functional costumes, most likely because the desire for serious play among them was stronger. Their aims to popularise such fashions were assisted by magazines aimed at middle-class women, like *The Queen: The Ladies Newspaper* and *Ladies Companion* that advertised tennis dresses for purchase or home-made production (Elks 2004).

Men's tennis fashions were not so closely tied to socio-political movements for physical emancipation, but developments were nevertheless conditioned by social conventions. Men's tennis costumes resembled those for cricket: long-sleeved white or off-white flannels and light, comfortable plimsolls, made of canvas or leather uppers and rubber soles. It was in the evolution of footwear where men most sought fashionable attire. The "Tenacious" tennis shoe manufactured by H.E. Randall of Northampton in the early 1880s was the first to enjoy widespread popularity, thanks to clever marketing and the employment of new techniques of mass production. By 1886, Slazenger had 16 different designs of tennis shoe on the market, and, much like women's tennis frocks in the 1920s, men's tennis shoes became mainstream fashion accessories for public consumption (Turner 2011).

Some females considered the impediments of fashion key to their playing inferiority to men, so much so they publicly challenged them to contests. Ernest Renshaw famously borrowed a corseted outfit from Mrs Hillyard for a match against two lady players in 1884, in what A. Wallis Myers (1903:98), the *Daily Telegraph* columnist, depicted as a humorous though perhaps derisive encounter. Renshaw won easily; the costume, apparently 'made not one iota of difference to his game'. In 1885, his brother William played two matches with Maud Watson, each winning one, but he gave her a large +30 handicap in each. Three years later, Ernest beat Dod 2–6, 7–5, 7–5 with that same handicap (*LT&B* 20 July 1911:400). It is unclear whether such encounters were meaningful for women at the time, or were simply indulged in for amusement. Likely the men attached little significance to the results, given that their physical superiority was assumed incontrovertibly.

Throughout the relatively liberal Edwardian era, changes to the dominant gender ideology had begun to influence women's access to sport and how it was played. There was a growing realisation, particularly after the Boer Wars, that 'physical fitness was essential to the ability of upper- and middle-class women to produce healthy babies' and maintain the nation's strength (Tranter 1998:85). Concomitantly, a new ideal of femininity emerged that regarded physical fitness as something that enhanced rather than detracted from women's attractiveness to men; a healthy woman was a greater asset in marriage than a perpetually sick one (Guttmann 1991). Chambers embodied this more dynamic and expressive femininity more than others. While often depicted as a conservative because of her traditional dress-sense, according to Gilbert (2011:196), she 'cut against Victorian "Corinthianism" through her intense and dedicated off-court training methods, which challenged the idea of women's tennis as a mere social practice'. These developments were matched by a mounting concern for, and display of, gender differentiation. Myers (1903:122) reminded female players:

> Ladies [cannot] be too particular about 'going into court' looking perfectly spick and span, for all eyes are on them. Many an onlooker understands nothing about the game, and the next thing generally is to criticise the player and her looks.

To underline the persistence of this tendency, Suzanne Lenglen (1920:99) made a similar comment in 1920: 'It must not be forgotten that neatness and style are also essential, since a woman is never more under observation than when on a court, especially if, as during a tournament, there is a critical gallery'.

Their persuasive dress sense complemented assumptions about physical deficiencies. Before WWI, women were thought incapable generally of executing complex tennis strokes, such as the overhead serve, volley, lob, smash and backhand. Often they were discouraged from attempting to learn them, perhaps as a means to differentiate the men's and women's games or to protect women's femininity. Female cricketers were discouraged from over-arm bowling apparently for similar reasons (Warren 1993); female archers used different bows and shot at closer targets (McCrone 1988) and female golfers shot from different tees (Lowerson 1989). Other more physical and confrontational sports like rugby and football segregated men's and women's sporting spaces almost entirely, whereas in lawn tennis men enforced subtle distinctions through conventions of playing style and etiquette (Lake 2012).

Regarding the serve, it was not until the 1910s when most elite-level women served overhead (Myers 1912). Previously, overhead serving was considered too tiring (Brownlee 1889) or a poorly executed 'caricature of a man's service' (Wilberforce 1889:269). Even Dod (1890:313) agreed that 'unless exceptionally good, and performed without undue exertion, I do think ladies' overhand service is a great waste of strength'. The volley was another contentious stroke. "What a pity ladies cannot volley", was a remark 'frequently made at tournaments', according to a *Pastime* correspondent; 'Could they do so, they would save themselves an immense amount of labour, and considerably curtail the almost interminable rallies in which they indulge' (25 June 1890:435). Ritchie (1910:75) considered it 'as a rule ... the average lady's weak spot'. Baddeley (1895) disagreed; for him, this (dis)honour went to the backhand. Wilberforce (1889:266) asserted: 'The efforts of most [women] to take a back-hander result in nothing more than a graceful swoop'.

Gender roles in tennis reflected those found in wider economic and industrial spheres, where men's 'virile' qualities were privileged: their 'creative energy, endurance, spirit of conquest and adventure, capacity for invention, taste for the rational and speculative intelligence' (Bédarida 1979:118). All found expression on the tennis court, particularly in mixed doubles, where men were instructed to take most of the shots and do most of the "work".

Female players should take a more submissive role, according to the broader notion that: 'It was up to the man, a being made for action and command, to protect the woman – frail flower, feeble creature, born to submission and devotion. ... To serve and obey, that was her duty' (Bédarida 1979:118). Thus, it was assumed that women in mixed doubles were only playing 'for the sake of appearances' (Ritchie 1910:75); subordinating her own pleasure in the game, a woman's chief responsibility was to make the game enjoyable for *him* (Lake 2012).

Hitherto, instructional guides had separate sections for women's play, women's doubles and mixed doubles, which implied different assumptions made of women's physical capabilities. Improved overall play throughout the Edwardian era, however, brought the following prediction from Vaile (1906:113):

> Before long it may be unnecessary to devote a special chapter to this game [mixed doubles], for when they have reached a certain state of expertness the rules laid down for men's doubles will govern the play in this class of matches.

He then went on to encourage women to 'try to play the game like a man', but added: 'she probably won't quite succeed, but she will play better than if she sets out with the idea that she is a mere woman and that the man has to do all the work and make the winning strokes'. The fact that a great deal was made of a publicised anecdote from 1887, when two women at a tournament apparently 'played in three or four successive matches with only a few minutes intermission', spoke volumes about the presumed physical (in)capabilities of women. It was said of this 'incredible' incident:

> The physique of the fair sex must be a great deal stronger than is generally supposed. ... Although they appeared much fatigued they played pluckily to the end, and set an example that many of the sterner sex might follow with advantage.
>
> (*Pastime* 27 July 1887:67)

Paternalism in mixed doubles meant displays of chivalry, and despite instructions urging men to take most of the shots, for example, they were supposed to 'ask the lady's permission' beforehand (Brownlee 1889:167). N.L. Jackson considered the gentleman's position more difficult, 'for he has to decide how many returns he may leave to his partner, while within his breast is being waged a fierce battle between the contending motives of politeness and expediency' (*Pastime* 2 September 1891:166). The greatest test of nerve came when men played shots toward their female opponents. Wilberforce (1890:267) recalled that 'in early days the tactics of placing the balls at the lady used to rouse great indignation'. Once, after he and his partner won using this tactic, 'the man on the other side came up to me in a great state of heat and said, "That sort of thing would never have been allowed at Wimbledon"'. Naturally, play of this type was not malicious or intended to frighten women; it was against custom, for example, to serve hard or hit an overhead smash at a female (Doherty and Doherty 1903). Instead, overplaying to female opponents became justified by chivalry; "giving the ladies a game", so to speak.

Overall, it appears men rarely took mixed-doubles games seriously or attached much significance to results. In fact, their growing popularity elicited public concerns regarding the future of the men's game and lawn tennis in general, as women were condemned for introducing an 'element of frivolity':

> Lawn tennis has been ruined by the favour of ladies. ... Feminine influence is a disintegrating force, and when women take up a game it is rather because it is new than because it of course answers to some deep-seated necessity in their organisation.
> (*Pastime* 9 July 1890:26)

Hinting at their supposed role in ensuring men's enjoyment ahead of their own, Dod (1890:314) instructed women to 'try to improve their play and not spoil the sport for men, as they too frequently do'.

The philosophy of paternalism made injurious judgements upon women's emotional stability and intellectual potential, neither of which was thought sufficient to overcome the complexities of lawn tennis. In the 1870s it was commonly thought that 'no lady could understand tennis scoring' (Dod 1890:307). Wilberforce (1890:266) repeated in 1890 that women were still 'greatly wanting in judgment; they seldom look beyond the particular stroke they are playing'. Off-court, McCrone (1988:164) reasoned: 'Only a few women were thought responsible enough to umpire, to be instructors or to serve as honorary secretaries or committee members of clubs, and even fewer to manage tournaments'. The genuine surprise captured by the following correspondent regarding a female umpire reveals the extent to which scientific and medical orthodoxy reinforced the social ideology of gender-separate functions and practices, and the notion of women's apparently smaller brains and 'psychological tendency to emotion [and] incoherence' (Tranter 1998:89).

> Hats off to Miss Blanche Williams! This young lady officiated as umpire in one of the principal championship matches, and in such an effective manner that many of those zealous young men who love to 'sit up aloft' must have felt particularly small. It was a daring experiment for Mr. Referee Jones to make, to put a lady in such a responsible position, but the fact that Miss Williams did not make more than one slight mistake throughout the match proved that his judgment was correct.
> (*Pastime* 23 July 1884:55)

Such notions of the "natural" innate intellectual inferiority of women were rooted in Victorian biological determinism, supported by Social-Darwinists like Havelock Ellis. He contended that physiological differences between the sexes resulted in behavioural and psychological predispositions; the female vasomotor system was alleged 'unstable and highly sensitive to stimuli, causing women to be mentally and physically more irritable than men' (Hargreaves 1994:46). Such scientific doctrines related to the inferior "nature" of women were internalised by both men and women to the extent that it became a "material reality", 'a part of everyday, commonsense consciousness, sustained by the practices and attitudes of women themselves [who] ... believed in their own inferiority' (Hargreaves 1994:47).

When it became known in 1886 that America had several women-only clubs, the report paid little attention to the notion, expressed by Hargreaves (1994), that such clubs were important locations for female bonding, where women were free from discrimination and sexism and developed a sense of control over their experiences that was otherwise lacking. Instead it was laden with mocking sarcasm: 'It is not recorded how long the deliberations at their committee meetings last, nor is it generally known whether the "tea and scandal" get mixed with the club business' (*Pastime* 27 October 1886:271). Women-only clubs also formed in Britain, but were only moderately successful at resisting male intrusion and persisting as enclaves of female empowerment. Sparkhill Ladies Cricket Club in Birmingham, with its thriving lawn tennis section, formed in 1889 but with two male committee members and a male president. Within four years they relented to allow men as members, provided they 'obtained their own pavilion and in no way enjoyed the privileges of the cricket section' (Pickering 1989:2). Other clubs and county associations accepted women as patrons; for example, Yorkshire LTA accepted the presidency from the Duchess of Devonshire from 1892–3.

There were also a handful of what appear to be exceptional clubs that appointed or elected women to club committees, as most were male-dominated. At times during the late nineteenth century, Ferryhilll LTC (Aberdeen), Carnoustie LTC (near Dundee), and Broadmead Baptist LTC (Bristol), for example, had a majority of female members on their respective committees, though it is unclear if most of the more important "officer" roles were reserved for men. Clubs like Bath LTA appointed a female "Lady Captain" in 1883, while Criterion LTC (Grimsby) and Doncaster LTC appointed a "Lady President" as distinct from the male role; at the latter, Mr and Mrs John Wintringham were the "President" and "Lady's President", respectively. Despite a two-thirds majority of female members at Braid LTC in Edinburgh, it continually declined to appoint women to its main committee, but relented eventually to provide a "ladies' committee", 'responsibly solely for the provision of refreshments on match days' (Tranter 1998:89). Lowerson (1993:207) contended: 'Where women were allowed into club buildings, as distinct from grounds, their role was essentially an extension of the domestic'. As if to reinforce these ideas, tournament committees sometimes offered domestic appliances to its female champions. One tournament in 1893 offered a new bride a "mincing machine", before offering congratulations to her 'lucky consort, on having found a wife who combines skill at lawn tennis with the cultivation of domestic virtues' (*Pastime* 6 September 1893:147). Hartswood LTC offered its 1914 male club championships winner and runner-up a cup and silver cigarette case, respectively, but for the ladies, a silver-backed brush and comb set and a case of fish servers (McLaughlin 2004).

As lawn tennis spread over time beyond its "fashionable" clientele to more serious players, dominant themes related to playing style, behavioural etiquette and fashion were challenged and replaced. This demonstrated the extent to which players from the 1880s onwards were responsible for creating a new "culture", in the sense that they modified aspects of the incumbent customs that lawn tennis initially slotted into, and in many cases went against common thinking. While this helped distinguish it from other sports and ensured its future popularity, it also brought new challenges to players and administrators. These took different forms between the sexes. As men pressed for stronger competition, and as the prestige of success in the leading tournaments grew, the traditional customs of amateurism were challenged from the inside. "Pot-hunting" emerged as a warning sign of imminent professionalism. For women, the push for greater on-court mobility through dress reform was matched with markedly improving playing standards, which helped lawn tennis lead other sports in its potential to emancipate the female body. It was in the growing number of clubs and tournaments across Britain where these developments were manifested most clearly.

Note

1. The height of the net at Wimbledon was lowered from 5 ft. (1877), to 4 ft. 9 in. (1878), to 4 ft. (1880), then finally 3 ft. 6 in. (1882).

Bibliography

Baddeley, W. (1895). *Lawn Tennis*. London: George Routledge & Sons.
Baker, N. (2004). Whose Hegemony: The Origins of the Amateur Ethos in Nineteenth Century English Society. *Sport in History*, 24(1), 1–16.
Barrett, J., and Little, A. (2006). *Wimbledon Gentlemen's Singles Champions 1877–2005*. London: Wimbledon Lawn Tennis Museum.
Bédarida, F. (1979). *A Social History of England 1851–1975*. London: Methuen.
Birley, D. (1995a). *Land of Sport and Glory: Sport and British Society 1887–1910*. Manchester: Manchester University Press.
Brownlee, W. M. (1889). *Lawn Tennis*. Bristol: J.W. Arrowsmith.
Chambers, D. L. (1910). *Lawn Tennis for Ladies*. London: Methuen & Co.
Collins, T. (2009). *A Social History of English Rugby Union*. London: Routledge.

Cunnington, P., and Mansfield, A. (1969). *English Costumes for Sport and Physical Activities*. London: A and C Black.
Dod, L. (1890). Chapter by Lottie Dod. In K. Duke of Beaufort and A. Watson, *Tennis: Lawn Tennis: Rackets: Fives*. London: Longmans, Green & Co.
Doherty, R., and Doherty, H. (1903). *R.F. & H.L. Doherty on Lawn Tennis*. London: Lawn Tennis.
Dunning, E., and Sheard, K. (2000). *Barbarians, Gentlemen, Players: A Sociological Study of the Development of Rugby Football*. London: Routledge.
Dwight, J. (1886). *Lawn Tennis*. London: Pastime.
Dyhouse, C. (1976). Social Darwinist Ideas about the Development of Women's Education in England, 1880–1920. *History of Education*, 5(1), 41–58.
Elks, S. J. (2004). *From Lycra to Whalebone: A Fashion Journey through Midlands Lawn Tennis History*. Birmingham: Susan J. Elks.
Elks, S. J. (2011). Tennis Fashions in the Frame. In A. Sumner, *Court on Canvas: Tennis in Art* (pp. 125–139). London: Philip Wilson.
Fletcher, S. (1985). The Making and Breaking of a Female Tradition: Women's Physical Education in England 1880–1980. *British Journal of Sports History*, 2(1), 29–39.
George, J. (2010). 'Ladies First'?: Establishing a Place for Women Golfers in British Golf Clubs, 1867–1914. *Sport in History*, 30(2), 288–308.
Gilbert, D. (2011). The Vicar's Daughter and the Goddess of Tennis: Cultural Geographies of Sporting Femininity and Bodily Practices in Edwardian Suburbia. *Cultural Geographies*, 18, 187–207.
Gore, S. (1890). Chapter by Spencer Gore. In K. Duke of Beaufort and A. Watson, *Tennis: Lawn Tennis: Rackets: Fives*. London: Longmans, Green & Co.
Greville, L. (1894). *Ladies in the Field: Sketches of Sport*. London: Ward & Downey.
Guttmann, A. (1991). *Women's Sports: A History*. New York: Columbia University Press.
Hargreaves, J. (1985). 'Playing like Gentlemen While Behaving like Ladies': Contradictory Features of the Formative Years of Women's Sport. *British Journal of Sports History*, 2(1), 40–52.
Hargreaves, J. (1994). *Sporting Females: Critical Issues in the History and Sociology of Women's Sport*. London: Routledge.
Haylett, J., and Evans, R. (1989). *The Illustrated Encyclopaedia of World Tennis*. Basingstoke: Automobile Association.
Heathcote, C. (1890). *Sports and Pastimes: Tennis*. London: Longmans, Green and Co.
Holt, R. (1989). *Sport and the British*. Oxford: Clarendon.
Holt, R. (2006). The Amateur Body and the Middle-Class Man: Work, Health and Style in Victorian Britain. *Sport in History*, 26(3), 352–369.
Lake, R. J. (2011a). Social Class, Etiquette and Behavioural Restraint in British Lawn Tennis: 1870–1939. *International Journal of the History of Sport*, 28(6), 876–894.
Lake, R. J. (2012). Gender and Etiquette in 'Mixed Doubles' Lawn Tennis 1870–1939. *International Journal of the History of Sport*, 29(5), 691–710.
Lenglen, S. (1920). *Lawn Tennis for Girls*. New York: American Sports Publishing.
Lowerson, J. (1989). Golf. In T. Mason, *Sport in Britain: A Social History* (pp. 187–214). Cambridge: Cambridge University Press.

Lowerson, J. (1993). *Sport and the English Middle Classes 1870–1914*. Manchester: Manchester University Press.

Mangan, J. (1989). The Social Construction of Victorian Femininity: Emancipation, Education and Exercise. *International Journal of the History of Sport*, 6(1), 1–9.

McCrone, K. (1988). *Sport and the Physical Emancipation of English Women 1870–1914*. London: Routledge.

McLaughlin, S. (2004). *Hartswood Lawn Tennis Club 1914–2004*. London: Shirley McLaughlin.

Myers, A. W. (1903). *Lawn Tennis at Home and Abroad*. London: George Newnes.

Myers, A. W. (1912). *The Complete Lawn Tennis Player*. London: Methuen & Co.

Park, J. (1989). Sport, Dress Reform and the Physical Emancipation of Women in Victorian England: A Reappraisal. *International Journal of the History of Sport*, 6(1), 10–30.

Pfister, G. (1990). The Medical Discourse on Female Physical Culture in Germany in the 19th and Early 20th Centuries. *Journal of Sport History*, 17(2), 183–198.

Pickering, J. (1989). *Sparkhill Tennis Club: The First Hundred Years 1889–1989*. Birmingham: The Club.

Ritchie, M. (1910). *Text Book of Lawn Tennis*. London: Health and Strength.

Schultz, J. (2014). *Qualifying Times: Points of Change in US Women's Sport*. Champaign, IL: University of Illinois Press.

Schweinbenz, A. (2010). Against Hegemonic Currents: Women's Rowing into the First Half of the Twentieth Century. *Sport in History*, 30(2), 309–326.

Simpson, C. S. (2001). Respectable Identities: New Zealand Nineteenth-Century 'New Women' – On Bicycles! *International Journal of the History of Sport*, 18(2), 54–77.

Sterry, C. C. (1903). Lawn Tennis for Ladies. In A. W. Myers, *Lawn Tennis at Home and Abroad*. London: George Newnes.

Summers, L. (2001). *Bound to Please: A History of the Victorian Corset*. Oxford: Berg.

Sumner, A. (2011). *Court on Canvas: Tennis in Art*. London: Philip Wilson.

Tranter, N. L. (1998). *Sport, Economy and Society in Britain 1750–1914*. Cambridge: Cambridge University Press.

Turner, T. (2011). The Social and Cultural Significance of Sports Shoes. *ICSHC Research Seminar*. Leicester: De Montfort University.

Vaile, P. (1906). *Lawn Tennis Guide or the Strokes and Science of Lawn Tennis*. London: British Sports Publishing Co.

Vertinsky, P. A. (1994). *The Eternally Wounded Woman: Women, Doctors and Exercise in the Late Nineteenth Century*. Champaign, IL: University of Illinois Press.

Wagg, S. (2006). Base Mechanic Arms? British Rowing, Some Ducks and the Shifting Politics of Amateurism. *Sport in History*, 26(3), 520–539.

Warner, P. C. (2006). *When the Girls Come out to Play: The Births of American Sportswear*. Amherst, MA: University of Massachusetts Press.

Warren, V. (1993). *Tennis Fashions: Over 100 Years of Costume Change*. London: Wimbledon Lawn Tennis Museum.

Wilberforce, H. (1889). *Lawn Tennis*. London: George Bell & Sons.

Wilberforce, H. (1890). Lawn Tennis. In K. Duke of Beaufort and A. Watson, *Tennis: Lawn Tennis: Rackets: Fives*. London: Longmans, Green & Co.

3 Social aspiration, social exclusion and socialites

Clubs, tournaments and "pot-hunting" in pre-war lawn tennis

The greatest and most notable boom in pre-war lawn tennis history was the marked proliferation of voluntary-run clubs, which replaced the private gardens of country houses as the key locations for upper-middle-class sociability. 'Local clubs' were, for Maclean (2013:1691), the 'basic unit of sports practice' and for Kay (2013:1655), the 'cornerstone of sporting activity', established in villages, towns and cities, and representing neighbourhoods, parks and workplace settings. According to Vamplew (2013:1569): 'They enabled people with a common purpose to come together, provided a basis for agreeing common rules and regulations, created a framework for competitive interaction and secured a location for participation and sociability.' Tennis clubs that were keen to establish themselves sought LTA affiliation. By 1900, almost 300 had done so, and by 1914, their number surpassed 1,000. Clubs adopted the function of representing middle-class interests and values; respectability and modesty were integral, but so was status competition. As visible representations of a particular community, and of a specific class within that community, clubs were constructed beyond strict necessities of functionality. Their conspicuous features helped in goals of social distinction, and at no time was this more apparent than during tournaments, which served the dual functions of allowing hosts to show off their grounds to visitors and of providing players with opportunities to enhance their status in different but no less pervasive ways. The aims of this chapter are to illuminate the peculiarities and complexities of the covert hierarchy of clubs and tournaments, and to consider the extent to which the latter's marked growth was responsible for the burgeoning professionalism notable among the nation's top male players.

Lowerson (1993) remarked on the importance of "clubability" and "hunger for space" in ensuring the immediate popularity of Victorian lawn tennis among the socially aspirational middle classes. The ways clubs were formed demonstrated the entrepreneurial qualities for which they were well known. Typically, a group of friends or enthusiasts that sought a dedicated space for their new-found passions would search for an accessible and affordable piece of land. This sometimes took the form of farmland or disused suburban land between residential areas or within neighbourhoods, which was most often rented from private usually upper-class landlords, the local council or land-owning religious organisations. Some clubs formed out of a syndicate, where members pooled financial resources to buy land and sustain control over its use. Just seven years after negotiating a lease in 1904, members of Hale LTC, for example, were able to buy their club's land outright and thus help to ensure its survival for over a century (Nelson 2004). Once clubs got off the ground, typically a constitution was written that alongside forming its rules also defined its primary functions. Clubs were invariably run with the interests of the amateur game foremost and governed by self-appointed voluntary committees that ensured the maintenance of its principal values (Baker 2004; Hill 2002). Running a club for profit was considered unacceptable; membership charges tended to cover only estimated running costs (Lowerson 1993).

Clubs attempted to avoid outside interference from "third parties", particularly government authorities (Heinemann 1984), though many tolerated religious influence by observing a ban on Sunday play. The AELTC was not one of these, permitting Sunday play after 2pm from 1888 onwards, but those with land rented from the Ecclesiastical Commissioners faced greater restrictions. £3 8s 4d was the hefty fine for John Berryman of Maida Vale for infringing bye-laws for Sunday play, and he protested: 'It was high time the rights of the community were not allowed to be subjugated to the will of an individual or two' (*LT&B* 18 June 1908:842). Such opposition reflected early movements towards the broader secularisation of Britain, and particularly England, in the late nineteenth and early twentieth centuries. There was a 'gradual disruption of the traditional balance between religion and society', argued Bédarida (1979:110), which witnessed the 'retreat of the Churches as institutions directing and controlling everybody's life', the decline of personal religious faith to a minority phenomenon due to the 'gradual decline of traditional Christianity', and the waning influence, generally, of religion as a 'cohesive force in the community'. Such developments, albeit gradual, continued to create conflicts deep into the interwar period, particularly with regard to Sunday play in tennis clubs (Kay 2013).

Overall, the process of "clubbing together" helped to reinvigorate community spirit among the expanding and increasingly socially and geographically mobile middle classes, who lived in new suburbs such as Gosforth, Wilmslow, Didsbury and Edgbaston (Holt 1989). Often, lawn tennis clubs were designed and decorated to kindle a sense of "rural" within an ostensibly "urban" environment, following the AELTC which promoted a quintessentially "English garden-party" atmosphere in what was essentially suburban south-west London (Jefferys 2009b). The core group of founding members were usually similarly socially positioned men and women of a particular locality, brought together through their love of lawn tennis and their desires to drink, socialise and possibly seek potential marriage partners. Other clubs were formed through a particular affiliation, such as churches and religious associations, athletic associations, schools, banks, hospitals, businesses, universities and colleges. The actual vocation of these reflected the relatively high class of their members. Companies like Lever Bros. Port Sunlight, W.D. and H.O. Wills (the Bristol tobacco company) and Cadbury Bournville went as far as providing lawn tennis facilities for their employees.

Regardless of their class composition, it is assumed that all clubs shared the common desire to promote internal atmospheres that fostered enjoyment and helped develop collective pride and an ostensible club identity. Some went about this by promoting an open and accessible culture with minimal membership restrictions, but were warned early on by a correspondent in *The Field* who described the potentially 'disastrous' consequences of committees resolving 'not to be so rigid in the exactments as to the position of candidates', or, in other words, of setting standards of exclusivity too loosely (14 February 1874:146). Most clubs tended to resist admitting lesser-bred members, thus lowering their credibility, but this was not always possible for those in greater need of financial security. The main qualification for membership at the Isthmian Club, for example, was "educational"; candidates must have belonged to the best public schools or have attended Oxford or Cambridge (Lowerson 1993). Other clubs judged a prospective member's suitability through choice of career. Holt (1989:113) suggested the 'rapidly growing cohorts of successful professional men' sought to 'pull [the social ladder] up behind them and set themselves apart from the massed ranks of the clerks, the managers, and the shopkeepers who made up the rest of the middle classes'. Todd (1979:9) elaborated:

> Careers in politics, the services, the diplomatic corps, the Church or the law were acceptable to [high] Society. Government service and financial activity, such as banking and the medical and other professions were a little lower down the scale. To be in 'trade', however successful, was undoubtedly middle-class and unacceptable.

West Worthing Club excluded people working in trade in the late 1880s: 'You had to be in one of the professions or services and certainly, for want of a better word, a "gentleman"' (West Worthing Club 1986:20). The exclusive measures used by some clubs to preserve their high-class membership composition were the ostensible manifestations of a class habitus that sought to maintain social distinction through action and association.

Membership of an exclusive club brought certain social advantages, affording opportunities to rub shoulders with highly placed people and accrue forms of cultural capital relevant to securing advances socially, politically or through employment. Peer approval conveyed prestige and brought individual honour. Like many others, Sittingbourne and Gore Court Archery and LTC maintained its exclusivity through personal invitations to certain 'ladies and gentleman of the neighbourhood', and 'in order to keep the society select all new members are elected by ballot after being proposed and seconded by a member of the committee' (*Pastime* 23 April 1884:261). Many clubs "blackballed" undesirables, while successful applicants served a period of probation.

The long-term survival of a club that enacted membership restrictions to all but the local elite was never guaranteed, of course. Some clubs with cheap running costs, their own land or generous landlords could afford such "luxury", but others trod a fine line, occasionally enlisting new members who, perhaps in an ideal world, they would rather have rejected. The perspectives of these particular members is near-enough impossible to obtain, and all evidence is anecdotal, but one letter of correspondence in the *Daily Telegraph* of 1891 revealed the unfriendly treatment experienced by one young couple during their first few months at a suburban club, which might have enlisted them out of some financial necessity. They made complaints of all but two of the other club members, who repeatedly ignored them, and subsequently, after having paid their subscriptions, felt forced to travel to another club in 'a distant part of London' in order to find partners to play with. The unfortunate new members were particularly perplexed by their exclusion given they, apparently, 'were not undesirable connections, and did not murder the Queen's English and so on' (cited in *Pastime* 8 July 1891:23). Poor treatment was perhaps a "rite of passage" for new members, as a means for more established members to ensure the maintenance of traditions and adherence to protocol.

If club members were carefully enlisted, committee members were even more assiduously chosen. This select group represented the club's principal decision-makers and ambassadors, and were responsible for making a positive outward impression. The role of the honorary tournament secretary was crucial, given that a club's annual "prize meeting" was the season's highlight and an occasion to showcase their club publicly. Many became as well respected as some of the leading players themselves. When Master A.H. Courtenay, the Fitzwilliam Club Honorary Secretary, intended to appear at the Championships in 1890, it was declared: 'Wimbledon will never, from a lawn tennis point of view, have welcomed a more distinguished visitor' (*Pastime* 11 June 1890:387).

Club patrons were equally cherished. The volunteer movement of the mid–late nineteenth century encapsulated upper-class values of fairness, association and solidarity, and lawn tennis clubs were attractive locations because of their polite civility and amateur status (Baker 2004; Hill 2002). Patronage for the upper classes was both a privilege and a duty and, though their actual day-to-day involvement was minimal – they were often merely figureheads – it stressed the need for 'maturity, ease of conversation and ability to deal with highly-placed people' (McKibbin 1998:97). Such a style came easily to public-school old boys, who were bred into leadership roles and thus accepted them as natural. The voluntary tradition reproduced 'dominant relationships of status and power' (Carter 2009:73). This arrangement also helped the middle class in their own goals of social advancement. 'Everyone loved a Lord', stated Holt (1989:111); '[none] more than the upper-middle class men who asked a succession of viscounts and earls to hold honorific office in their associations'. Aristocrats sometimes patronised several local clubs and associations as a means to enhance their status and influence. Budd's (2012) comprehensive research on pre-war Middlesbrough revealed that the ironmaster Arthur Charles Dorman found time away from his council (1897–1912) and mayoral (1903) duties to serve in one of his nine voluntary roles in sport as Vice-President of Nunthorpe LT & Squash Club. Theophilius Phillips, a successful grease and oil manufacturer, and also a Middlesbrough councillor (1884–7 and 1889–1904) and mayor (1895), was Captain of Linthorpe TC among six other positions. Though impressive, the Harrow and Oxford-educated Lord Desborough best exemplified aristocratic patronage, presiding over the LTA in the 1880s as well as the MCC, Amateur Fencing Association, Amateur Athletics Association and Amateur Wrestling Association. Throughout his lifetime he served on 115 government committees, including also as Chair of the newly formed British Olympic Association (BOA) in 1905 (Holt 1989).

Connections with royalty were particularly sacred, and the LTA through its official magazines repeatedly made attempts to locate tennis within broader nationalistic sentiments, as a means of asserting its prestige and attracting respectable patrons. To celebrate Queen Victoria's golden jubilee, *Pastime* (15 June 1887:406) gratefully recorded the Northern LTA's efforts to invite 'first-class players, ladies and gentlemen, to compete for special prizes', while for her diamond jubilee a decade later, the *LT&C* editor indulged:

> We have every reason to believe that lawn tennis players are among the most loyal of the Queen's subjects. We are sure, therefore, that we are only interpreting their feelings, as well as giving expression to our own, when we add our wishes to those which are everywhere being uttered for a long continuance of her Majesty's beneficent life and reign.
> (23 June 1897:114)

Some clubs and tournaments sought to use these connections by seeking royal patronage. Chingford LTC committee gained the patronage of HRH the Duke of Connaught in 1891, which prompted them to ask audaciously and ultimately unsuccessfully to change its name to the "Royal Essex". When, in 1884, the Renshaw brothers were honoured with an invitation to play before the Prince and Princess of Wales, *Pastime* exploited the opportunity by suggesting: 'The game is *the* fashionable pastime, and it would be charming indeed if royalty would set its seal upon it by appearing, say, at the championship meeting' (13 August 1884:108) (emphasis in the original). In 1902, it was proposed publicly for the newly crowned King Edward to grace Wimbledon during the Championships and thereby demonstrate his support for lawn tennis, as his contemporaries, the German Emperor and the King of Portugal, had done. He was never to do so, but his son, the

Prince of Wales, three years before being crowned King George, visited with his wife, Princess Mary. This came shortly after Commander Hillyard, who had served on HMS *Britannia*, had become AELTC secretary. This secured Wimbledon's royal patronage for years to come (Barrett 1986). In 1926, the Duke of York (later King Edward) actually competed at Wimbledon, partnering Wing-Commander Louis Greig in the doubles event. This, the jubilee year, also saw visits to Wimbledon from the Queen herself among other notably high-status guests, all of whom were listed on the front-page of *Lawn Tennis & Badminton* (*LT&B*) (3 July 1926). Royal attendance at events like Wimbledon or Ascot, according to Huggins (2008b:378), became 'repackaged as part of the traditional rituals of monarchy', and notices of royal deaths, coronations and jubilees provided excellent opportunities for tennis officials to reaffirm the sport's apparent royal connections, or make public appeals for patronage.[1]

Regardless of their social standing, all clubs shared the common desire for positive self-promotion, particularly when seeking to attract new members. Clubs used magazine advertisements and even match or tournament reports to describe their courts and other appealing features. Gainsborough LTC mentioned its regular dances, amateur theatricals and smoking concerts, while Victoria LTC (Liverpool) boasted a 'commodious club-house, containing ladies' room, smoking and reading rooms, a billiard room with two tables and the usual dressing and bath rooms … and a large concert room and conservatory' (*Pastime* 25 May 1892:332). Popular in Scotland were hardwood courts, while London's Hyde Park Club boasted the opportunities it afforded for indoor winter play. Despite their truer bounds, controlled light and no wind or sunshine interference, however, these courts met resistance from those who idealised the principle of outdoor recreation. A *Pastime* correspondent remarked: 'Indoor play … might be regarded as a retrogression, for there would be no denying that the game had reverted to a form of amusement, the disadvantages of which it had originally been intended to remove' (11 September 1889:182). Indeed, the depiction of natural and unspoilt rural surroundings was most common. Wirral Archers LTC illustrated its 'extremely picturesque grounds' and added it was 'well wooded nearly all round' (*Pastime* 16 January 1884:36). Stamford Brook LTC mentioned nearby 'fidds, orchards and picturesque old residences', before adding, 'with its noble elms and rustic hedging and fencing, [it] is probably one of the most beautiful [grounds] in the neighbourhood' (*Pastime* 13 February 1884:100). Dirleton LTC boasted its grounds as 'one of the most romantically situated in Scotland, being surrounded by yew trees of great antiquity, and close to the ruins of the old Norman castle of Dirleton' before adding, curiously, 'the finances of the club are in a satisfactory condition' (*Pastime* 27 February 1884:132). Southport LTC assured *Pastime* readers of its 'most satisfactory' financial position as well: 'there should be a future in store for it' (*Pastime* 13 February 1884:100). Given their infancy, it seems many clubs considered it necessary to assuage potential fears of an abrupt demise. Indeed, 'the best bred, most exclusive and most aristocratic of Englishmen do not regard any institution to which they belong, under such circumstances [of financial insecurity], with satisfaction', reported *The Field* (14 Feb 1874:146).

At times, this off-court competition between rival clubs was more important than on-court victories. Clubs fought for status as they competed for the highest socially ranked members and local elites as patrons (Huggins 2008b). Thus, matches between clubs were arranged principally for "social" reasons, 'drinking together in the early evening ... making and maintaining friendships with social equals' (Holt 1989:116). Clubs were careful to select the "right" opponents, judged not necessarily by their relative playing standard but by social rank. Scheduling mistakes in this regard often brought embarrassing consequences, as revealed in the following anecdote from 1889:

> In an old fashioned Kentish town there are two lawn tennis clubs, the one noted for its exclusiveness and the other numbering among its members many of the local tradesmen and their assistants. A neighbouring club, also of the genteel kind, had intended to invite the exclusives to a friendly match, but by some mischance the challenge was delivered to the town club, and they, feeling highly flattered, hastily accepted. The appointed day arrived, and the visitors, arrayed in bright blazers or smart gowns, journeyed to the grounds of the aristocratic ones, where they were delighted to find a champagne luncheon, with strawberries and cream and other seasonal dainties, in lavish profusion, awaiting their arrival. The hosts advanced to meet their visitors, but soon became aware of the mistake which had been made. The champagne luncheon, strawberries and cream, and the other delicacies were hurriedly removed, neither hosts nor visitors partaking of them, and a general coolness pervaded the scene. What was to be done? The home club had challenged the others, and the match must be played, so played it was. The full scores have not come to hand, but we are credibly informed that the lady milliners and *dames du comptoir* proved themselves much too good for the aristocratic ladies, but that the gentlemen, nerving themselves for great efforts, avenged their fair friends' reverses by defeating the townsmen handsomely, thus winning the match by the odd event. It was felt that some refreshment must be offered the visitors, who, instead of tasting the champagne, etc., were hospitably regaled on beer and bread and cheese.
>
> (*Pastime* 3 July 1889:3)

It was during tournaments that clubs went overboard to ensure their success, calling upon their esteemed patrons to distribute prizes and thus raise the occasion's tone. Local businessmen and other public figures used such events to boost civic standing and prosperity and accrue public revenue

48 *Pre-war lawn tennis clubs and tournaments*

from residents and visitors (Lowerson 1993). Provost Philip of Bridge of Allan noted in 1897: 'It is a duty to give ample facilities for bowling, cricket, curling, tennis, golf, etc. so as to induce visitors to come and bring prosperity' (cited in Tranter 1998:64). Tournament reports keenly boasted the appearance of aristocracy, who were attracted particularly to the most prestigious tournaments. The kudos of holding "championship" meetings was important, allowing tournaments such as those held at the Northern LTC, St. Andrews LTC, Fitzwilliam LTC and Buxton Gardens to be mentioned in the same breath as the AELTC, which hosted "The Championships", which by the mid-1880s had become integral to the social calendars of "society" alongside Lords, Henley and Ascot. As a regular event during the London "season", Wimbledon set the standard and style to which other tournaments aspired, as Todd (1979:193) illustrated:

> A ticket for the covered stand seat on the Centre Court – no queuing with the general public – and strawberries and cream, if possible in the members' enclosure, followed by a stroll around the grounds all offered a perfect setting for ladies dressed in the height of fashion, who were naturally accompanied by gentlemen correctly attired, to meet friends and engage in light conversation.

The Fitzwilliam Club in Dublin enjoyed the temporary status during the 1880s and 90s as 'the Wimbledon of Ireland', taking the opportunity ahead of the 1886 Irish Championships to spare few details to describe its tournament, club and surroundings:

> The houses surrounding the enclosed space are ... tenanted by Dublin "fashionables". ... In the centre of the enclosure is a splendid piece of turf ... surrounded by shrubs and trees now in their full spring foliage, their varied tints leading an additional charm to an already picturesque scene. ... The courts ... are arranged side by side, with military precision. ... A capital view of the play can be obtained. Tents for competitors and officials are pitched in convenient positions, while it is almost needless to say that the general arrangements are as near perfection as possible.
>
> (*Pastime* 26 May 1886:347)

When the Fitzwilliam hosted a match against Dublin University, the following review boasted the 'large and needless to say fashionable attendance... included in which were their Serene Highnesses the Prince and Princess Saxe-Weimar'; apparently, only the great horse show in Dublin could boast such a 'continuous stream of fashionable people' (*Pastime* 7 July 1886:5).

The Northern LTA was equally ostentatious in its declarations of social prominence, claiming 'the Wimbledon of the North', held alternately at Liverpool Cricket Club and "The Northern" club in Manchester, as surely 'one of the three great meetings of the year', typically attracting top players and large attendances. Another club that considered itself "leading" was Devonshire Park LTC in Eastbourne. At its tournament in 1885, it declared its daily attendance 'large and fashionable, in the latter respect probably excelling that seen at any other tournament, excepting perhaps the Championships' (*Pastime* 16 September 1885:201). From 1880, Buxton Gardens hosted the All England ladies' doubles championships until the AELTC commenced its own event, and throughout the 1880s and 90s it proudly boasted a direct train service from London provided by the Midland Railway Company. If not able to offer special transport, clubs like Durham Archery Club and Chiswick Cricket and LTC boasted their close proximity to train stations.

It is interesting that in match reports, clubs never shied from detailing catastrophic losses, but also never failed to make statements about their beautiful grounds, friendly members, competent referees, line judges and ballboys, the superb quality of their courts, facilities and refreshments and other superfluous details. This hints at the implicit prominence given to off-court features as a measure of prestige, though in some cases this was illustrated in more obvious ways. Weybridge LTC stated in an advertisement that 'it is intended *if possible* to play Oxford University' (*Pastime* 12 March 1884:163, emphasis added); a statement with no other purpose than to impress upon the reader where it ranked itself, or at least sought to.

Ultimately, for lawn tennis to survive, it needed to become more than simply "fashionable" among the social elites, and many of its staunchest supporters recognised the importance of carving out a lasting physical space for it. The press afforded considerable coverage to compare the relative merits of different sports, and debates about lawn tennis often became heated. The sternest rivalry came from cricket, whose exponents focused on the widespread participation of women in its constant torment of lawn tennis as 'effeminate' or 'namby-pamby'. *Cricket* magazine took issue:

> Many [cricket] matches have, not infrequently, had to be abandoned when a lawn tennis party is to be held in the neighbourhood. We may, as loyal cricketers, deplore this state of things, but we can do little more than offer a forcible protest against the sacrifice of a noble and manly game to the enervating influence of an effeminate pastime.
>
> (22 June 1882)

The article declared the growing interest in lawn tennis an 'evil' with 'pernicious effects'; cricket club secretaries were summoned to 'discontinue its practice on their grounds', otherwise suffer 'irreparable damage'.

When cricketers and lawn tennis players fought over rights to land use, amicable solutions were not always found and sometime underlying class or gender issues surfaced. Doncaster LTC formed in 1882 out of 'open hostility' between separate cricket and lawn tennis camps at their previous grounds. Recalling its formation,

> the meeting expressed unanimous opinion that the existence of such different games on the same spot was injurious to both; that it was a serious disadvantage to lawn tennis players to be controlled by a cricket committee; and that the exclusion of ladies from membership, on the cricket field, might be avoided on a separate ground.
> (*Pastime* 28 November 1883:436)

Particularly in Scotland, the arrival of golf, its 'natural enemy', affected the popularity of lawn tennis, but also in the south: 'at Exmouth, where links were laid down some two or three years ago, some whilom enthusiastic lawn tennis players have deserted the lawns for the putting greens' (*Pastime* 13 August 1890:131).

While undoubtedly tiresome, the tribulations associated with defending lawn tennis were managed confidently by its enthusiasts. Compared to golf and cricket, it was less land- and time-intensive and also the more active game, and claims to its effeminate nature were fervently quashed. Cricket clubs soon began setting aside patches of land for tennis courts, or proffering their ground for county tournaments, a situation not always welcomed. For the 1886 Edgbaston lawn tennis tournament, the cricketers had to 'swallow their indignation, and hand over their pitch to the Goths and Vandals of the ever-invading pastime, whose presence has already played sad havoc with the older game' (*Pastime* 30 June 1886:468). Numerous archery and croquet clubs also experienced the effects of its members wanting lawn tennis, but influences were undoubtedly felt in both directions, as all sports at this time vied with each other to attract supporters among a discerning middle class that was able to choose from a growing plethora of outdoor leisure activities (Lowerson 1993).

Competition with other sports was not the only challenge to lawn tennis in its early years. It also had to contend with huge swathes of social elites deserting the sport in search of more clear-cut opportunities for social distinction. Indeed, the increasing popularity of lawn tennis throughout the 1880s among the expanding and diversifying middle class, alongside the absence of crowd-pulling champions to stimulate general interest, actually caused a short-term drop in club memberships, tournament entries and spectator numbers. *The Standard* reported in 1890: 'There are thousands of Englishmen who are unable to repress a certain feeling of indifference, not to say of disdain, towards occupations or sports which are open to the whole world' (cited in *Pastime* 9 July 1890:26). Clubs like Earlsfield LTC in 1892 folded as a result of falling membership, and even Oxford University LTC experienced difficulties. In 1900, it issued an 'urgent appeal' for voluntary donations to 'save the club from extinction' after years of decline (*Lawn Tennis* 4 July 1900:173), and Cambridge University LTC followed suit in 1902. Tournaments in popular holiday destinations like Bournemouth, Bath, Cheltenham, Scarborough, Market Harborough, Dawlish and Clifton suffered temporary cancellations from lack of support, and the 1895 Wimbledon Championships reported, for the first and only time, a financial loss, of £33.

Through their collective action in ceasing playing, many social elites proved that it was not the sport itself but its social elements that held their interest. A combination of factors, including the instigation of new competitions at Wimbledon and the arrival of new exciting players, undoubtedly attracted attention from a more varied playing demographic, and lawn tennis could be said to have progressed through a general process of democratisation, downwards through the middle classes, over the following decades. The fact that some clubs were forced through economic necessity to open their doors to the middle-middle class, however, did not necessarily result in less exclusive practices. The further blurring of class lines merely gave them more reason to be conspicuous in their enforcement of rigid membership restrictions and other practices toward the exclusion of socially inferior players. Such actions formed part of the enduring legacy of British upper-middle-class conservatism that persisted well into the twentieth century.

In its first two decades, social exclusivity in lawn tennis helped to accelerate its rise to prominence, but in the early twentieth century this lingering element hindered its development. One *LT&B* correspondent wrote: 'One or two clubs may be attempting to discover talent, but even in clubs there are cliques, and any newcomer who shows promise is rather apt to be snubbed than encouraged' (4 September 1907:386). Another condemned further these practices:

> Many clubs are ruled by what amounts to an oligarchy, and it is bad for the game. They consider it infra dig. to be in touch with the ordinary members. They form a clique. ... Too many committee members ... seem to think they can regard the club as a sort of personal perquisite. They resent bitterly criticism of any kind.
>
> (*LT&B* 27 April 1911:116)

New members in many clubs were 'regarded with a jaundiced eye', according to another correspondent:

> If new members do not happen to be 'in' with any of the cliques outside the tennis club altogether, they stand but a poor chance of regular play and may come up to the club day after day without getting a game unless they happen to come across someone similarly placed to themselves. ... There are few [clubs], if any, from which [exclusiveness] is entirely absent. Whether the club be a large or a small one, we find the same thing.
>
> (*LT&B* 27 August 1914:935–6)

Growing class consciousness in British society during the Edwardian era evidently found its way into lawn tennis, facilitating the open criticism of social exclusivity among those victimised by it.

In 1891, 51 tournaments across Britain were scheduled at the start of the season. By 1900, the number had increased to 83, and by 1914, to almost 175. Initially, it was clear that tournaments were held for the enjoyment of a large number of players rather than a small and select elite. It was said of the bulk of tournament players, representing the 'backbone of tournaments', that 'not one of [them] ever has the remotest idea of becoming a champion, but merely of spending a week getting some jolly games, with the outside chance of winning a small prize in a handicap event' (*LT&B* 23 August 1930).

The marked expansion of tournaments proved a crucial testing ground for diehard amateurs who endeavoured to retain authority. Technological advances in transportation, such as the extension of suburban railway lines throughout the mid–late-Victorian period, improved access to club grounds and lowered travel costs for visitors and players, and improvements in communication, particularly the marked proliferation of cheap, mass-circulation newspapers and specialist sports publications, helped spread tournament news and assisted in making top players increasingly sought-after commodities. Tournament committees quickly realised the economic advantages of hosting top players, and at many events, their inclusion became an economic necessity. In the process, a shift occurred in public interest from seeing merely "good tennis" to seeing "the best players". The inclusion of foreigners added glamour to tournaments, and from the early 1900s, players found themselves under considerable pressure to compete *for* the spectators, instead of simply for themselves. When the Doherty brothers missed some important tournaments in 1907 for reasons publicly unknown, a correspondent in *The Sportsman* considered the 'peculiar circumstances' as 'an impertinence of the worst kind' (7 February 1908:3).

Regardless of widespread resistance to professionalism and commercialism, some were bound to exploit the economic opportunities of successful tournament hosting. Tournaments held in resort towns where tourist money represented a huge proportion of income were known to be particularly commercially oriented, often galvanising considerable support from private entrepreneurs (Durie and Huggins 2007). Some clubs went overboard when setting the value of tournament prizes to attract the stars. 'It is not considered safe at most of the best tournaments to dispense with [big prizes], and, in general, prospectuses bristle with "£'s" and "guineas"' (*LT&B* 22 July 1891:62). Outwardly, clubs refrained from attracting suggestions that they were encouraging "pot-hunting", which was the derogatory term for the practice of players entering tournaments for their prizes alone (Lowerson 1993). The behaviour of a "pot-hunter" signalled an impure abuse of the amateur sporting ideal: 'The tendency to run after big prizes only … seems to us a pity' wrote N.L. Jackson (*Pastime* 8 June 1883:24).

Lawn tennis was by no means alone with its problems of encroaching professionalism, and in fact remained free from some of the difficulties experienced in other sports like football, where the Football Association's (FA) legalisation of professionalism in 1885 led to the almost immediate collapse of amateur competition (Mason 1980). Athletics, pedestrianism, rowing and cycling were beset with betting and race-fixing, and rugby football with "under-the-table" payment for play (Bailey 1978; Dunning and Sheard 2000). Lawn tennis was protected in part because its leading players set such a fine example. The Renshaw brothers were said to 'as willingly play for the title of champion without a prize as for the most valuable trophy' (*Pastime* 11 July 1888:27). It was said of William: 'Although he could win prizes where and when he pleased, he has declined any but championship matches, leaving the many prizes for the encouragement of other players who cannot obtain that highest of honours' (*Pastime* 2 June 1886:367), and of Ernest, that 'he follows the game for its own sake, and treats prizes with indifference' (*Pastime* 1 June 1892:352). The Renshaws won 18 Wimbledon singles, doubles and mixed-doubles titles between them, and displayed the truest of amateur spirits. Their abhorrence to pot-hunting and their unimpeachable behaviour not only ensured their individual popularity but also put lawn tennis on a virtual pedestal of integrity. They set the bar that much higher for the players following in their footsteps, leading Wilberforce (1890:23) to declare that 'professionalism' was 'a taint from which the game has hitherto remained free', saying that 'fortunately ... there are no professionals at lawn tennis, or at any rate they are so few in number that they may be left out of account'.

Lawn tennis was a game to the Renshaws, not a means of securing financial stability, fame or recognition. Anecdotes were abundant of their impeccable sportsmanship, which sometimes bordered on absurdity. A match between William Renshaw and George Ball-Greene in 1892 was temporarily halted after both players repeatedly refused to accept the umpire's decision when given in their favour. It was said: 'The situation was highly relished by the spectators, but the umpire must have thought that excessive generosity was almost as inconvenient as its opposite' (*Pastime* 3 August 1892:70). In addition, William always conceded to his brother Ernest when they met outside of the major championships, setting a precedent for walk-overs and player concessions at many smaller tournaments. At the 1889 Taunton tournament, for example, 'W.L. Hancock obtained the first prize in the County Handicap after going through five rounds with only one match. Three of the walk-overs were given by others of the Hancock family, who declined to meet the youngster' (*Pastime* 7 August 1889:103). It was known also for players to split or 'toss' for a match if too exhausted to play, and full concessions were common as a courtesy to players seeking their third and final tournament win in order to take home a coveted trophy. Fans showed dissatisfaction with Barlow after he defeated Ziffo in the 1891 Eastbourne tournament final to deny him this honour: 'Among a portion of the spectators a feeling was prevalent that it would have been courteous in Barlow to refrain from the contest' (*Pastime* 16 September 1891:199). Evidently, some spectators would have preferred to pay and watch an award ceremony without it being preceded by any play.

At other times, players refrained from competing if no near rivals presented themselves, as James Dwight did at the 1885 Edgbaston tournament, or offered their opponents advantageous handicaps to keep it interesting. In 1888, Ernest Renshaw famously won the Torquay tournament giving the outrageous handicap of 'owe half 50' to every opponent he met. To the true amateur, none of these oppressive codes of behavioural etiquette or expectations of courtesy and generosity were approached with anything less than jovial compliance. This carefree attitude to competitive sport exemplified by the Renshaws epitomised the amateur ethos, which sought to emulate the frivolity of upper-class leisure but drive a wedge between the "working-class" attitude that was seen as impure, tainted with opportunities for corruption and driven by personal economic advancement (Allison 1980). This was the dishonour of professionalism, of which pot-hunting was its precursor. 'We simple country players regard the pot-hunter as worse than the professional, and from professionalism may the gods protect us', was how one enthusiast put it (*Pastime* 18 April 1888:232). Some correspondents suggested to eradicate pot-hunting by reducing the value of tournament prizes, while others were content to name and shame. C.W. Grinstead was derided publicly for securing 'a moderate balance to his credit', after converting his prize winnings to cash after the 1883 and 84 seasons (*Pastime* 23 September 1885:212). 'These tournaments are promoted', as the article continued, 'not for the special benefit of [Grinstead and others], but rather to give the general body of lawn tennis players an opportunity of displaying their skill, with a slight chance of now and again winning a prize'. Another correspondent even suggested: 'Winners of certain events should be penalised, so as to bring the second and third rank players a little closer together' (*Pastime* 2 July 1884:6). There was no sense that tournaments were restricted to the best players; instead, every player should have a reasonable opportunity to win occasionally.

The desire to control pot-hunting was almost universally held among players, fans and tournaments committees, but despite their efforts, the latter were unwittingly complicit in its escalation. In 1885, one member of the East Devon and Teignmouth committee demanded in *Pastime* that clubs 'keep their membership select and preserve open tournaments from any infusion of the rougher element of professional pot-hunting' (9 September 1885:184–5). Somewhat ironically, it was at this particular club's tournament some weeks earlier where a public complaint was made that their offer of money-cheques as prizes was tantamount to professionalism. Still, at least this was done in open honesty. Some cynics believed a culture of hypocrisy and corruption had begun to pervade lawn tennis by the late 1880s, with tournament committees and leading players in cahoots. In 1889, the Northumberland County tournament honorary secretary was asked by a wealthy local merchant whether 'there will be a good surplus to put into [his] own pocket' (*Pastime* 28 August 1889:151), and A. Wallis Myers (1903:110) noted the 'ignorant' public are 'apt to think the [players] make a business of the game, and stigmatise them off-hand as professionals or pot-hunters, or both! Now this is decidedly unfair criticism'. Regardless of whether allegations of "pseudo-amateurism" were true, it is more interesting to discover the motives behind why players and other supporters fought so resolutely to defend lawn tennis from such allegations. More than simply fighting to support their favourite pastime, they were attempting to assuage fears in the crumbling virtues of their social class in general; to deny the extent to which professional, i.e. lower-class, values were pervading an activity that reflected their class and culture. Such allegations threatened to damage the sport and the social, cultural and moral foundations upon which the entire middle class was positioned. Only when viewed in terms of a wider class contest can the passionate defiance against professionalism in lawn tennis be fully understood.

As these and other issues grew in importance, the need became apparent for stronger governance from a central organisational body, which would not only standardise rules of play but also bring order and structure to a sport that had hitherto been run in accordance with social and cultural norms largely derived from other sports. With increasing competitiveness among players, the necessity for democratic governance among clubs and the institutional promotion of amateurism was stronger than ever.

Note

1. See *LT&C* 6 February 1901:474; *LT&B* 12 May 1910:145.

Bibliography

Allison, L. (1980). Batsman and Bowler: The Key Relation of Victorian England. *Journal of Sports History*, 7(2), 5–20.

Bailey, P. (1978). *Leisure and Class in Victorian England*. London: Routledge and Kegan Paul.

Baker, N. (2004). Whose Hegemony: The Origins of the Amateur Ethos in Nineteenth Century English Society. *Sport in History*, 24(1), 1–16.

Barrett, J. (1986). *100 Wimbledon Championships: A Celebration*. London: Collins.

Bédarida, F. (1979). *A Social History of England 1851–1975*. London: Methuen.

Budd, C. (2012). *The Growth of an Urban Sporting Culture – Middlesbrough c.1870–1914*. Leicester: Unpublished PhD dissertation, De Montfort University.

Carter, N. (2009). Mixing Business with Leisure? The Football Club Doctor, Sports Medicine and the Voluntary Tradition. *Sport in History*, 29(1), 69–91.

Dunning, E., and Sheard, K. (2000). *Barbarians, Gentlemen, Players: A Sociological Study of the Development of Rugby Football*. London: Routledge.

Durie, A., and Huggins, M. (2007). Sport, Social Tone and Seaside Resorts of Great Britain, c.1850–1914. *International Journal of the History of Sport*, 15(1), 173–187.

Heinemann, K. (1984). Socioeconomic Problems of Sports Clubs. *International Review for the Sociology of Sport*, 19(3), 201–213.

Hill, J. (2002). *Sport, Leisure and Culture in Twentieth-Century Britain*. Basingstoke: Palgrave.

Holt, R. (1989). *Sport and the British*. Oxford: Clarendon.

Huggins, M. (2008b). Sport and the British Upper Classes c.1500–2000: A Historiographic Overview. *Sport in History*, 28(3), 364–388.

Jefferys, K. (2009b). The Heyday of Amateurism in Modern Lawn Tennis. *International Journal of the History of Sport*, 26(15), 2236–52.

Kay, J. (2013). 'Maintaining the Traditions of British Sport'? The Private Sports Club in the Twentieth Century. *International Journal of the History of Sport*, 30(14), 1655–1669.

Lowerson, J. (1993). *Sport and the English Middle Classes 1870–1914*. Manchester: Manchester University Press.

MacLean, M. (2013). A Gap but Not an Absence: Clubs and Sports Historiography. *International Journal of the History of Sport*, 30(14), 1687–1698.

Mason, T. (1980). *Association Football and English Society 1863–1915*. Brighton: Harvester Press.

McKibbin, R. (1998). *Classes and Cultures: England 1918–1951*. Oxford: Oxford University Press.

Myers, A. W. (1903). *Lawn Tennis at Home and Abroad*. London: George Newnes.

Nelson, J. (2004). *A History of Hale Lawn Tennis Club*. London: Hale Lawn Tennis Club.

Todd, T. (1979). *The Tennis Players: From Pagan Rites to Strawberries and Cream*. Guernsey: Vallencey.

Tranter, N. L. (1998). *Sport, Economy and Society in Britain 1750–1914*. Cambridge: Cambridge University Press.

Vamplew, W. (2013). Theories and Typologies: A Historical Exploration of the Sports Club in Britain. *International Journal of the History of Sport*, 30(14), 1569–1585.

West Worthing Club. (1986). *West Worthing Club Centenary Year 1886–1986*. Worthing: West Worthing Club.

Wilberforce, H. (1890). Lawn Tennis. In K. Duke of Beaufort and A. Watson, *Tennis: Lawn Tennis: Rackets: Fives*. London: Longmans, Green & Co.

4 The LTA's struggle for legitimacy

Early efforts in talent development, coaching and the retention of amateurism

Beyond the 1880s, what future lay in store for lawn tennis? The commanding exploits of the Renshaws demonstrated its potential to expand beyond restrained play and exclusive clubs, but with its rapid spread geographically, there would soon be demands for stricter rule standardisation and the control of tournament dates and prizes, not to mention the necessity of dealing with problems associated with the spread of professional and commercial impulses to the presumed detriment of amateurism. Connected to the latter issue was the new interest in identifying and fostering talent that was sure to emerge in the light of growing seriousness in play and keener interest taken in player performance and match/tournament results. The resolution of these issues would require a central authority, but to what extent were the AELTC willing and capable to fill this role? The aims of this chapter are to examine the process of shifting power in British tennis throughout the 1880s, leading to the formation of the LTA in 1888, and to discuss the push for talent development and emergence of paid coaches in this context. Unsurprisingly, social class features as an underlying theme, given the shift in authority between the elite AELTC and the supposedly more democratic LTA, and also in the context of how the new governing body dealt with escalating problems associated with the sport's modernisation.

In the early–mid-1880s, the first grumblings were heard publicly from leading players and club representatives about the need for a national association, not only for the purposes of championing the sport's expansion and dealing with disputes, but also to force the AELTC to relinquish their authority, as it had come to be regarded as crippling. In some respects, the desire to wrest power from this club reflected the cultural revolution that was taking place in the sport at this time, as the middle classes took control after widespread upper-class desertion. Much criticism was directed toward Julian Marshall, the 'colourful' but 'imposing' AELTC secretary, who inherited a very powerful position after the MCC relinquished its authority in 1883 (Haylett and Evans 1989). It was felt that while the AELTC had taken charge in standardising rules and setting precedents, it had done little to manage the sport on a national basis, popularise it outside of west London, or govern a democratic or representative system of decision-making. Meetings of club representatives were always held in the capital and convened by the club; they tended to attract southern clubs predominantly and consequently were broadly Anglo- and southern-centric in their focus. The 1883 meeting, for example, brought representatives from the Fitzwilliam Club, Liverpool, AELTC, Northern LTA, Manchester, Bath, Maida Vale, Redhill, Richmond, Finchley, Walthamstow, and Surbiton; geographically speaking, eight clubs from the south, three from the north, one from Ireland, and none from either Wales or Scotland. Also, the decision-making structure was such that proposals could neither be rejected nor accepted at the meetings themselves, but had to be referred back to Marshall's AELTC committee for final arbitration. One club representative remarked of this 'farcical' structure of authority:

> What practical results were likely to follow from all our deliberations? ... They had no binding effect upon the committee of the AEC, who were free to accept or reject them as they pleased. In fact, we were simply discussing and voting upon resolutions which were already foregone conclusions so far as that committee were concerned.
>
> (*Pastime* 17 December 1884:430)

Given that players from all clubs shared the responsibility of experimentation with rules, court designs and equipment, the idea of one club having the final say on all matters seemed unreasonable and dogmatic (Potter 1963). A correspondent in *Pastime* remarked: 'If the AELTC wishes to retain its premier position it must march with the times. The powerful lawn tennis associations which are springing up in various parts of the country will not be governed by an irresponsible body' (15 October 1884:259).

It is undoubtedly the case that the AELTC regarded their premier administrative position as prestigious, moulding themselves on the MCC and the Royal and Ancient Golf Club as not only their sport's leading club administratively, but also its cultural, moral and spiritual Mecca. Thus, in the early stage of proceedings to form a national "Lawn Tennis Association", first publicly proposed by Major General Bartlett of Exmouth LTC in October 1884, responsibility was passed respectfully to the AELTC. In keeping with the "amateur" principles that the majority of tennis players upheld, all correspondence showed deference, not resentment, to the club's efforts hitherto. *Pastime* wished to

> disclaim any idea of hostility to the AELTC, the members of which club are generally admitted to have done an immensity of good for the sport; and this unanimous approval of their efforts ... makes us cling to the hope that they will take the initiative, and organise a representative body to govern the game.
>
> (24 December 1884:446)

Such "hope" was short-lived. Instead of assuming responsibility, Marshall and the AELTC dawdled and resisted. Potter (1963:12) claimed: 'Marshall, impassive and dictatorial, scorned their interference. ... He refused to listen to suggested amendments'. This proved a counterproductive response. As time passed and reaction to their feeble efforts grew heated, the AELTC's public image and status declined. At best, they were viewed as incompetent; at worst, deliberately obstinate and transparently power hungry. What most hindered the club's chances of fair treatment was the partiality shown by the editor of *Pastime*, N.L. Jackson, who had become incensed personally at Marshall's 'rough-shod' approach to dealing with lesser-status clubs (Birley 1995a). Alongside running the game's premier magazine, he was also a leading tournament organiser, referee and handicapper. He described the AELTC as conspicuous in their lack of effort:

> Since last December ... at least two or three questions have arisen which required the decision of a governing body, but no steps have been taken to form one. ... I think lawn tennis players are justified in concluding that the Wimbledon Executive has no intention of taking action, and that other clubs should initiate proceedings.
> (*Pastime* 28 October 1885:296)

Daniel Jones, the President of Hyde Park Club, alluded to the AELTC's desire, despite widespread public disapproval, to 'cling with some excess of tenacity to the old order' (*Pastime* 11 November 1885:333), and, referring to the antiquated decision-making structure that remained in place, another correspondent queried:

> That [club representatives] should be summoned together, many of them from a distance, [to] discuss important subjects connected with the game, and that the representative of the AELTC should get up and say, 'I will refer these matters to my committee for decision', seems to many people absurd and intolerable. How long are we to be satisfied with the 'roma locuta est, cause finite est' [transl.: 'Rome has spoken, the cause is finished'] of the AELTC?
> (*Pastime* 18 November 1885:352–3)

At the meeting of club representatives a month later, the AELTC remained conspicuously silent on the matter. This was the final insult for external officials, who from that moment forward promised to wrest power from Marshall and bring the club down to earth. Revealing the extent to which the media had become a powerful influencer of public opinion, even by this time, they used correspondence in *Pastime* to fuel their campaign.

Public condemnation focused almost entirely on the Wimbledon Championships, the jewel in the AELTC's crown. The 1886 competition was criticised comprehensively for all manner of faults, including but not limited to the poor condition of the courts, the absence of linesmen, too few ballboys, no list of results and no published order of play. It was said: 'The AELTC occupies a leading position among lawn tennis clubs ... and yet its own meeting is so badly controlled that hardly one competitor has a good word for it' (*Pastime* 7 July 1886:10). In 1887, the Championships committee was criticised again for poor court conditions and also, embarrassingly, for not presenting the trophy to the winner until several weeks after the tournament had finished.

Next to be condemned was the AELTC's use (or abuse) of Wimbledon profits. It was said that a properly constituted governing body would 'turn to good account' the 'enormous receipts' of the Championships, but instead the profits were 'disposed of in some manner not known to the general public' (*Pastime* 13 July 1887:30). Frustration grew to the point that a public call was issued for 'some prominent player' to 'come forward and express his willingness to receive the names and addresses of sympathisers' who 'object to the domineering power of the AELTC' (*Pastime* 2 November 1887:299).

In 1888, correspondents took issue with the inconsiderate manner in which the AELTC set dates for Wimbledon: 'Little consideration for the convenience of other clubs is shown by this arrangement', wrote Jackson, regarding the AELTC's decision to schedule the Championships during the peak fortnight of the year, with an untimely two-day adjournment for the Eton vs. Harrow cricket match (*Pastime* 25 January 1888:49). Harry S. Scrivener, president of the Oxford University LTC, was asked to alter the standard date of its annual varsity match against Cambridge because of the assumed priority given to Wimbledon (Potter 1963). He was outraged. After garnering the support of over a hundred club representatives, a circular was posted to all club secretaries and prominent players criticising the AELTC's management of the affair and demonstrable lack of concern for lesser-status clubs, and urged everyone to attend a meeting on 26th January 1888 for the purpose of establishing a new and representative association. His efforts were successful, and the LTA was duly formed at the Freemason's Tavern in Dulwich that afternoon.

Marshall resigned shortly after the LTA's formation, but published criticism of his club and Wimbledon continued into the twentieth century, which demonstrated the extent to which its image and status had been irrevocably tarnished. In 1889 and beyond, there were repeated calls for the AELTC to remove its stranglehold on the All England Championships, to rotate the five principal meetings around three or four other leading English clubs. By this point, Buxton already hosted the ladies' doubles championships, while the Northern LTA controlled the mixed doubles championships. As spectator interest in the capital dipped in the mid-1890s, it was suggested: 'If the people in the suburbs around London do not care to see good lawn tennis, why not hold the Championships, at least occasionally, where the public have some appreciation of the skill and the difficulties of the game?' (*Lawn Tennis* 27 June 1900:158). In 1901, Wimbledon was said to have fallen below Edgbaston, Buxton, Eastbourne, Newcastle and Brighton tournaments in terms of crowds, entries and local interest. A visitor to Wimbledon in 1903 recalled:

> Never have I seen anything like the apathy of that crowd round the centre court. Half of them were watching another match ... and the other half were languidly chatting for all the world as if they were in a concert room while an indifferent pianist was performing.
>
> (*LT&C* 8 July 1903:225)

The sense of discontent was strongest from the northern contingent, where interest in lawn tennis compared to the south was apparently 'far greater'; it was said: 'Sandwich-men parade the streets, the papers advertise the day's matches, the railway companies run dozens of extra trains, and the people flock to the matches in thousands. It is a very different story around London' (*Lawn Tennis* 27 June 1900:158). Class differences played a part; the northerners depicted themselves as less restrained and traditional, but more gregarious and enthusiastic. Northern clubs and associations seemed also more inclusive and willing to promote junior competitions and develop talent. Singles competitions for boys younger than 17 years of age were held in St. Andrews and Scarborough from the early 1890s; the Yorkshire LTA held an under-17 competition for boys in 1895; and the Lancashire Association held a similar tournament for girls from 1902. When clubs from the south promoted junior tournaments, evidence suggests the initial take-up was rather poor. Ventnor LTC initiated a boys' under-17 competition in 1903 but received only three entries; the following year, just four. Following the 1905 Unemployed Workman's Act, which, among other local employment schemes, authorised the improvement of public parks, the city councils of both Bristol and Manchester built courts, but only in Manchester in 1909 did they form themselves into a Parks LTA. This pioneering effort was followed in Sheffield, Birkenhead, Liverpool, Derby, St. Helens, Sunderland and Scarborough. London, Cardiff and Birmingham constructed public courts as well, but were not sustained by an LTA-affiliated association. *Tennis in London* (1900) and *A Game of Tennis in Battersea Park* (1904) by the artist James Wallace support the contention that lawn tennis in public parks of the metropolis enjoyed considerable popularity around the turn of the century (Sumner 2011).

Geographically, lawn tennis developed strongly in certain "pockets", so wholesale north/south differences were imperceptible. Lancashire and Yorkshire were the first to found associations in 1884, four years prior to the LTA's formation. Northumberland & Durham (1885), Nottinghamshire (1889), Cheshire (1890) and Staffordshire (1893) soon followed. Lancashire and Cheshire organised an inter-club Challenge Cup in the 1880s; the first one in 1883 actually pre-dating the formation of both county associations. Sheffield and District LTA held the first inter-club league in 1891, which was unique also in offering both men's and women's competitions. Available evidence, however, suggests this was rare. The next women's inter-club league was not formed until 1909 by the Manchester & District Parks LTA. The North and Midlands were also well served by men's inter-club leagues forming in Nottingham (1893), Cheshire (1896), Derby (1896) and Northumberland (1896).

Unsurprisingly, the south was well represented with clubs and inter-club tournaments and leagues. By 1900, Kent, Essex, Surrey, Middlesex, Sussex, Gloucestershire, Warwickshire, Norfolk, Suffolk, Hampshire and the Isle of Wight had formed their own associations. The majority also organised inter-club leagues for men within a few years of being founded. The Home Counties Cup, inaugurated in 1899, was extremely popular, and lasted for almost a hundred years. There is no evidence of any inter-club competitions being staged for women before the Edwardian era. Middlesex was the first county to broaden its men's knock-out competition to women in 1902, and others followed over the following decade or so: Surrey (1906), Essex (1911), Kent (1919).

The Welsh LTA, formed in 1887, immediately introduced an inter-club Challenge Cup for the following year, but folded soon after, only to recommence operations in 1902. Its directives were split with the foundation of North Wales LTA in 1925, but it was not until the post-war period when specific associations formed to represent individual counties, like Flintshire (1949), Denbighshire (1960), Gwynedd (1960) and Clwyd (1974). Tennis in Scotland was on a much stronger footing. Fifeshire and Forfarshire formed in 1884 and 1887, respectively, and organised their own inter-club leagues, before the Scottish LTA was founded in 1895. Associations representing the East, West and Midland Counties of Scotland each formed in 1904 and held their first men's leagues the following year, while women's events were introduced periodically over the next few years. They were followed by associations representing the North of Scotland (1905), Stirling and District (1910), Ayrshire (1921), Central Districts (1921), Borders (1922), South-West Scotland (1924) and Wigtownshire (1927).

Despite the immense popularity of tennis across Britain, administratively "the south" retained its authority. Not only was London chosen for the Association's headquarters, but mostly southern clubs comprised the first provisional LTA committee meeting in 1888 that set about establishing official regulations. Clubs paid a small fee for affiliation in return for membership of a body charged with opening up new vistas of participation, developing new competitions and marketing lawn tennis in creative ways. The reality, however, was that the LTA had not established any concrete objectives, leading critics, within a few months, to label them an 'inert body', a 'phantom' and a 'myth': 'True, we have a LTA', said one correspondent, 'but since its formation it has fallen into a lethargy from which it gives no sign of awakening' (*Pastime* 12 September 1888). From the very start, therefore, it seemed their authority was undermined by inactivity and complacency, but also couched in a strong desire to sustain the "old order", by privileging class and prestige in the allocation of committee representation to only certain clubs within parameters they set themselves. Naturally, the AELTC had two representatives and Oxford, Cambridge, Dublin and Edinburgh universities each had one. It also privileged large clubs; those with at least 100 members were afforded representation, as were smaller clubs with tournaments offering at least £20 in prizes, because 'there are several clubs whose importance and whose services to the game cannot be fully measured by the number of their subscribing members' (*Pastime* 9 May 1888:276). This rule faced opposition as it excluded typically poorer clubs and inadvertently encouraged the practice of pot-hunting.

The LTA sought to promote inter-club competition in 1889 by introducing a Challenge Cup, but the matches proved a 'farce', played with 'apathy and lack of interest', and typical of an afternoon 'frittered away' (*Pastime* 8 May 1889:286). The competition brought an inordinate number of walkovers as clubs outside of London objected to the expense and time of travelling to the capital for matches. Only four out of eight teams appeared in the final stage of the 1891 Cup, which invited criticism:

> To the cup-tie mania ... the average lawn tennis player seems impervious. The entry for the cup was ... absurdly small in proportion to the number of clubs playing matches, and of this small entry ... as many ties were decided by the retirement of a competitor as by an actual meeting.
>
> (*Pastime* 5 August 1891:103)

As a way of improving take-up outside of London, one recommendation was to rotate the final stage among clubs in other cities, particularly in the North and Midlands. The LTA duly responded and staged the 1893 Cup in Edgbaston, but then many London clubs scratched in what was to be the last Challenge Cup held. Over the next two decades, the LTA experimented with more localised rounds and bigger prizes, but these minor adjustments proved ineffective. The same could be said for the LTA Inter-County Cup Competition, which was created to help better organise county tennis and bring together the nation's top talent, but complaints were raised soon after its inauguration in 1895. *Pastime* (15 July 1896:68) reported: 'When it comes to playing for their county, or to play for the honour and glory of the game alone, not one in ten [first-class players] comes up to the scratch'. For Britain's top players, lucrative club tournaments better held their interest.

The LTA's attempts to promote competitions and develop talent were earnest but found considerable opposition from the determined body of amateur players and administrators who resisted all "professional" impulses. The status of the professional across most sports at this time 'differed little from that of a servant or labourer' (Tranter 1998:71). Paid groundsmen had been utilised at some clubs from the 1880s, and their duties expanded gradually from court and clubhouse maintenance to instructing club members and training ballboys. Typically, wages were notoriously low and, even when supplemented by tips, rarely exceeded £1 a week. George Kerr was the first known club "pro", based at the Fitzwilliam LTC, and his genial and generous character secured him immense respect among the members despite his working-class background. Kerr's efforts were heralded as a chief reason for the club's early success, where he 'has done much to bring the Irish amateurs to their present high standard' (*Pastime* 20 August 1890:146). Kerr was soon joined by a small handful of other coaches. Charles Hierons began as a ballboy at Queen's Club in London before becoming professional there in the late 1890s; Tom Burke, another Irishman, based himself at the Lansdowne Club in Dublin; Tom Fleming resided at Queen's and Marshall at Craigside in Llandudno, North Wales, from 1899.

Exactly how coaches were treated by club members is difficult to ascertain, simply because they spoke out publicly so infrequently. Charles Hierons in 1924 became the first professional to author a book on tennis, but before the Great War their opinions were seldom sought in the press. According to Williams (2006:441), a similar 'exasperatingly scarce' body of evidence was found also among cricket professionals; very few wrote autobiographies or newspaper articles, and those that did tended to hold back from fear of losing privileges. Much like in late-nineteenth-century cricket, there is a sense that lawn tennis professionals "knew their place" within the rigid class structures of the time. Despite their often demeaning duties in and around their clubs, they were generally uncomplaining and deferent to middle-class authority. In terms of their behaviour and character, opinions of coaches tended to be largely positive. A leading amateur described them as 'quiet, respectful and keen opponents' (*Lawn Tennis* 8 August 1900:278). Similarly, Anthony Wilding (1912:41) considered the professional coach 'an excellent type of man, capable, intelligent and courteous', before expressing hope that 'every club [can] afford to place one on its staff'.

While some committees considered their services necessary, most deemed them surplus to requirements, and numerous authors of instructional booklets failed to acknowledge the need for, or the perceived benefits of, professional coaching as a means of acquiring proficiency, despite some of them having been coached themselves (e.g. Baddeley 1895; Dwight 1886; Heathcote 1890; Myers 1903; Wilberforce 1889). This lack of acknowledgement is a curious finding given the public praise received by the emerging class of professionals and the rising status of coaching as a profession. It was written in 1907:

> Why should a man hesitate to be a professional? If he loves the game, but cannot afford to play it without being paid; if the game helps him in body, mind or spirit; if it brings him precious companionship and friendship, and if he plays well enough to be paid for playing, let him,

for goodness sake, *be* paid, and be paid openly. ... What disgrace is it to be a professional?

(*ASI* 26 December 1907:309–10)

In 1890, the idea of staging a match between the leading amateurs and professionals was first proposed. 'Such games would certainly prove very interesting', responded a *Pastime* correspondent to the news (24 December 1890:439), yet there is no evidence of such an exhibition taking place until 1898, when Kerr, Burke and Fleming competed for a money prize in the Riviera. The Puteaux Club in Paris staged a similar event in 1900 attracting six professionals and, two years later, Nice held another tournament, sponsored by a wealthy American offering a $100 first prize. The first truly amateur-versus-professional tournament occurred in 1903, when Burke and Kerr were beaten convincingly by R.F and H.L. Doherty, the leading amateurs at the time.

This thwarted speculations of equality in playing standard, and amateur opposition to the event was so strong that the experiment was never again repeated. At no point subsequently did the LTA intervene to provide much-needed official sanctioning and, perhaps as a consequence, many of Britain's leading coaches moved abroad for better pay and conditions. Burke moved to France to teach at Nice and Paris, Kerr moved to Berlin, and Fleming plied his trade in Vienna and Cannes; *Lawn Tennis & Croquet* (*LT&C*) reported: 'they are well paid, and are bringing young players along very quickly' (27 April 1904:14–5). The Continental migration of coaches was not a phenomenon unique to lawn tennis but also occurred in association football and other sports (Taylor 2010).

The celebration of professionals was not shared by conservative traditionalists, who maintained their staunch abhorrence to money-making in sport and its apparent connection with the loss of 'intrinsic value' as well as 'greed and cheating ... gross ambition, gambling and moral laxity' (Gruneau 2006:572). Whigham (1909:740) maintained that it was 'essentially the mark of the bourgeois mind to specialise'. The fear of "professional contamination" was unmistakably present, but it was not the coaches themselves the amateur fraternity felt threatened by; rather, it was the exhibition of a "professional" mentality among amateur players, who might come to expect remuneration – if not money then fame or valuable prizes – for their efforts, place winning ahead of competing in terms of importance, and take new interest in training, specialisation and the cultivation of excessive muscular development. These were all contrary to the amateur ethos.

A path through these sullied waters was forged by the Doherty brothers, who were immensely talented but hard-working, and exemplified the burgeoning spirit of aggressive, attacking tennis and championed "professional" training methods. As exponents of the middle-middle-class value system that had slowly and silently crept into lawn tennis, they helped breed acceptance in the idea of victory through the physical domination of one's opponent. But, for most, the Dohertys were heralded as model amateurs of the new age when British successes could not be guaranteed. Thus, they offered a perfect solution to the growing problems associated with professionalism, because they maintained their endorsement of traditional standards of decorum through impeccable sportsmanship and their seemingly effortless on-court supremacy. The advancement of a more progressive and redefined amateur ethos had to be achieved in the context of established upper-middle-class authority, as strict amateur advocates scorned players who demonstrated a lack of humility. Self-restraint, magnanimity, generosity and honesty remained important character traits for players desirous of the fraternity's blessing.

Not all players were as gifted as the Dohertys in balancing such competing pressures, and unsavoury elements surfaced with increasing regularity in the early twentieth century. Some proposed stronger sanctions against professionalism, amidst fears that related problems in association football, boxing, cricket and golf might spread. Burrow lamented: 'The glorification of the professional ... always results and always will result in the introduction of commercialism, and the consequent spoiling to a greater or less extent of the game for the amateur' (*LT&B* 7 January 1909:50).

If it can be said that pot-hunting allowed professionalism to creep in the back door of the amateur establishment, then, correlatively, the sanctioned payment of players' expenses to compete abroad allowed it through the front door. Jefferys (2009b:2241) considered the establishment, worldwide expansion and growing national significance of the Davis Cup as a major factor in the growing "amateur problem": 'The imperative of extensive travel for leading players ... raised an awkward question about expenses. Was tennis to be confined purely to those gentlemen amateurs who could afford the time and money necessary to compete on the world stage?' National associations like the LTA set the precedent for paying travel and accommodation costs for Davis Cup competitors, but when clubs or tournaments offered the same, it was considered a different matter altogether. *Truth* in 1901 published fresh reports of "quasi professionalism", with top players (not including the Dohertys) accused of receiving free accommodation and expenses paid at certain events. Such occurrences would have directly contravened amateur conventions in other sports, but then British lawn tennis had no such rules defining appropriate amateur conduct. It was always, simply and unreservedly, expected. Worse still, the reports revealed that the LTA had sanctioned such behaviour several months earlier when it sent seven top male and female amateurs on an all-expenses-paid tour to Lisbon to play exhibitions for the Portuguese king.[1]

When comparing such an incident hypothetically to one in athletics, it was clear that considerations of social class underpinned the LTA's decision:

> I cannot imagine the Amateur Athletic Association for one moment entertaining the proposition that a team of English athletes should visit

Portugal and have all their expenses paid to run exhibition races. But then the runner is as a rule a man of a very different class to the lawn tennis player. Socially he is very often his inferior. But he is not allowed to have his expenses paid.

(cited in *Lawn Tennis* 6 November 1901:459)

The intimation here was simple: The LTA considered lawn tennis players superior to athletes in "class" and presumed qualities of honesty and integrity; thus, they regarded the payment of players' expenses as acceptable and an amateur definition unnecessary. The LTA's justification of the tour as a national duty 'in the interests of the game' was questionable – all the matches were played away from the general public behind closed doors – yet it still maintained 'there is no ground whatever for imputing the slightest impropriety to those who took part in the trip' (*Lawn Tennis* 4 December 1901:470–1). Indeed, fingers were pointed instead toward the LTA.

While support for the professional development of coaches was tepid, the LTA sought to make an influence in the area of talent development through promoting lawn tennis in public schools. They had long maintained that the entrenched unwillingness among public schools to recognise the sport was a major stumbling block, and in 1905 the LTA appointed a Special Committee to investigate the issue. The following year a letter was written and signed by the Association's Honorary Secretary, G.W. Mewburn, and sent to 29 schools in an attempt to encourage tennis court construction and initiate a public schools' trophy. Twenty-one replies were received: 16 unfavourable, 3 favourable and 2 undecided. Several reasons were cited for their refusals: lawn tennis would detract from the more established team sports of cricket, rugby and football and, moreover, was inferior in its potential to build character; lawn tennis was too tame and effeminate to be popular among schoolboys; and, according to Canon Edward Lyttleton, headmaster of Eton 1905–16, lawn tennis 'exercises only one side of the body, and causes lopsided growth' (*LT&B* 6 June 1912:324). Its adoption fared only marginally better in girls' schools. A headmistress of one leading high school replied that 'she considered it exceedingly wicked to encourage young people to waste their lives in frivolous amusement' (*Lawn Tennis* 27 August 1908:1187).

Such ignorant condemnation of the game by these revered public-school figures sparked widespread correspondence. Yet, interestingly, nothing was ever said about the provision of lawn tennis in grammar or state schools. Thus, while the LTA might have meant well in its early efforts in talent development, at best it showed a lack of foresight; at worst, they could be accused of sustaining snobbery and elitism. Meanwhile, schools and universities in America were reported to have introduced competitions from the 1890s. Bar just a handful of exceptions mostly from the north of England and Scotland, lawn tennis in Britain remained until the mid-to-late 1920s focused chiefly on adult participation and competition.

The overall outcome of the LTA's attempts to develop talent in the early stages of its creation, the initial point of which was to prove a more egalitarian and accessible body than the AELTC, was the sustained dominance of upper-middle-class authority. Thus, despite appearing to champion the philosophies of democracy and representativeness, the LTA ultimately differed little from the AELTC with regard to its underlying elitism. Its rules of representation privileged the largest and wealthiest clubs; its methods of promoting competitions to new populations lacked imagination; its support for the professional development of coaches was lukewarm at best; and, its endeavours to introduce lawn tennis to schoolchildren reflected an elitist worldview. It was only when the LTA involved itself in the promotion of international competitions that it demonstrated its potential to lead on a global scale and thus fulfil its administrative potential in a more deliberate way.

Note

1. The troupe consisted of Commander and Mrs G.W. Hillyard, Mr and Mrs Neville Durlacher, Miss M.E. Robb, H.S. Mahony and W.V. Eaves.

Bibliography

Baddeley, W. (1895). *Lawn Tennis*. London: George Routledge & Sons.
Birley, D. (1995a). *Land of Sport and Glory: Sport and British Society 1887–1910*. Manchester: Manchester University Press.
Dwight, J. (1886). *Lawn Tennis*. London: Pastime.
Gruneau, R. (2006). 'Amateurism' as a Sociological Problem: Some Reflections Inspired by Eric Dunning. *Sport in Society*, 9(4), 559–582.
Haylett, J., and Evans, R. (1989). *The Illustrated Encyclopaedia of World Tennis*. Basingstoke: Automobile Association.
Heathcote, C. (1890). *Sports and Pastimes: Tennis*. London: Longmans, Green and Co.
Jefferys, K. (2009b). The Heyday of Amateurism in Modern Lawn Tennis. *International Journal of the History of Sport*, 26(15), 2236–52.
Myers, A. W. (1903). *Lawn Tennis at Home and Abroad*. London: George Newnes.
Potter, E. (1963). *King of the Court: The Story of Lawn Tennis*. New York: A.S. Barnes.
Sumner, A. (2011). *Court on Canvas: Tennis in Art*. London: Philip Wilson.
Taylor, M. (2010). Football's Engineers? British Football Coaches, Migration and Intercultural Transfer, c.1910–1950s. *Sport in History*, 30(1), 138–163.
Tranter, N. L. (1998). *Sport, Economy and Society in Britain 1750–1914*. Cambridge: Cambridge University Press.
Whigham, H. (1909). American Sport From an English Point of View. *Outlook*, XCIII, 740.
Wilberforce, H. (1889). *Lawn Tennis*. London: George Bell & Sons.
Wilding, A. F. (1912). *On the Court and Off*. London: Methuen & Co.
Williams, J. (2006). 'The Really Good Professional Captain Has Never Been Seen!': Perceptions of the Amateur/Professional Divide in County Cricket, 1900–39. *Sport in History*, 26(3), 429–449.

5 British tennis as an imperial tool

International competitions, racial stereotypes and shifting British authority

The LTA did not demonstrate a serious interest in honouring their new responsibilities until they were able to sink their teeth into the challenge of promoting international competitions. This was an endeavour that reflected clearly an overall sense of supremacy driven by their sporting pedigree, and underpinned by imperialist notions of instinctive British leadership and racial superiority. The simple fact they organised themselves into what they called the Lawn Tennis Association, rather than perhaps the more modest *British* Lawn Tennis Association, speaks volumes about where in the global sporting hierarchy they considered themselves. What followed was an attempt to champion the sport's worldwide expansion, through setting standards and establishing rules for international contests and promoting codes of acceptable behaviour for amateur sportsmen. As this chapter aims to illustrate and explain, the LTA's endeavours in line with its amateur philosophy provided more contradiction than consistency at a time when Britain's need to supplant declining empire authority with other sources of national pride, like sporting success, was greater than ever.

Given its close proximity and long-established family and other personal ties, Ireland was naturally the first nation against which England sought competition, though sporting relations with the Emerald Isle were never entirely free of wider political significance (Bairner 2011). Lawn tennis developed there at a similar pace and among a similar demographic as in England and far more quickly than in Wales and Scotland, and mostly in geographical areas with a strong British settlement, such as Dublin, which staged the first Irish Championships in 1879. Clubs formed in variety, from the most exclusive 'county' clubs as in Limerick, Sligo, Kildare, Wicklow and Cavan, to those organised around churches or other community focal points (Higgins 2006). The Irish Championships were staged at the Fitzwilliam Club and attracted Dublin "society" throughout the 1880s and 90s, which helped sustain the sport's reputation and develop local talent. Willoughby Hamilton from County Kildare, Joshua Pim from Bray in County Wicklow and Harold Mahony from County Kerry were the pick of the Irishmen;

together they won four Wimbledon singles titles between 1890 and 96, leading *Pastime* to declare around this time: 'there is little to choose between the best men' of England and Ireland (1 June 1892:350).

Given its English roots, lawn tennis had a divided, largely Protestant following in Ireland (Higgins 2006). This fact did not prevent some Irish players from renouncing their British status, as John Boland did shortly after winning gold medals in singles and doubles at the inaugural Olympic Games in Athens. He declared: 'I refuse to forswear my "Hibernian origin" and the green flag in the field of sport' (*Oxford Magazine* 20 May 1896:173). Given the absence of formalised governing bodies in many sports before the war, Irish athletes were often included in British teams, though many endeavoured to distinguish themselves in their behaviour or clothing, often sporting green jackets or outfits when on international duty. Such attempts at social distinction, according to Llewellyn (2011b:654), reflected 'the broader historical struggle to achieve "Home Rule" from Britain'. The promotion of Irish sports generally in the late nineteenth century was unashamedly anti-British in sentiment. The Gaelic Athletic Association (GAA) that formed in 1884 signalled its intention to revive and reorganise ancient Gaelic games, like hurling, while excluding the British sports of rugby, cricket and association football (Bairner 2011; Polley 1998). In 1887, having galvanised large sections of Catholic Ireland to unite against the insurgence of British culture and the distribution of British goods and customs, the GAA enacted a ban: anyone who played British sports was prohibited from GAA-sanctioned events. In what Holt (1989:240) described as 'arguably the most striking instance of politics shaping sport in modern history', the spread of GAA prohibitions and philosophies represented a major stumbling block for the development of British sports in Ireland, even lawn tennis, which, along with golf and badminton, was officially spared in the ban given its unthreatening minority status (Higgins 2006).

Until 1908 when they formed their own association, Ireland was considered officially as a 'county' association of the LTA, and this patronising status impacted on its autonomy, to say nothing of its dignity in the unstable socio-political climate preceding Irish independence. Like most London-based amateur sport associations around this time, the LTA was a Conservative organisation and likely formed of committee members who opposed Home Rule for Ireland, as exemplified by Lord Desborough's (LTA President 1907–26) decision to switch his political affiliation from Liberal to Conservative after the Liberals lent their support to the Irish independence movement (Llewellyn 2011b). The Fitzwilliam members represented a politically Conservative and loyalist-Protestant minority in Dublin, so the club was not opposed in theory to forging links with British players or the LTA. However, much like the AELTC prior to 1888, the Fitzwilliam had adopted an autocratic position of leadership among Irish clubs. In matters of national or even tennis-related politics it was decidedly weak, though it ranked itself highly within the tacit club hierarchy, and as such demanded deferential treatment from all other associations. The club's sense of its own standing was revealed when the subject first arose of an international match against England. The question was: who should ask whom? The etiquette of extending invitations tended to allow the premier body the option of first refusal. Neither the Fitzwilliam nor the LTA wished to open themselves up to the possibility of embarrassment by an invitation being refused. Were it not for a handful of Irish players, who in 1892 circumvented the apparent stand-off by asking the LTA directly, a match might never have occurred. In the spirit of diplomatic back-slapping, the LTA 'hesitated to comply with their request until assured that the enterprise had received the sanction' of the leading Irish clubs, which of course it did (*Pastime* 11 May 1892:298).

The sport spread throughout continental Europe mainly via the popular holiday resorts frequented by wealthy Brits. It was recorded that two British visitors marked out a court in Bad Homburg in 1876 and were the first to play lawn tennis in Germany. Paris constructed the first tennis club in France in 1877, and was followed closely by Sweden, Italy, Belgium, Austria, Denmark and Greece. Many of the exclusive western-European holiday-spots held tournaments by the early 1880s, such as Bad Homburg vor der Höhe, Baden-Baden, Hamburg, Munich, Nice, Monte Carlo, Cannes, St. Servan, Boulogne sur Mer, Château d'Oex, Bordighera and Scheveningen. They were known for their 'irresponsible frivolity'; for example, at Dinard, where 'dances are too numerous, and the attractions of the Casino too great to permit of that strict course of living which is said to be necessary to success at this or any other game' (*Pastime* 12 September 1894:330). The Renshaws made Cannes their regular winter training location and, like numerous other British players, were treated like celebrities. The Dohertys developed a popular following among 'maidens in their teens' and were, according to Barrett and Little (2006:23), 'regarded as princes in the *haut ton* world of the Riviera and the imperial grandeur of the German tournaments'. Particularly after Queen Victoria's visits to the Cote d'Azur, winter holidays to the French Riviera became fashionable (Bédarida 1979), and, as Tinling (1983:16) suggested, 'the in-place for the stars and all the rich who surrounded them. Tennis, dancing and gambling were the catalysts of the high-fashion winter calendar'.

Outside of Europe, the sport spread first to areas frequented by British missionaries, servicemen and tourists. In Australasia, cricket featured as a gatekeeper for lawn tennis development. Melbourne CC in Victoria laid the country's first courts in 1878 and established a tournament two years later, and the first tennis club in Sydney also stemmed in 1880 from that city's cricket club (O'Farrell 1985). The game exploded especially in and around Melbourne, and by 1884, a women's competition had been established (Fewster 1985). The first inter-colonial challenge match was played in 1885, between Victoria and New South Wales, which had just played its first state championships, and further competitions were established in New Zealand (1886), Queensland (1889), South Australia (1890), Tasmania (1893) and

Western Australia (1895) (Tingay 1973). Tennis was popular among middle-class Anglo-Australian settlers around this time, who, Holt (1989:230) argued, 'never considered themselves anything but British at heart'. By the turn of the century, Australia and New Zealand were leading nations in tennis, producing Wimbledon champions such as Norman Brookes and Anthony Wilding. The 1908 Davis Cup Challenge Round, played in Australia for the first time, was particularly significant as a catalyst for the sport's boom; until then, lawn tennis had not managed to garner widespread interest or shake its effete image (Inglis 1912).

O'Farrell (1985) and Falcous and McLeod (2012) claim that popular conceptions of the sport's pre-war history in Australia and New Zealand, respectively, depict it as egalitarian, but they suspect its classless spirit has been overstated and point instead to its elite image sustained by exclusivity in clubs. Falcous and McLeod (2012:13–14) contend that tennis clubs in New Zealand were culturally moulded on the idea of creating a "better Britain", absent of class difference, affluent and equal, 'in contrast to a divisive British class hierarchy'; however, the reality was that clubs operated to 'create and sustain class-based inequity'. Similarly, in Australia, Vamplew (1994:2) contended that the adoption of British sporting practices were the result of 'deliberate attempts by the colonial wealthy and educated classes to replicate English social life, including its social structure'; thus, Australian sport, historically, 'has not proved to be an agent for social equality and indeed has more often than not emphasised rather than lessened differences of class, race and gender' (Vamplew 1994:14). Early players in Melbourne, for example, were chiefly derived from ambitious, middle-aged ladies and gentlemen who were keen to imitate elite British bourgeois cultural expressions, of which lawn tennis was one (Kinross-Smith 1987; O'Farrell 1985). In fact, Kinross-Smith (1994) suggested that lawn tennis along most of the Australian eastern seaboard, as well as in Perth and Adelaide, was the preserve of the wealthy and privileged, and O'Farrell (1985:74) contends that the creation and formation of clubs represented for those people a means to demonstrate symbolic forms of cultural attainment; it was 'a testament to a phase of civilisation achieved. ... Tennis was seen as a microcosm of a brave new colonial world in which this idea of energetic progress would be dominant'. In 1912, a correspondent from *The Referee* described the sport's social composition: 'Out here ... we luckily have no class distinctions. All that is asked of a player is that he shall be a pleasant fellow and a good partner or opponent. ... All are equal' (Austral. 1912:192). His description of a "typical" game involving 'the local doctor and dentist and one or two solicitors' suggests, like other elites in Australia and elsewhere, that he was blind to working-class realities of exclusion. That said, and despite the prevalence of elite clubs like Geelong LTC and the Royal South Yarra LTC, it appears that early players in Victoria, due in particular to fewer restrictions placed on constructing courts, were able to create for Australian tennis a uniquely egalitarian "flavour", which does offer an interesting contrast with developments elsewhere (Kinross-Smith 1987; Yallop 1984). Senyard (1996) also considered these assumptions of egalitarianism to ignore structural inequalities for women that privileged male experiences and excluded women from clubs.

Tennis also spread quickly to Canada. In 1874, just weeks after the game emerged in Staten Island, NY, a visiting Canadian by the name of I.F. Hellmuth returned to Toronto and established Toronto LTC, described by Kendrick (1990:10) as 'the haunt of Upper Canada's ruling elite'. A year later, Frederick Hamilton-Temple-Blackwood, the Governor General of Canada, constructed a lawn tennis court in Ottawa, though it was soon requisitioned as a banquet hall (Hutchinson 1996). Lawn tennis spread across the country throughout the late-Victorian period and further clubs were formed in St. John's, Halifax, Montreal, Winnipeg and Vancouver, as the sport enjoyed considerable appeal among the wealthiest classes. The Canadian National Championships, played in Toronto from 1881 onwards, garnered considerable attention and support from the best players, and despite an unsuitable climate for several months of the year, lawn tennis managed to sustain sufficient public and media interest across Canada to rival even lacrosse as its national summer sport (Kendrick 1990).

Outside of Britain's white dominions, lawn tennis made only a marginal infiltration into indigenous communities. Unlike cricket in the West Indies and rugby in parts of the South Pacific, lawn tennis failed in many cases to sufficiently galvanise "native" interest. Nevertheless, the sport took root in many of these locations, but seemed to remain the preserve of the occupying elite white populations. This seemed the case in much of South America and the Caribbean, where in the late 1870s / early 1880s, cricket clubs run by British expats were often the first locations where lawn tennis was played (Reay 1951). Tennis in Asia was thought to have first been played in Lahore, where the Punjab Lawn Tennis Championships were first staged in 1885 (Pal 2004). In South Africa, lawn tennis was available in the 1880s, but was organised from its inception by racial segregation (Odendaal 2003). Membership of early clubs and tournaments was held exclusively by the white minority, though blacks were exposed to the game through the missionary school system (Archer and Bouillon 1982), and even established "urban clubs" in Port Elizabeth, King Williamstown, Bloemfontein and Kimberley in the 1880s and 90s (Odendaal 2003). Port Elizabeth staged the first known lawn tennis tournament exclusive to whites in 1892 (Hutchinson 1996). Particularly in post-1910 South Africa, as mainstream tennis flourished, 'blacks remained on its periphery, confined to a tiny number of courts and prevented from competition with top seeds' (Khan 2010:78). The racial discrimination within South African tennis was, like in cricket and rugby union, also connected to its middle-class traditions (Booth 1998; Khan 2010).

Enthusiasm for sport in general was a widespread feature of the British elites that dominated the Empire during the late-Victorian era, and tennis served most certainly as a means to cement links between the British at home and abroad and perhaps even as an instrument of social control. The use of sports as vehicles to facilitate the compliance of indigenous populations across the Empire was particularly well appreciated, and sportsmen of repute were often stationed in such locations for these purposes (Holt 1989). Hutchinson (1996:121) noted, for example, that '300 British graduates were appointed to the Sudan Political Service in its 56 years of existence, and 93 of them were full Oxford or Cambridge Blues'. It was not necessarily the case that sportsmen were favoured for these positions, but rather that the entire culture of sport and upper-class lifestyles had become intertwined:

> The relationship between sport and empire became increasingly symbiotic as the Empire swelled. ... The confidence of one fed off the confidence of the other; they came to share not only the common goals of healthy Christian minds within healthy Christian bodies, but also vocabularies and structures.
>
> (Hutchinson 1996:122)

As Holt (1989) and Mangan (1992) discussed with regard to cricket and rugby, sport was often charged with helping to "civilise" indigenous populations and to bring them in line with British customs and ways of thinking and behaving. In the Asian subcontinent, Hutchinson (1996:104) remarked that sport was considered to help 'liberate the youngsters from the bound limbs and bound minds of their elders, and assist them towards seeing the world through Western eyes'. Though more research is needed, it is certainly plausible that in certain locations lawn tennis was charged with similar functions to those of cricket. The sheer speed and comprehensiveness of its global diffusion is indicative of its social significance.

Despite the rapid progress of competitions elsewhere, it was in America where British players discovered their strongest opponents, and almost as soon as the game had made its way "across the pond" in the mid-1870s and into the hands of affluent, land-owning, Ivy-League-educated Bostonians, Philadelphians and New Yorkers, the best Americans were keen to test themselves against the British (Rader 1990). Despite them establishing a prestigious national championship in Newport, Rhode Island, in 1881 and organising themselves into a governing body, the United States National Lawn Tennis Association (USNLTA), that same year – seven years before the LTA – American players remained comparatively inferior up until at least the late 1880s, if not later. *Pastime* (4 June 1884:358) wrote condescendingly of a visit by Americans as follows: 'Our visitors are here on a pleasure trip, and do not pretend to be equal to the Renshaw's, Lawford and others. They play to learn, not teach.' One American elaborated: 'The number of good players is continually increasing. When I say good players, I mean good for us. We have only two American players [Dwight and Sears] who compare well with the better class of English players' (*Pastime* 2 June 1886:369). Such a pessimistic view of their own relative physical capabilities reflected, according to Park (1985:8), a broader 'anxiety that Americans were physically inferior to their English contemporaries'.

Whether the difference in standard was as sizeable as some assumed, however, is beside the point. The debate is a moot one; Dwight and Sears lost heavily against the Renshaws in Cannes, but the courts could hardly be considered neutral given the long winters spent there by the English brothers (Clerici 1975). What is more interesting is the unfaltering and unquestioned British belief in their superiority. According to Llewellyn (2011a:631), 'the British held a robustly parochial and ethnocentric view of sport. They believed that sports were their sole property and displayed limited interest in playing against foreign rivals, except their own white dominions'. Indeed, while leading Americans like Dwight and Sears ventured across the Atlantic to compete at Wimbledon, the best British men did not go west until the mid-1890s, considering the American Championships unworthy of British interest. For a generation still not quite used to transatlantic travel, depictions of America were tainted unsurprisingly with hyperbole. Sensationalist reports exaggerated American deficiencies; they were described as inferior players, who used sub-standard rackets, balls, nets and posts, played on poorly maintained courts and according to inferior rules. British player Herbert Roper Barrett described the playing conditions at Longwood Cricket Club in Boston, where the first Davis Cup match was played: 'The grounds were abominable. The grass was long. ... The net was a disgrace to civilized lawn tennis, held up by guy ropes that were continually sagging. ... [The balls] were awful – soft and motherly' (cited in Myers 1908:243).

Remarks on playing style tended to reinforce stereotypes about national character. Americans were depicted as carefree, enthusiastic, well-trained and business-like but over-confident and temperamental, as Joshua Pim remarked:

> It is said to be more brilliant and aggressive than that of our own champions, but less certain. ... It may also be immature in other respects. ... The temperament of the average American athlete is more suited to flashes of superb effort than to steady effective excellence.
> (*Pastime* 31 July 1895:286)

Americans resorted to similar stereotypical comparisons, characterising the English by their endurance and self-restraint and the Americans by their technical brilliance but impatience:

> Broadly stated, the English principle seems to be to let your opponent beat himself by his errors, whereas the American system is to force the play and endeavour to score off the enemy all the time. The former is a waiting game, which commends itself to the temperament of the

visitors, and is profitable not alone in tennis, but in the world at large. ... We are more impatient here and cannot well control ourselves sufficiently to wait for things to fall into our laps. The consequence is that our tennis is incomparably more brilliant, but less profitable.

(*Town Topics*, cited in *LT&C* 6 January 1904:552)

For the British, apparent effortlessness was, naturally, the quality *de rigueur*. A *LT&B* correspondent remarked: 'The Americans are all for business and for getting the set over'; they play with 'no grace and no finesse, only business-like hard hitting, and hurry'. By contrast, 'Englishmen will generally try to do a stroke gracefully' (18 July 1906:260).

Such national stereotypes helped fuel the flames of international rivalry at a time when, according to Park (1985:8), 'Americans were asserting that they were the foremost nation, and that they were physically and technologically, if not intellectually and morally, superior to everyone. Sport – male sport – was frequently used in an effort to establish this presumption of superiority'. Throughout the 1890s, the Americans pursued a determined campaign to organise a match against the British, despite the latter remaining defiantly opposed. In an attempt to rile them, a renowned American newspaper declared that no player could claim "world's best" unless he/she had won the US National Championships. *Pastime* responded by questioning why 'the holder of the oldest established championship should have to travel to a comparatively new district to prove himself the best player in the world' (6 August 1890:111). In 1895, Tingay (1973) reported an exhibition "round-robin" singles tournament in America involving Joshua Pim and H.S. Mahony and four Americans, which was won handsomely by the British pair who lost just once each. Progress was being made, but when several leading British players competed unsuccessfully in an American tournament in 1897, blaming the "unfamiliar climatic conditions" for their comprehensive defeats, the USLTA's own *Lawn Tennis Bulletin* took the opportunity to challenge British sportsmanship in an attempt to bait them:

We all on both sides of the water expected the Englishmen to win ... but when ... it was demonstrated beyond a doubt that our two best American players are at least equal to the three English visitors, it comes with exceedingly bad grace ... to claim that the three players were ... ill all the time from the effects of [the climate].

(9 September 1897)

Such comments underlined the fact that the British could no longer continue to deny the Americans an officially organised match without seriously undermining their claims to supremacy.

Dwight Davis was the chief instigator for staging the first international match between them in 1900, but any threat of British defeat at this stage was tempered by a sense of its inconsequentiality. They considered it principally a social engagement to maintain cordial international relations and, given their simultaneous engagement in the Second Boer War and the absence of the Dohertys, Collins (2008:12) remarked: 'It was not the best British team.' Herbert Roper Barrett reflected candidly on his being chosen to play: 'There was no one else to represent England and I felt I had to go despite the inconvenience and personal expense to which we were put' (cited in Myers 1908:244). Any impressions that the Americans accorded the same triviality were quashed with their determined 3–0 clean sweep. Fielding their strongest team and playing as if victory brought more than personal prestige, they had rudely raised the stakes. Having waited patiently for the opportunity to overthrow their masters, the gauntlet had been well and truly thrown down for the British to show their mettle.

The following year, the LTA declined to send a team at all, citing at the eleventh hour the excuse of not being able to find a 'representative team'. The British were vilified in the American press for apparent cowardice. *American Cricketer* reported:

> The excuses seem childish and absurd ... Their players evidently changed their minds at the very last moment, presenting whatever excuses came handiest, and simply backed out. ... From all outside and unofficial sources are heard expressions of indignation and contempt for British sporting spirit.
>
> (cited in *Lawn Tennis* 4 September 1901:364)

In 1903, the British finally captured what was renamed the "Davis Cup", but only after another ignominious defeat on American soil the previous year. Keen to demonstrate lasting command, they fought accusations in the press of outdated attitudes to physical conditioning, playing styles, coaching and talent development, though occasionally they came across as defensive, complacent and short-sighted. The editor of *LT&C* summarised the 1903 season thus: 'In America our representatives have covered themselves with glory, and besides winning the Davis Cup, have annexed both the single and double-handed Championship of that country, so that now ... we have every reason to be satisfied' (*LT&C* 23 September 1903:470). Little concern was voiced about future prospects. In 1904, *LT&C* published a review of ladies' play, and stated: 'We may congratulate ourselves that ... it will be a long time before the gauntlet is likely to be thrown down and our position challenged' (27 July 1904:237–8). The very next summer, as if by poetic justice, May Sutton from California won the Wimbledon ladies' singles title for the very first time. Curiously, the opening speech at the dinner celebrating the successful British Davis Cup team just a few weeks later overlooked this result. Chairman H.W.W. Wilberforce toasted the Americans with the cheeky comment: 'They are a wonderful race. ... Long may they persist in coming over here unsuccessfully' (*LT&B* 26 July 1905:242).

This kind of self-satisfied overconfidence and belief in innate national supremacy must have been especially irritating to foreigners, alongside the apparent propensity to treat them 'as if they were creatures of a lower order, instead of being men infinitely better educated, and probably more refined than the swaggering tourist', as the disgraced *LT&B* editor put it (*LT&B* 4 July 1906:212). The impudent attitude of some British players when travelling perhaps reflected that of their own association. The LTA had over the years developed the habit of asking other Davis Cup associations to provide a financial "guarantee"; in effect, to reimburse them with gate money to pay their players' travel expenses. They assumed that other nations would relish the prospect of having the British on their own soil and would invest accordingly, as the Greek government did when generously donating £80 to the BOA in order to ensure Britain's participation in the 1906 Intermediate Games in Athens (Llewellyn 2011b). The Australians also had historically shown deference to visiting British sportsmen, according to Vamplew (1994:2), despite the fact that 'beating the mother country at her own sports became regarded as a sign of colonial maturity'. However, in 1910, the Australasian association rejected the LTA's request, declaring the proposed British team 'not good enough' to attract a decent gate. Publicly, the British were reproached for showing disrespect toward the three-time Davis Cup champions, not only proposing a weak team to face them but also expecting them to pay for the privilege. This act of defiance was a clear and visible illustration of the tables turning, and reflected years of on-court underperformance and off-court overconfidence.

Foreign victors at Wimbledon became increasingly commonplace in the decade before WWI. May Sutton repeated her success in 1907, alongside the Australian Norman Brookes, who became the first overseas gentlemen's singles champion. Back home, Brookes was heralded as a quintessential Australian sporting hero, cultured and refined but from a modest colonial background; his father was an English immigrant from Northamptonshire who made riches 'building railways and bridges, buying ships, paper mills and sheep stations' (O'Farrell 1985:76). Brookes' Wimbledon victory came at a key point in Australia's social and political history, just three years after they founded their own independent LTA and just six years after the country secured Commonwealth status with its own federal constitution. It came 'at just that time when Australian nationalism needed promotion. ... There were few international figures ... to whom Australians could attach a sense of national pride' (O'Farrell 1985:77). When Brookes and his Cambridge-educated New Zealand teammate Anthony Wilding captured the Davis Cup later that summer, it thrust tennis and the Davis Cup specifically to unprecedented heights of national importance (Kinross-Smith 1994).

Some lamented Britain's decline, particularly given the warning signs. A *LT&C* correspondent wrote, with evident frustration, that British players were 'content to ignore all signs of progress in other countries, and to flatter themselves that things are quite good enough as they are' (27 August 1902:382–3). They took their diminishing prowess with customary indifference, however; 'So much the better for everybody' was how another correspondent responded (*LT&C* 6 May 1903:36). Paternal sentiments were apparent in Myers' comments about the 'passing of the mantle' from master to apprentice:

> As missionaries in a good cause, Englishmen have sown the seed in every quarter of the globe. They have nursed the tender plant with heroic devotion and unremitting zeal. The fruit has now ripened ... Their joy at this bountiful harvest should be frank and wholehearted, and I believe it is.
>
> (*LT&B* 17 July 1907:178)

These conflicting positions on the decline of playing standards reflected contradictory understandings of Britain's global role more generally. While some considered performances by home players as the real barometer of the nation's health and status, others were happier to look toward the Empire as a whole for an assessment of Britain's standing. Taking pride in the performances of members of Britain's (crucially, white) dominions was customary; thus, Brookes and Wilding were accepted by many as *our* own.

Britain's relations with its non-white dominions were less than complimentary, however, at a time when "whiteness" was considered, unquestionably, as *the* racial standard against which all others were assessed. Early in the 1884 season, various sources reported the arrival of a top-ranked player from India. Clubs were quick to schedule "friendlies" with the man they referred to somewhat changeably as the "Hindoo player", the "cullured gen'man", the "dark man" or, by his supposed name, "Ajax". *Pastime* (3 September 1884:154) reported on his progress:

> The opportunity of seeing a "real Indian" playing was so attractive to some provincial clubs that arrangements were made whereby he played ... many of the best players ... and always [defeated] his opponents. His wonderful screws and twists afforded great amusement to the spectators, and altogether we must express our surprise that his services have not been more frequently requisitioned.

The extent that his visit provoked such excitement illustrates the British fascination with "exotic" indigenous populations at this time.

India was the "Jewel in the Crown" of the British Empire and sport acted as a form of "cultural imperialism", allowing Britain to 'impose its ideologies, values and behavioural norms on native groups'; sport was also considered part of a broader process in which 'colonial populations came to accept and even identify with the existing economic and political arrangements' (Taylor 2001:70–1). Pal (2004:454) contended that colonialists looked upon 'native prowess in European sports as symbolic of the success of the imperial agenda', so fascination, far more than abhorrence, would have characterised the British reaction to Indian players.

The same could not be said for the involvement of people of Afro-Caribbean descent, however. In a space taking up no more than two square inches, the following notice was printed in *Pastime* (20 August 1884:122) with regard to a proposed change to the following year's Exmouth tournament:

> They intend posting a notice at Exmouth, "No niggers allowed". One of these peripatetic minstrels turned up there and joined in chorus with the clear and well-toned voice, cultivated at sea. ... The umpire strongly objected, and flatly refused to proceed with the scoring until the "ebonite gentleman" was removed.

Also, in 1899, *The Telegraph* printed a short summary of the Great Yarmouth tournament, quoted in its entirety:

> Many people have betaken themselves to the lawn tennis tournament, which has been a great success. Several local amateurs were playing, but some of the competitors came from a distance. The tournament has been greatly appreciated by many visitors who have a preference for lawn tennis. There are also niggers.
> (cited in *Lawn Tennis* 30 August 1899:308)

That the perplexing final statement is made so unproblematically indicates race relations were secure rather than fragile. Such was the absence of an organised anti-racist agenda at this time that such comments provoked little public backlash.

Jews also faced discrimination but often in more covert ways. Applications for membership of numerous golf and tennis clubs were rejected in accordance with staunch anti-Semitic feelings (Dee 2011; Lowerson 1993). Underpinning overt discriminatory practices was an established British ethnic ideal against which most Jews were found wanting. The notion that Jews did not fully understand British sporting ideals of fair play, or were flashy and ostentatious in their displays of material wealth, translated into their rejection by the British mainstream as "outsiders" (Dee 2011).

The effects of centuries of colonisation left the British staunch believers in ethnic hierarchies founded on racist ideologies. The basic idea of imperialism was simple, argued Bédarida (1979:145): 'The English were a chosen race entrusted with a mission that was both human and divine, and which it was their duty to discharge'. H.F. Wyatt (1897:529), from the literary magazine, *The Nineteenth Century*, defined Britain's 'definitive duty':

> To carry light and civilization in the dark places of the world; to touch the mind of Asia and of Africa with the ethical ideas of Europe; to give

thronging millions, who would otherwise never know peace or security, these first conditions of human advance: constructive endeavour such as this forms part of the function which it is ours to discharge.

The effects of Social Darwinism and the popular Eugenics movement left whites in authoritative positions to dictate terms to native inhabitants, and associated ideas of "Nordic" racial supremacy based on scientific arguments continued to permeate in right-wing – though still relatively mainstream – contexts in Britain and North America until WWII (Dyreson 2001). While Canada, Australia, New Zealand and South Africa were accorded substantial autonomy in matters of self-governance, the populace from Britain's black dominions continued to be judged in inferior terms. Alongside the continued marginalisation of blacks within the South African Tennis Union's competitions, and the provision of poor or insufficient facilities and inadequate coaching (Khan 2010), a lawn tennis facility in Kitin, Uganda, was described in 1905 as attracting 'a host of local savages' (*LT&B* 3 May 1905:32). Racial discrimination toward non-whites reflected broader social, economic and political power structures. The "uncivilised" populace, as they were considered, would remain poor and uneducated without British assistance; this was argued to be an alleged consequence of inferior breeding and inadequate socialisation. British sporting relations with its dominions reinforced these beliefs, and tennis was not exempt from reflecting such structural inequalities.

In 1902, *LT&C* made the following comparisons between British and foreign training methods:

> Rightly or wrongly, [British] amateurs, as a rule, do not train specially for any game in which they have to take part. ... On the other hand, men on the Continent, in America, and in Australia will lay themselves out with the utmost seriousness to train for games.
>
> (28 May 1902:87)

There was little sense at this time that the extra seriousness mattered; the British were dominant *despite* the steadfast efforts of foreign competitors. Thus, arguments supporting the idea that Britain's sporting prowess was anything other than the product of national character found little challenge (Bailey 1978; Holt 1989; Mangan 1981). Advances abroad in coaching and technical development, principally in America, soon forced British administrators to revaluate their goals and training techniques, if not also the ideology that underpinned their sporting participation more generally.

The American eastern-seaboard elite that dominated sports including tennis until the early 1900s was soon superseded by more progressive, liberal west-coast Americans who were less inclined to sustain the antiquated amateur ideals of their transatlantic rivals. The 1908 London Olympics proved an important battle ground for the old versus the new, and represented a turning point in sporting prowess, as American athletes won the vast majority of track-and-field medals. The poor performances of Britain's athletes weighed heavily on their collective confidence, as their preparation methods and overall sporting ethos were challenged. British players won the majority of lawn tennis medals, assisted by the fact that no leading American or Australian players journeyed to London; unlike their track-and-field compatriots, they were not funded by their respective Olympic committees. American dominance in track and field, the marquee Olympic sport, mattered most; the *New York Times* (17 July 1908:11) claimed the Americans '[cared] nothing for the other sports'. Tales of British unfairness, unsportsmanlike behaviour, administrative failures and biased judging filled the headlines of American newspapers, which characterised the British as haughty and incompetent. The Americans meanwhile were criticised as "freaks" and "professionals" because they trained with new-found dedication; they received vast amounts of coaching and specialised with precision (Matthews 1980).

Llewellyn (2011c:692) felt that the Anglo-American rivalry at the 1908 Olympics and in other international sporting domains 'mirrored the battle being played out between the two nations for global, economic and cultural supremacy' in the early twentieth century. The competition between sporting ideologies was significant in the broader context of empire decline and escalating fears of national degeneracy more generally. The Boer War (1899–1902) brought rampant negative international press attention during and after its conclusion, whereby British preparations and tactics were comprehensively condemned (Holler 1999; Morgan 2002). Social commentators like George Shee (1903) diagnosed a deteriorating "national physique" among other broader social ailments as an outcome of Britain's industrialisation and urbanisation, and the initiation of the Boy Scout movement in 1908 by Robert Baden-Powell was in part a response to the sedentary lifestyles and subsequent declining physical health of the nation's young men (Springhall 1997).

While throughout the mid–late-Victorian era the Empire had achieved unreserved global dominance as an outcome of its commanding iron and steel production and world trade of manufactured goods, alongside Britain's soaring GDP and outranking currency, its position was challenged into the Edwardian era by assertive French, German, Belgian and Italian colonising missions throughout Africa, and the insurgence of Japan and Russia in the quest for territorial expansion (Warwick 1985). Of all their new rivals, the Americans had caught up fastest; the exploitation of their abundant natural resources, assisted by booming population growth and an innovative spirit of diligence and resourcefulness, pushed American goods into British homes and their capitalist ideologies into British workplaces (Llewellyn 2011c). Fears abounded not only of the growing influence of American values and ideologies in British society, but also the steady departure of Britain from its imperialist and Conservative, upper-class traditions. Arthur Balfour's embarrassing loss to the Liberals in the 1906 General Election signalled for some the end of traditional aristocratic authority in government (Cannadine 1999). These fears were matched in sport.

The sustained dominance of American athletes at the 1912 Stockholm Olympics pushed the French, German and Austrian sports federations, among others, to revaluate their training methods. The British considered their third-place medal-haul 'a humiliating blot on the imperial edifice' (Llewellyn 2011d:721), yet they continued to criticise American methods that apparently reduced sport to crass nationalism and espoused a win-at-all-costs formula that tarnished amateur ideals (Daniels 2000). Nevertheless, bubbling under the surface away from association boardrooms, there was 'a gradual push towards the more specialised "American" approach to athletic training' that embraced systematic coaching (Llewellyn 2011d:717). Defeats in rowing, cricket, athletics, cycling, football and rugby alongside tennis were considered more than just signals of Britain's failing sporting systems and ideology; they also contributed to fears of national degeneracy more generally.

In this context, their diminishing success in lawn tennis must have resonated quite powerfully among the entire amateur sporting fraternity. This was a sport in which many felt the British were owed success. Still, after losing on court, they attempted to consolidate their assumed position of global leadership administratively, and in this endeavour they were remarkably successful. The LTA's status was bolstered by the support of foreign clubs (e.g. Hamburg LTC, Moscow LTC, Santiago LTC) and associations (e.g. Swiss LTA, Belgium LTA, Bohemian LTA and New Zealand LTA) that sought affiliation to it. When the Swiss joined in 1897, *Lawn Tennis* (2 June 1897:66) reported: 'It would be well if the clubs of other continental countries would follow ... and form themselves into associations to be affiliated to the ... parent body'. Near its peak in 1913, the LTA had 17 overseas associations and 26 individual clubs from 15 countries affiliated to it (Collins 2008).

This approach of the British was not universally supported. The LTA were keen to avoid perceptions of weakness drawn from diminishing on-court successes, and were also wary of Wimbledon's growing popularity and the embarrassing fact that hitherto they had no authority over its management. While it might have been in the sport's "best interests" for the LTA to partly own or at least partly manage Wimbledon, the AELTC was an autonomous club and under no obligation to surrender its cash cow. Indeed, upon its formation in 1888, the LTA guaranteed the Championships complete autonomy from external interference. It was only through goodwill that, in 1907, the AELTC allowed two LTA representatives on its Championships Management Committee, and in 1913, they agreed to allocate some of their profits to the LTA. It was not until 1934 that a Joint Championship

Committee was formed between the two bodies that ensured the LTA received all Wimbledon profits.

Despite their powerful position abroad, there were calls for the British to get their own house in order, as fears of burgeoning commercialism threatened to undermine their administrative accomplishments. The Manchester-based sporting-goods company Slazenger relocated to London in 1881 and grew to lead manufacturing in lawn tennis balls and rackets. Dunlop Rubber emerged in 1889 as a tyre manufacturer in Birmingham and also entered the tennis ball market, but could not interrupt Slazenger's relationship with Wimbledon, as they became in 1902 – and have remained ever since – the Championships' official balls supplier. Their emergence as key players reflected the increasing extent to which sport was, in Joyce's (1999:157) words, 'inexorably sliding into the clutches of entrepreneurs', as sporting-goods and clothing manufacturers were joined by refreshment vendors, architects, engineers, labourers, watchmen, caretakers, bankers, lawyers, bookmakers, and those employed in other cognate areas including advertising, transportation, photography and equipment rental. While tennis officials were resistant in theory to business interests pervading sport, their desire for grander clubs and more lavish tournaments increasingly compelled their reliance on these enterprises.

In 1906, their first conflict of interest arose when the AELTC secretary, Mr Archdale Palmer, joined Slazenger as Joint Managing Director, but sought to continue his AELTC duties. This trade connection put the man and the club in a compromising position, reflecting more generally upper-middle-class anxieties over money-making. This sentiment was evident in the comments of Hon. Sec. of Middlesex LTA, John R. Burton: 'We are all in sympathy with the idea that trade influence should be eliminated from the game. ... Practically everyone feels that Palmer's position in connection with the AELTC and his position with Messrs Slazenger are, in principle, incompatible' (*LT&B* 5 December 1906:516). No allegations of corruption were made; calls for Palmer's resignation centred on hypothetical circumstances. The AELTC even declared that hitherto he had 'in no way affected, or indeed attempted to affect, them in regard to any measure in which the interests in his firm were in any way involved' (*LT&B* 5 December 1906:513). Palmer's appointment was 'a lucky moment for the club', according to his successor, George Hillyard (1924:43); he was by all accounts 'an ideal secretary'. Nevertheless, a climate of fear was created of the corruptive potential of trade influences, and in the process the LTA managed to score points against the AELTC in their campaign to assume greater authority over the management of the Championships (Birley 1995a).

There was contradiction in how the LTA managed this issue, however, which if anything underlined the lack of foundation in their anti-commercial sentiments. *LT&B*, the LTA's principal journal, was actually owned by Slazenger. Thus, by intervening, they were also involving themselves in this conflict of interest. In January, Palmer resigned from the AELTC. Six months later, Slazenger published its last issue of *LT&B*; the LTA resolved that it was not in the 'best interests of the game' that control of its 'official organ' be 'vested in the form of manufacturers of lawn tennis requisites' (*LT&B* 12 June 1907:10). Slazenger condemned the LTA's groundless accusations in their final issue:

> In our conduct of the journal we have been invariably actuated by a desire to forward the best interests of the game; and, although it has been inferred that trade influence has been allowed to permeate the management of the paper, we take this opportunity of giving an absolute disclaimer to such a suggestion, and of stating that our commercial interests have never been allowed to play any part or have found any ventilation in the columns of this journal.
> (*LT&B* 5 June 1907:93)

Birley (1995a:204) criticised the short-sighted and impetuous LTA, reasoning that, without trade influence, 'standards as high as Wimbledon's could hardly be maintained in an amateur sport'. At around this same time, news came that the USNLTA had revoked the amateur status of Beals C. Wright, a well-known player, because he worked part-time at his father's sporting-goods business. Although these charges were criticised publicly as 'preposterous, and contrary to the canons of common sense' (*LT&B* 5 December 1906:513), it was evident that an international witch-hunt had commenced to eliminate or at least curtail commercialism in lawn tennis.

Professionalism, as a connected feature, was also implicated. Throughout the early 1900s, the LTA had been pressed publicly to create an "amateur" definition and to realign itself with its cousin American and Australian associations that had formulated their own in 1889 and 1895, respectively. Hitherto, they were able to hide behind the claim that British lawn tennis was free from professionalism, but the enacting of restrictions on trade influence at the administrative level forced them to reconsider their position. In 1907, a correspondent in *Amateur Sport Illustrated* (*ASI*) wrote in to claim 'certain players have been for some time past indulging in practices which ... should concern the LTA, but ... nothing is done to combat the evil, which is a crying one, and calculated to disgust proper-minded people' (12 December 1907:244). Nothing was ventured until 1910, when fresh allegations of 'pseudo-professionalism' appeared in *Sporting Life*; the authors claimed players received travel expenses and free hotel accommodation at tournaments in Britain and southern France (21 April 1910:8). The Association's response, through their now trade-influence-free *Lawn Tennis & Badminton*, was defensive and arrogant. 'We beg most emphatically to deny that the need has arisen for an amateur definition', said the editor, before remarking: 'Lawn tennis players have good reason to be proud of the fact that their game has existed as long as it has without the necessity for an amateur definition' (28 April 1910:105). Growing pressure from the

International Olympic Committee (IOC) for an amateur definition for its Stockholm Games helped finally tilt the scales.

In 1911, the LTA made its first attempt, but instead of defining an "amateur", they preferred to define a "professional", or someone who was *not* an amateur. They seemed unable to effectively quantify what an "amateur" was with anything more than vague presumptions of one's "character" or personal motivations. It was felt an amateur should play 'for the sake of the game itself, the healthy exercise, and the exhilaration of pitting their strength and brains against those of their adversaries, without all the time mentally adding up the value of the prizes' (*LT&B* 6 April 1911:94). How they could ever determine a player's intent is beyond comprehension, and meant that any such regulations could never be watertight. Nevertheless, the LTA Council pressed onward to define as *not* an amateur someone who: played the game for money or a staked bet, taught the game for money, accepted travel or hotel expenses at tournaments, or accepted money or "requisites" from sporting-goods firms. Upon publication, correspondents immediately attacked its ostensibly idiosyncratic "grey areas". First, in a ruling that *American Lawn Tennis (ALT)* called 'absurd', British amateurs could write about, officiate or sell goods for all sports except lawn tennis, the only one where their expertise was actually valued. Second, a disqualification in another sport also stretched to lawn tennis, in what amounted to a "one drop" ruling that implied a strong likelihood that players would reoffend and a desire among the amateur establishment to eradicate professionalism rather than manage it respectfully. Third, the rules prohibiting prize money being given overlooked the possibility of players exchanging their prizes for items or services more useful to them. Rules of etiquette prohibited the purchase of 'necessaries', but, defining this term leads one to conclude: 'One man's necessary is another man's luxury' (*LT&B* 6 April 1911:94).[1] Fourth, free lodging at tournaments was allowed only if a "guest" at a "private house", but hotel proprietors were denied such opportunities. This brought criticism from the Continent, where it was reported, for example, that the vast majority of Homburg's 'most influential citizens' were hotel proprietors (*LT&B* 22 June 1911:276).

Unsurprisingly, these policies brought unintended consequences. One was the growth of resentment toward the Association by bona fide amateurs who were inconvenienced. Another was the discouragement of permissible commercial activities that might benefit the sport's development. Profoundly, these stringent rules of amateurism were geared toward stemming the onset of vulgar lower-middle-class influences, of which professionalism and commercialism were prominent, but it was clear they privileged the old and oppressed the new. It was argued: 'If the Council were to keep in touch more with the general rank and file, instead of letting themselves be guided so often by cranks, it would be better for all concerned' (*LT&B* 4 May 1911:133).

By the time of the 1912 Stockholm Olympics, which saw the defiant British send not a single lawn tennis representative because the event clashed with Wimbledon, the LTA had become overbearing at home, and the game abroad was flourishing to the extent that overseas governing bodies and clubs that were once affiliated began to relinquish their membership. The formation of the International Lawn Tennis Federation (ILTF) in March 1913 brought new challenges. Its headquarters were in London and the LTA undertook the lion's share of its early administrative duties, which allowed it to retain most of its former power (Birley 1995b). Also, as a goodwill gesture, Britain was allocated more votes on the Council than other nations, but these measures were still a far cry from their days of unquestioned authority. The Council's immediate decisions to introduce three "world championships" and to allow the payment of expenses to players competing in them brought a British boycott at the first event in Stockholm. Their bold stand of "splendid isolation" was, however, destined to fail. The LTA's opposition to the payment of expenses contradicted their policy in Davis Cup competitions, and their standing internationally would have suffered irreparably if Wimbledon suffered ILTF exclusion. Members of the LTA Council were begged, at its 1913 AGM, not to act like a 'small child who would not play unless he could get his own way in everything' (*LT&B* 11 Dec 1913:88). Nevertheless, the Americans supported the British in declining to join in early 1914, when ILTF affiliation was officially sought; the former cited a similar disagreement with the amateur rulings and a general uneasiness about how much their autonomy would be restricted in joining. In fact, the USNLTA remained outside until 1924, by which time the further shift in the global balance of power helped bolster their claims for greater respect in matters of sporting and non-sporting governance. Before that time, without full support from the leading associations, the desire for an effective international assembly was destined to remain unsatisfied. And so the onset of armed conflict in Europe brought a break from proceedings. When they returned in 1918 to a renewed climate of (allied) international solidarity, the Federation could operate with a grander sense of purpose. Until then, it remained an ineffectual body.

Throughout the troubled Edwardian period, the British elites retained a belief that 'what had worked in the past would continue to work in the future' (Tranter 1998:66). The idea that "natural" British qualities of pluck, courage, self-reliance and stoicism would eventually prevail was internalised as part of a ruling-class habitus (Holt 1989). Britain's loss of its virtual monopoly on production to the burgeoning industrialised nations of Germany and America created in Britain a crisis of confidence. Perhaps complacency, lack of innovation and a decline in entrepreneurship had set in within the national mindset, but also problematic was Britain's perceived unwillingness to modernise in accordance with foreign methods, to adopt new technologies, rationalise, undergo professional training and restore "scientific spirit" (Bédarida 1979). Inextricably connected to Britain's sense of self was its esteemed and once-revered amateur sporting philosophy, but the edifice of this also began to crumble. So evident was the need for an about-turn that by 1915, severe doubt was cast publicly on the supposed connections between innate British 'national characteristics' and sporting prowess, as an article in *Athletic News* revealed:

> Our plan has generally been to rely on the national aptitude, which we undoubtedly possess, for gaining or maintaining ascendancy in the field, and our racial talents and characteristics for winning a way somehow to the front. But in lawn tennis ... our muddle-through methods have lately found us out. ... The British ideal of a 'born' player with a natural aptitude for taking him to the highest position ... is ridiculously out of date, and if we are to maintain a place in the sun as a nation we must have something more practical.
> (cited in *LT&B* 1 July 1915:425)

Since the early Edwardian era when foreigners were criticised for taking their sport too seriously, fear had been generated among the conservative, amateur sport administrators of a shift away from their traditional approaches. Once news of how inveterate class and gender distinctions were transferred into rights to survival when HMS *Titanic* sank in 1912 and cost the lives of 1,500 people, the perceived need for fundamental social change strengthened. In its timing, the LTA's attempts to regain prestige and assert their status as world leaders in lawn tennis matters mirrored closely in its timing and emphases the same attempts made by the British government and the Foreign Office, British-based businesses, and social reformers. Undoubtedly, Britain's diminishing role in international sport came to represent something significant in itself, and its shifting position in lawn tennis was no exception.

The onset of war in Europe that accelerated processes of democratisation in both class and gender spheres had a notable impact on sport, with a growing public perception that amateurism was somewhat parochial. Recommendations for a more progressive model, akin to the specialised systems of talent development in America, flew in the face of British traditionalism. Yet, the increasing importance placed upon reclaiming lost sporting prowess in the 1920s brought new enthusiasm for "professional" approaches. The marked democratisation of tennis brought new clubs and competitions, new children's tournaments and the birth of public-school interest in lawn tennis, which helped forge a path toward the sport's greater public recognition more generally. The positive consequences of such affirmative action in the interwar period have often been summed up in one name, Fred Perry. However, the process was much more complicated than the exploits of a single player can illuminate, particularly when considering that Perry was disliked generally by the British fraternity. If anything, it highlighted the divergent opinions as to how Britain should move forward at this time.

Conservative Britain during the interwar years was a skeleton of its confident, dominant Victorian self, ripped of its economic and political stability and its indisputable sense of social, cultural and moral superiority. Its fears of imminent American usurpation as the new global leaders in industrial, economic and even cultural realms were realised. Thus, any motives to regain international sporting prowess were felt in the context of Britain's changing global position. While some clung ferociously to traditional ideals, the younger generations most particularly were learning to live in a new, more liberal and egalitarian world of open possibilities for women and the working classes. If public interest in the sport was the accepted measure of its success, the interwar period could be considered the heyday for lawn tennis, and yet it was the most turbulent and uncertain of all periods during which the sport was played, fraught with devastating internal disagreements related to the potential for full-blown professionalism and commercialism.

Note

1. An ILTF ruling was eventually accepted that placed restrictions on the "type of goods" that could be purchased with prize orders, which was not abolished until 1958.

Bibliography

Archer, R., and Bouillon, A. (1982). *The South African Game: Sport and Racism*. London: Zed Press.
Austral. (1912). *Lawn Tennis in Australasia*. Sydney: Eduards, Dunlop.
Bailey, P. (1978). *Leisure and Class in Victorian England*. London: Routledge & Kegan Paul.
Bairner, A. (2011). Sports Development, Nations and Nationalism. In B. Houlihan and M. Green, *Routledge Handbook of Sports Development* (pp. 31–41). London: Routledge.
Barrett, J., and Little, A. (2006). *Wimbledon Gentlemen's Singles Champions 1877–2005*. London: Wimbledon Lawn Tennis Museum.
Bédarida, F. (1979). *A Social History of England 1851–1975*. London: Methuen.
Birley, D. (1995a). *Land of Sport and Glory: Sport and British Society 1887–1910*. Manchester: Manchester University Press.
Birley, D. (1995b). *Playing the Game: Sport and British Society 1910–45*. Manchester: Manchester University Press.
Booth, D. (1998). *The Race Game: Sport and Politics in South Africa*. London: Frank Cass.
Cannadine, D. (1999). *The Rise and Fall of Class in Britain*. New York: Columbia University Press.
Clerici, G. (1975). *The Ultimate Tennis Book: 500 Years of the Sport*. Chicago: Follett Publishing Company.
Collins, B. (2008). *The Bud Collins History of Tennis: An Authoritative Encyclopedia and Record Book*. Chicago, IL: New Chapter Press.

Daniels, G. G. (2000). *The V and VI Olympiads: Stockholm 1912. Volume 6*. Los Angeles: Sport Research and Publications.
Dee, D. (2011). *Jews and British Sport: Integration, Ethnicity and Anti-Semitism, c.1880–1960*. Leicester: Unpublished PhD.
Dyreson, M. (2001). American Ideas about Race and Olympic Races from the 1890s to the 1950s: Shattering Myths or Reinforcing Scientific Racism. *Journal of Sport History*, 28, 173–215.
Falcous, M., and McLeod, C. (2012). Anyone for Tennis? Sport, Class and Status in New Zealand. *New Zealand Sociology*, 27(1), 13–30.
Fewster, K. (1985). Advantage Australia: Davis Cup Tennis 1950–1959. *Sporting Traditions*, 2(1), 47–68.
Higgins, T. (2006). *The History of Irish Tennis*. Sligo: Sligo Tennis Club.
Hillyard, G. (1924). *Forty Years of First-Class Lawn Tennis*. London: Williams & Norgate.
Holler, J. H. (1999). *The Boer Lessons that Changed and Prepared the British Army for WWI*. Pennsylvania: US Army War College.
Holt, R. (1989). *Sport and the British*. Oxford: Clarendon.
Hutchinson, R. (1996). *Empire Games: The British Invention of Twentieth-Century Sport*. London: Mainstream Publishing.
Inglis, G. (1912). *Sport and Pastime in Australia*. London: Methuen and Co.
Joyce, T. (1999). Sport and the Cash Nexus in Nineteenth Century Toronto. *Sport History Review*, 30(2), 140–68.
Kendrick, M. (1990). *Advantage Canada: A Tennis Centenary*. Downsview, Ontario: Tennis Canada.
Khan, F. (2010). Anyone for Tennis? Conversations with Black Women Involved in Tennis during the Apartheid Era. *Agenda: Empowering Women for Gender Equity*, 24(85), 76–84.
Kinross-Smith, G. (1987). Privilege in Tennis and Lawn Tennis: The Geelong and Royal South Yarra Examples but Not Forgetting the Story of the Farmer's Wrist. *Sporting Traditions*, 3(2), 189–216.
Kinross-Smith, G. (1994). Lawn Tennis. In V. Wray and B. Stoddart, *Sport in Australia: A Social History* (pp. 133–153). Cambridge: Cambridge University Press.
Llewellyn, M. P. (2011a). Prologue: An Indifferent Beginning. *International Journal of the History of Sport*, 28(5), 625–647.
Llewellyn, M. P. (2011b). Lighting the Olympic Flame. *International Journal of the History of Sport*, 28(5), 648–668.
Llewellyn, M. P. (2011c). The Battle of Shepherd's Bush. *International Journal of the History of Sport*, 28(5), 688–710.
Llewellyn, M. P. (2011d). 'A Tale of National Disaster'. *International Journal of the History of Sport*, 28(5), 711–729.
Lowerson, J. (1993). *Sport and the English Middle Classes 1870–1914*. Manchester: Manchester University Press.
Mangan, J. (1981). *Athleticism in the Victorian and Edwardian Public School*. Cambridge: Cambridge University Press.
Mangan, J. (1992). *The Cultural Bond: Sport Empire and Society*. London: Frank Cass.
Matthews, G. R. (1980). The Controversial Olympic Games of 1908 as Viewed by the New York Times and the Times of London. *Journal of Sport History*, 7(2), 40–53.

Morgan, K. (2002). The Boer War and the Media (1899–1902). *Twentieth Century British History*, 13(1), 1–16.

Myers, A. W. (1908). *The Complete Lawn Tennis Player*. Philadelphia: George W. Jacobs & Co.

Odendaal, A. (2003). *The Story of an African Game*. Claremont, South Africa: David Philip Publishers.

O'Farrell, V. (1985). The Unasked Questions in Australian Tennis. *Sporting Traditions*, 1(2), 67–86.

Pal, S. (2004). 'Legacies, Halcyon Days and Thereafter': A Brief History of Indian Tennis. *International Journal of the History of Sport*, 21(3/4), 452–466.

Park, R. (1985). Sport, Gender and Society in a Transatlantic Victorian Perspective. *International Journal of the History of Sport*, 2(1), 5–28.

Polley, M. (1998). *Moving the Goalposts: A History of Sport and Society Since 1945*. London: Routledge.

Rader, B. G. (1990). *American Sports: From the Age of Folk Games to the Age of Televised Sports*. New Jersey: Prentice Hall.

Reay, B. (1951, May-September). Lawn Tennis – The Game Britain Gave to the World. *Lawn Tennis & Badminton*, pp. 294–298.

Senyard, J. (1996). The Tennis Court: A Country Woman's Window to the Modern World. *Sporting Traditions*, 13(1), 25–41.

Shee, G. F. (1903, May). The Deterioration in the National Physique. *The Nineteenth Century and After*, LIII, pp. 797–805.

Springhall, J. (1997). *Youth, Empire and Society: British Youth Movements, 1883–1940*. North Haven, CT: Shoe String Press.

Taylor, M. (2001). Sport and the Empire. In F. Galligan, *Sports History* (pp. 68–73). London: British Society of Sports History.

Tingay, L. (1973). *A History of Lawn Tennis in Pictures*. London: Tom Stacey.

Tinling, T. (1983). *Tinling: Sixty Years in Tennis*. London: Sidgwick & Jackson.

Tranter, N. L. (1998). *Sport, Economy and Society in Britain 1750–1914*. Cambridge: Cambridge University Press.

Vamplew, W. (1994). Australians and Sport. In W. Vamplew and B. Stoddart, *Sport in Australia: A Social History* (pp. 1–18). Cambridge: Cambridge University Press.

Warwick, P. (1985). Did Britain Change? An Inquiry into the Causes of National Decline. *Journal of Contemporary History*, 20(1), 99–133.

Wyatt, H. (1897, April). The Ethics of Empire. *The Nineteenth Century*, XLI, p. 529.

Yallop, R. (1984). *Royal South Yarra Lawn Tennis Club: One Hundred Years in Australian Tennis*. South Yarra: Currey O'Neil.

6 Reconciliation and consolidation

Early struggles for British lawn tennis in the aftermath of war

The effects of WWI on British society were numerous, far-reaching and long-term. For a conflict that some predicted would be finished before Christmas 1914, its full scale certainly took many by surprise: 723,000 British servicemen were among the 9 million dead over the entire four years. *LT&B* gave weekly progress reports of top players in the war effort, noting with justifiable pride, for example, that Archdale Palmer, former AELTC secretary, accepted a commission as Captain of the Essex Regiment (8 October 1914:1011). Others were less fortunate. When the New Zealander and four-time Wimbledon singles champion Anthony Wilding celebrated his Wimbledon doubles victory with Norman Brookes in July 1914, he was blissfully unaware his life would end less than 12 months later at the battle of Aubers Ridge in France. The names of other players were to be listed in newsletters, newspapers and magazines or carved on plaques in clubhouses across the country over the next few years, as clubs and associations took solace in the righteous values these soldiers honourably died for.

The declaration of war prompted an immediate cessation of competitive play in some cases. It was reported that military personnel competing at the early-August Shanklin tournament, for example, were 'recalled at a moment's notice and had to leave in the middle of matches' (*LT&B* 6 August 1914:881). Handfuls of other tournaments and matches were cancelled over the following weeks and months, and membership lists dwindled as winter approached, which forced many clubs to suspend operations altogether. Friendly matches were sometimes encouraged to keep clubs afloat and interest keen, but debate raged in the national press. Some argued that watching and playing sport was 'unseemly and a discouragement to recruitment' (Huggins and Williams 2005:19). Those who preferred to play sport rather than enlist, called 'shirkers' or 'loafers', were vilified and felt the full force of a national media campaign against them (Collins 2009), but a good number of *LT&B* correspondents railed against the downbeat attitudes of those whose suggestions for ceasing competitions had no practical basis. One remarked:

> At a time like the present lawn tennis players may wonder if it would be considered correct to compete. For the life of us we cannot see why

they should not. ... We think that it would be a great mistake not to participate in tournaments. ... No good can be done by sitting still and twiddling one's thumbs.

(6 August 1914:875)

The stoic British attempted to remain composed and resolute at home, while also attempting to convey to their enemies a robust spirit. A correspondent in the *Referee*, so as not to 'assist our enemy' by producing 'widespread misery', urged Britons to continue their leisure activities: 'Be normal, spend wisely and amuse yourselves rationally, and so ease the stress' (cited in *LT&B* 24 September 1914:990). The opposition considered it an issue of decency, morality and patriotism. Even King George V got involved in the dispute – convenient, as he was also an LTA patron – by entering his horses in several races in the early part of the war, which legitimated the pursuit of other recreational activities.

As the war dragged on, and reports came back that illustrated in more certain terms the full material effects of human destruction on the once-picturesque landscapes of places like Ypres, Verdun and the Somme, personal morality and responsibility seemed to take over from public sanctions in determining what roles tennis players at home should adopt. The LTA published a series of advertisements urging donations to the Prince of Wales Relief Fund, and clubs were encouraged to dig deep into their coffers in search of 'unrealised assets' (*LT&B* 24 September 1914:986). Clubs certainly played their part; representatives from Newquay LTC, Grantown-on-Spey LTC and Criccieth LTC, for example, eagerly reported the sizeable whips they generated (*LT&B* 24 September 1914:990). Others like Hill LTC and Purley LTC keenly noted the names of respective club members who enlisted or were promoted as officers, and most clubs, including the likes of Teddington LTC, Twickenham LTC and Wembley and Sudbury Tennis, Squash & Social Club, offered free memberships to military personnel. The Weald LTC, like several others, hosted an exhibition match to raise money for the war-wounded, enlisting for its October 1915 event several top players such as Dorothea Lambert Chambers and M.J.G. Ritchie.

If anything, the trials of war certainly engendered among players the spirit of generosity, which would have helped open up the sport in the immediate interwar years to players from previously excluded classes. This process of "democratisation" had little impact on the development of British talent, though, given that the major crop from which its future success depended were killed or wounded. Reynolds (1991) reported that nearly 28 per cent of Oxbridge students that attended between 1910 and 1914 had perished in the war, becoming known thereafter as the "Lost Generation". Given their central role in supplying British talent across many sports, it is no wonder that a further decline in relative playing standards happened. Bill Tilden (1921:99) remarked that 'no good' sprang from the war, which 'placed its blight on the English game'. America was less affected in terms of number of troops and length and extent of involvement and, unlike Britain and France, it continued staging its national championships between 1914 and 1918. In these years, clubs and tournaments thrived and their players made considerable progress toward front rank. *ALT* reported that the war had affected municipal tennis in America more than any other branch of the sport, because of a 'shortage of labor and high cost of material imposed by the war', making it difficult to build new courts (15 February 1919:388). That said, the leading American men, among them Tilden, Bill Johnston and Vincent Richards, were able to capture most of the major honours, with US Open, Wimbledon and American Davis Cup victories.

Women were impacted less and in different ways. Their assumed war responsibilities limited their playing opportunities but not entirely. The budding Frenchwoman Suzanne Lenglen, for example, spent the entire four years at her family's winter home in Nice, practising in her back garden and across the road at her father's club. The Riviera continued as a lawn tennis haven and Lenglen played in numerous matches and tournaments against professional coaches and other male players, many of whom were servicemen on leave or convalescing from Western front-line action (Little 2007; Tinling 1983). Young British women enjoyed greater opportunities to play friendly matches than their male counterparts, and were assisted in part by the growing recognition of the importance of physical fitness generally. Hillyard (1924:17) described the role of tennis in this regard:

> During that time thousands and thousands of all classes had gone through physical training and grown accustomed to the taking of hard exercise, who had never known before, in the whole course of their lives, what exercise meant. ... Everyone, from the duchess to the shopgirl, had found the immense benefit conferred on their health by an hour's vigorous play.

After the war, British male and female players struggled to regain their premier ranking, though lawn tennis was not unique. In boxing, rugby, cricket, rowing, swimming, athletics and golf, the British declined in comparative playing standards and suffered defeats with increasing regularity, particularly to America and Australia (Birley 1995b; Hill 2002; Huggins and Williams 2005). Alongside the devastating impact of war, McKibbin (1998:380) considered this regression a result of 'excessive voluntarism' and the 'decaying ideology' of amateurism, though, for many with gruesome images of war still fresh in their minds, defeats were considered inconsequential at this time. 'So long as we win wars we can afford to lose games' was what one *LT&B* correspondent reasoned (15 January 1921:692). Such sentiments were reflected in early discussions about the possibility of sending British athletes to the 1920 Antwerp Olympics so soon after the cessation of armed conflict (Llewellyn 2011e). As time went on, the British were urged to approach lawn tennis with the same resolute spirit that had proved so successful in war. Arthur Batley at the 1924 LTA AGM, for example, in reference to recapturing major championships like Wimbledon and the Davis Cup, urged his compatriots to make a 'determined and deliberate effort to win back that which has been taken from us. That is the spirit we have always had in our history, and it is the spirit that manifested itself in the Great War' (*LT&B* 20 December 1924:910).

The aims of this chapter are to set lawn tennis in the broader social context of the immediate aftermath of war. British relations with its enemy nations revealed the extent to which sport was used as a political tool to register international disapproval. Allied solidarity among the leading tennis nations was also revealed in the increasingly strained relations with the IOC, which eventually forced tennis to remove itself from the Olympic movement. Nevertheless, responsibility for steering the ship of international tennis through the tumultuous interwar period was left to the LTA more than any other national association, whose moral leadership was by and large universally agreed. Soon, the British were forced to concede ultimate authority to the ILTF in the spirit of global solidarity, but also to some extent the USLTA, which became a key ally administratively and a chief influence culturally, as American developments that led to the advance of more determined, ambitious and competition-oriented players forced major changes to the organisational structure of tennis in Britain. As ever, Wimbledon, as the world's most prestigious tournament, remained a chief location where such developments manifested themselves.

World War I impacted Britain profoundly as a nation itself, economically, politically and in terms of its national identity. Its policy of widespread military and naval reform before the war had paid dividends in the light of Germany's threatening and impressive standing army, but the unexpectedly high death toll and a severely weakened economy left Britain in debt, with estimates from £7.5–£12 billion. Taxes were raised to repay the national debt, and after industrial production in shipbuilding, steel and cotton returned to its long-term structural decline after the artificial boost during the war, millions were left unemployed, particularly in the industrial North and Midlands, and the country was in the midst of economic recession (Bédarida 1979). Inflation doubled between 1914 and 1920, when it reached its peak, and the value of Pound Sterling fell by 61.2 per cent over this same period. Despite Lloyd George's ultimately failed public promises of economic payback through the Treaty of Versailles, Britain was unable to regain its lost power and influence globally, and as 'one began to lose confidence in the marvels of progress and science ... belief in Britain's primacy was beginning to shake' (Bédarida 1979:173). It was now forced to play second fiddle to its transatlantic cousin, the United States of America, to whom it owed a whopping £850 million from a war loan.

Britain's ultimate success on the battlefields of Europe helped counter claims of national decay, and renewed confidence in its methods. Britain's deep-rooted beliefs in its own racial superiority and ethical righteousness remained largely intact (Bédarida 1979). The pride of its people sustained their confidence despite the fact that the edifice of the British Empire was crumbling before them. British imperial sovereignty was threatened by the emergence of nationalist movements in the Middle East; the rise of the Indian Congress Party led by Gandhi that threatened Britain's imperial role; and, closer to home, Irish resistance that culminated in the bloody Easter Rising (Dewey 1997). Protracted negotiations and a bitter two-and-a-half-year civil war ensued over Irish sovereignty, with particular regard to Protestant-dominated Ulster, with the ultimate compromise of a divided Ireland finally ratified amidst great controversy in 1922.

Even closer to home, LTA councillors in Scotland began to voice objections to their lack of autonomy in running tournaments and administering finances. Given the specific composition of their clubs, which tended to be larger in size but fewer in number, they sought special financial arrangements that included the retention of a greater proportion of tournament fees and a smaller subscription for LTA affiliation (*LT&B* 29 May 1920:94). Dr Flavelle, who represented a southern-English club, criticised Scotland's position and claimed these financial arrangements actually created a deficit. Since a major expenditure arose from the payment of travel expenses for LTA Council meetings, he proposed that Scotland be represented by a Londoner. Outraged, and insulted by the insinuation that 'Scotland is the pampered child of the LTA', the Scotsman Mr Primrose proposed that future LTA meetings be held in Newcastle or Carlisle to reduce such expense payments, and demanded: Scotland should be represented 'by men who are in Scotland and who will understand its needs' (*LT&B* 6 Oct 1923:690). His colleagues agreed, voting overwhelmingly to shelve Flavelle's proposal. It is likely that wider political and economic matters inspired this discussion. After 1918, Scotland and the north in general were hit hardest by the economic recession and, from once leading the way in 'economic dynamism, technological advance, urbanisation and overseas expansion', these areas witnessed the south restore its dominance in terms of 'population, power and decision-making' (Bédarida 1979:178–9). Despite London being the administrative, economic and political centre of a declining empire, within Britain it remained its most prosperous city, and the LTA's administrative hub.

Despite these challenges, the strength of conviction to uphold and maintain the traditional British amateur sporting ethos remained strong. After all, the routine flouting of codes of gentlemanly conduct during the Great War by the Central Powers (Germany, Austria-Hungary, the Ottoman Empire (Turkey) and Bulgaria) provided an important stimulus to defeat them, and 'a principal rallying call behind the mobilisation of British pro-war sentiment', (Llewellyn 2011e:754). Moreover, it was the stoic, plucky and unflappable British spirit – the "stiff upper lip" – that held its own when confronted with the efficient German war-machine. It was often this conception of an unsporting German nation that fuelled anti-German sentiments. It was not long into the war, in fact, when Britons made their feelings known, with a strength of conviction that only the onset of horrific armed conflict could muster among the normally imperturbable British middle class. The British IOC representative Theodore Cook, who was knighted for his wartime anti-German propaganda effort, was particularly vociferous in condemning the gratuitous violence and terror enacted by Germany and its allies, and in 1915 threatened to resign from the IOC should they be included as part of the Olympic family (Llewellyn 2011e). Tennis correspondents supported this firm stance; one calling himself "Victim" was the most scornful, writing:

> The German soldier is the most pitiful creature that crawls on the face of the earth. Though a well-educated and intelligent man he deliberately places his very soul at the disposal of his superior, with the result that if his superiors are brutes he also becomes a brute. I regard it, therefore as probable that some of our German lawn tennis 'friends' have been actual accessories in the nameless outrages in question, and, further, I regard it an absolute certainty that *all* of them would unhesitatingly commit such acts if they were ordered to do so by superior authority.
> (*LT&B* 18 March 1915:241)

For these comments, "Victim" was accused of 'fanning the spirit of race hatred', thus demonstrating the full extent to which even lawn tennis could be dragged into the emotionally charged political minefield of warfare.

Associations like the LTA and ILTF refused to allow themselves to be pulled so deeply into this debate, but they did take positions on the issue of whether to allow the participation of ex-enemies. The general mood of the British public was strongly against any form of reconciliation, however trivial, and they pressed the ILTF to rescind German, Austrian, Hungarian, Turkish and Bulgarian membership. They denied their players the right to compete in the Davis Cup or in any tournaments held in allied or even neutral nations, and refused the right of allied players to play at tournaments located in enemy nations, or in neutral nations that did not enact the same restrictions. These extreme forms of exclusion sought to remove any chance of allied players coming into contact with them.

Considering itself to have pseudo-political responsibilities, and despite a track record of accepting international associations within their fold, the LTA refused affiliation to Argentina and declined an invitation to tour there because Argentina sought an exemption from resolutions against ex-enemies. The BOA and the respective Home Nation FAs also took stands against the inclusion of enemy nations in international sporting competitions, which led Llewellyn (2011e:755) to posit that such actions illuminated British hypocrisy:

> Claiming to uphold the purity of amateur sport, the British frequently condemned the intrusion of politics and nationalism into the sporting

arena. Yet … the British were the transgressors, violating their own lofty standards by transforming a sporting issue into a matter of far greater political significance.

Like the Olympics, the Davis Cup was initially created to serve the lofty ideals of promoting international relations and fostering goodwill, cooperation and mutual understanding between nations, but the inability of its organisers to separate sport from politics clearly demonstrated its limits.

It was several years before Germany and its former allies were welcomed back into the international fold. In 1925, the LTA allowed British players to play in tournaments abroad where ex-enemy players were invited, but did not allow British players to compete in Germany or allow ex-enemies to compete in Britain until 1928/29. In this environment, it was unsurprising that the Davis Cup should take on a new and deeper political significance. During the interwar years, particularly before the first football World Cup in 1930, the Challenge Round was rivalled only by the Olympics in terms of public interest and media attention (Jefferys 2009b). Representing one's country was a huge honour and successes carried much political weight, as battles of ideology played out in sport were important barometers of national vitality. LTA President Lord Desborough hinted at the political importance of fostering goodwill between allies: 'Whatever the destination of the Davis Cup… we feel that the actual winning of it is of small moment compared with the opportunities the competition affords of cementing the existing happy relations between the various challenging nations' (*LT&B* 26 June 1920:174). As a result of the growing popularity of tennis worldwide, ILTF membership numbers continued to increase. In 1927, 31 nations were affiliated to the ILTF, and by 1938, membership stood at 59. Consequently, the Federation enjoyed far greater reach and relevance than it had before the war, when it was perceived largely as an irrelevant and innocuous 'phantom' federation. At times, the Federation looked set to disband, but through conflict against those that threatened its autonomy it grew stronger.

While the IOC and ILTF agreed on the best course of action with regard to prohibitions against ex-enemy nations, their negotiations with respect to Olympic lawn tennis were less successful. The sport had featured in every Olympic Games but, while it had grown in popularity and significance, it failed to sustain the respect and attention of other sports like athletics and football. This was in part because national Olympic committees often placed greater emphasis on and provided more financial assistance to their track-and-field athletes than their tennis players. Timetable clashes chiefly contributed to the events failing to attract the world's best players and, for their part, the host cities often ran the events poorly. The 1920 and 1924 competitions were criticised heavily for the poor location of the tennis stadium, rudimentary dressing-room accommodation, lack of showers and poor umpiring, which forced the ILTF to propose having a greater say in the running of future Olympic tennis events (Cunnington 1988).

Similar requests had been made from other international federations, which in general were pressing now for greater authority and control over their sports. FIFA, for example, urged the IOC to change their attitude toward broken-time payments in 1927. Given the huge revenues generated by the football events – the most by far of any sport – the IOC was forced initially to concede, though this position was eventually annulled in 1930 under a weighty BOA protest (Llewellyn 2011g). Nevertheless, the IOC was clearly opposed to outside involvement, often limiting discussions on how events should be run to short consultations. The ILTF wanted direct representation on the IOC executive committee, however, and their own amateur definition used to qualify particular players. Pierre de Coubertin had been trying to create, since 1909, a "universal" amateur definition that applied to all nations and all sports, but this idea was controversial in forcing federations to fall in line or risk alienating themselves within the Olympic movement. In the case of tennis, the ILTF sought to allow once-professional-now-reinstated amateurs to compete, but this contravened the new amateur definition agreed at the 1925 IOC Congress in Prague. It appears also that the IOC blamed the ILTF for the poor entries and low standards of Olympic tennis events hitherto, so its proposal to raise the profile of Olympic tennis events involved cancelling all major national championships, including Wimbledon and the Davis Cup, during each Olympic year, and to herald the Olympic tennis event as the 'Championship of the World'.

Appalled, the ILTF refused to entertain such proposals. Siding with them, the LTA criticised the IOC for having 'little knowledge of the games which they wish to control', and 'fervently [resenting] any suggestion that they can possibly be wrong and fiercely [opposing] any attempt to put them right'. Given what was at stake, *LT&B* asked:

> Can any lawn tennis player do anything else but applaud the action of the Federation in replying to this with a direct negative? With the best will in the world, the points of view are so diametrically opposed that, so far as the ILTF is concerned, the prospects of lawn tennis forming a part of the Olympic Games in future are very remote.
> (27 March 1926:1105–6)

Unwilling to negotiate on such demands, the IOC and ILTF parted ways in 1927. The issue re-emerged on the ILTF agenda in 1939, but even after a 15-year hiatus, neither association was ready to compromise. By then, the Olympic Games and the major tennis championships were both considerably larger and more prestigious, to the extent that neither one needed the other. Tingay (1973:43) remarked: 'The Olympics added nothing to lawn tennis and lawn tennis little to the Olympics.' Moreover, from the tennis point of view, 'there were enough lawn tennis competitions already in existence without adding another every four years, which was at best a duplication of … those held at Wimbledon and Forest Hills' (*LT&B* 1 April 1939:1085). It was 1968 when both associations settled their differences, and tennis was chosen as a demonstration sport for the Mexico City Olympics, but due to further complications involving the IOC rules on amateurism, it was not until 1988 that tennis was reintegrated as a fully fledged Olympic sport.

Despite the LTA having assets at the war's end of just £1 15s, they remained convinced of their moral duty to lead the sport administratively through this new era; it was proud to claim that 'lawn tennis in this country is run on cleaner and honester lines than anywhere else' (*LT&B* 12 September 1925:611). Huggins and Williams (2005:147) argued: 'The selflessness and concern for others, modesty, honesty, courage and abiding by the rules that were involved with sportsmanship were interpreted as evidence that the English could be trusted' to exercise control for the benefit of all; they claimed *their* administrative leadership was necessary to preserve the high-minded goals of sportsmanship and to educate others of proper "sporting" ideals. This paternalist position was held also by the BOA, which claimed to have a "moral duty" to persevere with teaching the values of sportsmanship to athletes of other nations (Llewellyn 2011f). Polley (2006:460) argued that Britain's conviction to lead was reinforced by outsiders as much as from within; he cited an incident involving an international fencing tournament in Scheveningen in 1922, when a British diplomat was approached and informed that the organisers 'regarded the presence of an English team essential … because the fact of our team being there would raise the whole tone of the meeting'. Similarly, in tennis, there was a great deal of press correspondence about the importance of British leadership given that 'true sportsmanship' was its 'birthright' (*LT&B* 10 March 1923:899). Ideas associated with the LTA as the moral leader of international tennis found almost universal support.

Whatever their motives or beliefs, however, the ILTF's increasing size facilitated a loss of control for the British in actuality. Unlike FIFA, which was formed under the pretence of offering each member nation equal voting rights, the ILTF retained an organisational structure that allotted different numbers of votes to different nations. This was designed to ensure that Britain, America, Australia and France in particular retained control. While these nations undoubtedly were in favour of the sport's global diffusion, as it helped raise standards and make for more interesting contests, they must have realised this development would increasingly limit their own power to command. At this stage, however, the process of voting was such that most nations tended to follow majority opinion, which afforded the leading nations considerable power, so long as they agreed among themselves.

The allocation of votes often reflected an inclination toward Eurocentrism. In 1929, both Switzerland and Japan sought affiliation. The former had a fairly modest tennis set-up at the time; the standard of neither its tournaments nor its best players was particularly noteworthy, yet at the final moment their voting allocation was bumped up from two to three, because of 'the support and encouragement given by that country to the game of lawn tennis and to the ILTF' (*LT&B* 23 March 1929:1407). Japan was given just two votes, despite some remarkable international successes; Ichiya Kumagae (men's singles) and Kumagae and Seiichiro Kashio (men's doubles) both won silver medals at the 1920 Olympics and the following year, Zenzo Shimidzu made the semi-finals of Wimbledon.

Colonial bias was the curious shout of criticism voiced by the Canadian representative, E.H. Cooper, in 1934. He suggested that 'if Great Britain, France and Holland roped in all their dependencies they would be in a position to rule the Federation' (*LT&B* 24 March 1934:1280), but as a remedy that reflected Eurocentric bias, he proposed to offer all such dependencies just a single vote. It is highly unlikely that he meant to include the British dominions of Australia, New Zealand, South Africa and his own Canadian nation in this proposal. Thus, it smacks of imperialist paternalism, in condemning much of the Indian subcontinent and Asia, parts of South America and most of Africa to the sidelines with minimal voting powers. To be sure, many of these were weaker tennis nations, but to consider limiting their voting powers carte blanche uncovered a much more deeply rooted sense of what the leading tennis nations considered their responsibilities, and exposed fears regarding a potential loss of authority.

The British were already faced with burgeoning American power, which ultimately forced them to offer serious concessions to sustain friendly relations. As a sign of things to come, in 1920, the USLTA introduced entirely new laws regarding the "foot-fault". This assertive disregard for British-conceived laws was uncustomary, pushing the LTA to respond by asking whether 'Americans may possibly think that the obligation to defer to England's wishes no longer exists' (*LT&B* 25 March 1920:595). Evidently, the answer was that they did, and their growing influence was tacitly recognised. An article in *The Field* remarked: 'We consider the maintenance of complete harmony between the British and American governing bodies of prime importance at the present time, and nothing should be done to impair it' (cited in *LT&B* 8 April 1920:620). The Americans had still not joined the ILTF, but they knew they were in a powerful position to lobby and negotiate new terms, remarking in 1921: 'The complete success of a body like the International Federation is contingent upon its comprising *all* the leading lawn tennis nations' (emphasis added) (*ALT* 15 February 1921:622). The Federation could never function coherently or be taken seriously among other international sporting organisations with America's absence, so it was in everyone's interests to foster their cooperation. In 1923, British players took umbrage with the LTA for agreeing to accept the American foot-fault law, with the *LT&B* headline: 'Hands off our laws'. The author asked: 'Why should we forfeit our autonomy? We were the true inventors of lawn tennis' (*LT&B* 3 March 1923:883).

In broader spheres, it was evident that Britain considered their close "special" relationship with America politically expedient, economically rewarding and ideologically important. America had grown in status and confidence during and after the war. They now had the highest GDP, and their political stature as in-effect leaders of the free world was enhanced by Woodrow Wilson's post-war efforts to create the League of Nations and draft the Treaty of Versailles. The "Americanisation" of Britain was seen most notably in the industrial and commercial domains, where rationalisation and efficiency became bywords for American capitalist influences of mass production and consumerism. It was also seen in media and popular culture, through the erection of enormous cinemas and music halls, the spread of jazz music, and in the values and practices associated with advertising, marketing and publicity (Burk 2007; Campbell, Davies and McKay 2004; Taylor 1965). Not all were welcome influences. Bédarida (1979:176) contends that the ubiquitous "Woolworth" along English high streets symbolised 'cheapjack commercialism, of standardised and depersonalised mediocrity'.

What was most evident was American self-assurance, and this was seen as much in tennis administration as in other domains, showing courage and conviction to oppose joining the ILTF until some of their main proposals for reform were adopted. They objected to Britain's extra vote and the idea of Wimbledon permanently retaining the title "World Championships on Grass", particularly given that many of the world's best players were Americans whose presence in England each summer could not be guaranteed. Put under pressure, the LTA agreed with the AELTC to drop the word "World" as of 1st January 1924, and ILTF voting rights were redrawn to ensure the four leading nations received equal votes. A note of thanks was extended by the USLTA for their generosity, but any resultant feelings of goodwill likely did little to assuage British fears of waning administrative authority.

Lawn tennis was not spared from the need to introduce widespread and marked changes to its operational procedures in accordance with the new conditions of interwar life. In fact, developments were more marked in this 21-year period than in any other era. Most noticeably, the Wimbledon Championships underwent large-scale modifications, first to its geographical location and then to aspects of its tournament structure. In 1922, the AELTC moved from Worple Road to larger grounds on Queen's Road between Wimbledon Village and Southfidds. The necessary funds were obtained by forging a joint venture with the LTA in 1920, creating the All England Lawn Tennis Ground Ltd, whereupon both parties agreed, in effect, to split the financial burden of relocation and the Championships' profits for the foreseeable future. Demand for numbered and reserved seats for the new Centre Court far outweighed supply, so, for the LTA at least, the risk was calculated. Indeed, after the initial outlay, the Championships' surplus rose year on year from £2,950 in 1921 to £18,676 in 1927.

The first year of competition at its new site in 1922 also coincided with the commencement of "playing through" for the previous year's champion. The custom of the holder sitting out until the final match had become less prevalent at some of the smaller tournaments, which led one *LT&B* correspondent to remark in 1909:

> As time went on the idea that all competitors in a championship should start on an equal footing began to gain ground, and the practice of making the holder play through became more and more general, so that today the AEC, from having set the fashion in one direction, find themselves in the position of being asked to follow it in the other.
>
> (4 March 1909:71)

In 1911, the present singles champion Anthony Wilding even offered to relinquish his title in an effort to bring about this change, but the AELTC clung stubbornly to this tradition for a further decade, even after the USLTA reverted to the playing-through system for its national championships in 1912.

The introduction of seeding the leading players also commenced in 1924. The practice began in America in the early 1900s, when some tournaments separated the best players to ensure they could only meet in the later rounds when bigger audiences were attracted. The main objection to seeding was that it 'practically portions out the prizes between the best men, and doesn't give the second flight an outside chance of a prize' (*LT&B* 26 August 1909:579). Still, it was known that several British tournaments secretly "fixed" the draw out of financial necessity; for simple luck to jeopardise a tournament's financial success was an outcome considered too risky. The AELTC remained defiant against the trend, however; owing to its premier status, it could attract sufficient gates regardless of how the draw was ultimately distributed. It eventually caved when some of its cousin associations abroad objected to the possibility that two of their own could travel all the way to England only to meet in the first round. It was agreed therefore that each country could nominate up to four players who would be separated into four quarters of the draw. In 1927, the process of seeding changed to include also the top eight players of each tournament as decided by the committee.

The Wimbledon qualifying tournament was introduced in 1924 after several correspondents before the war voiced opinions that some players entered merely for the extra privileges obtained. One remarked:

> Experience has shown that to enter for the championships is one of the cheapest and best ways of witnessing them, apart from the fact that the entrant gets a game or two at least, and certain other privileges which are denied to ordinary ticket holders.
>
> (*LT&B* 7 July 1910:327)

Taken together, these moves represented a clear indication of the growing importance of gate money for the AELTC. They could no longer ignore the tens of thousands of paying visitors each summer and the wishes of the players who they came to see. As a means of ensuring the presence of top overseas players, at some point in the mid to late 1920s, the AELTC agreed to offer reimbursement for travel and accommodation. The grant subsidised only some of the competitors' costs; the balance was to be covered by the players' respective national association, which distributed the funds based on each competitor's individual needs (Macauley and Smyth 1965:281). As a result, Wimbledon boasted more of the world's top players than any other competition in the interwar period, which made it a very profitable fortnight for both the AELTC and the LTA. The club used its profits to improve and maintain its club grounds, courts and facilities, while the LTA concerned themselves mainly with funding British players in the Davis Cup and other international tours.

In these explicit ways, lawn tennis had become intensely and unashamedly commodified in the 1920s. The LTA and AELTC demonstrated at times the prioritisation of capitalist objectives, despite continuing publicly to champion the retention of amateurism and the somewhat empty rhetoric of anti-commercialism. The inability of British authorities to deal effectively with issues related to amateurism remained a point of contention throughout this period and beyond the next war. Early interwar recovery efforts continued to pull British tennis in seemingly opposing directions, emphasising the extent to which administrators sought the somewhat conflicting objectives of elite-level success and amateur authority. In this environment of change, while consumerism and commercialism threatened to undermine the ideals of amateurism upon which tennis was founded, previously marginalised groups made notable advances in gaining opportunities for participation and competitive success.

Bibliography

Bédarida, F. (1979). *A Social History of England 1851–1975*. London: Methuen.
Birley, D. (1995b). *Playing the Game: Sport and British Society 1910–45*. Manchester: Manchester University Press.
Burk, K. (2007). *Old World, New World: The Story of Britain and America*. London: Little, Brown Book Group.
Campbell, N., Davies, J., and McKay, G. (2004). *Issues in Americanisation and Culture*. Edinburgh: Edinburgh University Press.
Collins, T. (2009). *A Social History of English Rugby Union*. London: Routledge.
Cunnington, D. (1988). *75 Years of the International Tennis Federation 1913–1988*. London: International Tennis Federation.
Dewey, P. (1997). *War and Progress: Britain, 1914–1945*. London: Longman.
Hill, J. (2002). *Sport, Leisure and Culture in Twentieth-Century Britain*. Basingstoke: Palgrave.
Hillyard, G. (1924). *Forty Years of First-Class Lawn Tennis*. London: Williams & Norgate.
Huggins, J., and Williams, J. (2005). *Sport and the English: 1918–1939*. London: Routledge.

Jefferys, K. (2009b). The Heyday of Amateurism in Modern Lawn Tennis. *International Journal of the History of Sport*, 26(15), 2236–52.
Little, A. (2007). *Suzanne Lenglen: Tennis Idol of the Twenties*. London: Wimbledon Lawn Tennis Museum.
Llewellyn, M. P. (2011e). 'Olympic Games are an International Farce'. *International Journal of the History of Sport*, 28(5), 751–772.
Llewellyn, M. P. (2011f). 'Olympic Games Doomed'. *International Journal of the History of Sport*, 28(5), 773–795.
Llewellyn, M. P. (2011g). The Curse of the Shamateur. *International Journal of the History of Sport*, 28(5), 796–816.
Macauley, D., and Smyth, J. (1965). *Behind the Scenes at Wimbledon*. London: Collins.
McKibbin, R. (1998). *Classes and Cultures: England 1918–1951*. Oxford: Oxford University Press.
Polley, M. (2006). The Amateur Ideal and British Sports Diplomacy, 1900–1945. *Sport in History*, 26(3), 450–467.
Reynolds, D. (1991). *Britannia Overruled: British Policy and World Power in the Twentieth Century*. London: Longman.
Taylor, A. J. (1965). *English History, 1914–1945*. Oxford: Oxford University Press.
Tilden, W. T. (1921). *The Art of Lawn Tennis* (2nd edn). London: Methuen.
Tingay, L. (1973). *A History of Lawn Tennis in Pictures*. London: Tom Stacey.
Tinling, T. (1983). *Tinling: Sixty Years in Tennis*. London: Sidgwick & Jackson.

7 'New people' and 'new energy'
Advances for women and children amidst British decline

Britain's third Conciliation Bill in 1912 would have extended voting rights to a million property-owning women, but it failed to achieve the necessary majority vote. Shortly thereafter, the campaign for suffrage championed by the Women's Social and Political Union grew militant, bombing David Lloyd George's house, among other acts of vandalism (Bédarida 1979). Despite maintaining low profiles, tennis clubs in places like Birmingham, Dundee and Nottingham were targeted, apparently because of the high-class composition of their members (Kay 2008), and the AELTC would also have suffered were it not for a diligent night-watchman who apprehended women with intentions to "scrap" Centre Court. Such acts of defiance did little to change established power structures within tennis clubs or elsewhere, and in a broader context merely served to lose support from those women more inclined to wait patiently for constitutional change.

The onset of war thrust women into pits, mines and munitions factories, where they adopted traditionally male-dominated roles with widespread commendation. This provided the necessary opportunity for women to challenge their supposed physical and intellectual capacities, confront their limited education and employment opportunities and subordinated status within the family and to push for legislative change to improve their marginal social, political and economic positions (Hargreaves 1994). Suffrage was awarded in the Third Reform Act of 1918, but was initially limited to those over 30 years of age who were members or married to members of the Local Government Register. Not until 1928 did their rights tally with men's, as suffrage was extended to all women over 21. The "New Woman" movement that witnessed marked changes to how young women spent their time, dressed, displayed and used their bodies, was wrought similarly with inconsistencies and contradictions for interwar sportswomen (Skillen 2012; 2013).

Much like post-secondary educational opportunities, access to sport and leisure was confined more or less to affluent middle-class women who were unmarried and without children. Large numbers of married women considered sport 'irrelevant to their lives', given the physical debilitations suffered through 'multiple pregnancies, lack of medical attention and having overall responsibility for domestic labour and child-care' (Hargreaves 1994:114). Despite the institution of sport providing women with opportunities to challenge assumptions concerning gender roles and societal norms, it was not an explicit battleground for first-wave feminists. Its impact was more subtle.

In the interwar period, tennis enjoyed greatly increased popularity among women, as they came to successfully challenge widely held opinions of female frailty through advances in playing style and dress reform. However, the prevailing patriarchal ideologies that beset wider society continued also to position men's tennis on a higher plain of importance, as nearly all aspects of women's play were judged against men's, invariably unfavourably. Two important aims of this chapter are to critically analyse changes for women in tennis within the context of the sport's broader democratisation, and to examine the sport's impact on women's emancipation more generally. One final aim is to examine internal changes within the LTA and their affiliated clubs as they attempted to deal with these and other issues related to the provision of opportunities and talent development in the mid-1920s.

Alongside providing some measure of spatial freedom from parents and chaperones, women in sports clubs and educational establishments were afforded opportunities for physical emancipation, yet they tended to remain tied to domestic duties and largely excluded from decision-making committee positions (Hargreaves 1994). Even the British Wightman Cup team had a male (non-playing) captain for 1923, the first year of this all-female competition; the long-serving LTA councillor H.A. Sabelli was extended the honour of a glorified chaperone. From then until 1954, a male non-playing captain was chosen in eight of 25 years of competition. By contrast, the American team had only one male non-playing captain, Mr Cushman, serving in 1934 and 1936. Also, as far as records can tell, the ILTF failed to enlist a single female onto its Council during the interwar period. The LTA was only marginally better. Dorothea Lambert Chambers was the first known female on the LTA Council after being elected in 1923. She was followed by the London socialite Lady Wavertree, representing Dorset, in 1927, and Mrs M.S. Hazel, representing Staffordshire, in 1931. Following Wavertree's election, an *LT&B* correspondent commented:

> The ladies are in the majority in the multitude of players, and now there is a movement towards a more thorough representation for them. ... There is nothing in the world to prevent other counties doing as Dorset has done, and returning a lady member, nor to stop clubs, as they now do, sending a lady delegate to the [LTA] AGM. If it is true that in lawn tennis, as in politics, the feminine vote is the greater, it will prove itself.
> (18 January 1930:1145)

Some progressive clubs duly elected women into officer roles for the first time. Both Barrow LTC and Culford LTC in Suffolk elected a woman as secretary and treasurer in 1930, but these remained exceptional examples. At West Heath LTC, women comprised over 60 per cent of membership in the interwar period, but while the men's captain had been an official committee member since 1912, the ladies' captain was not extended the same privilege until 1927. This they did not seem to mind; apparently, lady members vied to provide the best Saturday afternoon teas (Berlin 2002). Despite having been integral to club operations since the club's formation in 1907, female members at Twickenham LTC achieved official recognition only after successfully lobbying for the creation of a "Tea Committee" in 1918. The following year, its name changed to the more official-sounding "Ladies Committee", but maintained as its main responsibility the serving of teas on Saturdays. They were not officially part of the main committee and as such had no executive decision-making powers, but had succeeded at least in organising themselves to provide women collectively with greater lobbying power. The club also continued to stipulate higher subscription charges for men, which was fairly common at the time and was likely due to an acknowledgement that women generally played less tennis or that women represented generally a class of lower-status members (Twickenham LTC 2007). Even the AELTC, despite its elite standing among clubs, did not elect its first female executive committee member, Virginia Wade, until 1982. Norah Cleather filled in as Acting Secretary during the six years of WWII, as all but four of the club's staff were called to service, but despite the 'warm appreciation and grateful thanks' extended for her services, the club committee agreed to advertise explicitly for a male secretary to replace her (Macauley and Smyth 1965:140).

In the early 1920s, inter-club competitions for women in many counties were either not in existence or poorly organised. Nottinghamshire LTA held its first women's tournament in 1921 (Lusis 1998), but little is known about competitions in other counties, either because they were low-key events or did not yet exist. Men's events continued to dominate proceedings and attract the most local attention, despite the fact that wartime losses meant that in most clubs in the early 1920s women outnumbered men (Wigglesworth 2007). For example, according to Norman Patterson (1921), only 20 per cent of tennis clubs in Tyneside and Wearside had a majority male membership.

At the elite level, there was widespread resistance to the idea of creating an international competition for women, similar to the Davis Cup. Just after the war, two such offers were extended: one in 1919 by Mrs Hall Walker and another the following year by Lady Wavertree. Neither was taken seriously. Across the Atlantic, in 1920, the four-time US Nationals champion Mrs Hazel Hotchkiss Wightman donated a cup for leading British and American players to compete for over a seven-match series, but the ILTF decided 'not to recognise this competition'; it was reminded that 'the Federation is opposed to the holding of a ladies' international team competition of any kind' (*LT&B* 25 March 1920:597). Like international competitions in other sports, e.g. the Walker Cup in golf and cricket test-matches, such contests were considered male privileges. Not until 1923 was the "Wightman Cup" extended ILTF sanction.

Despite these early frustrations, the story of women's tennis in the interwar period is characterised overall by significant advances. The sport became, according to Jensen (2010:37), a highly effective vehicle for the 'articulation of new women's roles' partly because 'it packaged subversive elements within the nonthreatening veneer of a sport that had long identified itself as suitable for women and had seamlessly incorporated many elements of traditional femininity'. While the involvement of women in politics, law or the sciences challenged inveterate patriarchal structures and ideologies, their participation in tennis did not, which gave its participants an ideal platform to challenge ideas and set new behavioural standards.

At the forefront of developments for female players was the flamboyant and talismanic Suzanne Lenglen, but even when she was elected a committee member of her own Nice LTC in December 1919 it went very much against established protocol (Little 2007). Her Wimbledon singles victory earlier that summer over the defending champion and seven-time winner Dorothea Lambert Chambers marked the beginning of a new era in women's tennis. *LT&B* (10 July 1919:178) wrote:

> Never has such tennis been seen in a ladies' single. There were a great many people who would never have believed such tennis could be played by women. ... Neither player showed the slightest trace of the old traditional womanly weaknesses.

A *Daily Mail* correspondent argued it was 'the greatest display by women in the history of the game' (7 July 1919:4).

The dominant "progressive" narrative of this match in journalistic and subsequent academic outlets provides some account of its social significance, but oversimplifies and exaggerates differences between the two players. For many, the 40-year-old Chambers represented 'the epitome of Edwardian backwardness and a supposedly conservative pre-war sporting culture' (Gilbert 2011:188); she advocated nothing less than dignified dress and demeanour, playing in traditional attire constituting a long, heavy dress and plain long-sleeved shirt. Lenglen, by marked contrast, wore a loose-fitting, short-sleeved, calf-length frock, which reflected the newly popular streamlined Art Deco-style sportswear of Jean Patou (Elks 2004). Despite her more cumbersome dress, Chambers' play was remarkably effective against Lenglen. At 6–5 and 40–15 up in the final set, she held, but lost, two match points, and eventually the match.

Though 'certainly not beautiful', argued Brady (1959:17), it was Lenglen's propensity to leap and stretch for difficult shots that most distinguished her; she defied convention in 'her grace, her vivacity and her exquisite clothes'.

Gilbert (2011:190) explained, 'there were some elements of the establishment that were shocked by Lenglen's dress and movement, and the way that parts of her body were revealed during play contravened notions of "respectability"'. Given the prudishness of the interwar period and the censorship of sexual material more generally, Lenglen's 'ballet leaps, the intermittent glimpses of bare thigh, and the sexual connotations of her very visible silhouette' were irresistible to men, argued Tinling (1983:25). In her looks and play she personified the next generation; described as a graceful player, elegant, attractive and 'awe-inspiring', yet like a panther, 'volcanic in action' and 'like a hungry man sitting down to dinner ... keen for the struggle, eager for action' (*LT&B* 12 Nov 1921:545). Undoubtedly, she helped facilitate a shift in notions of appropriate sporting femininity, '[fusing] athletic ability with heterosexual allure' (Cahn 1994:50). In her play, she defied those who felt that sport might "spoil" a girl's looks – something that the mannish Chambers could not do – but brought perhaps unwelcome scrutiny of her body for almost scientific objectification. Crawley, for example, contributed to the *Daily Mail* (4 July 1919:4) what he called a 'technical study' of Lenglen just before the 1919 final, and analysed her gait and posture, and focused on her shoulders, arms, wrists, legs and ankles for inspection. Such unwarranted attention on Lenglen's body reflected the sustained hegemony of men over women within 'a patriarchal culture that left women physically inhibited, confined and positioned', and undoubtedly preceded the more overt sexualisation of sportswomen that came later (Gilbert 2011:195).

Lenglen's role in accelerating dress reform during this period was also significant. In effect, she came to epitomise the modern "flapper" movement (Birley 1995b; Cahn 1994; Schultz 2014; Warner 2006), assisted greatly by her self-constructed public image. Gilbert (2011:192) explained, she was 'closely identified with a distinctly "continental" construction of glamour, associated particularly with the French Riviera, an impression strengthened both by her visible tan and her habit of sipping brandy between games'. Particularly to domesticated, suburban, young, middle-class British women, Lenglen and all that she represented must have seemed irresistibly enchanting. Her on-court successes merely added credibility to her mystique. It was no surprise, therefore, that her tennis outfits gained worldwide popularity and ushered in more comfortable and practical dress for play (Horwood 2002). Lenglen (1919:28–9) described the ideal tennis outfit: 'a simple "pique" dress, or one of drill or white linen, made in the old Grecian style, and fastened at the waist with a ribbon or leather belt. The sleeves should be short'. Her distinctive bandeau became a standard for women players and demonstrated how far Lenglen influenced fashions outside of tennis in an aesthetic, rather than merely practical, sense (Jensen 2010; Lumpkin 1981; Warren 1993; Warner 2006). Tinling (1983:26) stated that within weeks of introducing her bandeau at Wimbledon in 1920, 'for the next six years there was not a tennis girl who did not attempt some imitation'. When 19-year-old Joan Fry, from Staffordshire, met Suzanne Lenglen in the 1925

Wimbledon singles final sporting identically cropped hair, bandeau, loose-fitting short-sleeved, knee-length frock and white stockings, some might have thought she was mocking her charismatic French opponent, but in fact she was merely sporting the most fashionable look of the time.

During the interwar period, assisted by Lenglen and later Helen Wills and Alice Marble, tennis fashions became 'everyday fashions' for regular consumers (Horwood 2002; Schultz 2014). Wimbledon's "fashion milestones" made even bigger headlines, and images of popular tennis fashions continued to be advertised in the leading ladies' magazines and reproduced in photographic postcards and paintings of the top players, principally to accentuate their good looks and glamour (Elks 2004). Dorothy Wilding and the Bassano company exploited the natural beauty of players like Helen Wills, Helen Jacobs, and Englishwomen Betty Batt and Dorothy Round, who became pin-ups, posing wistfully often in sensuous positions with rackets as props (Sumner 2011). To some extent, they could be considered victims of the sexualised objectification of the female form, but Sumner (2011) felt that photography had a liberating function; it enabled women to 'control their own image ... [and] turned to such studios to show themselves to best advantage in their tennis attire'. Tennis champions were joined by Olympic swimmers and divers, such as Ethelda Bleibtrey, Helen Wainwright and Aileen Riggin, as symbols of new womanhood, combining athleticism and sexual attractiveness for consumption by eager male audiences (Dyreson 1996; 1999; Huggins and Williams 2005).

The British authorities were mostly concerned with ensuring that Wimbledon's female players appeared with utmost respectability. Their attempts to curb public enthusiasm for provocative photographs of Lenglen were met with widespread resistance from the tabloid press, which duly criticised their old-fashioned attitudes. One *Daily Mirror* correspondent commented on the 'pleasant pictures displaying the modern women's art in reconciling activity with grace' (18 July 1923:7), while another remarked: 'As long as they are suitably and respectably garbed I can see no reason why there should be any objection to photographs of respectable young women indulging in a thoroughly clean sport' (19 July 1923:5). The AELTC's actions in 1929 to ban the display of bare legs were born from similar sentiments regarding the preservation of female modesty, but were criticised by leading American players for being ultra-conservative. Alice Marble's shorts cut six inches above the knee created a storm in the late 1930s, being the shortest ever seen (Warren 1993), but by then clothing was becoming more functional.

While stressing modesty, the authorities were concerned also to ensure that women appeared as attractive models of refined heterosexual femininity. Thus, when Lili de Alvarez, in a pair of white trousers, faced off against the stocking-less Joan Lycett for a Centre Court match in 1931, the incident created widespread public commentary, as both actions re-articulated fears about the masculinisation of women (Horwood 2002). In 1933, Helen Jacobs appeared at the US Nationals in a pair of tailored shorts, similar to Bunny Austin's, and commentators questioned her motivation to 'dress like a man'. She responded in the *New York Times* (15 August 1933:21) that shorts offered a 'tremendous advantage ... they are cooler and enable one to get around so much faster, particularly in the latter stages of a hard match'. Gradually, Jacobs' dress styles became more acceptable to the British middle-class public because as a crowd favourite her off-court actions conformed to traditional notions of femininity. Huggins and Williams (2005:158) argued: 'Apologists for women's sport were still eager to stress that playing sport did not masculinise women and that it would not diminish their physical appeal to men'. Artwork at the time helped a great deal to reinforce the important balance between athleticism and beauty. *Tennis Under the Orange Trees, Cannes* (1929) by John Lavery and *Tennis in the Park* (1930) by Eric Ravilious, in particular, displayed female players wearing loose clothing and in athletic, commanding poses, but ensured they remained elegant and distinctly feminine with their long hair and fashionable accoutrements (Sumner 2011).

Hargreaves (1994) suggested that the continued emphasis placed on physical attraction frustrated the women's emancipation movement in the interwar years, as women continued to measure their self-worth by the extent that men found them sexually appealing. In this guise, they offered an incomplete challenge to male authority and hegemonic masculinity. Not only was their on- and off-court behaviour and appearance still conditioned by broader male-centred notions of appropriateness, but also their playing styles and overall attitudes to competition.

From this viewpoint, it is argued that the ultimate extent of Lenglen's impact on women's emancipation was contingent upon male acceptance of the new type of femininity she advocated. Her relentless and aggressive on-court attack was counterbalanced by an ebullient off-court personality. The extent that her playing methods were accepted is revealed by the fact that new tennis instructional books published during her tenure had altered chapter formats; no longer did authors specify different conventions for women's play as compared to men's. Crawley (1922:48) felt the tone of 'old-fashioned' sections on "ladies' play" was 'either flippant or compassionate, a relic of the primitive male view of women', and Aitken (1924:42) argued: 'Women no longer need a book on lawn tennis to themselves; they play in the same style as men.' When playing exhibition matches against men, Lenglen beat all but the very best. She had a comprehensive repertoire of strokes, and in mixed doubles was known to adopt the traditional male position as chief antagonist and poacher. *LT&B* reported a match involving Lenglen and her teammate, the number-one-ranked Frenchman William Laurentz. It described how she took charge and poached many of his volleys and smashes, before commenting on the evitable outcome: 'The amusement was heightened by the fact that he proved very disobedient' (*LT&B* 3 July 1919:150). He was embarrassed to allow his female teammate to dominate play, as traditional conventions prescribed him to do so. Lenglen's stubborn self-reliance epitomised the independent and ambitious "new woman" of the 1920s, presenting an alternative version of middle-class womanhood that was accepted by proponents of women's physical activity but offended against dominant ideologies of domesticity, particularly because of the 'unrelenting public manner' in which she lived her life (Jensen 2010:36).

Despite the advances that Lenglen oversaw in women's play and in her personal endeavours not to be marginalised in mixed doubles, conventions here did not change immediately. Different expectations were sustained by men in the mixed game (Lake 2012). For example, Beamish and Beamish (1924:76–7) recommended: 'The man … is expected to play more shots from every part of the court', including most of the lobs, overheads and volleys. Ritchie (1928:70) recommended for female players: 'attend to weak over-head shots, side lines, drives and dead straight balls, leaving everything else to her partner'. Retired army officer-turned-coaching-professional Major Rendall felt that mixed doubles for men was a poor substitute for "real" tennis because the players are not 'equally matched':

> [A woman] has not the physical strength to keep up the tussle, stroke for stroke, of a rally in which the man is urging forth his full, untempered force. Thus, it happens that a man does not bang a ball at a woman as hard as he can when the tennis calls for it. Instead, he either softens his shot, or he sends it elsewhere.

In this case, 'the male is under restraint [and] … strokes that would be true tennis must be sacrificed because they may not properly be played against a woman'. Thus, he stressed that the inclusion of women 'inevitably lowers the standard' overall (Rendall 1926:132–3).

Other disparaging comments were found frequently in *LT&B*. One columnist opined that women were 'hopelessly caught' when it came to speed, were at a 'very great disadvantage' in service, and 'hopelessly inferior' at volleying (5 January 1924:918). Meanwhile, the leading American player, Molla Mallory, advised girls to 'learn to serve overhead' and 'acquire skill at volleying' like the men, but admitted many 'cannot move fast enough … or think quickly enough'; they 'seldom finish off a volley decisively' and 'are weak in anticipation' (10 February 1923:839). British girls in particular were condemned for being lazy; one correspondent remarked that girls 'can't be fagged' to learn proper technique (*LT&B* 7 August 1919:252). This suggests 'that some women players were conforming to expectations surrounding the female athlete's physical ability: conscious of the public gaze they chose not to put their bodies through excessive physical strain' (van Someren 2010:12).

Such comments from both sexes served to sustain women's subordination and assuage men's fears of declining masculine prowess. Undoubtedly, some were threatened by women's notable advances, to the extent that in 1930 a suggestion was made that "men's only" clubs be formed. Apparently, these would serve as better locations for talent development, attract more men from university and provide tougher competition; given the presence of women 'greatly lowers the standard of play as a whole', mixed doubles was considered the chief culprit and 'really rather a farce' (*LT&B* 1 November 1930:886). It was elite-level play that set the tone for social change, however, and the continuous stream of fashionable and attractive female players brought new enthusiasts to the sport and increased media exposure.

Chambers' defeat to Lenglen in 1919 represented more than just the figurative "passing of the torch", but the end of Britain's 40-year reign of women's tennis success at Wimbledon. From 1919–26, the Frenchwoman remained untouchable on grass and, barring the occasional defeat often due to illness, she continued to dominate women's competitions in Europe both in singles and in doubles with her American partner Suzanne Ryan. Molla Mallory and Helen Wills took most of the spoils in the US National Championships of the early interwar period. The Brits Kitty McKane and Betty Nuttall led Britain to Wightman Cup victories against America in 1924, 25, 28 and 30, and served up occasional successes against the big names in the major championships, but these performances compared unfavourably against Lenglen, Mallory and Wills. In reality, such comparisons revealed huge disparities; while the latter were globetrotting superstars, capable of galvanising thousands of spectators and commanding huge under-the-table payments from tournament committees, McKane (née Godfree) and Nuttall were typical British players of this period, relying on the financial support of their families and the goodwill of their employers to afford their tennis opportunities (Hargreaves 1994).

British decline was most apparent among the men and had begun before the war. Although they managed to reach the final in 1919, being defeated by Australia 4–1, Davis Cup results from 1920 to 1929 highlight British regression. From once being in the top tier, Britain was now only narrowly defeating teams from Belgium and Hungary and losing to those from Spain (twice), Denmark, Italy and Germany. Hitherto, none of these other nations had won the Davis Cup, nor produced players close to winning any of the four major championships.

By the early–mid-1920s, the excuses of war had worn thin among a public expectant of success, and there was a growing feeling among administrators, particularly those outside the LTA Council, that fundamental structural change was necessary. Blackmore (1921: xvi) criticised the 'autocratic' LTA for 'misgoverning' the game, while Burrow (1922:204) claimed it was 'out of touch with the players of today and their requirements'. At the end of 1922, after the British defaulted to Spain in the Davis Cup second round because they could not field a sufficiently strong team, a mutiny was staged within the LTA administration by an activist group calling itself the "Lawn Tennis Reform Committee" (LTRC). They aggressively campaigned to unseat a significant proportion of LTA councillors, and wrote to all affiliated clubs and associations stating their aims that included: 'to restore the prestige and influence of this country as the leading lawn tennis nation', to 'train up and encourage by every means consistent with true amateurism British players capable of regaining the Davis Cup and the championships of Wimbledon', to give more voice and power to the county associations, and to develop tennis in the universities, public schools and parks (*LT&B* 2 December 1922:667). Their chief platform seemed to be international rivalry and the need to embark upon a more ambitious project to restore British glory. Twenty-one LTA councillors signed a published response, but this offered little substance to counter claims of negligence. Perhaps consequently, LTRC campaigners secured 21 of the 36 seats contested at the next AGM, which prompted a well-known *LT&B* correspondent to ask the obvious question: 'Is there any reason why Englishmen should throw over their traditional policy of "the game for the game's sake", and subordinate everything to the production of world beaters?' (*LT&B* 30 December 1922:743).

Incumbents blamed escalating American competitiveness for the increased seriousness with which the British were forced to participate. This was something that administrators of other sports like athletics had also voiced, and comparisons between American and British approaches often criticised the more scientific methods of the former for compromising true amateur values through the implementation of "artificial" means of skill enhancement, i.e. systematic coaching, talent identification and development (Carter 2010; Huggins and Williams 2005; Wrynn 2010). According to Queen's Club professional Charles Hierons (1924:103), the Americans embraced professionalism far more comprehensively than the British by adopting a more serious and progressive approach: 'No nation takes lawn tennis so seriously. ... Not only has [America] a greater number of young players to draw upon, but she takes hold of them at school, trains them with professional teachers'. Similarly, British Davis Cup player Gordon Crole-Rees commented on the American propensity to 'specialise to a very marked degree' and 'let nothing interfere with their determination to get to the top', but concluded defiantly: 'if it were possible to arrange a lawn tennis match between the first 2000 players in this country and the first 2000 in any other, England would win by an overwhelming margin' (*All Sports Weekly* 7 May 1927).

Britain's failure in 1923 to defeat Spain in Manchester in the Davis Cup second round was likely the wake-up call needed for LTA councillor Arthur Batley to compose a comprehensive treatise accounting for Britain's recent failings. Sections were published in *LT&B* throughout 1924, pressing the point that fundamental flaws in the British sporting 'mentality' were to blame. For a young Englishman, he wrote:

> lawn tennis is a game, and not one of the serious activities of life. ... It is not to be confused with work, or to be made too much like it. ... Exercise and pleasure are its true objects and greatness merely one of the attractive incidences of it. ... He may take a few lessons if he can get

them, and practice a little occasionally, but the regular dogged practice which makes perfect is rarely indulged in.

In comparison, 'the overseas player ... takes the game more seriously than we do, and goes in search of greatness, while we are inclined to wait for it to come to us' (*LT&B* 16 February 1924:1015). Throughout his diatribes, Batley spoke in clichés, remarking, for example, that the LTA should lead with a 'progressive spirit', to generate 'an atmosphere charged with enthusiasm and ambition to succeed by deliberate methods', and to 'dispense active encouragement, help and inspiration to the players' (*LT&B* 23 February 1924:1035). At the 1924 AGM, Batley took the floor again, this time urging those present to show support rather than fear or contempt for overseas associations that specialised and approached tennis with greater seriousness. Talent development in Britain, by comparison, he said, was 'haphazard, spasmodic, purely individual', and his overall recommendation was to 'scrap the old machine' (*LT&B* 20 December 1924:910).

Batley's delivery was passionate, but like many of his contemporaries, he articulated little more than vague proposals for change. In fact, mere platitudes were ubiquitous in published discourse from *all* sides. Even the LTRC, having usurped some authority from the "old guard", did little to advance lawn tennis in the following years and, like Batley, preferred to point fingers at decaying aspects of the British national character than actually devise a workable action plan. For sure, the LTA's inability to produce champions was an unwelcome signal of national degeneracy, and those with the power to change the system were growing desperate. Thus, Batley's most significant contribution to the debate came from his articulation of distinct "camps" in lawn tennis administration, divided in their outlook. One stood for 'active, energetic and progressive methods, supported by deliberate effort, and keen personal interest', and included most of the leading players and LTA Council members; the other stood for 'strict adherence to methods and practices of a bygone generation, clinging tenaciously to the belief that standing still is the best way to progress'. Despite being numerically outnumbered, the paralysing grip of the latter, which he described as 'a small group of obstinate men, deeply and securely dug in' within the Council, seemed to have considerable constraining influence overall (*LT&B* 8 November 1924:814). He noted the 'smug complacency' of the present leadership and remarked: 'A complete change of policy and methods controlled by new people and backed by new energy would create a fresh and invigorating atmosphere of inestimable value to the game and the players.' (*LT&B* 15 November 1924:830). He was right in that a substantial proportion of LTA Council seats were filled by senior citizens, many of whom were once expert players, but from the bygone era of weak overseas competition and honest adherence to amateur values. It is likely they lacked the necessary experience and ingenuity to design and implement programmes that paved long-term progress for players in the 1920s.

Advances for women and children

Shortly after the war, Burrow (1922:5–6) offered a frank appraisal of Britain's relative playing standards:

> There is undoubtedly a dearth among home players at the present time. ... Other countries are producing outstanding players ... mainly because [they] begin to play at a much earlier age than ours do. ... In America, Australia, France and many other countries, boys play lawn tennis while still at school, and not only play it but *learn* it. They have had ... at the very least five or six years' start of the English boy.

Indeed, the nations mentioned were now in a "different league", thanks in part to their more comprehensive talent-development schemes. The USLTA initiated a nationwide system of talent identification for under-18 boys as early as 1917, yet the LTA remained laissez-faire in its approaches until after WWII. 'We shall never produce champions capable of holding their own against foreign competition and winning back the Davis Cup until general interest is more widely stimulated in Junior lawn tennis', argued Lowe (1924:126); '[junior] events are still kept too much in the background. ... The fact remains that for every promising youngster we turn out there are at least a dozen in America, Australia and France'.

The Championships of 1924 witnessed the delectable Jean Borotra, nicknamed the "Bounding Basque", win the singles title and usher in a new era of unequivocal dominance from the "four musketeers". The group that also included Henri Cochet, René Lacoste and Jacques Brugnon was nurtured by the Fédération Française du Tennis (FFT) into the most successful men's tennis team ever assembled. Between them, they won six Davis Cups, and 20 singles and 13 doubles titles across the four major championships. Moreover, they each became cultural symbols and objects of national affection, as Faure (1996:91) described:

> The French doted on Borotra, who confirmed their own image of themselves, admired the artist and magician of the courts in Cochet, felt considerable esteem for the altruistic team spirit of Brugnon, [and] they respected Lacoste who personified the essential virtues of courage and determination.

Their resounding success in spite of France's own post-war economic problems left Britain with few remained excuses for its own dismal failures. Now, more than ever, the LTA needed to implement fundamental changes to how they identified and developed talent.

To their credit, a new emphasis was placed on children's talent development, broadly speaking, for the purposes of raising general standards and achieving international success. Through its affiliated county associations and clubs, the LTA set aside increasing amounts of time, energy and money to organise and run children's tournaments, fund coaching sessions and pursue talent-development programmes in schools. Surrey was exceptional in holding its first junior tournament before the war, in 1914 (Noel 1954; Paish 1996), as most commenced these efforts in the 1920s and 30s. The Scottish LTA contemplated a junior championship event in 1910, but the idea did not materialise until 1921, followed by a junior event at the Scottish Hard Court Championships at St. Andrews in 1927 (Robertson 1995). Bedfordshire held its first junior tournament in 1924, Sheffield in 1925, Nottinghamshire in 1930, and Warwickshire in 1933. Many clubs also began staging junior tournaments in this period, such as Felixstowe LTC in 1923, Radyr LTC in 1926, Edgbaston Priory TC in 1933, Dinas Powis LTC in 1935, Bexley LT & Squash Rackets Club in 1936 and Bowden LTC in 1939.

These developments coincided with shifting relations between adults and children in wider British society. The long-term effects of NSPCC lobbying, the publication of findings from humanitarian social reformers like Booth and Rowntree, and various legislative reforms involving children's education and health,[1] brought about a transformation and redefinition of "childhood" into a distinct stage of moral and intellectual development (Hendrick 1997). What occurred, in simplistic terms, was a revaluation of children's rights and a strengthening of emotional bonds between children and adults, in the context of declining birth and infant mortality rates, improvements in health care, housing and domestic technology and general standards of living (Elias 1998; Hendrick 1997). It follows that children figured more centrally in adults' decision-making, both on a personal scale in relation to family planning and more broadly through the basic notion of children representing "the future". Increasingly in sport policy, as in educational, health-care and housing policies, the provision of resources for children was considered a worthwhile investment.

As county LTAs and their affiliated clubs recommended the institution of junior tournaments, authors of instructional booklets on talent development urged coaches and parents to invest more heavily in children. As the interwar years progressed, the recommended age to commence training fell noticeably, from around 14 (Hierons 1924:97; McKane 1925:20) to 12 (Godfree 1929:38), or, as Doeg and Danzig (1932:12) recommended, 'the earlier the better ... as soon as he is able to hold a racquet'.

Despite these advances, children continued to be denied equal rights and opportunities in tennis clubs across the country, and this partly reflects the prevailing sense that tennis remained an adult sport. The LTA's emphasis on talent development was undermined in many cases by entrenched age prejudice that manifested itself in anti-child club cultures. In some cases, the only children allowed within club grounds were the ballboys, who were not members but essentially servants, and treated as such. When clubs did lower the minimum age of membership from 18 to perhaps 14 or 15, they continued to restrict their numbers and also when and where children could play. In Nottinghamshire, Radcliffe-on-Trent TC allowed 15–19-year-olds membership from 1924, but play on Saturdays, match days or after 6.30pm every night was forbidden. Boys and girls aged 15–17 were welcomed at Woodthorpe TC from 1928, but again were subject to limited playing opportunities. In 1929, Musters TC permitted junior play but only from 2.30–5.30pm and, on Thursdays, Saturdays and holidays, not at all (Lusis 1998). At Sparkhill TC in Birmingham, only one child per family was allowed on the premises at any time, and a junior section was not initiated until the 1930s. At Waverley LT&SC in Edinburgh, junior members were admitted in 1934, but were forbidden from playing after 5.30pm. In some clubs, children not only had restricted hours, but also restricted courts; both Cullercoats LTC in Tyne and Wear and Bowden LTC in Cheshire denied children access to its grass courts. Similar to other clubs, Myddleton LTC in north London introduced reduced-price membership for under-16 "juniors" in 1933, but they were forbidden from playing if adult members wanted the courts. Those clubs that pressured their committees to improve access to children or to allocate older members to assist them were exceptional cases. Also, it seems in the majority of cases, the rationale for introducing junior membership categories, alongside others for senior, family, student/young adult, honorary, winter/summer, daytime, weekend or social/non-playing members was purely financial (Kay 2013). Largely autonomous and independent of LTA jurisdiction, clubs decided for themselves whether or not to foster junior talent. Despite some window-dressing, many clubs continued to marginalise and numerically limit junior members until well beyond WWII.

The LTA were forced to turn to the next generation as a means to achieve success vicariously, and their efforts were assisted in part by the sport's widespread democratisation. Advances for women and children came as a result of liberal developments in wider British society, but while their greater inclusion ultimately helped raise standards, the swathe of new players introduced to the game in clubs and schools brought new influences some considered unsavoury. Britain's simplistic and monolithic model of talent development was increasingly perceived as redundant, given new emphases on professionalism and expedience. Faced with an association that was considered out of touch with "modern" conditions, players from this new generation pushed the boundaries of acceptable behaviour, demanding the LTA respond to their desires for greater resources and personal freedom. In part, this was evidence of the shifting class demographic among players as well as shifting middle-class attitudes and values in itself, but it was evident nonetheless that wider societal developments were brought to bear upon lawn tennis in these respects.

Note

1. These included the Elementary Education Acts (1870, 1880, 1891 & 1893) that raised school-leaving age from 10 to 13; the Prevention of Cruelty to, and Protection of, Children Act (1889); the Education (Provision of Meals) Acts (1906 & 1914); the Education (Administrative Provisions) Act (1907), which saw the creation of school medical inspections; the Children Act (1908) that helped establish a juvenile justice system, and the Maternity and Child Welfare Act (1918) and Education Act (1918) that raised the school-leaving age to 14.

Bibliography

Aitken, A. (1924). *Lawn Tennis for Public Courts Players*. London: Methuen.
Beamish, A., and Beamish, W. (1924). *Lawn Tennis for Ladies*. London, Mills & Boon.
Bédarida, F. (1979). *A Social History of England 1851–1975*. London: Methuen.
Berlin, L. (2002, 1 May). *The First Half-Century of the West Heath Lawn Tennis Club 1902–1952*. Retrieved February 23, 2009, from History of West Heath Lawn Tennis Club: http://www.westheathltc.co.uk/whhistry.htm
Birley, D. (1995b). *Playing the Game: Sport and British Society 1910–45*. Manchester: Manchester University Press.
Blackmore, S. P. (1921). *Lawn Tennis Up-To-Date*. London: Methuen.
Brady, M. (1959). *The Centre Court Story*. London: Sportsman's Book Club.
Burrow, F. R. (1922). *Lawn Tennis: The World Game of Today*. London: Hodder & Stoughton.
Cahn, S. (1994). *Coming on Strong: Gender and Sexuality in Twentieth-Century Women's Sport*. Boston, MA: Harvard University Press.
Carter, N. (2010). From Knox to Dyson: Coaching, Amateurism and British Athletics, 1912–1947. *Sport in History*, 30(1), 55–81.
Crawley, A. E. (1922). *Lawn Tennis Do's and Don'ts*. London: Methuen.
Doeg, J. H., and Danzig, A. (1932). *Lawn Tennis*. London: Eyre & Spottiswoode.
Dyreson, M. L. (1996). Scripting the American Olympic Story-Telling Formula: The 1924 Paris Olympic Games and the American Media. *Olympika: The International Journal of Olympic Studies*, V, 45–80.
Dyreson, M. L. (1999). Selling American Civilization: The Olympic Games of 1920 and American Culture. *Olympika: The International Journal of Olympic Studies*, VIII, 1–42.
Elias, N. (1998). The Civilising of Parents. In J. Goudsblom and S. Mennell, *The Norbert Elias Reader* (pp. 189–211). Oxford: Blackwell.
Elks, S. J. (2004). *From Lycra to Whalebone: A Fashion Journey through Midlands Lawn Tennis History*. Birmingham: Susan J. Elks.
Faure, J.-M. (1996). National Identity and the Sporting Champion: Jean Borotra and French History. *International Journal of the History of Sport*, 13(1), 86–100.
Gilbert, D. (2011). The Vicar's Daughter and the Goddess of Tennis: Cultural Geographies of Sporting Femininity and Bodily Practices in Edwardian Suburbia. *Cultural Geographies*, 18, 187–207.
Godfree, K. (1929). *Lawn Tennis Simplified*. London: Thornton Butterworth.
Hargreaves, J. (1994). *Sporting Females: Critical Issues in the History and Sociology of Women's Sport*. London: Routledge.
Hendrick, H. (1997). *Children, Childhood and English Society 1880–1990*. Cambridge: Cambridge University Press.
Hierons, C. (1924). *How to Learn Lawn Tennis: A Simple Instructive Treatise* (2nd edn). London: Ward, Lock & Co.
Horwood, C. (2002). Dressing like a Champion: Women's Tennis Wear in Interwar England. In B. C. C. Breward, *The Englishness of English Dress* (pp. 45–60). Oxford: Berg.
Huggins, J., and Williams, J. (2005). *Sport and the English: 1918–1939*. London: Routledge.
Jensen, E. N. (2010). *Body by Weimar*. Oxford: Oxford University Press.

Kay, J. (2008). 'It wasn't just Emily Davison!' Sport, Suffrage and Society in Edwardian Britain. *International Journal of the History of Sport*, 25(10), 9–13.

Kay, J. (2013). 'Maintaining the Traditions of British Sport'? The Private Sports Club in the Twentieth Century. *International Journal of the History of Sport*, 30(14), 1655–1669.

Lake, R. J. (2012). Gender and Etiquette in 'Mixed Doubles' Lawn Tennis 1870–1939. *International Journal of the History of Sport*, 29(5), 691–710.

Lenglen, S. (1919). *Lawn Tennis for Girls*. London: George Newnes.

Little, A. (2007). *Suzanne Lenglen: Tennis Idol of the Twenties*. London: Wimbledon Lawn Tennis Museum.

Lowe, G. (1924). *Gordon Lowe on Lawn Tennis*. London: Hutchinson & Co.

Lumpkin, A. (1981). *Women's Tennis: A Historical Documentary of the Players and Their Game*. New York: Whitston.

Lusis, A. (1998). *Tennis in Robin Hood's County: The Story of Tennis Clubs in Nottinghamshire*. Nottingham: The Author.

Macauley, D., and Smyth, J. (1965). *Behind the Scenes at Wimbledon*. London: Collins.

McKane, K. (1925). *Lawn Tennis: How to Improve Your Game*. London: Ward, Lock and Co.

Noel, S. (1954). *Tennis in Our Time*. London: Sportsmans Book Club.

Paish, G. L. (1996). *Surrey County Lawn Tennis Association: The First 100 Years*. Brockham, Surrey: Taylor Lambert Advertising.

Patterson, N. (1921). *Lawn Tennis by Tyne and Wear*. London: T. & G. Allan.

Rendall, J. (1926). *Lawn Tennis: A Method of Acquiring Proficiency*. London: Cassell and Co.

Ritchie, M. J. (1928). *Lawn Tennis: The Modern Game*. London: Athletic Publications.

Robertson, G. (1995). *Tennis in Scotland: 100 Years of the Scottish Lawn Tennis Association 1895–1995*. Edinburgh: Scottish Lawn Tennis Association.

Schultz, J. (2014). *Qualifying Times: Points of Change in US Women's Sport*. Champaign, IL: University of Illinois Press.

Skillen, F. (2012). 'Woman and the Sport Fetish': Modernity, Consumerism and Sports Participation in Inter-War Britain. *International Journal of the History of Sport*, 29(5), 750–765.

Skillen, F. (2013). *Women, Sport and Modernity in Interwar Britain*. London: Peter Lang.

Sumner, A. (2011). *Court on Canvas: Tennis in Art*. London: Philip Wilson.

Tinling, T. (1983). *Tinling: Sixty Years in Tennis*. London: Sidgwick & Jackson.

Twickenham LTC. (2007). *Twickenham LTC – The First 100 Years*. London: Twickenham LTC.

van Someren, J. (2010). *Women's Sporting Lives: A Biographical Study of Elite Amateur Tennis Players at Wimbledon*. Unpublished PhD dissertation, University of Southampton.

Warner, P. C. (2006). *When the Girls Come out to Play: The Births of American Sportswear*. Amherst, MA: University of Massachusetts Press.

Warren, V. (1993). *Tennis Fashions: Over 100 Years of Costume Change*. London: Wimbledon Lawn Tennis Museum.

Wigglesworth, N. (2007). *The Story of Sport in England*. London: Routledge.

Wrynn, A. M. (2010). The Athlete in the Making: The Scientific Study of American Athletic Performance, 1920–1932. *Sport in History*, 30(1), 121–137.

8 'Demand for the game was insatiable'

Interwar developments in club/recreational tennis

The war made a significant impact on class relations, as cobblers, artisans, bankers, doctors and other ranks of men fought side by side against a common foe. Certainly, the wealthiest classes had their eyes and hearts opened to some realities of working-class life, but the outcomes of post-war efforts did not necessarily make for sweeping changes. The 1918 Education Act, for example, made education compulsory for children up to 14, but this had the unintended outcome of dividing more clearly boarding-school education for elites and mass education for everyone else (Bédarida 1979). Family background continued to distinguish those destined for the best schools from the rest (Taylor 1965). Nevertheless, an increase in direct taxation from 33–49 per cent throughout the 1920s led to slow but steady transfer of wealth from rich to poor (Cannadine 1999), and with rising unemployment, particularly in some of the staple industries like coal and cotton, working-class issues reached the forefront of public attention. In 1923, Ramsay MacDonald's victory won Labour its first right to govern, with their mandate to manage inequalities in income, education, housing and health provision. The TUC General Strike two years later has been recognised as the culmination of Labour's power in the interwar period, but its overall impacts have been debated. Bédarida (1979:183) claimed the strike a 'debacle' and 'total fiasco', given the eventual 'capitulation by the unions' and their submission to even greater state intervention, yet Cannadine (1999) recognised its impact in prompting middle-class sympathies toward manual labour and working-class issues more generally. Regardless, the period afterwards until the Wall Street Crash of 1929 represented clearly one of political consolidation and compromise between Labour and the Conservatives. More pertinently, improved working-class living standards resulted from the noticeable hike in "real wages" (Bédarida 1979).

All governments of the 1920s, even Labour, overlooked sport as a key policy priority, but undoubtedly it was influenced by wider political fluctuations. Just days after the General Strike, a *Times* (19 June 1926) editorial called for the provision of more playing fields, principally so that the working-class boy could be moulded into 'a strong and happy and helpful citizen'. Llewellyn (2011g:797) made the connection between 'rising democratic sympathies' and the selection of the former Liberal MP Lord Rochdale as the BOA's first non-Conservative leader in 1927. The same could be said for the LTA's decision to elect that same year a more left-leaning president, Right Hon. Viscount D'Abernon (Edgar Vincent), to succeed the mild-mannered Conservative Lord Desborough.[1] Typically, LTA presidents acted as little more than figureheads; they were selected primarily to add prestige to the Association rather than, necessarily, to spearhead policy change, but D'Abernon outlined several new initiatives from his opening speech:

> Earlier training in schools; more coaching and more practice in later life; a reduction in the cost of playing – opening the game to wider classes and to younger players; more hard courts to improve accuracy and develop the new aggressive tactics; more opportunities for first-class practice; and more strict training for our leading players.
> (*LT&B* 11 June 1927:200)

Hitherto, LTA efforts to develop talent had been formed of disconnected schemes: notably, the negotiation with public schools for tennis provision; the establishment of coaching and competitions in public parks; and the creation of inter-club and county competitions. Into the 1920s, the public schools continued to limit access for tennis. They stuck by their traditional excuses, such as the need to protect from interference the more established and "manly" team games of football, rugby and cricket. Lawn tennis of the pre-war era was overlooked by headmasters because it was considered not physically strenuous enough, but the marked advance in its physical demands as displayed annually at Wimbledon afforded it new legitimacy, which had the effect of making such excuses seem increasingly antiquated. Repton was the first public school to build courts in 1921, supported by an LTA grant of £100, and was quickly followed by Haileybury and Charterhouse. Harrow showed early enthusiasm, but resisted until 1925. The cause was assisted by the formation of the Public School Old Boys LTA in 1929, yet some schools like Liverpool College, Merchant Taylor's, Crosby, Ruthin and Rydal played no tennis against other schools (Jones 1983). By 1933, 32 public schools had adopted lawn tennis, 21 of which utilised LTA coaching services. But it was still claimed by Fred Lohden, LTA Chairman, that 'the youths of every country excepting ours start lawn tennis at the age of 10 or 11 and play no other games' (*LT&B* 18 March 1933:1224). The idea was that public schools should come to represent only a small part of their talent-development programme, which in general needed to be more comprehensive, creative and dynamic, and be implemented at a younger age. It was not until the late 1940s that a more comprehensive programme was instituted that included coaching provisions in public, grammar and state secondary and primary schools.

Fortunately for the LTA, improving lower-middle-class access provided opportunities to discover new talent, and also reflected ideologically and politically the popular ideas, principles and sentiments of mass consumption.

Parks tennis blossomed throughout the 1920s (Kay 2012), and tennis clubs increased numerically and in many cases changed culturally by inviting greater membership diversity in terms of social class. Liberalising developments as a connected outcome of growing consumerism also impacted on attitudes to Sunday play and on- and off-court behavioural etiquette. In this context of widespread social change, the LTA were fearful of new commercial influences, and so commenced their laboured and oftentimes misguided efforts to avoid pitfalls experienced in other sports. This chapter aims to discuss these connected developments.

Broader societal changes helped to facilitate a shift in the social composition of tennis players during the interwar years. Enhanced opportunities for geographical and social mobility resulted from periods of economic prosperity and growth, particularly in the south and Midlands, where unemployment was lowest. There were considerable shifts in employment patterns and conditions that improved working-class access to leisure. The long-term and gradual decline of the traditional British export markets of coal, textiles, iron, steel and shipbuilding forced them into new industries like vehicle manufacturing, electrical engineering and energy, which tended to have better working conditions. White-collar occupations increased and offered the working classes new opportunities, and, even during the depression years, "real wages" rose for those in employment, which provided most families with greater expendable income and higher living standards (Cannadine 1999). Motorcars became affordable for many middle-class families and witnessed increased supply even during the depression years, and both the railway and major road networks were greatly improved (Bédarida 1979). The abundant newly developed neighbourhoods on city outskirts became key sites for relocation as 'setting up house in the suburbs' became representative of 'moving up the social scale', argued Bédarida (1979:232–3). Particularly for the lower-middle and upper-working classes, 'a "semi-detached" in the suburbs seemed the ideal way to independence and social consideration', yet it was often 'a dull, narrow, restricted world', as the 'frigid and selfish privacy of "we do like to keep ourselves to ourselves" [was] a privacy of loneliness and tedium'; standardised houses were matched by 'the people who lived in them – the endlessly repeated humdrum pattern of existence creating its own form of anonymity'. Given the strains that "artificial" suburban life exacted on its residents and the lack of established kinship ties, the enthusiasm with which clubs were established is unsurprising (Hill 2002; McKibbin 1998).

Thousands of new tennis clubs formed during the interwar period, many of which affiliated themselves to the LTA. From just over 1,000 in the early 1920s, there were more than 3,200 affiliated clubs in 1939. Paish (1996) recorded that in Surrey, the number increased from 70 to 200. Of Nottinghamshire, Lusis (1998:30) wrote: 'For every club that had closed there must have been at least ten new ones. By all accounts the demand for the game was insatiable'. Based on extensive research, he made an interesting supposition that less than 20 per cent of Nottinghamshire clubs were affiliated to its county LTA in 1928, and though this increased toward the late 1930s, it suggests a much greater amount of tennis was being played than affiliation statistics suggest. Meanwhile, neighbouring Derbyshire had a far higher proportion of clubs affiliated to its association, which exposes the difficulties of making national generalisations (Kay 2012). Indeed, Scottish LTA club affiliation rates fluctuated markedly throughout its history, at times and in some districts recording more unaffiliated than affiliated clubs (Robertson 1995).

Evidence suggests that many clubs were in no rush to affiliate themselves in the 1920s, often being unaware of the associated benefits. Teddington LTC formed in 1908, but only sought LTA affiliation in 1926 because it needed financial assistance to obtain the freehold on its land, which it got in the form of a £400 low-interest loan (Medway 1958). Its west London neighbours, Twickenham LTC, waited until 1927 to affiliate when it had reached near its membership peak, whereupon it entered teams in the Middlesex County Inter-Club league and sought the services of a coach. It is posited that considerable increases in affiliation coincided with the LTA's efforts to boost perceived benefits. Such was the case in Sussex, whereby the allocation of Wimbledon tickets from the late 1920s represented a 'very big inducement to clubs to become affiliated' (*LT&B* 8 February 1930:1218). Kay (2012) uncovered numerous clubs, particularly in the north and Midlands, connected to "works" sports associations, public parks and churches that were unaffiliated but successfully ran their own independent leagues and competitions. The mass production of tennis equipment made it more affordable, such that blue-collar workers were no longer excluded carte blanche as before the war (Birley 1995b). The boom in tennis not only facilitated growth in new clubs but the enhanced competition between clubs for recruitment of new members also pushed many established clubs to relax their membership requirements.

Increased lower-middle-class involvement in tennis also coincided with growing momentum in socialist and communist movements, which brought forth the British Workers' Sports Federation, the National Workers' Sports Association and the "Workers Olympics" in 1931, 35 and 37 (Jones 1988). Reading also staged a "Workers Wimbledon" during the 1930s (Wheeler 1978). In this environment, parks, churches and works sports associations that catered for tennis flourished. The first parks LTA formed in Manchester in 1909, and by 1920 had established coaching opportunities for 'the industrial and artisan classes' (*LT&B* 8 May 1920:30–1). They remained an exceptionally progressive body, though parks associations in London and Birmingham, and others in Leeds, Sheffield, Bolton, Liverpool, Glasgow, Edinburgh and Dundee, also progressed notably (Huggins and Williams 2005; Kay 2012). In 1920, the London City Council, with LTA backing, initiated a scheme to build park courts and introduce 'The Civic Lawn Tennis Cup', donated by the distinguished newspaper publisher Sir Edward

Hulton, and six months later they formed the Public Parks LTA with H. Roper Barrett as president (*LT&B* 15 April 1920:627). The Birmingham Parks LTA (BPLTA) was singled out for special praise for its provision of over 380 courts for public use. Although it was admitted that it had not produced anyone near capable of winning an open title, nor added much to the 'stature' of the game, and that the standard generally was 'not a high one', they had nevertheless improved "baseline" standards and the overall understanding of rules and laws of a 'vast number of players' (*LT&B* 5 June 1926:138). The parks associations never sought to create champions, yet they often replied defensively when forced to make comparisons with America, which had achieved great success; public park courts, particularly in California, had already brought to prominence players like George Lott, John Doeg, Bill Johnston, Ellsworth Vines, Don Budge and Helen Jacobs. The upshot was that some in Britain questioned the investment of parks tennis given the lack of elite-level talent generated there. The BPLTA disbanded after only two years due to financial troubles, and other parks associations also struggled to sustain activities during the interwar years.

Lusis (1998) reported an increase in clubs connected to Anglican, Baptist, Methodist denominations and the Church of England, many of which, like their established counterparts, continued to restrict Sunday play, despite the adoption of more broad-minded approaches to Sabbath observances elsewhere. Members of Hale LTC passed a motion in the early 1920s to permit play from 1.30–6.30pm, with the curious stipulations that 'no teas could be served, the gas stove and china etc., could not be used and balls could not be retrieved from neighbouring gardens' (Nelson 2004:13). Members of Teddington LTC began lobbying for Sunday play in 1917 but, after repeated votes at annual meetings, this luxury was not granted until 1923. Like many others, the club was founded by benevolent members from the local church, and many of them felt forced to resign after reaching this decision. Medway (1958:6–7) contextualised the problem: 'Without Sunday play the club could not have survived in the face of competition from other clubs'. McLaughlin (2004:13) provided an account of difficulties experienced by clubs in Stamford Brook in this regard. In 1919, Hartswood LTC galvanised support from local residences and approached their landlords, the Ecclesiastical Commissioners, claiming: 'It is difficult to imagine a more suitable manner in which the latter half of a Sunday can be spent than in healthy exercise in the open air.' However, it was not until 1926 when Sunday afternoon play was allowed, and a further eight years before the allowance extended into the morning. At the Stamfordian TC, permission was granted in 1928 to allow players just two hours' court access on a Sunday afternoon, but only after a bitter five-year battle. The letter written to the Commissioners in 1923 warned that 'the club will be forced into liquidation' if this concession is not granted, given that work commitments prevented most members from playing on weeknights. Their fears were realised; permission came too late in the day and the club was forced to close after the 1928 season. Even public park courts faced restrictions. Chiswick Borough Council prohibited play at its Stamford Brook park courts until 1925, and only then after 2pm.

It appears clubs remained diverse in terms of their affiliations. Lusis (1998) reported in Nottinghamshire an increase in urban, suburban and rural "village" clubs, alongside those connected to hospitals, teachers' associations, military groups and political organisations like the Young Conservatives. Also enjoying a 'great boom' were clubs connected to companies, mills and mines, such as the pump manufacturers Worthington-Simpson, the Kelham Sugar Factory and Welbeck Colliery. These tended to provide tennis facilities within multi-purpose club grounds, as a means to enhance 'efficiency and productivity', attract and retain staff, establish 'closer collaboration between white- and blue-collar workers', inculcate a 'sense of loyalty to the firm', and contribute to the 'industrial peace in the workplace' (Kay 2013:1662). The boom in workplace tennis clubs that arrived in the interwar years and peaked in the 1950s found its greatest concentration in the Midlands (Kay 2012), and Kay (2013:1666) also discovered that almost a third of all affiliated clubs in 1956 were 'attached to places of employment'. The connection between the expansion of new industries, sustained economic growth, lower-than-average unemployment figures and the growing popularity of tennis within particular geographical regions is plausible, yet while some clubs were removing barriers to membership, others were tightening them. Lawn tennis remained a sport for socially aspirational young people, just the kind willing to move across the country for work and confident enough in their abilities to make friends and "get by".

In these times of greater democracy and improved lower-class accessibility, public opinion often turned against clubs that enacted elitist restrictions. Some were criticised for not encouraging the interaction of new members better; Chapel Allerton LT & Squash Club, in Leeds, for example, recognised that its reputation for "snobbishness" was gained during the interwar years. Females were often identified as the worst offenders for cliquishness: 'It is recognised that womankind as a body are more conservative than men folk; they have a circle of acquaintances at clubs, and it is often difficult to induce them to widen the circle' (*LT&B* 19 May 1923:71). Fry and Doust (1926:40) noted this unfortunate tendency, whereby 'it is practically impossible for the young player to obtain "knocks up"'. In 1920, the secretary of Bromley Wendover LTC made a formal appeal to club members not to form cliques (Lynch 2006). Alongside encouraging clubs to be more welcoming to new members, they were urged also to improve their clubhouses, which were often like 'glorified dressing rooms' or 'miserable shanties' (*LT&B* 30 June 1923:303).

Such conditions related to exclusivity arose as a consequence of broader societal changes. The widespread democratisation of tennis, coupled with greater opportunities for social and geographical mobility, increased the unstable and transient nature of club memberships, and likely propelled established members to tighten up on behavioural transgressions as a means to preserve customs of rules and etiquette. In his discussion of the 'undermining of hierarchy' throughout the twentieth century, Cannadine (1999:131) noted the 'corresponding undermining of the ubiquitous states of mind on which hierarchy had depended and served to inculcate'; in essence, in the context of societal democratisation, the codes of conduct differentiating the classes had eroded. In tennis clubs, the enactment of stricter conditions of membership and the greater insistence on "proper" behaviour or some heightened form of deferential treatment likely corresponded to attempts made by established members to retain structures and customs that afforded the differentiation of status. Alongside playing in private and often secluded confines, the customary rigmarole associated with gaining membership, the hierarchical structure of club committees, the persistence of noble patronage, the giving of awards, honours and titles to prominent members, and the celebration of these practices in recurrent rituals and ceremonies, there were strong demands made of members to "know their place" and behave toward others in accordance with their relative social position. Such practices would have helped promote among club members of an increasingly mixed social demographic, in the words of Cannadine (1999:126), 'a hierarchical cast of mind'. It could be argued that tennis clubs, seen in this way, fulfilled an important function in sustaining or redefining class divisions and hierarchy at a time when widespread changes in employment and educational opportunities were less effective at doing so. It points to their importance in helping to articulate class boundaries and reinforce class distinctions in the interwar period. Indeed, far from disappearing throughout this period, available evidence suggests that codes of deferential conduct according to status and rank remained embedded in many clubs, whereupon the systematic adherence to these codes by the established membership and their constant reaffirmation helped socialise new members into these traditional behavioural conventions. The general adherence to etiquette served a few practical purposes, but it functioned primarily to reinforce hierarchy and unwritten behavioural conventions.

One example of an unwritten rule widely adhered to was that weak players should not ask far superior players for a game:

> Tennis is stimulating and satisfying only when played between players of the same class. This does not prevent a better player playing with 'rabbits' for instructional purposes, or just for fun; but it is not for him lawn tennis as he plays it. The knowledgeable player realises this and no more seeks to play with those above his class, save as a useful experience, than he does with those below it.
>
> (Noel 1954:17)

A breach of this unspoken and seemingly innocuous rule posed more than just the potential for embarrassment, but instead, at a time when playing standards among amateur members became an increasingly significant barometer of status, such an act could be considered offensive or disrespectful. Satirist Art Hoppe (1977:9–10) elaborated:

> No tennis player, no matter what his calibre, wants to play tennis with any other tennis player who is not better than he. ... If they are seen playing with inferior players, superior players with whom they wish to play will identify them with the inferior players ... and will never invite them to play. Worse yet, players slightly inferior to the inferior players with whom they are playing will make the same identification and will besiege them with invitations to play. Such a path can only lead inexorably downward to the depths of degradation.

To avoid such humiliation by raising general standards, and to facilitate better play in inter-club competitions, many clubs introduced "playing-in tests". Twickenham LTC enjoyed steady membership growth in the early 20s and introduced such tests for prospective members in 1926, but after reaching a peak in 1928, membership fell by approximately 25 per cent by the mid-30s, leaving the club needing to relax these restrictions and advertise widely for new members.

Other features of club etiquette were more explicitly discussed as club committees keenly displayed rules of etiquette on noticeboards or in newsletters. Advice for new members was also offered in *LT&B* (12 February 1921:743): 'buy the very best racket and balls you can possibly afford', in terms of appearance 'have nothing strange about you', 'look agreeable and at ease', 'be willing to take part in anything that is proposed', 'do not talk of past achievements', and, most importantly, 'do not criticise established rules or players' or 'sit and grouse'. *ALT* (15 May 1921:60) also published a list of general rules of etiquette, which included points such as making sure the receiver is ready for the serve, be 'prompt and decisive' when calling balls, avoid repeatedly disputing the score, return balls when not in play straight to your opponent, don't 'stall or hurry the game unduly' and, above all, remember to 'conform, as far as possible, to the wishes of your opponent'. Helen Wills (1928:151) published a list of rules for spectators she discovered on the back of a tournament programme, which included sanctions against: applauding before rallies have finished, moving about during play, using parasols, using hand gestures to attract the attention of friends, making negative remarks about players, and questioning the decisions of umpires. She suggested that conduct and procedure, both on and off the court, made 'a perfect sportsman', before offering specific advice when dealing with visitors, toward whom 'every consideration must be shown': the visitor enters the court first, calls the "toss" for court, and also, should both players meet at the net during a changeover, the visitor should be allowed to pass first. 'Little things like this help the match to run smoothly and pleasantly. They are the expression of a natural feeling of goodwill toward the opponent'

(Wills 1928:149). Such public recommendations appeared more frequently from the 1920s onwards.

Dress was another feature that afforded similar treatment by clubs. Like others, Hale LTC only made their regulations explicit after the war; the 1919 AGM minutes recorded that gentlemen members and their visitors were reminded to wear white trousers, white shirts and rubber-soled shoes (Nelson 2004:12). Members of Teddington LTC expressed disapproval of the length of women's shorts in its 1936 AGM minutes, which concluded by suggesting the ladies' captain investigate the issue (Medway 1958). For Huggins and Williams (2005:127), 'the constant reiteration of values of amateurism, sportsmanship and decorum were an expression of elitism, but also ... a sign of anxiety'. These reminders of respectability reflected middle-class fears over declining behavioural standards more generally, alongside their loss of distinction in an environment increasingly characterised by class intermixing.

Players demonstrated new-found skills of gamesmanship in the early 1920s that caught the public's attention. Some *LT&B* correspondents sought to call their bluff by revealing these in explicit detail, while those less amused considered this regressive development a serious danger to the sport and its gentlemanly ethos.[2] The etiquette of "throwing points" after a bad call was made in one's favour came to be questioned. Though once considered "sporting", Burrow (1919:26) now declared: 'The thing is cheap. ... You have swaggered; you have obtained credit to which you are not entitled, you have in effect behaved rudely to the umpire; and you have deliberately played to lose'. Consequently, in 1924, a new LTA rule prohibited players from questioning an umpire's call, even if wrongly given in their own favour. This is one example of how unwritten rules of "amateur" etiquette, which placed a premium on the self-regulation of behaviour, came to be replaced by written rules that took away any need to exercise personal ethics. One could argue that this development was as important as any other in inviting a "professional" approach to the sport.

Particularly at a time when Britain's sporting failures gained as much attention as their successes, the promotion of sportsmanship was important for British pride. A *LT&B* correspondent remarked: 'The birth of the game was with us. Let us retain our birthright of behaviour, and in our turn we shall regain championships' (14 November 1925:789). Into the early 1930s, disputes regarding etiquette and manners rose frequently in the press, and the increasing extent to which behaviour fell foul of British expectations suggested that the correspondents themselves, most of them ordinary fans, players or administrators, had failed to appreciate the pressures associated with top-flight tennis.

Handfuls of new inter-club competitions were created in the interwar years that afforded opportunities for clubs to enhance their prestige, reaffirm their own identity and gain a one-up on local rivals. In Surrey, LTA-sanctioned inter-club tournaments for men first began in the 1920s (Paish 1996) and, in Nottinghamshire, the first men's league formed in 1924 (Lusis 1998). These often suffered from a lack of support from top-level players, who, understandably by this stage, preferred prestigious tournaments and international matches over obscure club or county fixtures. Who could blame them? Many of these competitions were poorly organised, with no line judges or umpires. One *LT&B* correspondent questioned whether, in fact, 'the county championship [was] to be a tea party knock-up or a test' (29 August 1925:567). Further and more direct criticism of the county championships appeared throughout 1928 and 29; the Surrey LTA Honorary Secretary claimed, 'the cost to the LTA in providing free railway fare for six players of each county is enormous and a great waste of money', especially when often the best players they could muster were 'elderly gentlemen who have no chance of improving' (*LT&B* 4 August 1928:510). Given these and other failings, there was a dire need expressed for a special committee to place the Inter-County Championships on a 'proper footing': 'The existing committee has proved itself not only dormant but incapable' (*LT&B* 23 November 1929:962).

At a time when competitive tennis was exploding in a new direction, pulling up playing standards and lending an air of seriousness to events, undoubtedly there were some who sought to sustain their chief emphases as frivolous and "social" rather than competitive. Huggins and Williams (2005:87) argued that recreational sporting participation continued to provide for most a range of satisfactions: 'release from everyday routine, the joy of exercising the body, the edge of competition ... the sociability of playing with and against others, receiving admiration and possibly consolation for lack of status and achievement in other areas of life'. Some of the more modest inter-club tennis matches remained little more than excuses to eat, drink and share company with social equals amidst a mildly competitive sporting occasion, with the hosts making tremendous efforts to entertain guests and provide good cheer and merriment. Frivolity and the opportunity for playful social intercourse and even romance remained as chief attractions for many participants. John Betjeman subtly depicted these features in his famous poem, *A Subaltern's Love-song*, from 1941:

> Miss J. Hunter Dunn, Miss J. Hunter Dunn,
> Furnish'd and burnish'd by Aldershot sun,
> What strenuous singles we played after tea,
> We in the tournament – you against me!
> Love-thirty, love-forty, oh! Weakness of joy,
> The speed of a swallow, the grace of a boy,
> With carefullest carelessness, gaily you won,
> I am weak from your loveliness, Miss Joan Hunter Dunn.

The irresistibly charming depictions of "social" tennis also remained in interwar artwork, though Sumner (2011) lamented its post-war decline; given the sport's professionalisation and increasing seriousness, arguably the sport's social settings became less interesting to depict artistically. Modernising trends at the elite level were inevitably counterbalanced with the continuous endorsement of simple pleasures found in light-hearted recreational sport.

Given their alternative social functions, most clubs were not in the business of producing champions, and so many resisted LTA interference or new developments generally that might alter internal club cultures. Regardless, the LTA seemed unfazed by the aversion of many clubs to work alongside them to develop talent and, according to a report in 1930, actually seemed proud of working 'quietly' and 'behind the scenes' with regard to enhancing opportunities for children. Was this a front or did they lack vision? For the annual junior championships in 1930, it was smugly proclaimed: 'It has not been the official policy to blazon the meeting or do anything which might encourage undue publicity for young players'; they were happy that 'the spectators [were] mainly those who are directly interested in the competition' (*LT&B* 6 September 1930:668). It is hard to fathom how the LTA could perceive greater public/media attention or commercial support as unhelpful to the long-term development of junior tennis, particularly considering its possible benefits. It demonstrates a principled rather than pragmatic approach to talent development and a general reluctance to adapt to the inevitable hardships of the ensuing economic depression. At such a time, who were the LTA to refuse partnerships that could help foster tennis competitions? It is undoubted that the LTA's anxieties were underpinned by a suspicion of commercialism more generally. There was a widespread belief that all such impulses should be curtailed, however seemingly innocuous, and particularly given the endemic "pot-hunting" of top players. The LTA were keen to avoid the problems that plagued other sports, though changes in the social composition of tennis players and the LTA's heightened enthusiasm for talent development pointed toward a battle between competing cultures: conservative, traditional and amateur versus progressive, inclusive and professional. Despite their best efforts, the LTA were forced to deal with new challenges brought about by the changing world around them.

Notes

1. Though elected as a Conservative for Exeter in 1899, Vincent actually opposed numerous Tory policies, including Tariff Reform, and in 1910, switched affiliations and stood (unsuccessfully) for the Liberal seat in Colchester. Liberal PM Herbert Asquith made him a peer in 1914.
2. See *LT&B* (15 September 1923:616; 22 November 1924:847).

Bibliography

Bédarida, F. (1979). *A Social History of England 1851–1975*. London: Methuen.
Birley, D. (1995b). *Playing the Game: Sport and British Society 1910–45*. Manchester: Manchester University Press.

Burrow, F. R. (1919). *Lawn Tennis Hints*. London: County Life.
Cannadine, D. (1999). *The Rise and Fall of Class in Britain*. New York: Columbia University Press.
Fry, J., and Doust, S. (1926). *Lawn Tennis: How to Master the Strokes*. London: W. Foulsham and Co.
Hill, J. (2002). *Sport, Leisure and Culture in Twentieth-Century Britain*. Basingstoke: Palgrave.
Hoppe, A. (1977). *The Tiddling Tennis Theorem*. New York: Viking Press.
Huggins, J., and Williams, J. (2005). *Sport and the English: 1918–1939*. London: Routledge.
Jones, K. (1983). *Physical Education in Four North West Public Schools from 1920 to 1930*. Liverpool: Liverpool University, Unpublished M.Ed. Thesis.
Jones, S. G. (1988). *Sport, Politics and the Working Class*. Manchester: Manchester University Press.
Kay, J. (2012). Grass Roots: The Development of Tennis in Britain, 1918–1978. *International Journal of the History of Sport*, 29(18), 2532–2550.
Kay, J. (2013). 'Maintaining the Traditions of British Sport'? The Private Sports Club in the Twentieth Century. *International Journal of the History of Sport*, 30(14), 1655–1669.
Llewellyn, M. P. (2011g). The Curse of the Shamateur. *International Journal of the History of Sport*, 28(5), 796–816.
Lusis, A. (1998). *Tennis in Robin Hood's County: The Story of Tennis Clubs in Nottinghamshire*. Nottingham: The Author.
Lynch, P. (2006). *Bromley Wendover Lawn Tennis Club: Centenary 1906–2006*. London: Bromley Wendover LTC.
McKibbin, R. (1998). *Classes and Cultures: England 1918–1951*. Oxford: Oxford University Press.
McLaughlin, S. (2004). *Hartswood Lawn Tennis Club 1914–2004*. London: Shirley McLaughlin.
Medway, A. (1958). *Teddington Lawn Tennis Club: The Souvenir Jubilee History 1908–1958*. London: Teddington LTC.
Nelson, J. (2004). *A History of Hale Lawn Tennis Club*. London: Hale Lawn Tennis Club.
Noel, S. (1954). *Tennis in Our Time*. London: Sportsmans Book Club.
Paish, G. L. (1996). *Surrey County Lawn Tennis Association: The First 100 Years*. Brockham, Surrey: Taylor Lambert Advertising.
Robertson, G. (1995). *Tennis in Scotland: 100 Years of the Scottish Lawn Tennis Association 1895–1995*. Edinburgh: Scottish Lawn Tennis Association.
Sumner, A. (2011). *Court on Canvas: Tennis in Art*. London: Philip Wilson.
Taylor, A. J. (1965). *English History, 1914–1945*. Oxford: Oxford University Press.
Wheeler, R. (1978). Organized Sport and Organized Labour: The Workers' Sport Movement. *Journal of Contemporary History*, 13(2), 191–210.
Wills, H. (1928). *Tennis*. London: Charles Scribner's Sons.

9 "The Goddess" and "the Monarch"

Lenglen, Tilden and the "Amateur Problem" in lawn tennis

There was no denying that players in the "golden age" of lawn tennis in the 1920s were the most flamboyant, exciting, talented, artistic, voracious, committed and enthusiastic ever seen. They were also the most impressionable; the doom and gloom of war was replaced by rampant collective confidence, and Britain was remodelled increasingly in the image of American popular culture, which promoted individualism and mass consumption. Top-class athletes sought to develop and enhance their images, and new media sources were ready to exploit them to an audience thirsty for sports consumption. Sales of daily morning newspapers increased by 80 per cent between the wars, and also their emphases shifted from merely presenting news to making it interesting and, in the process, generating profits (Huggins and Williams 2005). Leading newspapers like the *Daily Mail* and the *Daily Mirror* increased their sports coverage, while *The Times* and *Daily Telegraph* consolidated their position as the two principal dailies covering lawn tennis. Also, *Mitchell's Newspaper Press Directory* revealed that tennis-specific periodicals increased five-fold from 1926 to 1940, which demonstrated this period as key in terms of growing public interest (Huggins and Williams 2005:41). The BBC's influence also grew, as the distribution of radio licences quadrupled from two to eight million from 1926–39, meaning 71 per cent of all British households owned a wireless (Holt 1989:311). Sir John Reith, first Director-General of the BBC from 1927–38, sought 'to establish a range of sporting events ... deemed to be of *national* significance', and by suppressing regional variations and ignoring more local sporting traditions, the BBC sustained unashamedly its southern-centric, paternalist and elitist image for decades to follow (Holt 1989:312). The AELTC strived to ensure the Championships became part of this coveted collection. When the club moved to its new grounds in 1922, according to H.R. McDonald, reporters were to be well catered for, with numerous press seats on the main courts and a press room, good telephone facilities and access to the dressing rooms for interviews. BBC radio coverage of Wimbledon commenced in 1927, with first live broadcasts from 1937, and it soon followed that the BBC would retain exclusive rights to Wimbledon broadcasts (Whannel 1992). Reflecting on this relationship in 1952, the BBC's Head of Outside

Broadcasts, Seymour Joly de Lotbinière commented: 'I have never attempted to conceal my belief that "Wimbledon" treated us generously. I assumed it was the deliberate policy of an amateur sport towards a "public service"' (cited in Briggs 1979:859). A BBC survey conducted in 1939 found that 34 per cent of the general population listened to Wimbledon on the radio. This was an impressive figure given de Lotbinière's (1942) complaints that for tennis commentary it was 'almost impossible to prescribe any treatment that is wholly satisfactory', given the fast play and 'sameness of strokes'.

Enhanced press and radio coverage was matched by shifting emphases, as the more populist and sensationalist approaches of American sports reporting spread to Britain. Despite the BBC clinging to its conservative approach, university-educated, middle-class emphasis and southern-centricity through its unique speech patterns and language, it did aim to offer more entertaining broadcasts (Haynes 2009; Huggins 2007). Sports coverage played a growing role in this endeavour, and the 'creation of heroes' was an important outcome of editorial pressures for "human interest" stories, which was particularly prevalent in America (Bingham 2004). Reports of Bill Tilden's off-court exploits, for example, put him alongside film stars like Katherine Hepburn, Charlie Chaplin and Douglas Fairbanks (Clerici 1975). A small, high-brow, but vociferous minority judged American influences negatively, as commercialised, mass-produced and vulgar, but throughout the 1920s and 30s, newsreel footage of American sports stars helped ensure their transatlantic popularity (Huggins and Williams 2005).

It was a highly probable outcome that the attitudes and behaviours of top players would change as a consequence of the increasingly globalised and commercialised context within which elite-level tennis came to exist. The improving status of players and the increasing opportunities available for them to set their own terms for competing merely complicated matters. No longer were they silent, passive or entirely complicit in adhering to regulations set forth by their associations to restrain their behaviours, but instead they were active, vociferous and sometimes confrontational in opposing rules designed to suppress what they perceived to be their unequivocal rights to share in the spoils they helped generate for clubs, tournaments and associations. Rumours began circulating before the war about illicit secret payments to players, and the French Riviera in particular was known as a haven for such activity. In the 1920s, such allegations were numerous. In 1922, Lenglen's presence at tournaments was said to have had 'a remarkable influence on the gate' (*LT&B* 29 April 1922:931). Clerici (1975:151) reported that organisers 'would go to any lengths to insure her presence', oftentimes ingeniously wagering her father that Suzanne would *not* participate. When travelling between tournaments, Lenglen often used a private railway coach and, arriving in Saint Moritz one year, was met by 'a carriage and eight horses' (Clerici 1975:151). In 1926, when Lenglen met Helen Wills at the Carlton Club in Cannes in what was their first and only ever meeting, speculation was widespread about the huge under-the-table payments and luxury accommodations offered to both players. John Tunis, the sharp-tongued *ALT* reporter, expressed his disgust by asking 'what the hell' happened to the balance of 150,000 francs from the match, before questioning: 'Why was it that Miss Wills went to a small pension at Cannes on her arrival and the next day moved up to a grand Palace Hotel where a tennis tournament was just starting?' (Tinling 1983:40; *LT&B* 3 April 1926:1129).

Over time, these charges increased in frequency and became harder to deflect. Before long, correspondents exposed an organised ring of deceit that implicated tournament and club officials, representatives of sporting-goods firms, media outlets, and even national association executives. An anonymous writer in *John Bull* claimed the LTA actually condoned breaches of amateurism; 'owing to their share of the gate-money, they are compelled to show a blind eye to malpractices at the Wimbledon Championships'. Top players apparently demanded 'excessive expenses' at local tournaments and were seen 'lolling at ease in borrowed Rolls-Royces and flitting from country house to country house in the midst of society'. Clubs reportedly offered top players free membership to represent them, and hotels were blamed for failing to present bills; the LTA were said to be either 'too lethargic to apply its rules or consciously an accessory both before and after the act' (cited in *LT&B* 17 August 1929:585). Frank Poxon, from the *News Chronicle*, suggested several top players made 'four-figure salaries' from the game (cited in *LT&B* 23 August 1930:606); another correspondent described how one particular American player received free board, lodging and travel expenses at 22 tournaments in 1930 (*LT&B* 21 March 1931:1371–2).

To explain these developments, Norah Cleather (1947:86) remarked of the 'longer journeys and longer absences from home' that top players endured, which necessitated 'a cash allowance for their expenses' and 'every necessity – and many luxuries – put at their disposal free of charge'. Racket manufacturers negotiated secret deals to ensure top players used their equipment and clothing, and ball suppliers offered money to clubs in return for the guaranteed entries of top players (Cleather 1947). Many of the leading Americans from the late-30s/early-40s era admitted receiving "bonus" expenses, often directly from USLTA officials (Budge 1969; Hart 1985). Tournament directors offered undisclosed incentives to attract top players, and secret payments were hidden in hotel rooms, left in jacket pockets or in boxes of chocolates or other gifts (Cleather 1947). By all accounts, the age of the sham-amateur or "shamateur" player had arrived.

The issue of players receiving, and tournament officials giving, illicit expenses was just one aspect of the growing fear of commercialism, and the national associations that hitherto had retained almost complete control lamented their loss of authority. Each was at the mercy of global developments, given the widespread extent of such unscrupulous practices. The LTA responded in ways that reflected a confusing mixture of motives. On the one hand, they were motivated to improve their British players' performances and guard against player withdrawals, declining standards and falling gates at British tournaments, but on the other, they sought to retain amateur traditions and authority. Thus, the LTA was charged with curtailing the growing tendency for players to "serve two masters", which they attempted through a two-pronged approach. To keep players in check they tightened amateur rules and placed greater restrictions on players' freedoms, but their greatest challenge was how to enforce rules and sustain their authority without limiting the potential for developing talent by alienating players or curbing legitimate employment opportunities. So, to keep their players sweet, they gradually increased the expense allowances for LTA-sanctioned competitions. This commenced with the Davis Cup in the mid-1920s, as a means to reimburse players for their weeks or months away from paid employment.

This bilateral approach met with opposition for being ill-advised and half-hearted, a consequence of contradictory thinking that on one level questioned the personal morality and integrity of anyone connected commercially with tennis, but on another sought higher playing standards that were aligned inevitably with modern professionalised methods. The Victorian stigma that considered professionals as a tainted sort, greedy and less than entirely honest, was challenged by a growing progressive contingent that demanded changes in vision and attitude to ensure Britain's standards did not slide further downwards.

In 1920, A.E. Crawley demanded the LTA recognise its contradictory legislation that condemned a player who worked for a tennis manufacturer but not one who produced other tennis-related products or who worked as a paid club secretary or tournament umpire: 'The ramifications of business are so intricate that such pettifogging legislation is absurd'; he called for 'more sensible and sporting spirit' (*LT&B* 11 December 1920:621). By legislating at all, the LTA were dipping their toes into murky waters, but the arbitrary shaming of only some jobs as inappropriate for an amateur created confusion. Moreover, their decision in 1925 and 26 to deny professionals from other sports the right to play in amateur lawn tennis tournaments was thinly disguised class snobbery. The LTA councillors who originally proposed the idea claimed they wanted to remain consistent with their sister national associations from rowing, gymnastics, swimming and boxing, but under colleagues' pressures they revealed a different intention. The anonymous regular *LT&B* correspondent "Simplicitas" stated that a man who had acquired a habit of 'playing for gain' in one sport might 'perhaps unconsciously ... do something which would not be done by a man who has played games as an amateur all through his career' (12 December 1925:852). If professionals from other sports were to be welcomed in amateur lawn tennis tournaments, it was said, 'you are going to admit an undesirable class of person ... A professional he is at heart, and a professional he will remain at heart' (*LT&B* 19 December 1925:872). As a stigmatised creature who is by definition untrustworthy, unprincipled, and potentially open to dishonourable behaviour, claimed the *Sydney Referee*, 'the professional is suspect and resembles the case of the man-eating tiger, which can never be cured' (cited in *LT&B* 18 March 1933:1230). Despite the LTA reversing this 'archaic and anachronistic' ruling in 1946, it was not until 1951 when the ILTF ratified the decision and allowed professionals from other sports to play in lawn tennis tournaments (*LT&B* 15 December 1951:640).

Partly as an outcome of differing views on how athletes and their achievements should be rewarded and celebrated, contrasting understandings and definitions of amateurism emerged globally. The main aim of this chapter is to use the case studies of Suzanne Lenglen and Bill Tilden to highlight the new opportunities and challenges presented for elite-level players, alongside some of the problems faced by administrators, many of whom were ex-players attempting to protect their sport from commercial and professional influences, and sustain the lofty ideals of amateurism amidst marked societal change. What is revealed most clearly is the extent to which the actions and opinions of elite-level players came increasingly to garner greater interest and influence, as amateur definitions were repeatedly modified in attempts to control the actions of a small handful of players, but came increasingly to frustrate the masses. The image of the LTA and its partner associations globally would forever be forged from their inabilities to find real solutions to the "amateur problem".

Administrative decisions in lawn tennis during the interwar years reflected a strong and almost universal desire to sustain amateur ideals. Both the LTA and USLTA tightened their respective amateur definitions throughout the 1920s, but in so doing somewhat misread public desires for democratisation and liberal political reforms. In pursuing such a course of action, they found themselves pulled in opposing directions by two equally pervasive forces: ethics and integrity on the one hand, prestige and power on the other. The numerous half-measures introduced by the LTA and its partners designed as compromises failed to hold water, however, and acted ultimately to the overall detriment of both amateur and professional tennis globally.

The prejudices shown by the tennis establishment toward professional players and the "professional motives" of amateur players themselves were deep-rooted. More than any other player of this era, Bill Tilden personified the "amateur problem" and his ongoing battles with the establishment illustrated the diverging cultures in lawn tennis. Frank Deford (2004), his posthumous biographer, recalled the era that Tilden began his amateur career as one of "old country clubbers". By the 1930s, elite-level players no longer approached tennis as a frivolous summer attraction but as an avenue for social mobility. Through tennis and associated endeavours, they competed for their livelihoods and showed a level of seriousness toward competitions, training and preparation hitherto unseen. Feeling unable to continue playing within a system that was increasingly considered outdated and impracticable, one player after another departed amateur competition to take economic advantage of their respective gate-drawing potentials that the establishment continued to deny them upfront, and which players of this new and more assertive, expectant and individualistic generation felt they deserved. In their wake was a decrepit amateur ethos that held back players' egos alongside their bank balances.

Of all the male players of this era, Tilden was *the* colossal figure, pursuing the limelight and embracing new commercial and media opportunities presented to him. Compared to his more affable compatriot, 'Little Bill' Johnston, 'Big Bill' Tilden was less favoured by the American public and the USLTA, who did not appreciate his 'arrogance and air of superiority', nor his affected posturing and effete masculinity, which challenged dominant notions of American manliness (Tinling 1983:63). The British, in contrast, were fascinated with Tilden's refined mannerisms and clipped, east-coast upper-class accent; he appeared as if from a Hollywood film-set (Baltzell 1995).[1] For this, Tinling (1983:70) called him 'the absolute monarch', and for his tennis prowess he has been called the greatest of all time (Maskell 1988). From 1920 onwards, he achieved back-to-back Wimbledon singles victories, six straight US Championships singles titles and seven straight American Davis Cup wins. Arguably, though, his most significant impacts were felt off-court, in committee boardrooms where administrators dealt with issues related to something the sport's first true male superstar had said or done.

Tilden was threatened repeatedly with bans for various amateur-rule breaches, many of which sought to curtail new wage-earning opportunities for players. From 1923–5, the USLTA threatened to suspend Tilden three times: for profiting from producing instructional films; for writing newspaper articles for money; and for giving press interviews about tournaments he was playing in. These restrictions on artistic/journalistic endeavours frustrated Tilden, who was essentially reprimanded for earning money simply because of his name. Moreover, Tilden was actually trained as a journalist, fully qualified and quite skilled, so these rulings countered the advice frequently offered that players should seek employment to allow them to remain as amateurs. Regardless, these early suspension threats for Tilden never materialised, often because of his solemn apologies to the USLTA.

Quite astutely, concerns were voiced at the 1926 LTA AGM that restrictions on press contributions from amateurs might lower journalistic standards. Non-players or, worse still, professionals might come to dominate, which Colonel Kingscote feared would corrupt article content:

> You will get professionals laying down the ethics of the game. You will get them describing the Championships in the manner in which they can get the most money and in the way in which it suits them to do it.

A. Wallis Myers, himself a journalist, warned against passing legislation that encroached upon the personal liberties of amateurs more generally, however:

> Penalties and threats will not make amateurs. They will only tend to damp loyalty and engender mistrust. ... Amateur lawn tennis players, I

content, do not require to be surrounded by barbed wire. Fortifications are worse than useless if they inspire in the garrison only a desire to walk out.

Self-assuredly, he then asked whether the LTA felt 'justified' in pocketing £14,000 from the 1924 and 1925 Championships, but then seeking 'to deprive the large outside public ... of the interest and education which it derives from reading comments on Wimbledon written by players?' (*LT&B* 18 December 1926:926).

Come 1928, Tilden was skating on thin ice, and the USLTA decided enough was enough and went for his 'jugular' (Deford 2004:89). Allegations surfaced that Tilden had written for the *San Francisco Chronicle* and *New York World* about the Wimbledon Championships that he was still competing in, so the USLTA banned him from the upcoming Davis Cup Challenge Round match against France. Support for Tilden came immediately and forcefully: the FFT president appealed for the USLTA to reconsider, stating how important Tilden's appearance was to help fund their newly constructed Roland Garros stadium; the LTA president assured the USLTA via cablegram that no breaches of British amateur laws had been broken; René Lacoste announced his intention to withdraw from the upcoming US Nationals despite being defending champion, should Tilden be excluded; Joseph Wear, Davis Cup committeeman, actually resigned in direct protest; and Myron Herrick, the American Ambassador in France, warned US President Calvin Coolidge of potential damage to USA–France relations. Remarkably, these collective interventions forced the USLTA to back down. Tilden played and won the only rubber in a 4–1 defeat, but his greatest triumph was the off-court moral victory against the USLTA (Tinling 1983). Upon returning home, he was immediately (re)suspended and missed the US Nationals that September. However, in galvanising such high-profile support, he demonstrated the new-found power that star players wielded; no longer could national associations assume their passive compliance. *LT&B* (1 September 1928:614) reacted to the incident by saying that the USLTA 'cannot be congratulated on the way in which they dealt with the matter. ... This is not a fair and proper way to treat any man, and evinces a vacillation which cannot but do harm to any constitutional authority'.

Understandably, tennis administrators globally were torn by the "Tilden conundrum", given inherent contradictions in the ways he lived life and played tennis. Despite his public support for amateurism and its adjacent values of honesty, personal integrity and sportsmanship, he continually walked the line of appropriate actions and behavioural etiquette both on- and off-court. Although he outwardly appeared to be the sportsman, Tilden's opponents recognised his less-than-altruistic motives. During matches, he was known to "play" the crowd by throwing points and sometimes entire sets to orchestrate a spectacular comeback, 'for the sole purpose of showing spectators how he could then demean his opponent at will' (Tinling

1983:69). His propensity to glare at officials and line judges for bad calls pressed the USLTA in 1928 to propose a penalty for such actions. 'Only the best in travel, hotel accommodation, and food' satisfied Tilden, but tournament officials knew that his name 'kept the turnstiles clicking merrily', so most obliged his insatiable demands (Tinling 1983:70). Oblivious to the contradictory way he approached amateur tennis, living like a pampered prince out of administrators' pockets, he still maintained a defiant objection to professionalism. He claimed teaching professionally 'is perfectly analogous to a young lady turning whore' (Deford 2004:15). He obviously recognised an important difference between coaching as a professional and touring, as he played on and later promoted professional tours after relinquishing his amateur status in 1930.

Unquestionably, Tilden was at the time the highest profile player moonlighting with journalistic work, but the problems he created for administrators did not disappear when he turned professional, as the mutual mistrust between associations and the press was inveterate (Gray 1974). At their 1931 AGM, the LTA criticised the press for failing to address the shameful practice of "ghosting", and labelled the entire industry disreputable. Former LTA President H.H. Monckton condemned the oftentimes devious nature of journalistic work before questioning the integrity of journalists who also represented the LTA:

> How is a man who is on the public press going to differentiate between his duty as a Councillor and his duty to his paper, if he comes to a meeting where information is given to him which perhaps the chairman of the meeting does not intend should be broadcasted?
> (*LT&B* 19 December 1931:1014)

Not willing to be a scapegoat for the LTA's inability to legislate effectively on amateurism, tennis-writers and their supporters immediately challenged the notion of journalists as 'irresponsible'. Myers was particularly vociferous, reminding those present of past journalists who had rendered considerable service to amateur sport, including J.H. Walsh, first editor of *The Field*, who offered a cup for the inaugural Championships, Harry S. Scrivener, an original LTA founder, and other distinguished committeemen in cricket and golf. He also challenged the idea that professionals manipulated the media to corrupt readers' minds, by highlighting, using Tilden as an example, how professional writing standards had improved markedly.

These supportive comments, and an apology made earlier by the LTA Chairman of his general 'ignorance of Fleet Street', contributed chiefly to the Association's decision *not* to exclude tennis writers from LTA administration (*LT&B* 19 December 1931:1014). Passed by just one vote, the clear split nevertheless highlighted the extent of divided opinion on the perceived integrity of journalists. Unwilling to surrender, the staunch traditionalists returned to debate in 1934, but by then, a growing number of LTA councillors had become frustrated with continual amateur legislations. J. McCabe remarked: 'I cannot help feeling that we are getting into difficulties in continually extending and elaborating the things that an amateur tennis player cannot do' (*LT&B* 15 December 1934:890). His point was well received; perhaps without much forethought, the LTA had infringed increasingly on personal liberties.

Alongside restrictions on writing were prohibitions against players receiving free or subsidised playing equipment. Despite the ILTF's acknowledgement that many young players on low incomes 'found it increasingly difficult to follow the game thoroughly and supply themselves properly with rackets for first-class play' (*LT&B* 29 March 1930:1397), a majority within the LTA considered obtaining free rackets a breach of amateur regulations.

The extent of the LTA's declining faith in amateur players was revealed unequivocally when they proposed a player "declaration", similar to the IOC's Olympic Oath introduced in 1925, to be signed by all players before entering a tournament, stating they were not violating amateur regulations. For some, the proposal was ineffectual at depriving rule-breaching foreigners their amateur statuses, rooted in fear and suspicion of malpractice without evidence, and counterintuitive to fostering trust and goodwill among players. For Myers:

> This declaration sends a cold shiver down the spine. It suggests that at every tournament in this country there is a pitfall for the young player. It conjures up a vision of commercial men lurking in the dressing-room ready to offer [money] to a player.

He ended by stating this resolution simply advertised the LTA's 'weakness as administrators ... while casting suspicions on the great majority of honourable amateurs. In the words of Pope, they are "willing to wound, yet afraid to strike"' (*LT&B* 17 December 1932:933–4).

This was persuasive, but Monckton's response was equally determined; he used an incident from 1930, when a leading manufacturer circulated a letter to numerous tournament committees enticing them with guaranteed gates in exchange for using their equipment, to highlight the problem's pervasiveness. The letter read:

> It is our privilege to claim personal friendship with a very large majority of the leading players, and we wish to emphasise that as a result of our efforts during the past season, we arranged many attractive entries and partnerships at meetings where the – ball was in use. It is our intention to concentrate on this important aspect of tournament service, and to extend our efforts to ensure, as far as possible, the greatest success of meetings we are privileged to supply.
>
> (*LT&B* 7 January 1933:994)

In this, as in other similar issues, the LTA was trapped between two equally unattractive potential outcomes: (i) allow negative commercial influences to creep into the sport; or (ii) demean and frustrate the amateur players they intended simply to protect.

Demonstrating their primary intention, the LTA chose to retain control even if it meant adopting a contradictory position. They opted for players to sign an entry form – apparently not a declaration – that asked whether they understood the amateur regulations and associated penalties for receiving funding or free equipment without special permission. Despite admitting rightly that players were now in greater financial need than those from decades previous, this was yet another LTA regulation that made it harder for such players to fund themselves and also, concomitantly, more likely to push them toward considering illicit financial inducements, or toward turning professional outright. It was a sad example of "biting off your nose to spite your face", and signalled, certainly for Fred Perry (1935:96), the growing hypocrisy within the amateur establishment:

> It is all very well for tennis legislators all over the world to exclaim 'what a pity it is that tennis is such a "business" these days', when all the time they are helping to make it a "business" – and for the associations they represent, a very profitable one.

There was no simple solution, but arguably administrators had brought some of these consequences upon themselves by failing to adapt to wider social developments. Did they honestly expect world-renowned players to win a major competition one day, and then return contentedly to their city day-jobs the next? The idea must have seemed farcical, but some players did attempt such an arrangement, though often unsuccessfully. This begs the question: What kinds of careers would have allowed players repeated sizeable breaks from work? Certainly, those sports-related, e.g. with sports writing or sporting-goods firms, would have been the most accessible, but these were precisely the areas prohibited (Potter 1936).

Tilden's exploits paved the way for others to follow, and even as a professional, he remained for national associations the symbolic face of the "amateur problem". Yet, it was the indomitable Suzanne Lenglen who pioneered the professional tennis tour, signing a contract with Charles C. Pyle, the versatile American promoter, in 1926. Her decision further fuelled anti-commercial sentiments, to which Tilden and others were then subjected.

Lenglen's contractual arrangement worth a guaranteed $50,000 was to play exhibition matches at 39 venues across North America with a six-player troupe that included Vincent Richards as the male star. Lenglen was initially hesitant because she feared 'losing friends and social position', but was reminded by Pyle: 'Money never hurt anyone's social standing' (Bowers 1999). Public reaction to her bold move was mixed. Some offered condemnation, claiming she thought of tennis as a 'commercial proposition' instead of playing for 'love' (*LT&B* 28 August 1926:549); she had, in effect, "sold out" and 'betrayed the cause of sport' (*LT&B* 4 September 1926:582). In *Life Magazine*, Lenglen was caricatured as big-nosed, crooked-toothed, and spindly-legged, swatting balls with $ symbols on them (see Tingay 1973:47). Other condemnations were less subtle. One *LT&B* correspondent considered her 'unbridled temperament' and 'years of unchallenged supremacy' as bad for the game: 'Not only Wimbledon, but all tournaments ... will be all the more peaceful and pleasant in consequence of her withdrawal' (14 August 1926:489).

Another body of players and fans were more supportive of her desire to capitalise economically on her talents. The editor of the FFT's *Tennis et Golf* magazine praised Lenglen for having 'rendered the greatest services to the game', putting herself 'at the disposal of Associations' and 'keeping appointments when duty more than pleasure called them' (cited in *LT&B* 4 September 1926:595). For Lenglen, turning professional was an act of 'self-emancipation' (Jensen 2010:35); in an interview for the German magazine *Sport und Sonne* (March 1928:152), she explicitly expressed the need to look after herself: 'Why shouldn't I think about my future now that everyone for whom I've played has made their fortune? Will the people who have become rich through me one day take up my [cause] when I need them?' Lenglen appreciated her exploitable commodity status, but had been less generously rewarded compared to some of her contemporaries in other sports, like Babe Ruth, Jack Dempsey and Red Grange. Even non-sport-related businesses began to profit from associating themselves with successful athletes (Smart 2005; 2007), as Pierre du Pasquier, from the FFT, described in *Tennis et Golf*:

> In the US one of the leading chocolate companies, having placed on the market the 'Red Grange Chocolate Bar' ... sold more than six million bars during the [first] month. ... Huge profits are realised from the staging of certain events which the use of the players' names make possible. The desire to share in these profits and the fact that their names are universally known are the two motives which induce amateur players to consider the step to professionalism. ... All amateur players of any note at all have an indisputable 'professional' value.
> (cited in *LT&B* 5 March 1927:1108)

Despite occasional lucrative under-the-table bonuses and the immense pressures players felt when representing their associations and nations, both income and status were unstable for tennis players. Cleather (1947:177) noted that "expenses" depended on players maintaining high profiles, and oftentimes 'the moment they were beaten hospitality ceased. It was literally a matter of life and death ... It was a tough and merciless life'. Examples were numerous of players being booed by spectators for losing or, worse, for forfeiting for what appeared an unreasonable excuse. Lenglen was castigated for months in *ALT* for conceding to Molla Mallory from a losing position in the 1921 US Nationals, and Helen Wills endured similar treatment for retiring when 3–0 down in the final set against Helen Jacobs at the 1933 US final (Tinling 1983). *LT&B* (2 September 1933:571) proffered a reminder:

> What these critics seem to forget is that lawn tennis is an amateur game, and that the player is under no obligation to provide the crowd with a spectacle, and that the player has the right to retire or even concede a walk-over.

Spectators and associations demanded the display of both sportsmanship and a professional attitude to achieve success, yet this necessitated intense training and pre-match preparation with professional coaches and even scouts. For all their efforts and successes, players were poorly rewarded with what amounted to merely trophies and honour. "You can't buy groceries with glory", Harpo Marx, brother of Groucho, famously said to Fred Perry in 1934 (cited in *Telegraph* 11 September 2012). Yet administrators and tournament officials of amateur tennis prospered handsomely. Lenglen stated, in the exhibition programme for her inaugural professional match at Madison Square Gardens in 1926, that players were exploited by the 'shrewd businessmen [who] saw to it that these tournaments netted them a handsome profit. With few exceptions, the proceeds from these amateur exhibitions went into private pockets' (Lenglen 1926:15). However, given her "professional" status then, it is likely her words had little impact beyond the 13,000 paying New Yorkers who might have read them.

The slight on her character that turning professional revealed was extended to criticisms of her anticipated level of effort. The format of repeated matches involving the same players departed from standard practice, and accusations abounded that players would deliberately and routinely manipulate play to keep matches and series scores close (Bowers 1999). In syndicated articles written before the tour commenced, Lenglen assured readers that whether amateur or professional, she would 'always try to play that same brand of tennis'; Richards professed similarly: 'I intend to play just as hard as when I was an amateur' (Bowers 1999).

Despite early uncertainties, fuelled by Richard Lowenthal's criticisms in *ALT* that spiritless play and a lack of concern for the end result would render the tour concept a certain failure, public support grew as the tour progressed. One fan from Denver, Colorado, wrote:

> I had never before seen tennis of this grade, and two minutes after they started playing I was unconscious whether they were pros, amateurs, or royalty! I didn't care. I was simply carried away by the wonderful tennis; that was all.
>
> (cited in Bowers 1999)

Bowers (1999) confirmed that crowds from the Lenglen-Richards tour could not tell if players' efforts wavered, and 'didn't seem to mind' the staged circus-like atmosphere.

The influential LTA councillor, Fred Lohden, felt certain that no professionals were worth £30–£40k for six months exhibition play, and that:

> Such stunts as exploited by Mr. Pyle cannot attract a public for any length of time. ... There is no doubt that professionals at lawn tennis are a necessity, but only a necessity as regards teaching people how to play the game; the circus performer is not a necessity.
> (*LT&B* 26 February 1927:1091)

On this issue, Pierre du Pasquier was more open-minded, but speculated: 'Professional lawn tennis will only live if it is of a sporting quality equal or even superior to amateur lawn tennis' (*LT&B* 5 March 1927:1108). Certainly, it was this outcome the leading amateur associations were so desperate to avoid, particularly given the uncomfortable reality that tennis players, their attitudes, ambitions and the world around them were changing.

From her first professional tour, Lenglen was awarded an extra $25,000 bonus on top of her guaranteed fee, and Pyle himself cleared at least $80,000. *LT&B* reported the tour fairly as a financial success, but avoided implying that other players might equal her achievement. Lenglen's unmatchable talent and international repute set her above the rest, but then so did Tilden's. Upon turning professional in 1930, he created Tilden Tours Inc., which came to manage all the leading professionals before WWII. His troupe toured mostly in North America where the press and public were most receptive, and competed in numerous formats, including the normal knock-out structure, the Davis Cup format as a team event with one doubles and four singles matches, round-robins and also one-night-only exhibitions. From 1931 onwards, tours were staged in major cities in Western Europe, including Berlin, Paris and Amsterdam. Because of institutional resistance they were not played in Britain until the autumn of 1934, when two professional tournaments were organised: one four-man round-robin tournament in Southport, which included Tilden and the British coaching professional Dan Maskell, and another six-man round-robin competition at Wembley, which included the 1932 Wimbledon and US Nationals champion Ellsworth Vines (Bowers 2003a). By the end of the 1930s, according to Bowers (2003b), this Wembley event had become the most hotly contested of all the world's professional competitions, which signalled the growing popularity of professional tennis among the British public.

After an unsuccessful tour involving two lesser-known American women in 1936 (Bowers 2004a), Tilden came to recognise what basic necessities ensured the survival of professional tours, namely: meaningful, honest competition; the occasional introduction of new ideas and formats; and, most importantly, the launch of new high-profile players (Bowers 2002).

Unsurprisingly, he considered Wimbledon and US Nationals champions as key recruitment targets, which brought anxiety upon the national associations, which recognised the possibility of a mass exodus of amateur talent and the subsequent declining quality and thus profitability of amateur competitions. They attempted to counter this trend with carefully orchestrated propaganda that exposed ex-amateurs as immoral and corruptible beings. Administrative actions that were intended to punish ex-amateurs and deter current amateurs from turning pro were comprehensive and immediate. Honorary memberships to clubs were rescinded, often without notice; official national and international rankings overlooked ex-amateurs, and news reports often ceased reporting on their performances. When mentioned, ex-amateurs were portrayed as disgraced outcasts or money-grabbing sell-outs, and labelled 'dissenters', 'defectors' or 'circus acts'. As a final betrayal, national associations used their own media outlets to depict professionalism itself as an evil and wicked thing. Vincent Richards noted that, as an amateur, he was 'showered with hospitality' but, after turning pro, was invariably 'ignored' and outlawed by the USLTA (Jefferys 2009a).

Through their actions, the elderly gentlemen who ran the national associations often disregarded the real-life conditions of their own players who came from less affluent backgrounds. To all intents and purposes, it seems the LTA and its sister associations globally were embarking on 'class legislation', as Monckton later put it. But in the midst of their battles with players, press representatives, manufacturers, tournament directors, club committees and professional tour promoters, an unlikely ally emerged. Coaching professionals enjoyed greater opportunities for competitive play and an improved position within the LTA's talent-development agenda. Moreover, while they emerged as an independent force, by the mid-30s, coaches were welcomed into the LTA fold, which was equally significant and intriguing given their typically modest and often working-class backgrounds. An analysis of their changing status and role brings broader class relations to light.

Note

1. His image as an American hero became increasingly incongruous when word of his homosexual tendencies, which resulted in several scandals involving young boys, came to press.

Bibliography

Baltzell, E. D. (1995). *Sporting Gentlemen: Men's Tennis from the Age of Honor to the Cult of the Superstar*. New York: Free Press.

Bingham, A. (2004). *Gender, Modernity and the Popular Press in Inter-War Britain*. Oxford: Clarendon.

Bowers, R. (1999, 31 October). *Suzanne Lenglen and the First Pro Tour*. Retrieved April 11 2014, from Between the Lines: An Analytical and Sometimes

Controversial Look at the Pro Tennis Tour: http://www.tennisserver.com/lines/lines_99_10_31.html

Bowers, R. (2002, 3 March). *History of the Pro Tennis Wars, Chapter 3: Tilden's Year of Triumph: 1931*. Retrieved from Between the Lines: An Analytical and Sometimes Controversial Look at the Pro Tennis Tour: http://www.tennisserver.com/lines/lines_02_03_03.html

Bowers, R. (2003a, 1 March). *Forgotten Victories: The Early Pro Tennis Wars*. Retrieved April 11, 2014, from Between the Lines: An Analytical and Sometimes Controversial Look at the Pro Tennis Tour: http://www.tennisserver.com/lines/lines_03_03_01.html

Bowers, R. (2003b, 1 December). *Forgotten Victories: History of the Pro Tennis Wars, Chapter IV: Vines's Second Year: 1935*. Retrieved April 11, 2014, from Between the Lines: An Analytical and Sometimes Controversial Look at the Pro Tennis Tour: http://www.tennisserver.com/lines/lines_03_12_01.html

Bowers, R. (2004a, 25 July). *History of the Pro Tennis Wars, Chapter VII: Awaiting Perry, 1936*. Retrieved from Between the Lines: An Analytical and Sometimes Controversial Look at the Pro Tennis Tour: http://www.tennisserver.com/lines/lines_04_07_25.html

Briggs, A. (1979). *The History of Broadcasting in the United Kingdom: Sound and Vision* (vol. 4). Oxford: Oxford University Press.

Budge, D. (1969). *A Tennis Memoire*. New York: Viking Press.

Cleather, N. (1947). *Wimbledon Story*. London: Sporting Handbooks.

Clerici, G. (1975). *The Ultimate Tennis Book: 500 Years of the Sport*. Chicago: Follett Publishing Company.

de Lotbinière, S. J. (1942). *Some Notes on Commentary*. London: BBC Archives Centre R30/428/1.

Deford, F. (2004). *Big Bill Tilden: The Triumphs and the Tragedy*. Toronto: Sportclassic Books.

Gray, D. (1974). The Press. In M. Robertson, *Encyclopedia of World Tennis* (pp. 176–180). New York: Viking Press.

Hart, S. (1985). *Once a Champion: Legendary Tennis Stars Revisited*. New York: Dodd, Mead.

Haynes, R. (2009). 'Lobby' and the Formative Years of Radio Sports Commentary 1935–1952. *Sport in History*, 29(1), 25–48.

Holt, R. (1989). *Sport and the British*. Oxford: Clarendon.

Huggins, J., and Williams, J. (2005). *Sport and the English: 1918–1939*. London: Routledge.

Huggins, M. (2007). Projecting the Visual: British Newsreels, Soccer and Popular Culture 1918–39. *International Journal of the History of Sport*, 24(1), 80–102.

Jefferys, K. (2009a). Fred Perry and British Tennis: "Fifty Years to Honor a Winner". *Sport in History*, 29(1), 1–24.

Lenglen, S. (1926). Why I Became a Professional. In C. C. Pyle, *Professional Tennis: Souvenir Exhibition Programme* (pp. 14–15). New York: Charles C. Pyle.

Maskell, D. (1988). *From Where I Sit*. London: Willow.

Perry, F. (1935). *Perry Wins! Expert Advice for All on Lawn Tennis*. London: Hutchinson.

Potter, E. (1963). *King of the Court: The Story of Lawn Tennis*. New York: A.S. Barnes.

Smart, B. (2005). *The Sport Star: Modern Sport and the Cultural Economy of Sporting Celebrity*. London: Sage.
Smart, B. (2007). Not Playing Around: Global Capitalism, Modern Sport and Consumer Culture. *Global Networks*, 7(2), 113–134.
Tingay, L. (1973). *A History of Lawn Tennis in Pictures*. London: Tom Stacey.
Tinling, T. (1983). *Tinling: Sixty Years in Tennis*. London: Sidgwick & Jackson.
Whannel, G. (1992). *Fields in Vision: Television Sport and Cultural Transformation*. London: Routledge.

10 Developments for professional coaches and the early (failed) push for "open" tournaments

In 1934, the *LT&B* editor clarified an important distinction between two types of "professionals" that had been emerging in lawn tennis:

> The genuine professional player [i.e. coach] is accorded full recognition in his own sphere of livelihood. It is the other class of professional, the exhibitionist, usually an ex-amateur, who is causing dissension in the game. He tours the world seeking to put into his own pocket as much as he can in the least possible time. Of what benefit is he to lawn tennis? He is commercialising the talent which has very often cost amateur associations thousands of pounds to mature.
>
> (1 December 1934:837)

By this juncture, it was clear that the homogeneity of "professionals" was being challenged, as coaches and ex-amateur touring players sought to develop their own distinct identities. In 1934, the latter formed the International Professional Players Association, which, having recognised that most coaching professionals added little to the success of professional touring events, excluded them from joining (Bowers 2003b). Equally, in order to obtain institutional support and elevate themselves socially, coaching professionals were keen to distinguish themselves; by outlining their commitment to develop amateur talent, they emphasised their loyalty to amateur tennis, its associations and clubs. Conversely, touring professionals were regarded as leaches upon the amateur game or, as a writer in *The Field* called them, the 'vanguard of an invading army in lawn tennis' that pinched players from amateur competitions (cited in *LT&B* 1 December 1934:845). Coaches ostensibly gave something back to amateur tennis and were perceived as a lesser threat.

The LTA demonstrated their growing appreciation for talent development as a means to restore British prestige by offering greater support to professional coaches. Once regarded as outsiders, they were eventually brought into LTA jurisdiction, which represented a major shift in emphasis toward professionalism. Historically speaking, the very notion of coaching challenged the inveterate amateur philosophy of sport, which held a strong suspicion of professionals as lacking moral integrity and sportsmanship (Huggins and Williams 2005). Some believed they had a questionable level of 'commitment to victory and to the codes of the game' (Bowers 2001). Thus, while coaches did come to enjoy greater opportunities for employment and an improved level of respect and status as a result of their efforts, inveterate class antagonism continued to prevent their full inclusion in the amateur fraternity. This chapter aims to discuss developments for coaches in the context of intensifying disagreements surrounding appropriate talent-development methods. Shifts in the status of coaches in clubs are discussed, alongside the early push for "open tennis" in the 1930s.

Clubs began hiring "professionals" to teach members with greater regularity during the interwar years, but it was said that 'you might count them almost on the fingers of one hand' (*LT&B* 10 February 1923:837). Coaches in Britain generally tended to derive from less privileged working-class backgrounds (Carter 2010), so they were often treated like paid servants and denied liberties that club members enjoyed. In 1922, the LTA Council allowed coaching professionals to become members of clubs, but they were forbidden to represent their club, county or country in formal competitions. They could compete in "friendly" matches against other clubs, but even this token gesture found opposition. One LTA councillor objected to clubs fielding professionals in matches or offering them free memberships so they could represent them: 'Such conduct is not amateur in theory or in practice, and is only a short way removed from the action of getting a professional team to play for the club' (*LT&B* 13 December 1924:894).

For the most part, coaching professionals were kept in their place by strict class protocol. The social hierarchy within many clubs naturally resembled country houses; while scullery maids deferred to house stewards in the latter, in tennis clubs ballboys accepted the seniority of the head professional, and undertook whatever menial or demeaning tasks that accompanied their positions. Alongside coaching duties, they strung or repaired rackets, and looked after courts and club grounds. Age and class prejudice combined to make the lot of the ballboy particularly meagre, as club members often took opportunities to insist on deferential treatment and respect from these social inferiors. Such hierarchies were mirrored in other sports, even for the head professionals. Williams (2006:430) noted of cricket: 'at almost all county grounds amateurs changed separately from professionals … [who] were also expected to perform ancillary duties'. Similarly, McKibbin (1998:360) described how golf "pros"

> were often working in an environment which was hostile to them and to professional sport. … [His] function … was to coach and to run a small golfing shop attached to the club. He was a servant of the club and usually denied entry to the clubhouse. Some were treated not much better than caddies.

At Stanmore Golf Club, 'social inferiors' included club servants, caddies, green staff and professionals. Their organisation was formalised in 1922 with the creation of an 'Artisan Section', which offered severely limited playing opportunities and a separate 'hut' adjacent to the main building (Holt 1989:85).

Lawn tennis coaching professional Dan Maskell recalled the 'upstairs downstairs' days at Queen's Club in the 1920s when professionals were not allowed into the members' dressing rooms or lounges. Alongside coaching, Maskell strung rackets and completed other menial tasks. The professionals had their own recreation room, a dark and dingy basement beneath the clubhouse, but this evident subordination they happily accepted. Maskell earned seven shillings and sixpence for each 75-minute lesson, which corresponds to just over £10 at today's value, but despite the less than generous financial remuneration and lack of job security, he considered himself incredibly fortunate to be privy to the 'charmed world of privilege' from where most members came (Maskell 1988:39). In 1929, after several years at Queen's, Maskell became the AELTC head professional. Escorting him around the club on his very first day, Secretary Major Dudley Larcombe offered Maskell a locker in the members' dressing room. His recollections of this moment tell a story of deeply entrenched class segregation:

> I could hardly believe my ears. It is difficult today to realise the impact of Major Larcombe's suggestion. When, later, I told my fellow professionals at Queen's they refused to believe me. With one blow Major Larcombe had swept away centuries of protocol, redefining the social order.
>
> (Maskell 1988:72)

As a reflection of how the status of professionals had improved in the interwar years, there was evidently a desire among some at the AELTC to admit specially selected working-class affiliates, and Maskell was an ideal candidate for this honour given his Queen's Club experience that successfully reared him in the art of mixing with highly placed people. He was liked among the elite fraternity because of his deference and modesty; he "knew his place", posed little threat to established order and idealised the amateur philosophy. His status improved throughout the interwar period, as he was commissioned with increasing frequency to coach the leading amateurs and offer opinions on various tennis-related issues. In 1936, Maskell was praised by Davis Cup captain H. Roper Barrett as a "gentleman" by behaviour if not by class: 'that excellent sample of a professional who ... learns to impart his knowledge to the team rather than fill his own pockets' (*LT&B* 8 August 1936:463). It would be imprudent to suggest that Maskell's enhanced persona reflected the wholesale erosion of class barriers more generally; it was more likely that Maskell's knowledge and expertise had become increasingly important commodities to the tennis establishment seeking to fulfil performance objectives (Lake 2010a).

Coaching professionals were careful not to "forget themselves", as strict etiquette between themselves and club members sustained their differing social positions often without the need for official sanction. Coaches were called by their first names, but were expected to refer to members as Mr or Mrs. When a young Fred Perry referred in 1927 to an old friend who had become the Queen's Club dressing-room attendant as 'Mr. Jenkins' within earshot of an apparently 'rather pompous official', he was told, 'We don't address attendants like that here' (Perry 1984:19). In most cases, waged working-class labourers in tennis clubs had an acute understanding of the social hierarchy within which they operated and a keen sense of their "station" and what could or could not be said or done. Those with ambition were cognisant of what behaviour was necessary to gain acceptance among the privileged gate-keepers whom they served. It seems for most ballboys, becoming the head professional at a prestigious club was the most ambitious aspiration to have in tennis. Maskell (1988:42) recalled: 'To my young eyes there could be no finer achievement than to … become the head professional'. Few ballboys would have considered themselves suitable to actually play the game competitively as an amateur. In truth, likely the closest they would ever get to the grass on Centre Court was behind a lawnmower.

Dan Maskell was the most outspoken of all British coaching professionals, championing the cause of improving their expertise and status. His struggles to persuade the LTA to invest the required time, money and energy into coach development, because it was in their best interests to do so, reflect the Association's initial lack of conviction. One notable problem for coaches was their lack of competitive match-playing opportunities. For most, their daily grind consisted predominantly of instructing middle-aged beginners with simple stroke practice; most club members were incapable of stretching their coaches as players. 'We are daily engaged in playing ordinary friendly games, and also in coaching. This does not conduce to improvement, and if such contests were arranged we should be able to prepare for them in a proper way', argued Hierons (*LT&B* 7 August 1920:333). The logic was sound: What good was a coaching professional who never competed? How could he/she advise pupils about winning matches when rarely competing him/herself? The LTA responded late in 1920 by creating an official register of coaches and sanctioning a professional championship. Throughout the 1920s, professional events grew in number and popularity, and before long they attracted the best coaching professionals from across Europe. In 1927 Dan Maskell won his first British professional championship while still at Queen's, and he dominated over the next decade, winning 16 in total. Despite being open to *all* professionals, this and its sister events in America and Germany attracted mainly coaches, as touring professionals tended to play separately (Bowers 2003b).

The LTA also sanctioned doubles matches between amateurs and coaching professionals. The first tournament at Queen's in 1924 was limited to just three matches. Won 3–0 by the amateurs, the LTA nevertheless considered it a major success and organised a further five such events in Eastbourne, Manchester, Leeds, Paignton and Teddington (Maskell 1988:50). The amateurs were naturally advantaged with regular match practice, so won most of these, though pundits predicted closer matches in future. The professionals had a bumper year in 1925, winning singles matches against the amateurs at Dulwich and other venues, leading one *LT&B* correspondent to remark: 'It is doubtful if there is an English amateur capable of beating the best of the professionals at the present time' (*LT&B* 20 June 1925:228). Another stated: 'There is no amateur belonging to this country who could owe 15 to Read [professional champion], and I feel that there are, at least, three or four other professionals who are good enough to beat our best amateurs' (*LT&B* 15 August 1925:515).

These matches were popular among the paying public, and soon there were calls for officially sanctioned open tournaments. Monckton first suggested this in 1929:

> The general idea of what I would describe as an open championship in principle seemed to us to be advisable, because we have got to the stage when, as you know, there are some leading professionals who are very anxious to try their skill in what I suppose is commonly known as a blood match between themselves and the amateurs.
> (*LT&B* 14 December 1929:1028)

On this issue, the LTA's firm anti-professional stance wobbled, as they came to recognise coaching professionals as important partners in their long-term talent-development plans. At the 1930 ILTF AGM, the LTA proposed holding one open tournament per year in each participating country, so an official national open championship could be created.

Britain's support for open tournaments rested on a clear-cut status distinction between coaching and touring professionals; given their proven loyalty to the amateur game, only the former were alluded to in the proposal. Travel expenses and prize money were considered investments, as long-term gains could be achieved by developing their playing standards and coaching abilities, which could then be displayed publicly. For these reasons, the open tournament idea underpinned Britain's strategy to regain its lost prominence.

America also proposed open competitions in 1929, just two years after Vincent Richards spearheaded the formation of its own tennis professionals' association, but it is suspected that their underlying motives were directed less toward overcoming problems of declining standards but more toward capitalising on commercial opportunities. Their notion of open competition was more inclusive than Britain's as it welcomed the participation of touring professionals. Richards' enthralling matches against the Czechoslovakian coaching professional Karel Kozeluh prompted other coaching and touring professionals to compete with them at tournaments in New York (Forest Hills), London (Queen's Club) and Beaulieu, in the French Riviera. Debates about how professionals might fare against the top amateurs raged in the tennis press, and public interest in the idea of open tournaments underpinned USLTA support (Bowers 2001).

The USLTA's idea for open competition afforded them greater control over the flow of money in tennis. They could divert it back into amateur tennis, which, from their perspective, was an infinitely more desirable outcome than allowing it to pass through the hands of entrepreneurial promoters. The USLTA shared the LTA's open opposition to money-making in tennis, but in America the problems of professional touring were more acute. This is possibly one reason to account for their comparatively stricter amateur definitions in the mid–late 1920s. The USLTA refused to sanction post-war charity matches and also disqualified players for a number of reasons: converting prize vouchers into necessities like food or clothing; allowing his/her name or initials to be used to advertise sport-related products, even if no remuneration was received; obtaining a free club membership in exchange for pecuniary benefits; competing in an event where gate money was charged, even if no remuneration was received; and, even engaging in unsportsmanlike conduct (*LT&B* 10 January 1925:962). The USLTA's hard-nosed, anti-commercial stance quite cleverly, but entirely hypocritically, concealed their reliance upon gate receipts.

In the lead-up to the ILTF AGM in March 1930, British newspapers, including the *Daily Sketch*, offered their support for open competition, if only to right the wrongs of "shamateurism". In America, a poll among 42 elite amateur players revealed that 36 expressed enthusiasm for open competition, five abstained and only one disapproved (Bowers 2001). These offers of moral support likely counted for little, however, in an international context when a two-thirds majority vote across all member nations was necessary. Indeed, the resolution was defeated comprehensively; only Britain and America voted in favour against 20 nations in opposition. The chief opposing argument, in the *LT&B* editors' words, was that 'lawn tennis had its own public, which had been built and grown up round it. Democratic though the game was, this public was particular. The "open" championship would make it general'. Regarding open tournaments, he said: 'What more certain way could be devised to tempt young amateurs from the true path' (*LT&B* 29 March 1930:1397). Thus, it seems the exclusion of a lower-class public and the preservation of amateurism were key reasons for opposition to open tournaments, putting these priorities ahead of developing coaches, advancing playing standards and promoting tennis to new audiences. At this juncture, at least, the British were championing the cause of open tennis competition but were halted by cumbersome ILTF legislation.

The open-tournament idea was returned to repeatedly over the next few years, but defeated at every opportunity with either tenuous or anachronistic arguments. In both 1932 and 33, opponents claimed the top coaching professionals were of inadequate standard to challenge the top amateurs: 'With the exception of one or two players, the professional standard of match-play is so much below that of the leading amateurs that their ranks would be decimated quite early in the tournament' (*LT&B* 25 February 1933:1558). This opinion contrasted, however, with new viewpoints that stressed 'the greatly improved form of the professionals' (*LT&B* 12 August 1933:482), or predicted 'the professionals are getting gradually nearer to victory' (*LT&B* 1 September 1934:540). At the 1934 ILTF AGM, the open-tournament proposal was defeated again; this time, the key concern was to protect players from the 'bad features of sham amateurism'. Charles Barde, Chairman of the ILTF Committee on Amateurism, claimed:

> Most of the trouble has been brought about by the competition between clubs and other promoters of lawn tennis tournaments for the presence of amateurs of high skill, who have responded only too readily to the lures dangled in front of them. … The game has ceased to be a game … and has become a business, with enticing possibilities of profits for all concerned.

Alluding to the idea of open competition, he remarked: 'Nothing should be done to encourage a state of professionalism which can be tolerated in some sports, but not in ours' (*LT&B* 24 March 1934:1279).

In 1936, the LTA and USLTA were joined in their efforts by the All-India LTA, which argued that 'the time was ripe to press for the institution of one open championship per annum' (*LT&B* 5 December 1936:889). Their proposal came just three weeks after Fred Perry had announced his retirement from the amateur game, and the timing was important in lending a nostalgic air to one councillor's subsequent remarks:

> An open tournament in this country would mark their appreciation of all that F.J. Perry had done on behalf of Great Britain in the Davis Cup. Perry would have an opportunity of opposing his old friends on the court again. … Why was Perry to be an outcast?
> (*LT&B* 5 December 1936:889)

It is unclear whether his comments about Perry were shared by his LTA colleagues, but they certainly supported the open tournament idea. Their proposal was defeated, but by a narrower margin this time. At this pace of change, open competition was predicted to arrive by the early 1940s.

Where were coaches positioned on the open-tournament debate? How did they consider their relations with touring professionals? Answers to these questions are difficult to fathom, simply because very few expressed their views in a critical or detailed way. Tending to speak in clichés and avoid controversy, they observed the etiquette of remaining tight-lipped. Professional cricketers did the same, according to Williams (2006:441); very few before WWII wrote autobiographies and those that did, 'may have been tempted to write not what they felt but what they imagined readers wanted to hear. ... Criticizing amateur captains was risky for professionals'. Moreover, 'some counties vetted articles written by professionals before they were sent to newspapers'. Athletics literature was equally dominated by an 'Oxbridge elite', so few working-class coaching professionals would have contributed (Carter 2010). Tennis was also characterised by amateur privilege and paternalism, and most LTA policy directives implicating coaching professionals were discussed and enacted often without consulting them. This arms-length relationship was indicative of broader class relations, alongside the coaches' lack of formal organisation.

In 1925, Dan Maskell worked with Charles Hierons to form an autonomous professional coaches' association that aimed to work with the LTA to improve coaching standards. However, their progress was limited by their forced exclusion from LTA boardrooms, alongside others who made money through tennis, like referees or journalists. In 1931, the LTA made a failed attempt to placate coaching professionals by creating a 'Contact Committee' for the purpose of discussing issues arising with their association, but this offered no solution to the problem of their denied representation and voting powers on the main council. Dissatisfied with 'the manner in which the LTA controlled their side of the game', the leading coaching professionals convened a secret meeting, whereupon they publicly vowed to sever relations with the Contact Committee. They also asked for more funding, beyond small donations from the LTA and AELTC and meagre membership subscriptions (*LT&B* 12 December 1931:987). These moves reflected the growing collective confidence of coaching professionals, who by now must have appreciated their enhanced bargaining power as a consequence of increased LTA demand for their services. This did not prevent the LTA from making further hollow statements, creating the Coaching Professional Committee (CPC) in 1934 to replace the independent association and take coaching professionals under its wing. Administratively, however, coaches remained a visible minority, and as such were still denied representation on the LTA Council. The CPC's ultimate ineffectiveness is hinted at by the fact that Dan Maskell entirely fails to mention its existence in his lengthy autobiography, despite him sitting on it.

On a positive note, the CPC did manage to squeeze the LTA for £3,000 in its first year, for the purpose of reigniting several floundering county coaching schemes. Throughout the late 1920s, Bedfordshire offered free coaching to several promising young players but was apparently 'not in a position to [give] sufficient lessons to do real and lasting good'. Similarly, Hertfordshire reported that 'some of the junior clubs have taken no part in the coaching scheme, as they do not understand its value, nor do they know if they have any players worth coaching' (*LT&B* 25 January 1930:1171). Surrey also faced difficulties: a great difficulty was experienced in utilising the coach's time; several centres defaulted and often players far outside their target age-group were coached, in one case an elderly 55-year-old man (*LT&B* 12 November 1932:810). According to *Tennis Illustrated* (April 1931), of the 4,800 players coached across Britain in 1930, only about 1,000 were under 18. Overall, it was apparent that partnerships between the LTA, its county associations, clubs and coaches needed reformulating.

Despite assurances that budding talent would not be overlooked, class barriers remained. One *LT&B* correspondent urged:

> Boys and girls in elementary schools should be given the same opportunity as the children whose parents can afford to send them to public schools, if the governing body are sincere in their wish to make lawn tennis really democratic.
> (4 February 1933:1087)

Fred Perry was utilised as a non-public-school-boy role model within a slightly exaggerated working-class rags-to-riches narrative, though some pointed to his raw talent, natural physical abilities and determination as principal reasons for his success rather than the apparent erosion of class barriers. Davis Cup captain, H.A. Sabelli, remarked of Perry: 'It is obvious that you cannot keep a good man down. Any boy or girl, no matter what their social standing, has a chance to climb to the top of the tree if they are keen enough' (*LT&B* 4 February 1933:1087). Such claims indicated the extent of LTA blindness to class-based inequities. Moreover, many of the coaching schemes for non-public-school children offered paltry amounts of actual coaching time; in many cases, just thirty minutes per child, which was scarcely long enough to determine an individual's relative potential. The Middlesex LTA felt compelled to acknowledge this regrettable situation by disclaiming:

> The scheme ... is intended to sow the seed of enthusiasm and study of the game amongst the very ordinary young club player. The county associations are quite aware of the fact that this scheme probably does not result in the immediate and direct improvement of any one individual.
> (*LT&B* 2 November 1935:794)

Two years later, the national coaching scheme was criticised as a poor investment: 'three quarters of the amount allocated by the LTA for coaching is practically wasted' (*LT&B* 25 December 1937:947).

Another issue was ineffective coaching. In the early 1920s, coaches were criticised publicly for "over-coaching" or, more specifically, 'suppressing all originalities; discouraging individuality of style; condemning the subtle power of mannerism' (*LT&B* 22 April 1920:640). In his translated autobiography, René Lacoste (1926:40) discussed the tendency among many coaches to commence with 'the idea that every stroke in a certain category must be played in precisely the same way; [thus], the instruction he gives will cramp, instead of develop, individual talent'. Fry and Doust (1926:57–8) also warned:

> The ordinary paid coach is not to be recommended, if only for the fact that as a rule he has not the ability to impart to a pupil the knowledge that he himself possesses. ... [The professional] plays each stroke in a certain manner, and deems it expedient that his pupil should slavishly copy his methods. Such coaching has little or no real value.

These views were not new, but reflected subtle, deep-rooted class-based socio-cultural distinctions, whereby individual flair and the scope for creativity were considered products of elite upbringing.

Connected to this, a key predicament was the unregulated proliferation of new coaches. In 1927, a coaching certificate was recommended as a means to manage the 'wholly incompetent class of self-styled instructors whose only concern in life is to take money from beginners while giving an entirely inadequate return' (*LT&B* 15 January 1927:989). The LTA also introduced an official "register", but in practice this was just a list of names; hitherto, they had held no information as to their coaches' comparative abilities. Only in 1934 was it proposed that they be tested beforehand to ensure they were suitably qualified, though Maskell's suggestion that a sub-committee be formed for the purpose of ranking coaches was not taken seriously. The LTA claimed weakly in their defence: 'there could be no stereotyped method of coaching' (*LT&B* 8 December 1934:860).

Over the following two years, complaints about bad coaches being chosen for LTA coaching schemes and players being instructed to adopt changes that damaged their games appeared frequently in *LT&B*. Again, Maskell proposed a grading system to differentiate experienced instructors from beginners, but the LTA's response made them appear incompetent and amateurish. First, they made the feeble claim that 'it was impossible to test all professionals' by way of a short course of instruction, yet there were only 155 of them (130 men, 25 women) across Britain. Second, when asked how a coach would get him/herself on the register, they replied, 'the authorities [would] institute enquiries as to a candidate's proficiency and general character'; in other words, relying on subjective estimations of relative ability and personality. Third, it was considered that having a classification system was 'impracticable' and less than necessary since 'the problem really solved itself as the good man invariably came to the top' (*LT&B* 5 December 1936:887–8). Further indecisiveness delayed the adoption of Maskell's proposal to classify coaches until 1938, when it was pushed forward to the agenda for 1940. With the intervening war, measures were not taken to classify or qualify coaches until 1946, 12 years after the initial proposal was made, which was probably presented a full 15 years after it was needed.

The LTA's lackadaisical attitude toward the institution of a comprehensive coach-development system was indicative of their hands-off paternalist relationship with coaches generally. They sought to maintain ultimate control over coaches' actions, but from such a distance that negated full responsibility. In 1932, their position was defended by the *LT&B* editor, who claimed the LTA had provided 'a large number' of coaches with employment opportunities and financial assistance to 'keep their association together', and helped 'to improve the standard of play for the professional so that he will able to take his proper place in the game, namely to teach the young player' (*LT&B* 25 June 1932:240). In truth, however, LTA employment opportunities for coaches were scarce; only 30 were hired within their County Coaching Scheme, which earned them just 10 guineas a week and only for several months of the year. This represented a paltry investment from the LTA when considering their revenue for 1932 totalled £13,500. One *LT&B* correspondent countered: 'Limiting the opportunities of professionals for tournament play is not doing everything "to improve the standard of play for the professional"', before noting: 'Where we essentially differ here is on our view as to the "proper place" of the professional. You assume ... that his proper place is in the basement. I maintain that such assumptions are behind the times' (*LT&B* 23 July 1932:377).

It was evident that some disparity existed between the LTA and the growing body of coaches whose ambitions often extended beyond the head professional job, but the timing of this burgeoning discontent among coaches was poor. In 1931, Britain reached the Davis Cup inter-zone final for the first time since 1919, thanks partly to Maskell's extensive training prior to the team's departure to France, and Bunny Austin reached the 1932 Wimbledon final. Any criticism directed toward the LTA regarding coaches not being properly supported would likely have fallen on deaf ears and been countered with the ample evidence of Britain's rising standards. The LTA could be forgiven for their complacency at this time. In 1933, they finally regained the Davis Cup, retaining it until 1936, and in 1934 Perry won the first of his three consecutive Wimbledon singles titles. Margaret "Peggie" Scriven was the first overseas player to win the French Championships singles title in 1933, and won again in 1934. Dorothy Round reached the US Nationals' women's doubles final with Helen Jacobs and the singles semi-final in 1933. She reached the Wimbledon singles final in 1933 before winning it outright in 1934 and 1937, and she also won the 1935 Australian Championships – the first overseas player to do so. Austin reached the Wimbledon singles final again in 1938 and Kay Stammers did the same in 1939. These successes provided a much-needed injection of confidence for the British amateur lawn tennis establishment, but they masked underlying problems for coaches.

However, the most pressing issue for the LTA in the 1930s was not related to coaching or talent development, but rather to sustaining playing success alongside their lofty amateur ideals. Critical analysis of this period highlights the precarious compatibility of professional-driven success within an amateur-rewards framework, alongside the incredible extents to which national associations like the LTA were willing to compromise their integrity in order to promote a positive image.

Bibliography

Bowers, R. (2001, 1 March). *History of the Pro Tennis Wars, Chapter 2, Part 1: 1927–1928*. Retrieved April 11, 2014, from Between the Lines: An Analytical and Sometimes Controversial Look at the Pro Tennis Tour: http://www.tennisserver.com/lines/lines_01_03_01.html

Bowers, R. (2003b, 1 December). *Forgotten Victories: History of the Pro Tennis Wars, Chapter IV: Vines's Second Year: 1935*. Retrieved April 11, 2014, from Between the Lines: An Analytical and Sometimes Controversial Look at the Pro Tennis Tour: http://www.tennisserver.com/lines/lines_03_12_01.html

Carter, N. (2010). From Knox to Dyson: Coaching, Amateurism and British Athletics, 1912–1947. *Sport in History*, 30(1), 55–81.

Fry, J., and Doust, S. (1926). *Lawn Tennis: How to Master the Strokes*. London: W. Foulsham and Co.

Holt, R. (1989). *Sport and the British*. Oxford: Clarendon.

Huggins, J., and Williams, J. (2005). *Sport and the English: 1918–1939*. London: Routledge.

Lacoste, R. (1926). *Listening to Lacoste* (J. Pollock, Trans.). London: Mills & Boon.

Lake, R. J. (2010a). Stigmatised, Marginalised, Celebrated: Developments in Lawn Tennis Coaching 1870–1939. *Sport in History*, 30(1), 82–103.

Maskell, D. (1988). *From Where I Sit*. London: Willow.

McKibbin, R. (1998). *Classes and Cultures: England 1918–1951*. Oxford: Oxford University Press.

Perry, F. (1984). *Fred Perry: An Autobiography*. London: Arrow Books.

Williams, J. (2006). 'The Really Good Professional Captain Has Never Been Seen!': Perceptions of the Amateur/Professional Divide in County Cricket, 1900–39. *Sport in History*, 26(3), 429–449.

11 New British success and renewed issues of amateurism in the 1930s

Seen in the context of waning British on- and off-court dominance throughout the 1920s, broader opportunities to reaffirm the collective strength of empire were of crucial importance. The British celebrated the global spread of lawn tennis, but frustrations were plainly visible among those with interests in restoring British prowess. Wimbledon's sustained prestige and the LTA's administrative leadership were key to pursuing international respect, but it was not until the arrival of Perry and Austin that British on-court success matched claims to off-court supremacy. Perry's rather modest social background played a crucial part in the overall narrative, and highlighted contradictory viewpoints regarding precisely who the British amateur officials desired as their flagship champion. Class antagonism revealed itself as the story unfolded.

The aims of this chapter are to assess the British revival of the early–mid-1930s in broader social, cultural, political and economic contexts, and to assess the overall impact that British successes had on the LTA's leadership and prevailing attitudes toward amateurism and professionalism. Britain had been relatively cosseted from any negative effects of professional tours until 1936, when Perry eventually signed, and this chapter concludes with an examination of this period when the promise of full-scale professionalism threatened to engulf the entire sport.

In the early 1930s, amateur sport organisers rallied behind the newly created British Empire Games as a means to showcase imperial solidarity and British vitality (Moore 1989), but tennis administrators sought to resist its political manipulation by way of not taking part. Alongside wanting to protect the prestige of the Davis Cup, national associations also opposed in principle direct government involvement in sport. It was argued: 'If [the LTA] were to be subordinated to the changes incidental to politics', its position of leadership would be 'untenable'. However, it was generally agreed that: 'It would be to our advantage to devote more thought to the game at home and in the Dominions' (*LT&B* 15 February 1930:1242). This position was defended in 1933, when LTA Chairman Fred Lohden insisted overseas tours be continued, 'or else foreign players would not come to England'. Accordingly, Wimbledon, 'the pride and envy of the whole world', would suffer; 'attendances would fall, the receipts would drop, income would be seriously affected and the Council would find it impossible to carry out [their] far-reaching and ambitious programme' (*LT&B* 18 March 1933:1223).

In this sense, the LTA's attitude toward tennis as a diplomatic tool reflected broader political appreciation for sport in Britain (Polley 2006), but their stance is of particular interest given the historical context from whence it derived. Britain and much of the Western world were in the midst of the Great Depression, yet the LTA showed considerable concern – some might argue more concern – for its dominion relations and matters of international prestige. The Wall Street Crash on 24th October 1929 that signalled the end of free-flowing American capital and investment and sent global markets to a virtual standstill, hit British export industries hard, and unemployment almost doubled from one to two million by July 1930, before rising still further. Confidence in the economic markets was low and few areas of British cultural life were spared its effects. Huggins and Williams (2005) noted widespread loss of revenue and declining fortunes across horseracing, cricket, football and rowing, yet the Great Depression remains something of a misnomer in reference to British tennis.

The Championships continued to enjoy profits; for example, an impressive £18,408 was made in 1931, its toughest year that decade. The LTA might have considered seeking supplementary income for tournaments, but confidently continued to refuse commercial support, and paid travel and subsistence expenses for overseas tours. In 1931, nearly three million Britons were unemployed, huge dole queues were a regular scene along high streets and, following a run on sterling, a national coalition government was formed as an emergency measure to rekindle economic growth. Just weeks later, the LTA President, Lord D'Abernon, opened the Association's AGM with an apology of its favourable finances; it was said: 'he hardly liked recording such a cheery financial outlook in the face of the general gloom' (*LT&B* 19 December 1931:1003).

Outside of the LTA headquarters, unsurprisingly, the picture was not as rosy. Throughout 1932, numerous charitable appeals were published asking for used tennis balls and other equipment for children of the unemployed; those in the poorest circumstances would be given priority. Middle-class clubs were also forced to adapt and evolve to changing social and economic conditions or risk falling by the wayside. Some waived entry fees, reduced subscriptions or released groundsmen or coaches (Kay 2012). Very few avoided a fall in membership, and as a result of income lost, many resorted to converting grass courts to hard courts to extend their playing seasons. Most intensified their efforts to advertise for new members, particularly children, and extend social events and entertainment. Clubs like Oakleigh Park LTC in Barnet were rewarded for their resourcefulness; it responded assertively to the growing challenge of playing fields 'falling gradually into the hands of the builder' by amalgamating with another club and obtaining a flexible lease with sufficient land provisions to construct more courts and build a first-class pavilion (*Barnet Press* 5 April 1930). As an outcome of intensifying pressure on land use, due to marked suburban residential expansion and rising government taxation, which meant for some clubs a three-fold increase in expenditures since before the war, many counties witnessed a trend toward fewer but larger clubs. The *Barnet Press* (5 April 1930) reported:

> It is no longer possible to rent a field at a moderate rate, or to move at will to another across the way. A club is now fortunate if it can secure a permanent home at a cost which it is able to pay.

As a consequence of heightened financial concerns, the emphasis on club tournaments shifted from largely social enterprises to key revenue-generating ventures. In the ensuing competition to attract the best players and the highest gates, many ceased operating, as *LT&B* (11 September 1937:585) reported:

> One hears more and more of tournaments ... on the brink of extinction. The sufferers appear to be the smaller country tournaments, where one or two lean financial years can be ill afforded, for no protests have so far come from our larger tournaments.

The number of LTA-sanctioned tournaments fell from 184 in 1930 to 167 in 1932, and there was also a 17.5 per cent fall in tournament entries over the same period (*LT&B* 24 December 1932:953). To help struggling clubs, the LTA reduced tournament fees, as it was agreed:

> In these difficult times, when it is desirable to get people to spend their holidays in this country, we do not wish to put any obstacle in the way of anyone who wants to do anything helpful connected with the game.
> (*LT&B* 19 December 1931:1015)

Their offers of meagre financial assistance did little to halt the downward trend, however. As the 1939 season commenced, the number of scheduled LTA-sanctioned tournaments had fallen to 151.

Despite the LTA's communicated rhetoric about clubs and tournaments being a key priority, evidence from 1937 illustrated falling numbers and entries but an increase in investment in elite-level players on international tour duty. Their efforts reflected increased interest in elite-level tennis, arguably at the expense of recreational-level concerns.

From being considered throughout the 1920s and early 30s as a staunch advocate of amateurism, from the mid-30s onwards, the LTA demonstrated efforts to loosen the amateur definition and accept some mild forms of professionalism. A chief cause of this U-turn, undoubtedly, was the improving fortunes of

Britain's top players and subsequent fears they might desert the amateur ranks to pursue professional careers. The LTA were known to condemn amateur rule breaches from overseas players, yet when problems arose in Britain, they lobbied for certain rule relaxations to protect their own players. Undoubtedly, the coming of Perry, Austin and Round to global prominence represented an important milestone. Perry's rise in particular not only challenged inveterate class structures and boosted the confidence of British amateur authorities, but also kick-started the professionalisation of British tennis.

The signals were already there in 1931 when Britain reached the Davis Cup Challenge Round, losing narrowly to the indomitable Four Musketeers in Paris. Two years later, they would finally accomplish this elusive goal. Perry's comeback four-set victory against the stand-in André Merlin that clinched the 3–2 win sparked widespread euphoria. It was reported that 5,000 people met the team upon their return to Victoria station. Fundamentally, their success helped to validate national training methods, given criticisms made beforehand of Britain's decadence, incompetence to lead and flawed national character (*LT&B* 12 August 1933:483). Thus, the winning Austin–Perry combination of 1933 was retribution personified, and also justified the controversial and costly world tour in 1928 that Austin took part in.

For Dan Maskell, it must have been a particularly sweet moment. He was recruited as the squad's private coach, the first ever professional to travel abroad with a touring team. The venture challenged deep-rooted traditions of anti-professionalism, and paid off spectacularly. Still, the LTA could not allow Maskell to enjoy the full complement of plaudits enjoyed by the rest of the team. He described in his autobiography his and the players' collective embarrassment at him being put up at a different and, naturally, inferior hotel in Paris; this inconvenience was surely something the LTA saw fit to arrange in order that Maskell did not "forget himself". Although invited to the formal celebration dinner afterwards, he was not allowed to pose in official team photographs alongside the players and non-playing captain (Maskell 1988).

Numerous international telegrams were received to congratulate the British team, many of which were published in *LT&B*. The defeated French were perhaps surprisingly generous: 'If France were to lose the Cup, there was no one to whom they would rather lose than to their friends the English' (12 August 1933:485). Wartime alliances were recalled in a similarly sentimental message made earlier:

> The friendly feeling between the two nations had been enhanced by these encounters on the lawn tennis court, that they were good allies in sport as they had been in the Great War, and Lord Tyrell [British ambassador to France] expressed the hope that every English man or woman present would assist the "Entente Cordiale" by conveying that message to their friends at home.
>
> (5 August 1933:447)

Dwight Davis messaged the team: 'Every lover of sport will give the British full credit for their splendid triumph. ... It is a splendid thing for the game and a tribute to the proverbial British sportsmanship' (5 August 1933:442). It was a truly sweet celebration for the British, but for their superstar, even greater things were to come.

Fred Perry overcame the upright Australian Jack Crawford five weeks later to win his first major singles title, the US Nationals. The following summer, he beat Crawford again, this time in a one-sided straight-sets victory to claim his first of three straight Wimbledon singles victories. For Perry it was the culmination of years of fearsome dedication and perseverance. He worked diligently to reach an unmatchable level of physical fitness and perfect his unique method of striking the ball early. The former became Perry's key weapon, couched in the belief that he could outlast most players in the fifth set. E.J. Simpson of the *Manchester Guardian* called him 'immune to fatigue'. Perry was also a pioneer in pre-match preparations; he scouted opponents and studied their games in order to exploit weaknesses. In forcing opponents to match his efforts, he pulled the entire men's game up with him, which was probably Perry's most notable impact on tennis.

His Wimbledon singles victory was the first by a British male since 1909, but reactions from the class-conscious establishment were lukewarm at best, and openly hostile at worst. Jefferys (2009a:2) surmised 'there was little instinctive rapport between Perry and his audience'; in their eyes, his uncompromising ambition, dedicated training regime and playing style that gave primacy to fitness above elegance perhaps marked him as lacking true gentlemanly qualities. His was not the "right" way to win a tennis match, as Perry (1984:78) expressed himself:

> The Wimbledon crowds ... had never seen an Englishman of this era who didn't like to lose. ... You have to try to impose your superiority on him as forcefully as you can. Give him a beating to remember. Well, I don't think this was an approach generally favoured in England at the time.

The deep-rooted snobbery revealed itself in Perry's famous anecdote of when he received his AELTC tie just minutes after winning.

> Out in the dressing room, I overheard the distinctive voice of Brame Hillyard, Club committee man, talking to Crawford. 'Congratulations', said Hillyard. 'This was one day when the best man didn't win'. I couldn't believe my ears. ... Hillyard had brought a bottle of champagne into the dressing room and given it to Jack. ... There, draped over the back of my seat, was the official acknowledgement of my championship, an honorary All England Club member's tie. ... Instead of Fred J. Perry the champ, I felt like Fred J. Mugs the chimp.
>
> (Perry 1984:10–11)

Crawford, the "best man" who lost, was a refined sportsman who played with effortlessness, 'elegance and ease without crushing power anywhere. There was an atmosphere of majesty and magnificence in his approach' (Brady 1959:92). He exuded more obviously than Perry the old-fashioned "gentleman-amateur" ethos; he 'brought back to Wimbledon the aura of wholesome Victorian days', argued Clerici (1975:181). Tinling (1983:167) recalled that Crawford was 'the most modest and unassuming champion', while Baltzell (1995:266) considered his 'stylish tennis form and courtly manners ... classic examples of old-school majesty and grace'. More than this, in his movements and posture, he presented aesthetically an alternative masculinity. It was said of the popular Australian:

> We look upon him as more or less our own. ... He is a constant source of pleasure to watch with his fine range of strokes and artistic touch. ... His game ... does not depend on mere force and speed; but rather on the gradual manoeuvring of the opponent out of position by placement and strategy. It is thoughtful lawn tennis.
> (*LT&B* 2 July 1932:278)

The celebration of Crawford's playing style latently reinforced the upper-class "gentlemanly" values of behavioural self-restraint, emotional control and tactical foresight; these same qualities that were consistently admired in earlier players, alongside modesty and sportsmanship. Perry *did* demonstrate modesty and sportsmanship in his 1934 Wimbledon post-match speech when he suspected defeat to Crawford the following year, but hoped to 'lose in the same charming manner as Jack did' (*Daily Mail* 9 July 1934). Perhaps some doubted his sincerity. Jack Kramer (1979:59) described Perry in his autobiography as 'an opportunist, a selfish and egotistical person' who used to infuriate opponents by crying out "Very clevah" if they played an unreturnable shot against him, and later castigated him for "tanking" matches when touring as a professional. Tinling (1983:193) also described his ruthless tactics of gamesmanship:

> He was a master on one-upmanship. ... He had a sharp tongue and took every opportunity to make cutting comments, sometimes to the point of being extremely personal. ... He was never averse to using a caustic one-liner to distract an opponent.

For the British establishment, Perry was considered to lack the qualities and virtues befitting a gentleman and the necessary cultural capital that came easier to men born into affluence, like Crawford.

Samuel Perry, the father of Stockport-born Fred, began as a cotton-spinner, but involvement in trade unionism and left-wing politics led him to become a Labour MP for Kettering, back in the time when, according to Fred, 'labour was a dirty word' (Perry 1984:25). He moved the family to Brentham near Ealing, where Fred played local tournaments and developed his talents at the Herga and Chiswick Park clubs. He was financially supported by Samuel and his own part-time work at a sporting-goods store, until the LTA selected him to tour America. When representing the LTA and Britain abroad, Perry was warned to appear and behave immaculately or risk being sent home, and, surrounded by ex-public schoolboys, he remarked feeling like an outcast and loner. Despite his family background, however, it would be wrong to exaggerate Perry's poverty-stricken "working-class" roots; Perry was bred into an upwardly mobile working-class family, or what Bédarida (1979) termed the "labour aristocracy". Due to his father's success as a union president and later MP, the Perrys enjoyed some affluence and likely aspired to a modest but comfortable lifestyle. Indeed, Perry attended Wallasey Grammar School in the Wirral and then Ealing County School upon his relocation to the leafy west-London suburb at age nine. This allowed him to live in relative ostensibly "middle-class" comfort, far removed from the working-class poverty experienced by his father. Nevertheless, it was clear that Perry was awestruck by much in the lawn tennis world. Touring America, his team travelled first-class, stayed in top hotels and were wined and dined by "society" folk. Class differences were not lost on him; Perry (1984:43) recalled: 'After the snobbery and class divisions of the tennis set-up, and life generally, in England, America in 1931 was like a breath of fresh air'. Over the following years, the alluring tennis stardom tasted in the States only further fuelled his inner drive to excel. Now fully funded by the LTA on overseas tours for major competitions, and offered "personal terms" by tournament committees of many others, Perry was able to devote himself to full-time training.

Despite Perry being encouraged by his own association, the principle of full-time training was not widely accepted among international tennis administrators. The Davis Cup, in particular, had been subject to numerous criticisms related to the insatiable demands it placed upon players. H.J. Crocker, President of the South African Lawn Tennis Union, considered it:

> one of the principal causes of unrest in the tennis world, entailing as it does a strain upon amateur players and a threat to their vocational careers which exposes them to risks and stresses and to temptations of an insidious nature.
>
> (*LT&B* 20 April 1935:1309)

Given the event's growing cultural and political significance, however, not to mention the substantial economic gains made from competing in later stages, all administrative efforts in the mid to late 1930s to curtail the event's development for the sake of amateur ideals were half-hearted. Leading administrators openly admitted that some players lived from tournament expenses alone or were unable to secure employment due to heavy playing schedules, yet collectively they failed to appreciate their role in this broader development or acknowledge a need for change.

A. Wallis Myers, now in his late fifties, recognised the issue as simple greediness among players, and suggested that tennis success could be achieved without full-time training. He cited H.L. Doherty, A.W. Gore and H. Roper Barrett as examples of ex-champions who 'found it possible to mix business in the City with championship honours' (*LT&B* 27 April 1935:1330). He was correct, naturally, but all were examples from the pre-war period, when overall pressures to train and succeed were weaker, because of the sport being less commercialised and politicised and the rewards less significant. Thus, Myers' argument seemed both outdated and untenable. Indeed, Perry claimed top players of his generation simply could not sustain the lifestyles of pre-war amateurs. To be a world beater, you needed 'almost unlimited time for the game' (*LT&B* 27 April 1935:1330). Even Austin, a Repton public schoolboy and Cambridge graduate from affluent means, agreed; a 'would-be champion' should be prepared to 'devote all his energies to the game' or at least 'to give up everything which may in any way impair his ability as a player, and to do everything which may increase that ability' (*LT&B* 6 June 1936:166). It was apparent the "sport" played by the elite-level players now differed markedly from the "game" played by its administrators from the previous generation.

In an early autobiography, Perry (1934:148) sympathised with players who considered exploiting their own talents: 'Is it any wonder that when the chance comes to join the "Tilden troupe" some of them take it? ... Can they really be blamed for turning their tennis into cash *now* while youth remains?' Such comments provoked fear among some administrators that Perry, the top-ranked British player and tournament "cash cow", was wavering as an amateur. For the LTA, their goal now was to retain him, notwithstanding the burgeoning professional tours which, according to LTA President Sir Samuel Hoare,

> would not only become a very formidable danger to every Association, but would strike at the very root of lawn tennis as a game and a sport. ... If nothing were done and a number of the best players drifted into the ranks of this kind of professional, the result would be the very opposite of that which everyone wished to achieve, namely, it would weaken and not strengthen the amateur game.
>
> (*LT&B* 2 February 1935:1025)

Up against the widespread cultural changes that helped make professional tennis a more lucrative and sustainable career choice, administrators' positions were tenuous. Tennis players of Perry's calibre were pulled in opposing directions, but without a full appreciation of key difficulties that beset them, the LTA were bound to make unsound policy decisions.

In 1933, the LTA had vehemently opposed an ILTF resolution to allow amateur players to profit from film-making, the result of which almost cost the popular Frenchman Henri Cochet his amateur status. Two years later, Perry began entertaining offers from the likes of Paramount Pictures, and some on the LTA Council saw fit to assist him in this regard, by supporting a new proposal made by the Czechoslovakian Association that called for part of ILTF's Rule 23, which banned amateurs from making money through tennis films, to be deleted. They noted the recent relaxation of rules for amateurs who worked for manufacturers and wrote educational books and articles, and considered that film-making warranted the same treatment. G.F. Goodman, LTA Chairman, remarked:

> [A] player may have definite ability for film work, and it would be unreasonable for us to try to prevent him using that ability in earning his living. ... It does not seem quite fair that a player should give his time to lawn tennis and then be deprived of the opportunity of earning money in quite a legitimate way.
>
> (*LT&B* 26 January 1935:1013)

The verbalisation of such liberal thinking from the Association premier's mouth seemed incongruous with the LTA's previously tough and conservative anti-commercial/anti-professional stance, yet this urge for change was shared among his colleagues, who voted with an overwhelming 57–4 majority to support the Czech proposal. It is suggested that Perry's recent disagreements with the ILTF over his own film-making endeavours prompted this response. Thus, it appears the LTA's principles were discarded as quickly as the lure of money, prestige and glory from Perry's successes became appreciated. The USLTA, less emotionally involved, declined to support the Czech resolution, which they considered would

> insert the thin end of the wedge and break down fundamental standards which have prevailed for years. ... We cannot agree that the way to preserve the amateur game is to open the door to professionalism, as has been suggested.
>
> (*LT&B* 16 February 1935:1070)

They were proved right.

Perry, meanwhile, continued as an amateur out of his own personal sense of loyalty to the LTA and British tennis, but he continued to draw attractive offers from businesses like Simpson of Piccadilly. Jefferys (2009a:14) explained: 'He held back in the hope that the LTA might come up with a scheme allowing him to make a decent living while remaining in amateur ranks', but by the end of 1936, Perry had lost respect for the LTA's President, who he was convinced had tried to 'thwart' rather than 'help' him during this trying time. Hoare, an upper-class statesman and politician of international repute, was likely less swayed by Perry's desires to commercially exploit himself than some of his more progressive LTA associates, and also probably considered his duties with British tennis of lesser consequence than preventing war against Mussolini's Italy, as his role as British Foreign Secretary in 1935 demanded.[1] Unsurprisingly, after his third and final US Nationals victory, Perry sold himself to the highest bidder and was gone from amateur lawn tennis. America was his target.

Perry's decision to turn professional was covered with great interest by all the major tennis publications, particularly those in Australia, America and Britain. Some correspondents paid tribute to his incredible triumphs and to what he achieved both in and for the sport. Dan Maskell (1988:179) remarked: 'He had served his country magnificently. ... The time had come for him to capitalize on all the hard work and dedication that had made him the greatest champion of his generation.' Others considered his move a great loss, with accounts of his legendary training methods and playing style often written in the past tense as though memories of a dead player. Phrases like "Perry's passing" were interspersed with others that used words like "abandoned" or "deserted". *The Times* (10 November 1936) asked what player 'would forego the opportunity of making a fortune ... if he had Perry's ability to earn it?'. Pierre Gillou of the FFT was equally unsurprised by Perry's departure, and asked:

> Are we to regard this as a disaster for British amateur lawn tennis? Certainly not ... Nobody need be afraid that the Wimbledon tournament will suffer at all from the absence of the great champion. ... Spectators will continue to hurl themselves in serried ranks at the turnstiles.

He went on to predict Davis Cup defeat the following year but reasoned that it 'will not be accompanied by sad regrets. There will be no tears' (*LT&B* 9 January 1937:996). He was proved correct on both counts; not only did Wimbledon entries remain buoyant in the last three tournaments before the war, but the Americans led by Don Budge recaptured the Davis Cup in the 1937 Challenge Round, with what amounted to little public surprise.

Perry's professional debut was well documented. Professional tours had developed a good reputation as entertaining and of a high standard, but the timing of Perry's arrival after the slump of 1936 proved crucial to sustain public interest (Bowers 2004b). The arrangement was to tour North America in a four-month, head-to-head contest against Ellsworth Vines, with Tilden joining them in the bigger venues, and Americans George Lott and Bruce Barnes making up the sideshow events. *LT&B* noted the opening crowd of 17,630 at Madison Square Gardens and immediate gate receipts of over £11,000, but used Perry's early dominance to denounce claims of professional superiority:

> Amateur lawn tennis, supplying as it does greater variety and experience of opposition in all kinds of conditions, is more conducive to the highest

class of play than in the professional exhibition field where opposition of the best class is numerically limited.

(*LT&B* 16 January 1937:1019)

By the tour's end, Vines had secured a 32–29 match lead, and the pair decided to embark on a tour of Europe that summer, with Tilden as manager. Aside from successful exhibitions at Wembley and a handful of other select venues, however, the troupe was met with firm opposition from associations, including the LTA, which forbade them from staging professional matches on the courts of affiliated clubs. Perry (1984:117–18) recalled: 'There was an unavoidable feeling that although we were playing the game we loved, we couldn't appear in the places we would have loved to play. In European tennis "pro" was still a dirty word'. In Britain, the troupe was forced to erect courts at football stadiums in Liverpool, Bristol and Lincoln, and play in gymnasiums and town halls.

The typical format for tours involved recruiting the latest Wimbledon or US Nationals champion, who matched up against the previous winner, with the newest recruit making the lion's share of the profit in the first tour. For the Perry–Vines North American tour, for example, Perry grossed $91,000 and Vines $34,000 (Bowers 2004b). After Budge won both major championships in 1937, many expected him to turn pro, but like Perry he was torn by the prospect of letting his nation down. Budge was warned by his compatriot Bill Johnston, however, that a delay in signing could have devastating consequences; for "Little Bill", in fact, it proved fatal. Johnston told him:

> I was offered thirty-to-forty thousand to sign a few years ago, and I thought I would … then a lot of people started telling me not to. They gave me that line about … the country needed me to play for the Davis Cup. … Well, you know what happened. A year or so later, I came down with Tuberculosis. I needed money then, but I couldn't get my hands on it. All those friends who had urged me to stay amateur for the sake of Uncle Sam turned their backs on me as soon as I needed them. Take the money Don. The pats on the back don't last very long at all.
>
> (Budge 1969:129)

Just days after winning the US Open again the following autumn, Budge signed. Over time, players seemed less willing to risk forgoing the increasingly lucrative financial opportunities of professional tennis.

National associations were also forced to deal with rumours of "shamateurism" among star players. Early in 1934, the ILTF passed a rule that allowed players to claim legitimately up to eight weeks of expenses from their national associations but, with an overwhelming majority vote, the LTA opposed its adoption. At that time, Britain was the top-ranked nation and there was no sign of their best players turning professional, but by

1937, other leading nations, most notably France and America, had already adopted it. British Davis Cup doubles specialist G.P. Hughes fumed at the obvious disadvantage that British players faced because of the LTA's refusal to provide equal support. Why did the LTA consider a rule passed officially by the ILTF and accepted by most other nations as 'contrary to amateurism', yet accepted and profited from the participation of financially supported foreigners at Wimbledon each summer? These were players who, if British, would be deemed professional and forbidden to enter (*LT&B* 4 December 1937:868).

Instead of adopting the eight-weeks rule, the LTA charged tournaments with furnishing receipts and expenditures as a deterrent to secret payments being made. This was despite it being pointed out that tournaments were under no legal obligation to provide reliable data. H.H. Monckton feared that any decision appearing to make it more difficult for any but the 'gilded youth and the idle rich' to play would be considered 'class legislation' (*LT&B* 8 January 1938:979). In part, he was right. A regular *LT&B* columnist remarked:

> Lawn tennis is no longer a preserve for the well-to-do, and ... the present rules do tend to prevent the adequate exploitation of some of our best potential playing material. It is futile to prate of the "good old days" when a champion did his job in the morning and won at Wimbledon in the afternoon.
>
> (*LT&B* 26 November 1938:716)

Supporting this view were the leading amateurs, realistic and logical in their advances toward a more equitable, fair and just system of support, recognition and reward. Their main objectives were to survive financially and remain competitive internationally, but Hughes was vociferous in condemning apparent inequalities in LTA legislation, criticising them for being out-of-touch and short-sighted in their policy-making:

> The present position is obviously unsatisfactory. Rules have remained the same whilst conditions have changed. Ideas at headquarters have not moved with the times, and the small "Inner Cabinet" of the LTA continues to rule with its ultra conservative and old fashioned methods. ... It is no good trying to bluff the world that amateurism is any purer in this country than anywhere else, because it is not so. Those on the Council who think otherwise are living in a fool's paradise.
>
> (*LT&B* 3 December 1938:737)

The AELTC representative on the LTA Council, Ted Avory, also waded in, claiming the LTA was 'more to blame for the present deplorable condition of amateur lawn tennis in England than the "shamateur"' (*LT&B* 3 December 1938:738).

Amidst heated debate, the 1938 AGM failed to produce the necessary two-thirds majority to pass the eight-weeks rule. While some considered it a necessary evil to prevent further amateur rule breaches that undermined LTA authority, others wondered whether the ruling could guarantee players stopped claiming at eight weeks. The Council's failure to agree allowed present rule breaches to continue unchecked and ensured foreigners at Wimbledon enjoyed positive discrimination at Britain's expense. Harold Lee, late advisor on the LTA Selection Committee, fumed:

> Is it necessary or ethically right for our LTA to make substantial grants for expenses to Associations of other countries, in order to persuade players not regarded by our LTA as amateurs to come to Wimbledon to produce bigger and better Wimbledons, and all the while for members of the LTA to refer to England as the last stronghold of amateurism?
> (*LT&B* 14 January 1939:863)

The LTA's spineless leadership on issues related to amateurism, professionalism and commercialism came at its own expense, as both Avory and Lee resigned their positions as a consequence of recent events; the latter argued his Association had displayed 'a most regrettable lack of knowledge, understanding and imagination' (*LT&B* 14 January 1939:863). The LTA certainly demonstrated a lack of poise, which was a far cry from when it emerged cautiously yet confidently after the war with its moral integrity, political clout and social prestige intact. Instead of pursuing consistency, they forged ineffective middle-ground policies; they enforced some amateur rules but not others and made examples out of some players but not all. As a sad consequence, they presided over an intensely hypocritical administrative system and came to appear ostrich-like, feeble and fickle. Only the onset of war helped divert attention away from their failings.

Britain in the lead-up to WWII was a shaken but resolute nation. The death of King George V, the hasty abdication of his eldest son and the surprising resignations of Prime Ministers Baldwin and Chamberlain were cause for concern, but in matters of warfare, Britain was in its element, confident and poised. Hitler's Germany had responded to the global recession by adopting staunch right-wing politics, in the course of which they blamed Jewish greed. Anti-Semitism even crept into German tennis administration, as evidenced by the defamation of their leading Jewish player, Daniel Prenn, for apparent charges of professionalism, and the failed attempts to manipulate blond-haired, blue-eyed Baron Gottfried von Cramm as a propaganda tool (Jensen 2010). These hints of Nazi ruthlessness confirmed, for any initial doubters, the extent to which sport was now subject to political manipulation.

Tennis administration remained bound by ILTF rules, which limited national autonomy to enforce regulations specifically to deal with their own socio-cultural and economic conditions. Greater flexibility might have been desirable, but after America joined in 1924 there is little evidence to suggest that any of the leading nations considered leaving the Federation to forge their own path. This illustrates the extent that ILTF authority was secure, even if at times the cumbersome bureaucracy was considered an impediment to progress. Only in the late 1960s would their authority be challenged by renewed British desires for sovereignty on the "open tennis" issue.

It is undoubted that the six-year hiatus of war slowed the professionalisation process in tennis. By the late 1930s, the leading players had formed themselves into a coherent professional troupe, touring in North America and Europe, galvanising public support and drawing spectator revenue and players from the amateur game. The growing incidents of "shamateur" corruption from officials and players had become a source of widespread embarrassment, but it seemed an increasing number of amateur officials wanted to accrue greater control over professional tours instead of shunning them altogether. Communication channels between amateurs and professionals were at times testy but still nevertheless open, but by the 1950s the entire professional tennis structure had become far more threatening. Had amateur administrators managed to gain some say in its organisation, not only might amateur–professional relations have been characterised less by mutual distrust and bitterness, but open tennis might consequently have arrived earlier than 1968. As it was, the interruption of war afforded sporting traditionalists an ideal opportunity to demand a return to glorified ideals, which, after the prolonged gloom of war, must have seemed only too attractive to those desperate for peace and a return to normality.

Note

1. Jefferys (2009a) reported that Hoare's personal account of his 1930s public life, *Nine Troubled Years*, makes no reference to his spell as LTA President.

Bibliography

Baltzell, E. D. (1995). *Sporting Gentlemen: Men's Tennis from the Age of Honor to the Cult of the Superstar*. New York: Free Press.
Bédarida, F. (1979). *A Social History of England 1851–1975*. London: Methuen.
Bowers, R. (2004b, 3 December). *History of the Pro Tennis Wars, Chapter VIII: Perry and Vines, 1937*. Retrieved April 11, 2014, from Between the Lines: An Analytical and Sometimes Controversial Look at the Pro Tennis Tour: http://www.tennisserver.com/lines/lines_04_12_03.html
Brady, M. (1959). *The Centre Court Story*. London: Sportsman's Book Club.
Budge, D. (1969). *A Tennis Memoire*. New York: Viking Press.
Clerici, G. (1975). *The Ultimate Tennis Book: 500 Years of the Sport*. Chicago, IL: Follett Publishing Company.
Huggins, J., and Williams, J. (2005). *Sport and the English: 1918–1939*. London: Routledge.
Jefferys, K. (2009a). Fred Perry and British Tennis: 'Fifty Years to Honor a Winner'. *Sport in History*, 29(1), 1–24.

Jensen, E. N. (2010). *Body by Weimar*. Oxford: Oxford University Press.
Kay, J. (2012). Grass Roots: The Development of Tennis in Britain, 1918–1978. *International Journal of the History of Sport*, 29(18), 2532–2550.
Kramer, J. (1979). *The Game: My 40 Years in Tennis*. London: Andre Deutsch.
Maskell, D. (1988). *From Where I Sit*. London: Willow.
Moore, K. (1989). 'The Warmth of Comradeship': The First British Empire Games and Imperial Solidarity. *International Journal of the History of Sport*, 6(2), 242–251.
Perry, F. (1934). *My Story*. London: Hutchison.
Perry, F. (1984). *Fred Perry: An Autobiography*. London: Arrow Books.
Polley, M. (2006). The Amateur Ideal and British Sports Diplomacy, 1900–1945. *Sport in History*, 26(3), 450–467.
Tinling, T. (1983). *Tinling: Sixty Years in Tennis*. London: Sidgwick & Jackson.

12 'We must face the hard facts that confront us'

Early post-war recovery efforts in British tennis

Within weeks of VE Day in May 1945, Churchill's Tories were displaced by a new Labour government in a landslide victory. It signalled for some an opportunity to create a new more equitable and ultimately prosperous Britain. The post-war era represented a period of considerable social, political and economic fluctuations. It began as an age of compromise rather than conflict, as emotional and physical wounds from the war were devastating reminders of the human potential for self-destruction. The high-minded policies that followed were based largely on broad socialist principles outlined in the Beveridge Report, and were invested with a collective egalitarian spirit of social unity. Over the following six years, Clement Attlee's government introduced the most wide-ranging and comprehensive social reforms ever seen, inspired by the perceived political, economic and cultural necessity for "nationalisation" and the creation of the "welfare state" (Bédarida 1979).

The increase in industrial output and rising employment levels during the war convinced even those on the political right of the merit in coordinated central planning, and there was a push for state-funded and publicly owned and regulated services and industries, ranging from iron and steel to the Bank of England (Kynaston 2007). Solutions to the increasingly visible problem of poverty among Britain's poorest included the creation of a free National Health Service; a comprehensive National Insurance scheme as a safety-net against sickness, unemployment and old age; a growing long-term commitment to state pensions; urban slum clearance and the erection of new council housing; and expanded access to non-fee-paying secondary education (Kynaston 2007). There emerged a general political consensus between the Labour and Conservative parties; thus, it could be put, rather crudely, that after the war, Britain in general moved somewhat to the political left. The legacy of such sweeping reforms remain today in some measure, particularly in the protectionist principles of state intervention that sharply contrasted with the laissez-faire and liberalism of the pre-WWI period (Bédarida 1979).

The same was true for tennis. As in WWI, many clubs offered their land for military use, while others recognised their roles simply as facilitators of recreational opportunities for convalescent soldiers or those on leave. Roehampton

LTC offered free memberships to as many as 600 American soldiers, and the AELTC extended invitations to the Australian Air Force and British and American Forces (Cleather 1947). Queen's Club also had an influx of overseas service members, alongside foreign ambassadors and others seeking refuge in Britain (McKelvie 1986). Other clubs sought simply to survive. The Cumberland Club discussed its difficulty finding balls, the decline in membership to a quarter of its pre-war level, and a lack of refreshments. Nevertheless, its "spirit" was celebrated; 'we carry on' they said (*LT&B* September–October 1944:19). Certainly, the rationing of petrol, clothes and basic food supplies played havoc with players wishing to return, but the real problem for clubs was a shortage in human capital, namely labourers to undertake renovations and repairs, groundsmen and dressing-room attendants (Barrett 1986). The shortage of coaches was mentioned repeatedly, and the LTA issued a public request for new recruits, but stipulated they must have 'athletic ability and some culture' (*LT&B* September–October 1944:23).

The eagerness to return was encouraging, as were the LTA's immediate efforts to rekindle its talent-development programmes. At this time, when more pressing political, economic and social concerns demanded attention, theoretically speaking, nothing could have been less important than playing tennis, but equally nothing could be more essential than playing sport to the millions of Britons desperate to recommence normal lives. Playing lawn tennis was valued, meaningful to people and thus socially significant principally because it offered a diversion from the stresses of rebuilding a war-torn country. The statistics in many ways speak for themselves. In 1946, with many clubs still unable to open, an impressive 49 open tournaments took place with a total of 5,250 entries. A year later, almost 2,000 clubs had affiliated themselves to the LTA. By 1950, the number of clubs including those formed in schools had eclipsed the number from 1938, reaching an all-time high. The demand for tennis was growing. The aims of this chapter are to answer the following questions: How did tennis recover from the war, and what new opportunities and challenges presented themselves? What role did tennis play for those who were recovering personally and collectively from the war? How did the LTA attempt to rekindle growth, stimulate talent development and enhance performance standards, and with what overall results?

Toward the end of war, many top players were given leave to play charity exhibitions. Bill Tilden claimed that he and Vincent Richards played 77 matches from May–September 1945, most at armed-forces bases (Bowers 2007b). Clubs also played their part. The AELTC hosted a match between the British Empire Forces and US Forces in June, just a few weeks after VE Day, which was attended by Queen Mary and the Duchess of Kent, as well as the American Forces Championships later that summer, which conveniently coincided with VJ Day celebrations (Macauley and Smyth 1965). Not surprisingly, most of these contests were won by the Americans, which hinted at their future dominance. The vast majority of amateur competitions across Europe and in the southern hemisphere had ceased during the war, yet the US Nationals continued to be played, though it could scarcely consider itself representative of the world's top talent.

The LTA commenced its campaign for post-war recovery with renewed promises of social reform, but couched with a hearty plea for patience. With depleted reserves and modest tournament income, it had little expendable funds to help clubs repair war-damaged facilities. It stressed, 'the rehabilitation of clubs must be the concern of the members themselves' (*LT&B* June 1945:100). Such efforts at "make do and mend" stretched also to the county associations, which were congratulated en masse at the 1947 LTA AGM for not asking the LTA for money and asked to continue these efforts until the LTA's reserves had replenished. Lincolnshire reported numerous clubs that had not survived the war, some that struggled through and others that actually grew. Nottinghamshire made sterling efforts to recommence its inter-club league in 1946, though Lincolnshire declined, given that so many of its young players had not played since before the war. Staffordshire noted that recommencing its inter-club league was crucial to stimulate greater club affiliation. Staffordshire also aimed to institute a coaching system for young players but on a grander and more efficient scale (*LT&B* 15 December 1945:363). It was evident that both clubs and their county associations considered the resurrection of regular play a key priority, though pre-war participation levels were not returned to until the late 1940s. The *LT&B* editor, L.H.J. Dorey, remarked with delight in 1949 that many of the largest tournaments had regained, and in some cases exceeded, their pre-war levels, like Eastbourne, Ilkley, Bournemouth, Bognor, the Priory Club and Tunbridge Wells (*LT&B* 15 December 1949:725). Much of this work was done by industrious committee members who worked independent of LTA financial assistance.

The LTA's relationship with the AELTC had proved costly during the war, given the bombing of Centre Court; repairs and renovations were funded from "LTA investments". Still, Wimbledon went from strength to strength, managing in its first post-war Championships to profit £25,000; still more than in 1939. Its ultimate economic success depended on sustaining the tournament's high-quality field, but given the club's small operating budget and unwillingness to explicitly commercialise the event, they had to rely on the LTA for subtle promotional assistance. New executive committee members were appointed and the Royal Navy were called upon to provide stewards (Barrett 1986). The Association's decision to advance the goal of restoring Wimbledon as its key priority proved crucial, though Hon. Treasurer Sir Clarence Sadd defended this decision on pseudo-political rather than economic grounds:

> It is essential that we should continue to compete in the Davis Cup, to send teams abroad and to enter our players in official championships, in

order to maintain the representative character of the entry at Wimbledon. That great meeting is the Mecca of lawn tennis and the admiration of the whole world, and we are bound in our own interest to reciprocate and so maintain that prestige and goodwill.

(*LT&B* 1 January 1948:10)

The LTA's continuing intervention paid dividends; the enthralling play of the leading American players helped rekindle interest. In 1949, the tournament made a surplus of over £35,000, which allowed the LTA to operate in the black for the first time in 13 years.

This mutually beneficial relationship between the AELTC and LTA lent the former considerable economic freedom, which they used in the following two decades to raise ticket prices and thus make spectator entry more exclusive. From 1946 to 1967, regular Centre Court tickets increased from 14s to £1 12s 6d; a whopping 132 per cent rise during a period when inflation fluctuated from just 1–10 per cent (December 1966–January 1967:23). Wimbledon profits also increased from an average of £30,000 to £50,000. The combined AELTC/LTA actions that facilitated these impressive figures somewhat contradicted their rhetoric about the desire for greater inclusivity. In his Presidential address at the 1955 LTA AGM, Viscount Templewood reflected on the last decade of British lawn tennis:

There had taken place so profound a revolution in our social life that the old conditions in which lawn tennis was played before the war had disappeared. Our problem, therefore, was … to adapt British tennis to the new conditions … to turn a game that had been mainly played by the leisured classes into a national game played by all classes … to increase the pool from which we can draw potential winners in the future.

(*LT&B* 15 December 1955:605–6)

It certainly warrants questioning whether AELTC/LTA actions were geared entirely toward this goal or whether the restoration of Wimbledon by whatever means necessary came at its ultimate expense. Though they were justified economically in their decision to support the Championships and to promote and fund tours under the veil of international diplomacy, these decisions did not necessarily sit well with the county associations and clubs, which considered their own survival of greater consequence than the status of Britain's premier tournament or the fortunes of top British players abroad. Still, this agenda was pushed ahead of reinstating coaching grants and other financial assistance for county associations, which had to wait until 1949 for LTA funding. If nothing else, it smacked of overbearing leadership and signalled a growing divide in priorities between the LTA and its affiliated clubs and associations. By the mid-50s, the budgetary imbalance still remained. In 1956, for example, the LTA spent £540 on 'coaching of affiliated organisations' and a further £800 on the 'training of juniors', but this paled in comparison to the massive £4,000 spent on international matches, which included a world tour for their elite players (*LT&B* 1 January 1957:13). It was certainly a costly enterprise to enhance British prestige in these ways, but Wimbledon was at stake: the LTA's cash cow and financial crutch that consistently provided over 80 per cent of its annual income.

How smaller clubs and tournaments fared was another matter. Rising overhead costs and government taxation, particularly through the Ratings and Valuations Act, pushed many into very precarious positions. In her analysis of post-war clubs, Kay (2013) noted the problems of increased costs associated with grass-court maintenance, repairs and restorations and compulsory purchase orders. To survive financially, most clubs were forced to hold fund-raising events and install a bar, while others merged together to split costs (Kay 2013). For clubs without such opportunities, two or three lean years often spelled disaster, but in 1953 the "Tournament Mutual Assistance Fund" was created by leading administrators from the largest and wealthiest clubs. A small subscription ensured some insurance against a particularly bad year. The scheme was a true example of post-war class solidarity and philanthropy, moulded in the charitable spirit of social welfare. The LTA played no part in it, though reported at its 1954 AGM: 'The purpose of the fund continued to justify itself ... with many tournament finals delayed or abandoned owing to the weather' (*LT&B* 1 March 1955:92).

The LTA offered low-interest loans to clubs desirous of undertaking redevelopment projects, like resurfacing courts or erecting a new clubhouse. Floodlighting became an increasingly popular alternative to covered courts, and even received wholehearted support from the London Electricity Board, which agreed to offer reduced-priced tariffs (*LT&B* 15 December 1954:668). Cottingham Club, for example, reportedly lit two courts for £350 and welcomed 35 new members in the first two months. Thus, the LTA were prompted to make floodlighting projects a funding priority, and loans at 3 per cent interest were offered for up to half of the entire cost (*LT&B* 15 March 1961:117). It is noteworthy that such funds tended to be reserved for clubs in strong positions, where investment most likely would lead to some ostensible return, i.e. those looking to expand and develop rather than those simply trying to stay afloat. By 1956, which was a full half-decade after the LTA began offering these loans, only 96 of their 3,755 clubs – just over 2.5 per cent – had actually received an LTA loan, and for what amounted to a tiny average of just over £400 per club (*LT&B* 1 January 1957:13). Undoubtedly, the LTA would have contributed more, were it not for their divergent funding priorities.

In what appears a token gesture of goodwill toward clubs, but also a clever way of increasing affiliation, the AELTC and LTA jointly agreed to offer clubs small allocations of Wimbledon Centre Court tickets. The issue was first raised at the 1947 LTA AGM, when Colonel G. Warden of Sundridge Park LTC proposed that club members be given priority over the general public for tickets. 'To witness tennis of the highest standard, and thus gain knowledge as well as entertainment', he argued, was a suitable 'reward' for those loyal to the sport. He asked why club members, who contributed to the 'hard-pressed finances' of their clubs and 'whose keenness and subscriptions' made the LTA's continuance possible,

> should [not] be granted a privilege over the general public, who were not members of clubs, did not play tennis and had no interest in the game, except the desire to take part in the social event of Wimbledon … [and] who make no contribution to the welfare of the game.
> (*LT&B* 1 January 1948:23)

Cynically speaking, the LTA's decision to support this idea might have derived less from a sense of duty and more from the good business sense to promote one's product to its chief target market. Possibly as a consequence, LTA affiliation rates improved. They peaked in 1959 at 3,788, but then fell year on year throughout the 1960s and 70s, which Kay (2013) posited was partly because of diversifying middle-class leisure pursuits.

Tournament entries peaked in 1950 at 14,309 amidst changing conditions. In 1938 there were twice the number of tournaments but only 3,000 more entries, which suggests that tournaments were getting larger but fewer numerically (*LT&B* 15 December 1950:715). This suspicion was confirmed statistically when 99 tournaments were staged in 1953, 11 more than in 1950, but had almost 2,000 *fewer* entries. In his summary of the shifting fortunes of post-war tournaments, columnist Lance Tingay remarked: 'Many happy meetings exist no more and from year to year the tournament list tends to become shorter rather than otherwise'; it was Tingay's assessment that those tournaments in between the 'big' and 'small' were struggling most (*LT&B* 1 March 1959:89).

Small tournaments tended to survive because they catered exclusively to local players who were loyal and had no realistic ambitions of competing in the bigger arenas; they offered small prizes, paid no expenses, and were supported enthusiastically by local residents and club members. The chief issue with these tournaments was timetabling; the earliest rounds were played during the week when the majority of players were at work. In itself, this problem illuminates the shifting class composition of players alongside changing middle-class working conditions more generally. Former referee-turned-columnist A.K. Trower surmised:

> Fifty years ago the competitors, with very few exceptions, either did no work or were on holiday. Today? The proportion of the entry that can give – and enjoy giving – full-time attendance has shrunk to nothing. Of a normal big-town tournament more than half the entry require to have their times fitted in; most of the men and many of the women work in offices and can play 'only after 5:30'.
> (*LT&B* 1 December 1947:1237)

Late-comers and their requests to play evening matches subsequently became the bane of many tournament organisers, but to compromise, some clubs experimented with separate competitions. After the Cumberland Club recorded a dismal tournament in 1948, with numerous unfinished matches, it decided the following year to introduce two tiers, selecting the best 16 players for the major event and leaving everyone else to compete for the lesser honours. The result was recorded as 'an immediate success, bringing larger attendance and better publicity' (*LT&B* 1 March 1954:113). Other clubs took a different approach, and acted on their temptations to seek out more "full-time" players who were more readily available. Despite promising higher standards, their performance or even their ability to draw spectators could not be relied upon. Typically, "expenses" were paid for appearances, regardless of performances, so such ventures carried a significant risk if a star player was eliminated early in the tournament. Organisers must have looked upon the larger, high-profit-grossing tournaments with envy, but they were likely ignorant of the unique pressures the organising committees faced.

The big tournaments were embroiled in an often cut-throat competition to recruit players. They also had to be more inventive with marketing to spectators, likely weighing the merits of offering creative ticket packages, enhancing bar or catering takings and even simply raising ticket prices against the likelihood of higher gates. Overall, this had the consequence of many clubs attempting to provide facilities and pay expenses to players they could not afford. Naively, the LTA recommended: 'Cooperation and mutual agreement are essential, otherwise the spiral of expenses will lead to a deficit everywhere' (*LT&B* 1 March 1955:87). The logic was theoretically sound, but practically it was difficult to envisage a level of mutual trust and reciprocity between all tournament committees that would prevent some clubs offering "improved" expenses to attract better players. Put simply, tournaments could not afford to let their positions slip or their profits fall through an ill-advised attempt to be cooperative. In 1960, a meeting with tournament committee representatives took place where it was agreed in theory that such off-court competition between tournaments was harmful, but nothing was ever done to halt the process and the LTA was unable to effectively legislate on it. Another attempt 'to get a limited number of tournaments to work co-operatively' was made in 1964 by John Archer, Hurlingham Club chairman, but, according to Tingay, 'the project did not get off the ground' (*LT&B* 1 February 1965).

These problems were not confined to Britain. A.J. Mottram commented that Continental tournaments had long been 'skimming the cream off Wimbledon's rich entry, leaving [British] tournaments with a few lesser-known players to bolster up a weaker home field' (*LT&B* 1 March 1956:85). Continental tournaments, because they were often subsidised by wealthy benefactors or local municipalities, tended to offer more lavish hospitality and better prizes, and paid higher expenses, as Gordon Forbes, the South African Davis Cup player, recalled: 'Europeans ... were far more inclined to flash a bit of the folding stuff at tennis players whom they felt might add weight to their tournaments'. Tournament secretaries employed 'cloak-and-dagger methods' to 'settle up', perhaps taking the players into 'a small windowless room' and withdrawing a 'money box', or 'slipping a sheaf of bills into the player's trouser pocket' (Forbes 1978:152–3). American tournaments were also able to offer lucrative expenses, but many British tournaments that attempted to compete in this environment simply fell by the wayside. Hence Tingay's assessment that medium-sized tournaments suffered worse than the others; they often alienated the local players but could not always afford to host the stars. Between 1953 and 1961, the number of LTA-sanctioned tournaments fell by 22 percent.

Elite-level players came to view tournaments outside of the major championships according to their financial prospects. Given they offered lower expenses, the second-tier county or club tournaments were considered by most players as little more than stepping stones to Wimbledon, where exposure could improve their stock. According to the ILTF President, loyalty toward tournaments declined as players often entered for many tournaments concurrently but 'waited as late as possible before giving a definite decision in the hope that they would receive more generous expenses'. Last-minute cancellations were not uncommon; the prestigious Italian Championships of 1967 apparently lost four star players to a lesser-known tournament in Berlin because, simply, 'they were offered more money' (*LT&B* February 1968:14–5). Tournament committees were often at the mercy of players' whims, but felt compelled to make certain "arrangements" to ensure their participation. There was little alternative to these underhanded tactics.

As a way to curtail such practices, officials discussed lowering the value of prizes, to take the opportunity offered by the war – i.e. the necessity to reduce prize values – to push an agenda for permanent change. Demonstrating innocent naivety, one *LT&B* correspondent speculated:

> The day of the big money-value prize has gone, and probably never to return. ... The tennis player after being deprived of his game for six years will return to it with such new zest that the bait of a money-value prize will not be necessary to ensure his entry for a tournament.
> (1 April 1946:501–2)

Ultimately, such lofty idealism proved short-lived, as tennis became ever-more popular as a commercially exploitable spectator sport.

As these interrelated developments occurred, which had the combined effects of forcing many clubs to fold, sell their land, merge with their neighbours or diversify by offering facilities for other sports, the LTA sat on their hands. Like other associations, they were constrained by increased expenditure, but undoubtedly their Wimbledon and elite-level funding priorities brought consequences to clubs and their relationships with them. The final insult came in 1958, when they proposed to levy a new tax on clubs, indiscriminately.

The "LTA Contribution" represented a charge of one shilling per club member. Clubs in severe financial difficulty were particularly vociferous in their opposition; Tingay reported: 'That so many were loath to add so small a trifle … was symptomatic of the difficulties besetting club treasurers' (*LT&B* 15 February 1962:72). Two years later, he reported non-compliance still among one-third of clubs. Alfred Knight, a Council member from United LTC in Northampton, criticised his LTA colleagues for having 'no knowledge of the financial difficulties … [of] many small clubs … [that] are finding it hard to attract new members, and have to run football totes, bingo, dances, etc., to meet the ever-rising costs of running expenses'. He predicted an exodus of clubs from affiliation as a direct consequence of this scheme, and added: 'It was only after strenuous canvassing by county officials that these clubs were affiliated in the first place'. Reaching the crux of the matter, he concluded with candour: 'The individual members of these clubs have no interest whatsoever in the LTA or its activities, they are only concerned with their own recreation and enjoyment in the game' (*LT&B* 1 July 1964:361).

Tingay, who had once supported the scheme, soon grew opposed; he criticised the LTA for its less-than-expert "public relations" with clubs, particularly their laissez-faire attitude and perceived lack of concern for smaller clubs. Knight's prediction was proved accurate, as LTA affiliation numbers were down almost two hundred the following year. Many clubs expressed disappointment in their lack of say in LTA operations and the fact that much of their income went to projects they considered inconsequential. This act of dissent proved that clubs were no longer blind followers of policy as the LTA might have thought. Their unequivocal support had been compromised, and struggles with disengagement among clubs only intensified over time.

How did the LTA's early post-war policies translate to on-court performances? First and foremost, the British women made a terrible start, losing 7–0 on home soil in their first post-war Wightman Cup. Their play was comparatively so poor that *Daily Telegraph* journalist John Olliff suggested the Cup be opened up immediately to other nations (*LT&B* 15 September 1947:1092). The competition had become heavily one-sided; 1930 was the last year the British women won. Numerous excuses were made for their comprehensive 7–0 thrashing in America the following year. 'If Kay Menzies and Jean Bostock had spent the war in America', argued one defiant correspondent, 'they would be numbers one and two in the world today'. As it was, they were unable to deal with the famous American "kick" serve and were soundly beaten. Other excuses ranged from a comparative lack of match practice, hectic travel arrangements, 'strange' courts and balls, to biased press attention, a crippling inferiority complex and problems associated with the fact that their non-playing captain was a man. One correspondent highlighted physical differences between the players on account of continued food rationing in Britain, while another, rather oddly, *complained* of the 'strangely abundant food' in America (*LT&B* 15 October 1947:1153–5).

Over the next few years, performances only marginally improved against the Americans, spurring Hazel Wightman herself to dispatch instructional films to Britain followed by a tour with talks and demonstrations to improve standards and thus help make the Cup more competitive (*WT* April 1969:22–6).

After sporadic victories in the preceding years, including Susan Partridge's win in the 1952 Italian Championships and Joy Mottram's victory in the 1954 German Championships, the major breakthrough for British women came in 1955, when Angela Mortimer won the French Championships, Pat Ward was champion of Italy and reached the final of the US Nationals and Mortimer and Ann Shilcock won the ladies' doubles at Wimbledon. The following year, Angela Buxton was the first British woman since Kay Stammers in 1939 to reach the Wimbledon singles final and, though losing, she eventually won the doubles with the American Althea Gibson. After Mortimer reached the Wimbledon final in 1958, she did one better four years later, and Ann Haydon-Jones and Virginia Wade also won Wimbledon in 1969 and 77, respectively. Wade also achieved success at the 1968 US Open and the 1972 Australian Championships, winning "down under" 14 years after Mortimer was the first British woman to do so since Dorothy Round in 1935. The French Championships were the most successful for British women, registering a further five victories after Mortimer's: Shirley Bloomer, 1957; Christine Truman, 1959; Ann Haydon/Haydon-Jones, 1961 and 66; and Sue Barker, 1976. Also, having not won it since 1930, the British women recaptured the Wightman Cup in 1958, and won it on five further occasions from 1960–78.

Mandatory conscription did not begin to wind down until 1957, which stunted the men's progress. Despite the top three British boys, Bobby Wilson, Billy Knight and Michael Davies, showing immense promise in the early 1950s, at the senior level they had far less success. Wilson won the 1951 British Junior Championship at age 15 and won Junior Wimbledon the following year. Knight won there in 1953 and the Junior Australian Championships in 1954. Swansea-born Davies won the Welsh Junior Championships four times as a teenager and impressed selectors enough to be included with Wilson and Knight in several tours to Australia in the early 50s. Templewood boldly claimed in 1952 that they were the 'best boy players in Europe', and many predicted they would return senior national titles to Britain, but this was not to be. Wilson excelled furthest at the elite level, reaching the quarter-finals of Wimbledon four times between 1958 and 63, and a further three quarter-final finishes in France (1963) and the US (1960 and 63). Knight's best result in a major championship was reaching the quarter-final in France in 1959, but at Wimbledon he could go no further than the fourth round, where he was defeated four times between 1957 and 64. Despite being the top-ranked Brit for most of the period 1957–60, Davies' best performance in a major championship was his fourth-round defeat at Wimbledon in 1954. Still, all three made top 50 amateur rankings and Davies even went on to tour professionally in 1960.

The relative failure of the British men to live up to high expectations was cause for concern. It was their performances that were used as barometers of success overall; victories for women at this time were considered bonuses. For every positive forward step, it seemed foreign players, particularly from America and Australia, progressed quicker and more assertively. This fall from grace was seen across many sports, and brought national mourning in the context of Britain's declining world position more generally. Both athletics and cricket suffered severely declining attendances at national meetings, and a series of embarrassing defeats for the England football team in the 1950s and a poor showing at the Helsinki Olympics brought accusations of ineffectual central sport policy and funding, alongside outdated training methods (Polley 1998). In tennis, the general reaction to decline was a mix of denial and bitterness. The excuses of post-war austerity were continually made, which frustrated the realists by deflecting the problem away from its perceived root-cause, that is, a defective sporting mentality and general lack of commitment. It was urged: 'We must face the hard facts that confront us and ... rely on British skill, British sportsmanship and British determination to bring us once again to the top of the game that we invented' (*LT&B* 1 January 1950:13).

'Partly as a result ... [of] flying the flag of "true blue" amateurism', another correspondent argued, however, Britain is 'now near the bottom of the lawn tennis ladder' (*LT&B* 15 December 1947:1281). While undoubtedly a drastic measure, departing from Britain's deeply engrained but crippling amateur philosophy represented the only viable means of reinvigorating British sport, via new methods and greater accessibility. One of the most outspoken realists was Mary Hardwick, who wrote of the different class composition of players that America enjoyed in comparison:

> Perhaps 90 per cent of the young [American] players do not come from families who can afford to contribute anything financially to a tennis career, so it is surely only natural that the rewards dangling ahead and the inspiration and desire for success, is *always* present in [their] eyes.

American players, she argued, trained harder and more aggressively, supported up-and-coming players more, and benefitted from better coaching (*LT&B* 1 March 1950:141).

While advocated by some progressives, the adoption of America's sporting mentality was far from universally favoured. It was claimed: 'One gains the impression that present day American life regards it as of far greater importance for a person to excel in sport than to succeed in attaining eminence in the professions or in science' (*LT&B* 15 December 1947:1281). The unashamed competitiveness of their athletes was less than attractive, and publicly the British rejected it. However, behind closed doors and in the hearts of amateur officials, their desires for international success were fervent and unrelenting. That they cared more for success than they cared to admit was evident in the often inconsistent positions adopted on amateur rulings and in their denouncements of opponents' tactics or training methods only after losing to them. In truth, despite preaching the virtues of modesty, self-respect, behavioural restraint and quiet dominance, the British played as much for prestige as any other nation, the difference being their opponents were less ashamed to admit it.

Increasingly, they fell back on the performances of other nations or players who were seen to adopt qualities and traits widely admired in Britain. The Australians were natural targets for this reclaiming of heritage, given their widespread successes in the 1950s and 60s. After winning the 1950 Davis Cup, for example, Templewood remarked: 'We have come to regard the Commonwealth front as one and indivisible. The victory of any one of our partners is therefore the victory of all' (*LT&B* 15 December 1950:719). The British did the same with Jaroslav Drobny, a Czechoslovakian-born nationalised Egyptian who happened to play like an Englishman. His Wimbledon singles victory in 1954 at 32 years of age was widely accepted as a home victory, which speaks to Britain's declining world position and their deeply entrenched love for unassuming and modest success. World-renowned tennis historian and former journalist Alan Little recalled it was the only time in his entire life when he cried after watching a player triumph at Wimbledon, and the euphoric ovation Drobny received on Centre Court was reportedly the largest seen in living memory. Drobny's playing style and personality seemed to complement British ideals; he was a shrewd and cunning player, classy, reserved and showed 'complete harmony between hands, feet and head' (*LT&B* 15 July 1954:405). He was a great sportsman and a solid competitor, respectful of Wimbledon and its traditions, and even after his victory was unwilling to turn professional, unlike many of his contemporaries. After losing the finals of 1949 and 1952, and with the odds stacked against him in the 1954 final, he played like a quintessential home-grown plucky underdog and galvanised British sympathies like no foreigner had ever done. Peter Wilson from the *Daily Mirror* (2 July 1954) described the atmosphere around Wimbledon the day of his final against the Australian Ken Rosewall:

> Everyone seemed to be waiting for the men's singles final this afternoon – like the man who came all the way from Norfolk and set up his deck chair outside the ground with the intention of seeing just this one match. One man only has caused this state of almost suspended animation in the world's greatest lawn tennis tournament, thirty-two year-old Jaroslav Drobny.

Tom Phillips from the *Daily Herald* (3 July 1954) recalled his victory:

> Almost everyone in Britain had wanted to see 'Drob' win. When he did, the Centre Court crowd rose, cheering, clapping, as he ran to console

his crest-fallen opponent. In the Royal box Princess Margaret and the Duchess of Kent clapped their hands, smiling broadly and bobbing up and down excitedly. ... Like thunder the applause broke out again as the Duchess of Kent walked on to the Centre Court to present the championship trophy which Drobny had at last won after trying, trying and trying again in 11 attempts since 1938.

With similar sentiments, the *Daily Mail* described fans openly weeping as he left the court. More than just a popular hero, Drobny remarked feeling 'at home' in Britain, and that the British 'have taken me to their hearts' (*Sunday Graphic* 5 July 1953), so much so he moved to Britain and was granted citizenship in 1959.

Britain's post-war efforts to provide moral leadership, define on-court behavioural etiquette and form national and international policy reflected a sustained sense of ordained leadership. Their efforts to judge foreign methods and players according to British norms and values, using Wimbledon as their main stage, remained a powerful means to influence the global development of tennis, despite their dwindling on-court successes. Their sustained efforts to protect Wimbledon's prestige and aura paid dividends off-court, but at the expense of their relations with other clubs and tournaments as club affiliation numbers dropped, tournaments folded and entries dwindled. Growth was demonstrated in junior tournaments, affiliated boys' and girls' schools and children's coaching schemes, however. The number of affiliated school clubs rose rapidly year on year from 108 in 1947 to 1,598 in 1966. In 1963, there were more junior tournaments (113) held than senior ones (85). The following chapter discusses talent development at club level, and considers British schemes and methods in the context of advances abroad. The democratisation of tennis in this period was a widespread phenomenon, and it brought changes to the commercial structure of tennis and player conduct.

Bibliography

Barrett, J. (1986). *100 Wimbledon Championships: A Celebration*. London: Collins.
Bédarida, F. (1979). *A Social History of England 1851–1975*. London: Methuen.
Bowers, R. (2007b, 27 October). *Forgotten Victories: A History of Pro Tennis 1926–1945, Chapter XIII – The High War Years 1943–45*. Retrieved April 11, 2014, from Between the Lines: An Analytical and Sometimes Controversial Look at the Pro Tennis Tour: http://www.tennisserver.com/lines/lines_07_10_27.html
Cleather, N. (1947). *Wimbledon Story*. London: Sporting Handbooks.
Forbes, G. (1978). *A Handful of Summers*. London: Heinemann.
Kay, J. (2013). 'Maintaining the Traditions of British Sport?' The Private Sports Club in the Twentieth Century. *International Journal of the History of Sport*, 30(14), 1655–1669.
Kynaston, D. (2007). *Austerity Britain 1945–51*. London: Bloomsbury.

Macauley, D., and Smyth, J. (1965). *Behind the Scenes at Wimbledon*. London: Collins.
McKelvie, R. (1986). *The Queen's Club Story, 1886–1986*. London: Stanley Paul.
Polley, M. (1998). *Moving the Goalposts: A History of Sport and Society Since 1945*. London: Routledge.

13 Shifting attitudes toward talent development, coaching, commercialism and behavioural etiquette in post-war British tennis

Toward the end of WWII, the British government signalled its intentions to improve general educational standards across society with the 1944 Butler Act, which propelled legislative change for free secondary education, and initiated a major overhaul that also witnessed the creation of comprehensive schooling to replace the elitist tripartite system (Bédarida 1979). Aligned with welfare-state ideals, a new era commenced for children, as their rights and needs were subject to greater state intervention, and the responsibilities of adults to ensure these rights and needs was paid more attention by government (Hendrick 1997a, 1997b; Hill and Tisdall 1997).

Unsurprisingly, the LTA's post-war talent-development policies mirrored to some extent the broader welfare-state-inspired government objectives for reform, with emphasis on promoting enhanced opportunities for, and allocating more of their overall budget toward, children. By 1950, the LTA had launched a nationwide talent identification programme for school-aged children, set up a training school for the most talented youngsters and devised a comprehensive tennis training scheme for school teachers. In their mission, they were joined by numerous correspondents who wrote with ostensibly greater urgency about the need to advance children's playing standards, both to enhance public provision of tennis-playing opportunities and to achieve elite-level success.

The stronger emphasis on children at an administrative level was complemented often, though not always, by improved access in clubs. The Junior LTC founded in 1942 facilitated children's talent development at a time when adult competitions were near impossible to organise; six school-holiday tournaments were held that year, followed by eight the next. Children played a vital role in keeping clubs with predominantly adult membership afloat during the unsettled early post-war period, and the likes of Queen's Club and Northwick LTC in Worcestershire initiated new programmes of children's talent development. Some clubs instituted junior tournaments, often held early autumn when less likely to disturb adult members. Tunbridge Wells LTC commenced its first in 1941, Bramhall Lane LTC and Pit Farm LTC in 1948, Frinton-on-Sea LTC in 1950 and Hoole LTC in 1953, though Lymm Lawn Tennis & Cricket Club waited until 1955, and Finchley Manor

Lawn Tennis & Squash Rackets Club until 1961. Juniors were first allowed membership at Bridgnorth LTC in 1946 but were restricted to play from 10am–3pm, and at Aberaeron TC in South Wales juniors were forbidden to play after 6pm.

The shift in emphasis was by no means comprehensive, and the extent that individual clubs felt compelled to provide greater access for children was related often to local conditions and/or the personal desires of committee members. Post-war economic growth in some communities meant marked changes in employment conditions, creating a more geographically and socially mobile, and thus transient, populace, which impacted upon local sports clubs that relied upon long-term memberships, posing difficulties for established club members who were unsettled by the unpredictable nature of membership (Bale 1982). Margaret Stacey suggested that many of Banbury's post-war newcomers were often either uninterested in their new community and its associations or did not 'share any common social system or system of values and customs'. Conversely, new immigrants 'found it difficult to adapt themselves', finding Banbury 'unsociable', 'self-centred' or 'self-important'. These feelings permeated through voluntary associations and clubs, and created tensions for both new and established members; the latter would 'accept their position and behave with the manners appropriate to it', while newcomers 'come in with quite other systems of values and customs and [develop] new ways to meet the changed circumstances of their life and work' (Stacey 1960:13–14).

The *LT&B* editor was compelled to urge existing club members to ensure they looked after new members and did not leave them 'sitting about … [having] no opponent with whom to play' (*LT&B* 1 July 1945:50). The idea of forming special sub-committees to look after newcomers was proposed, and female members were especially encouraged to be more welcoming. It was argued: 'A satisfied member is a walking advertisement for a club' (*LT&B* 15 August 1945:226). Clubs were also advised to provide more comfortable facilities to entice new members (*LT&B* 15 March 1946:472), yet the reality was that many were precariously situated financially, compared to their Continental, North American or Australian counterparts. They could only afford the most modest of refurbishments, as Tingay grumbled: 'Where we have wooden building they have marble. … While the average British lawn tennis enthusiast is prepared to spend one pound his continental counterpart is prepared to lay out ten' (*LT&B* 15 February 1962:72).

Undoubtedly, the LTA would have welcomed any club improvements that afforded greater access, but it is likely they overestimated the extent that clubs actually desired new child members for anything more than economic necessity. The LTA's creation of the Lawn Tennis Foundation (LTF) in 1961 was aimed at managing grass-roots tennis, but sought more specifically to combat the problem that 'many [club] secretaries refuse to face the fact that the future of the tennis club is in the hands of boys and girls now at school' (*LT&B* 15 November 1963:595). Indeed, if this was *not* the case, the LTA President would *not* have felt compelled to ask for a change in attitude:

> Nothing is more irritating for the old gentleman, who for years has enjoyed his doubles match from 2.30–4.30 on a Saturday afternoon, to find his favourite court occupied by some lithe and laughing youngster, [but] it is a small price to pay for giving that schoolboy and his friends the desire to join and be part of the club.
>
> (*LT&B* 1 January 1965:15)

Tingay remarked that some clubs looked down upon children, running junior tournaments not for love but for profit. He posited that 90 per cent of club members 'have no interest in juniors or junior tournaments … [yet] it is these same people who would be the first to say "It's a scandal that we haven't got any promising players in this country"'. He urged senior members to make it their 'first duty' to

> help the juniors at your club in every way [because] it is far more enjoyable and rewarding than using the club as a place where you might impress someone with an old club tie and blazer and your own importance.
>
> (*LT&B* June 1967:170–1)

Despite the refutation made by the Northern LTC President that most clubs, like his, *did* run junior tournaments for altruistic reasons (*LT&B* July 1967:213), the reality was that "NIMBY-ism" characterised general attitudes toward junior development; most considered it a positive thing, just not at their own club.

Regardless of any policy directives, the LTA could not force club committees to change their attitudes, and they could offer few incentives to entice them to. As such, many clubs continued to organise themselves for "social" rather than "competitive" purposes and retained some practices of active exclusion, either through traditional membership restrictions, regulations on clothing and behaviour, or the institution of "playing-in" tests to judge standards prior to entry. Stacey (1960:18) reported that in one Banbury tennis club, for example, frictions arose between new members, who sought to improve playing standards, and traditionalists, 'who wanted the social atmosphere preserved'; the 'serious friction' eventually compelled many of the non-traditionalists to resign in protest. As another example, it was reported in the local *Hunts Post* (19 July 1979:14) that two players were denied membership at St. Neots LTC, despite it being 'the only [club] in the area', because their respective playing standards were considered 'too weak'. The club captain reasoned that the minimum playing standard existed 'to ensure that every player could play with others', yet the pragmatic functions of these rules masked the systematic rejection of those players lacking an early tennis education. It is likely that adults without the necessary tennis proficiency would not have attended the best schools where tennis was available; thus, clubs that enacted such rules ensured distinction along playing standard and social-class lines.

Much of the emphasis on "social" rather than "competitive" tennis was reinforced through subtle behavioural norms and expectations above written rules. Tennis club memberships continued to represent a visible status symbol, so the demand for respectable behaviour and the patronage of high-status individuals were two features that many clubs sought to retain deep into the post-war period. Stacey (1960:88) remarked that 'Banbury people', for example,

> do not engage in sport as an exercise in competitive athleticism, but as an occasion for social intercourse: as a competitor remarked of a tennis tournament in which he was playing, 'these do's are 75 per cent social and 25 per cent tennis'. With this attitude dominant the 'right atmosphere' and fellow members who are the 'right sort' are more important considerations that the standard of play.

Noel (1954:14) stated similarly: 'Up to county standard in England the game is still very much a relaxation. People play in clubs and parks, and although some play more than others and get better, they regard it purely as a pastime'. McKibbin (1998:382) explained that in most clubs, 'anything which disrupted sociability, like over-competitiveness, was deprecated'. At Bramhall Lane LTC, for example, "afternoon teas" were of paramount importance: 'It was an unwritten rule that once teas had started then anyone continuing to play tennis would be reprimanded by club officials and all present. So it was just not done' (Gare 2000:15).

Local elites who patronised clubs might have been conspicuous in their lack of physical presence in its day-to-day running, but were influential in enhancing prestige, preserving the high social tone of a club, and in prioritising sociability over competitive success (McKibbin, 1998). The extent of their disproportionate leadership within voluntary associations is revealed in numerous studies. In Gosforth, Northumberland, according to Williams (1956:124):

> Status within the village organisations tends to reflect the status system within the community generally. ... The position of President ... Chairman, Vice-Chairman and Vice-president are distributed in such a way that the upper class, who form little over 6 percent of the total population, occupy more than half these positions.

Frankenberg (1966) highlighted a similar pattern in Glyn Ceiriog, in northeast Wales, where higher-status outsiders often patronised voluntary associations; working roles like club secretary were filled by "intellectuals" who had valuable clerical skills. Similarly, in Banbury, the committees 'tend to have a higher social status than the membership. ... The higher occupational-status classes concern themselves with voluntary associations to an extent out of all proportion to their numbers' (Stacey 1960:81).

The local elites who were afforded opportunities to reassert their hereditary claims to civic leadership by patronising sports clubs did so during a period of continuing economic and political decline of aristocratic authority (Cannadine 1990). Given their cohesiveness, it remained common for elites to occupy positions on several committees simultaneously. Meller (1976) gave numerous examples of Bristol families that held multiple positions on the city council, and two further examples of upper-class individuals who operated in over ten different associations, ranging from sport to politics. Williams (1956:128) noted: 'A small minority are able to exert considerable influence on the affairs ... [sitting] on nearly all the committees of village organisations. Since they are mainly upper-class people this influence is naturally in accordance with upper-class standards'. Arguably, Disraeli's famous contention that Britain was not governed by the aristocracy but by aristocratic principles still held true deep into the post-war period.

The combined outcomes of middle-class philanthropy and social welfare helped to blur class distinctions as it had in the early interwar period. Competency in business and administration, marked by qualities of leadership, diligence and efficiency, alongside formal qualifications, ascended in importance, yet the consciousness of "them" and "us" was still strongly felt. The requisite qualities of club presidency, such as 'maturity, ease of conversation and ability to deal with highly placed people', came more readily to ex-public-school boys, argued McKibbin (1998:97). Class demarcation in this more meritocratic, fluid and socially mobile society therefore still rested on a 'lively consciousness of status', which continued to be informed by birth, breeding, occupation, education and way of life, alongside appearance, behaviour, gestures and accent (Bédarida 1979:282). As a reflection of the divided currents of political and social thought, tennis was similarly pulled in two directions. Some clubs continued to remove participation barriers, reduce relative costs, and promote an inclusive culture. Others retained exclusivity, enacted rigid membership restrictions, and sought only to attract higher-class new members. Regardless of their respective stances, it was clear that tennis clubs remained important locations where social distinctions were normalised and formalised. Moreover, given their presumed positive functions that complemented social policies, voluntary-run sports clubs as a whole remained protected by government, which sustained their relative social, political and economic autonomy for decades. Vamplew (2013:1575) declared: 'Social legislation designed to reduce discrimination and improve equality has tended to exclude private clubs from its provisions'. This allowed them to develop fairly organic internal cultures; they could enact their own rules, exclude whomever they wished, elect whomever they chose to positions of power, and serve their local communities however they desired.

Despite its rhetoric, the LTA was equally internally torn between tradition and expediency. Their new talent-development programmes implied a desire to remove elitism and class prejudice, yet evidence suggests some internal resentment to these changes, a preference for retaining traditional amateur methods that closeted social discrimination, and resistance to the sport's democratisation and progress toward greater inclusivity. This chapter attempts to position this period of change in the broader context of post-war socio-political developments. It aims to critically assess the various LTA talent-development programmes, and discuss the opportunities and challenges presented by new government funding for sport alongside commercial sponsorship and television exposure in general. Changes for coaches, and in particular their social positions and responsibilities, are discussed, alongside shifts in behavioural etiquette among elite-level players, both of which are understood as outcomes of the sport's professionalisation.

As Britain emerged from the immediate post-war austerity period and entered the 1950s, the optimism of the nation's government was shared by its people. Though a crude generalisation, the decade represented for many a time of conformist trends, reflecting a belief in moderate politics and social welfare. Petrol rationing ended in May 1950, as did most food rationing in 1953 and 54. While the decade was celebrated by some, for many others it was characterised by stifling conservatism and mono-culturalism (Murphy and Smart 1997). Despite conflicts in Korea, the Suez and Cuba, the Marshall Plan and the establishment of NATO promised, and in some cases delivered, economic prosperity, global stability and consensus among "Western", i.e. non-communist, nations. In many ways, the decade represented an attempt to return to a projected glorified past, and 'everything seemed to point to calm and stability' (Bédarida 1979:249). Britain was ready to set a new course to consolidate its increasingly marginalised global position in the light of decolonisation. As overseas technologies, particularly from America, began flooding British markets, the increasingly consumer-minded middle classes were supplied with new time-, money- and energy-saving conveniences (Bédarida 1979). The 1951 Festival of Britain and the ascent of Everest in 1953 helped renew British pride in itself, all of which led Prime Minister Harold Macmillan to claim in July 1957: 'Most of our people have never had it so good'. He was likely referring collectively to the white, middle classes, who were the wealthiest and healthiest they had ever been. They had a great deal to be happy about.

This optimism was shared by the LTA, which began the decade registering a healthy and growing number of affiliated clubs and tournaments. This was the start of a boom period for tennis, and although the LTA's budgetary allocation for grass-roots talent development was comparatively small, it was spread thinly across many different projects. Alongside grants to county associations, universities and the public schools for coaching, the first major nationwide training scheme to receive support, conceived in 1946, was for school teachers. A total of 174 "proficiency certificates" were awarded in its first year, and by 1949 this rose to 679. In an inspired attempt to create external partnerships, the LTA co-opted the Ministry of Education and the Central Council for Physical Recreation (CCPR) to help expand the scheme, and the following year alone issued over 1,500 certificates. By 1952, the total was over 4,000. Costing approximately £1,200 per year, the scheme was considered a sound investment, given the huge pool of young players introduced to tennis. Though directed only for teachers in boys' schools, the scheme's greater comprehensiveness – the fact that it was not merely limited to public schools – was heralded as a major breakthrough in the LTA's aim to "cast its net" a little wider. Templewood confidently proclaimed: 'I am convinced that we shall see increasingly good results from this wide effort to improve the general standard of tennis teaching, and to extend the game to every class in the community' (*LT&B* 15 December 1950:719). Theoretically at least, this made sense, given Fred Perry's modest background.

Alongside teacher training, associations for school tennis formed and children's coaching programmes were initiated. The Preparatory Schools LTA formed in 1948 in order to extend tennis opportunities beyond the public schools. It catered solely to boys' schools, but the schoolgirls' counterpart formed in 1952 and grew rapidly. The Aberdare Cup for schoolgirls grew from 90 schools in 1947 to a peak of 384 in 1968 (LTA 1974). In 1947, Perry and Maskell commenced a nationwide coaching tour called "Focus on Tennis" that gave demonstrations and mass-coaching sessions to an estimated 30,000 boys and girls (*LT&B* 1 August 1949:463). It is worth noting that, of the 14 towns visited on this apparently "nationwide" tour, none were in Scotland and just two were in northern England. The most promising talent was invited to attend the LTA's first annual "training school" over the 1949 Christmas holidays, located at the Southdean Sports Club in Sussex. The six-day intensive course involved physical training, coaching sessions, lectures and viewing instructional films, which some heralded as 'a landmark in lawn tennis history', and 'the most important cog in the wheel of [the LTA's] long-term training plans'. However, L.H.J. Dorey boldly highlighted the uncomfortable fact that 17 of the 21 children chosen were boys and 'most ... had a background of a good tennis centre' (*LT&B* 15 January 1950:35–6). Thus, the scheme failed in its aim to actually *discover* talent; it merely provided those who had already played with further opportunities. Of the total, ten hailed from the south, seven from the Midlands, and only four from the north, but it was still claimed: 'the fact that pupils came from all parts of the country emphasises the widespread roots of British stock' (*LT&B* 15 January 1950:36). After further expansions, Templewood praised the LTA's 'pioneering' efforts and opined: 'These training schemes represent in my view the most important activities of the LTA' (*LT&B* 15 December 1950:719). The 1956 winter training school unearthed future British stars, Michael Sangster and Roger Taylor.

These new programmes aimed also to extend the LTA's radar beyond the most privileged schools and clubs, but their success in this regard is difficult to assess. Undoubtedly, progress was influenced also by the falling cost of tennis equipment, and the establishment of more egalitarian clubs and free public park courts. Alan Mills, the Wimbledon referee, noted a shift in class composition when reflecting on his early playing days in the 1950s: 'most of the players appeared to have come from relatively humble origins – not quite from "the ghetto", but the majority of them certainly could not be described as rich or privileged'; he even recalled the Welshman Mike Davies once 'slept under a hedge travelling to a tournament because he couldn't afford even to stay in a cheap bed and breakfast' (Mills 2005:69–70, 73). Such anecdotes illustrated the new-found enthusiasm and will-to-win that young middle-class players had for the game, but behind the scenes, it seemed that many LTA officials cared little for the democratisation of tennis. Maskell (1988:192) admitted the LTA's declining image across Britain:

> It was quite apparent ... that people felt the LTA were not terribly concerned with the development of the game. Park superintendents felt that they were being neglected, some schools felt much the same and all too often some of the counties were not really trying to spread the game to a new generation of players.

In an anecdote that Mills (2005:71) claimed was 'nothing extraordinary' at the time, and 'par for the course', he recalled as a 15-year-old around 1950 standing on a platform, tennis gear in tow, waiting to board a train heading for Southdean's LTA training camp. Standing right next to the LTA Chairman, Mills recalled, 'it could not have been more obvious that I was heading to the same destination as him, but he completely ignored me before getting into a first-class carriage. (I was in third class.)' After disembarking, 'and without so much as a "Hello young laddie, see you at the camp", he breezed straight past me and climbed into a taxi while I bumbled off in search of the bus stop'. This experience for Mills, a future British Davis Cup player, taught him what he called 'the LTA attitude', which came to mean the Association's tendency to look down upon the very players they claimed publicly to be supporting. Moreover, being from Lancashire, Mills always felt that 'there was some real substance to the talk of a North–South divide', and he claimed: 'If you came from the North it was certainly more difficult to catch the eye of the national selectors' (Mills 2005:173).

Anecdotal evidence suggests that female players were subjected to different but equally subjective selection criteria for national squads. In 1946, Joan Hughesman (née Curry) upset two male British Wightman Cup selectors because twice she comprehensively defeated the highly favoured "blue-eyed girl" Betty Hilton during trials. Eavesdropping on their conversation shortly afterwards, she heard one of them say: 'We won't have any trials again; the wrong people always win' (cited in van Someren 2010:89).

The sense that male tennis officials continued to operate within an "old-boys" network was reinforced quite literally in 1948, when the public-school old boys sought somewhat controversially to enhance their standing within the LTA. Having reached a peak affiliation of just 45, the Public Schools LTA (previously Public School Old Boys' LTA) nevertheless considered itself worthy of direct representation on the LTA Council and so proposed such a motion. It was carried with an 80 per cent majority vote, but the ensuing discussion revealed deeply embedded elitism. One councillor admitted with candour: 'I think this is a difficult question because we – most of the people here – have been public schoolboys. That is apt to bias us in favour of any public schools approach'. Indeed, it probably did. In a statement smacking of class snobbery, the well-known and long-serving Scottish representative G.B. Primrose commented:

> I hope that outside bodies who also covet a place upon the Council will not think this is the thin edge of the wedge, and think they have established the right to come in too. If next year the National Coal Board or the Electricity Board think they have a right to a representative of their tennis clubs they would not have a very strong case.
> (*LT&B* 1 January 1949:22)

It was unclear if he was being deliberately facetious.

Despite all of their rhetoric about expanding tennis to a broader playing demographic, it was evident the LTA was still riddled with southern-centric, patriarchal and elitist ideologies promoted among an elite body of officials who thought their young players beneath them. This was not something that would disappear easily.

Coaching also progressed through a marked process of change in terms of its practices and coaches' relative social statuses. Ostensibly at least, the LTA were encouraging in their support, agreeing in 1945 to assist in the creation of the Professional Contact Committee (PCC) within the LTA, headed by Maskell, to better organise coaches throughout Britain. Over the next few years, they also offered a group insurance package and a regular allocation of Wimbledon tickets. These advances suggest a heightened respect for coaches, and for their craft, which was gaining credibility as a legitimate vocation. However, coaches were still marginalised in their status as "professionals", and the prejudiced view of coaches as "money-grabbing" was still held by some LTA councillors, which forced on one occasion a firm rebuttal from the PCC Secretary, who declared: 'the vast majority ... had a more genuine interest in the game's welfare than in mere pecuniary reward' (*LT&B* 1 February 1946:415). Still, when one coach asked, at the 1946 LTA AGM, whether he could take part in local tournaments to gain match practice, as was customary during the war when amateur–professional distinctions were abolished, he was summarily reminded that such events had returned to being amateur privileges. On other occasions, the LTA rejected proposals to reinitiate the once popular amateur vs. professional matches that had ceased during the war. When another PCC member asked whether they should press the ILTF to modify such rules, the aging LTA stalwart, H.A. Sabelli, replied matter-of-factly: 'such suggestions were tantamount to opening up the amateur game indiscriminately' (*LT&B* 1 February 1946:415). For some councillors, a "professional" remained a stigmatised, second-class citizen, regardless of whether he/she coached or toured, and this attitude was often carried into clubs. Alan Mills remembered an incident from the exclusive St. George's Club in Weybridge in the early 1970s when the club "pro" had been invited for a drink in the bar after a coaching session, but 'was asked to leave and finish his drink outside in the hallway'. Mills (2005:72) recalled: 'It was as if he were a leper or had a personal hygiene problem.'

Certainly, in terms of respect and status, some coaches had it better than others. In 1953, Dan Maskell became the first professional honoured with AELTC membership, and in 1956, Templewood made special mention of him in his closing speech after 24 years as LTA President, noting that he had 'done so much during these years to raise the general standard of tennis in the country' (*LT&B* 1 January 1957:12). Maskell's progress, however, masked the deep-rooted structures of subordination that many coaches were everyday faced with. Their vocation's precariousness was highlighted after allegations surfaced of illegal canvassing in clubs from teachers who disguised mere "proficiency certificates" as formal coaching qualifications (*LT&B* 15 March 1954:142). Feeling aggrieved, the coaches responded en masse by withdrawing their support for the LTA's teacher-training scheme, which forced its disbandment. Stronger unionisation was consequently prompted, and the independent British Professionals' Association was duly founded as an extension of the PCC, to protect coaches' livelihoods and 'administer their affairs as a properly constituted body with rules and regulations' (*LT&B* 1 May 1956:193–4). They maintained their links with the LTA, because they considered respect and recognition from them as important as institutional autonomy to manage their own affairs.

These developments complemented changes in the coaching craft, as it progressed from being highly subjective, based on "feel" and a coach's "discerning eye" for correct technique, toward a more systematic and empirical-based endeavour (Day 2011). Australian scientists in the 1950s began experimenting with more "scientific" training tools that stressed a highly rationalised, mechanistic view of the 'sporting body' as a 'machine' and 'an object to be mechanically conditioned, tuned and managed to improve performance' (Phillips and Hicks 2000:215). This notion contrasted noticeably with traditional British coaching methods, but the LTA took a more active interest in training methods and the sporting culture "down under" as Australia rose to become the premier tennis nation. In every Davis Cup competition between 1938 and 1968, Australia either won or was runner-up and, from 1950–67, won it 15 times from 18 attempts. In the four major national championships from 1946–69, Australian men and women posted a phenomenal record of winning 85 of the total 192 singles events contested; this represents an Australian victory in over 44 per cent of all major national championships.

Unlike the LTA, which derived profits from Wimbledon, the Lawn Tennis Association of Australia (LTAA) relied upon perennial appearances in the Davis Cup Challenge Round to fund their various coaching programmes, clinics and overseas tours (Fewster 1985). Their successes prompted the LTA from the early 50s to send their best players to Australia to learn the secrets of success. Long periods of instruction were arranged with the legendary coach Harry Hopman, who had a personality 'halfway between a military strategist and drill sergeant', and epitomised the Australian's new enthusiasm for "sport science"; his players ran endless miles, lifted weights and performed interval training, alongside enforcing strict regimes that demanded discipline and the abstinence of smoking and alcohol (Clerici 1975:249). The LTA hired the Australian George Worthington, a former Hopman squad member, as its chief national coach, and most of Britain's best young players, including Knight, Davies and Wilson, were recipients of Australian hospitality. After a trip over in 1961, Michael Sangster observed the importance of variable conditions, courts and opponents for improvement. He commented on the stronger bonds between junior and senior players in Australia, which positively impacted the juniors' confidence and motivation, and described the tendency for British juniors to raise hopes, but decline between 15 and 18, perhaps as a result of over-coaching or lack of effort (*LT&B* 1 May 1961:207). These comments came just two months before Sangster defeated the second seed, Rod Laver, and the up-and-coming American, Clark Graebner, during his best ever Wimbledon run to the semi-finals. His performance justified the LTA's Australian tours but also, ironically, added weight to his scathing condemnation of British methods.

Other commentators remarked similarly. In 1950, Mary Hardwick decried Britain's prescriptive and inhibitive coaching methods. American players, she claimed, are never told 'this is the style of play that wins', but rather are allowed to develop '[their] own idea as to "how" to hit the ball' (*LT&B* 1 May 1950:269). In the early post-war period, Maskell attempted to 'unify' national coaching methods under key fundamentals, but admitted the idea of standardised teaching styles had its 'detractors' (Maskell 1988:187). It was suspected that such methods might stifle creativity and individuality, and retard the development of "spirit" and "personality". Britain's highly respected Davis Cup captain, John Barrett, also took to criticising the 'national traits' of laziness and disinterestedness as being more damaging to Britain's prospects for success:

> We in this country have been some-what half-hearted in our attitude to training for tennis. ... Our leading players have tended to conform to the national trait which ... [treats] casualness in sport as a virtue. ... A

much more realistic and professional outlook on the part of the individual player is needed.

(*LT&B* 1 April 1962:146)

Similarly, Christopher Brasher, of *The Observer* (8 April 1962:18), explained the 'state of stagnation' in British tennis talent development as an outcome of: weak talent-identification methods, where stroke quality is made paramount ahead of 'strength of character and determination'; the LTA's desire to force their most promising players to switch from their original coach to one under the LTA's jurisdiction; and the tendency to stifle the ambition of their most promising young players with free training, equipment and tours. Such commentaries spoke to the need for fundamental cultural change in British tennis, including modernised coaching/training methods; stronger, more inclusive, child-focused and performance-oriented clubs; and clearer talent-development pathways. Australian successes revealed what an apparently egalitarian sporting culture could produce, as indicated by the humble social backgrounds of their best players (Fewster 1985). Lew Hoad (1959:72) remarked that Australian clubs welcomed 'any workingman's son', which somewhat contrasted with their counterparts in Britain. Australia's climate, moreover, 'favours outdoor sport and outdoor living', and creates 'abundant' leisure opportunities (Menzies 1972:3).

By modelling itself on the inclusive Australian system, it was assumed Britain would produce champions across all sports. A key component was the new Lilleshall Sports Complex that opened in 1955, after a £59,000 donation from the King George VI Memorial Fund. It signalled impending change to the social conditions of sport, particularly in the push for mass recreation. Run by the CCPR alongside the National Playing Fields Association, their remit was to coordinate a campaign to improve national fitness. Tennis was to be well served there; the complex housed two indoor courts and placed at its helm J. Eaton Griffith, back fresh from his stints as ILTF President and LTA Chairman.

Parks tennis in America was boosted thanks to President Roosevelt's personal appreciation for tennis (Baltzell 1995), and in Britain enjoyed a brief resurgence after being in decline since the interwar years. In 1957, representatives from the Parks LTAs of Sheffield, Manchester, Leeds, Bradford and Burnley formed the British Parks Amateur LTA, as a result of

> a generally expressed feeling in the North that more could be done for the players, the clubs and the associations which pursued the game on Parks courts. It was thought that a nationally organised tournament might stimulate interest in parks' tennis, particularly amongst juniors.
>
> (*LT&B* 1 January 1958:7)

Cooper (1959) considered better organisation of parks tennis important given the growing competition from private clubs with better facilities, and advocated extending the association outside of the north. By 1959, Bournemouth and Brighton & Hove had joined but remained the only two southern representatives in an association that also grew to include Dumfries, Glasgow, Nelson (Lancashire), Fenton (Staffordshire) and Walsall. Unfortunately, it seemed the British Parks Amateur LTA's southern expansion facilitated its demise, as parks clubs struggled to attain the necessary funds to travel south. The Association folded within five years, though their efforts to expand mass participation were taken over by the LTF, which aimed to 'bring death to [the] old tradition' of tennis being perceived as a 'snob sport' (*LT&B* 15 February 1961:72).

Progress for these new associations was assisted by emergent government funding for sport. The CCPR's Wolfenden Report from 1960 stressed sport's usefulness as a means of social control, cohesion and discipline, which resonated at a time when social commentators voiced concerns over increasing juvenile delinquency (Polley 1998). Wolfenden's recommendation to establish an Advisory Sports Council was commended by associations including the LTA, and came to fruition five years later after the Council of Europe presided over a debate on the right of all individuals to participate in sport (Phillpots 2011). The Sports Council's initial aim was to cater to both mass and elite-level objectives, which the UK government supported because of its perceived potential to address concerns over crime and health, alongside the possibility of enhancing prestige through international sporting success (Green and Houlihan 2005).

For Houlihan (1991:98), 'there was little discernible tension between the interests of the elite and the mass'. The belief that both objectives could be delivered simultaneously was widely held, and underpinned the "pyramid" model that provided a common framework for sport development, as Kirk and Gorely (2000:122) explained: 'The broader the base of support, the higher the pinnacle of achievement.' Despite this logic coming to be regarded as self-evident, the model itself proved too primitive; based on 'lazy and muddled thinking', it overlooked the myriad ways that athletes developed, and conflated two distinct cultures of sport: one oriented to achievement and the other to sociability and physical fitness (McDonald 2011:373). At the time, nonetheless, it found considerable support. The LTA persisted with the basic philosophy that more children playing tennis meant greater chances to develop elite-level players. For them, the twin aims merely represented two sides of the same coin, both of which required more and better-quality sports facilities and central government support delivered at a local level (Phillpots 2011).

One unintended consequence of this general process was to push sports governing bodies to more closely align themselves with central government policies (Polley 1998). The new emphasis placed on grass-roots tennis, as shown through the LTF's activities, indicated the mirroring of LTA strategy with government policy (Lake 2014). It was expected that open communication channels between state and sport could bring more funding and better facility provision. After two years of delivering successful programmes, which included staging numerous tennis festivals, demonstrations and a national tournament, and the creation of coaching and information centres, the LTF stressed the importance of creating partnerships, to 'make as many contacts in as many places in Great Britain as possible, with authorities, and people interested in the development of the game'. This explicit emphasis on partnerships was remarkable for the LTA, and they also urged for more coaches, the 'decentralisation' of decision-making and, in another landmark move, an approach to 'big business for donations to finance it' (*LT&B* 15 November 1963:595). The following year, as if to acknowledge the benefits of commercial sponsorship in particular, the LTF accepted funding from the Scottish Milk Marketing Board and the Scottish Council of Physical Recreation to stage numerous rallies and demonstrations for children (*LT&B* 1 May 1964:225).

British tennis took the lead from government with respect to the increased perceived acceptance of commercial sponsorship for sport. The food manufacturing giant Nestlé initiated its own Sports Foundation in 1960, putting forward £15,000 over three years. Arguably its greatest achievement was to launch a national tennis tournament that grew to become the biggest of its kind in the world (*LT&B* 1 November 1962:536). By 1963, the Nestlé National Tennis Championship had catered for over 14,000 children, 6,000 in that year alone, which forced the advisory committee, which included notable figures like Basil Reay (LTA Secretary), Clarence M. Jones (editor of *British Lawn Tennis*), Jaroslav Drobny, Dan Maskell and Angela Buxton, to divide the competition into four distinct age groups and create two schools' singles events. Prizes included equipment, coaching grants and overseas training, but 'as the tournament expanded, costs became higher', reported David Gray when announcing Nestlé's plans to abandon its sponsorship after just seven years (*Guardian* 17 November 1966). Sponsorship was nonetheless forthcoming from tobacco firms Rothmans, W.D. and H.O. Wills, Embassy, Benson & Hedges, Player's and Silk Cut, whisky distillers John Dewar and Sons, and petroleum giant BP. The tobacco companies were the major sponsors from the mid-60s, assisting the British Hard Court and Covered Court Championships among dozens of other tournaments, while the Dewar Cup, instituted in 1968 for £12,000, offered enhanced prizes and helped reinvigorate events in Scotland (Perth) and Wales (Aberavon). The BP International Tennis Fellowship, also inaugurated in 1968 with £10,000 investment, supported John Barrett in his coaching efforts to develop British hopefuls Mark Cox, Gerald Battrick and Paul Hutchins.

These rapid developments represented a sharp turning point for British attitudes and upper-administrative support for commercialism in tennis. Lance Tingay noted that 'thought is changing fast' in the matter of commercial sponsorship; he believed that new investment would inject 'vital blood' into British tournaments, which had suffered from under-capitalisation and had numerically declined for seven straight years (*LT&B* 15 September 1962:480). Between 1962 and 65, almost half of all British tennis tournaments sought and obtained financial backing from sponsors, saving many from 'certain extinction', according to Tingay; the total number of tournaments increased from 77 in 1961 to 87 in 1964 (*LT&B* 1 February 1965:56).

Despite this growth and the perceived need to reduce their reliance on Wimbledon by securing alternative income sources, the LTA initially were reluctant to fully support tournament sponsorship. While they backed firms like Nestlé and supported talent-development schemes for children, their official position was to encourage nothing more than 'discreet' partnerships for the sponsorship of tournaments; blatant commercialism was condemned, as was using corporate money to fund players' expenses (*Guardian* 20 November 1962:12). Tingay considered this an 'utterly unrealistic' hope, given the obvious pull that well-backed tournaments had on players' loyalties: 'The chances are overwhelmingly that the highest bidder will get the player. It is virtually impossible for money from sponsorship to be used for anything else but the expenses of players' (*LT&B* 1 February 1965:56). The LTA overturned their ban on sponsorship of national championships in 1967, but that year's prestigious Covered Court Championships at Queen's Club was cancelled – for the third time in ten years – because it could not attract enough quality players, despite Rothmans putting forward £1,750. Still, the £5 per day expenses offered by Queen's compared pathetically to the "going rate" of £600 per week that top male players made in Europe, but when the idea of matching these amounts was raised, Rear-Admiral Sir Antony Miers, chairman of the organising committee, summed up Britain's old-fashioned position by responding: 'We are not prepared to break the rules of amateurism. After all, we're British aren't we, and we play to the rules' (*Guardian* 7 January 1967:1). Alongside more relaxed amateur rules and expenses, European tournaments also typically offered more flexible terms for sponsors, including allowing named tournaments (i.e. title sponsorship) and advertising within club grounds, which made the attraction of sponsorship in Britain more challenging. The economic downturn of the late 1960s made attracting sponsorship more a survival mechanism for clubs than a means to secure profits (Polley 1998), and from 1966–83, sport sponsorship revenue in Britain grew from £1 million to £100 million (Whannel 1986).

The push towards creating partnerships with government and corporate sponsors was certainly influenced by broader developments in sport. Television and the development of televised sport was clearly the most important change (Whannel 1992), and Smart (2007) linked the gathering momentum of consumer culture to the commercialisation of sport, as lucrative opportunities opened up for star athletes and their managers and/or agents to exploit. Mark McCormack's International Management Group (IMG), established in 1960, was the first of numerous associations to represent the growing number of sports celebrities.

Other British sports associations differed in their approaches to commercialism and professionalism, but none were protected from their influences. The maximum wage for professional footballers was abolished in 1961, while cricket removed its amateur–professional distinction in 1963 as a consequence of declining income from traditional playing formats (Polley 1998). Golf was divided somewhat by the well-established PGA, which failed to budge from the idea that professionals were anything more than skilled artisans employed to serve club members. As income from television and sponsorship increased yearly, the PGA was forced in 1976 to split into two distinct divisions, one representing the club professional and another for tournament players (Physick and Holt 2000). Coaching methods in British athletics remained antiquated until the 1970s, according to Porter and Smith (2000), but in 1981, the payment-for-performance idea was adopted, which conveniently coincided with the arrival of a new golden era of British dominance in athletics (Polley 2000). Avery Brundage also managed to deflect commercial input within the IOC throughout his 20-year reign, but by the 1970s, the global success of major team sports revealed the lucrative opportunities provided by corporate sponsorship and television broadcasting. Growth in the betting industry was a key development, particularly after the 1960 Betting and Gaming Act that facilitated the rise and spread of betting shops like Ladbrokes and William Hill (Polley 1998).

During this period of sport's rampant commercialisation, the LTA were forced to move quickly on these issues, facing an insurmountable problem should they pull back the reins in tennis. They feared appearing outdated or being overtaken by other sports' associations if they condemned entirely the use of sponsorship, but equally they sought to avoid the wholehearted abuse of commercial money so tournaments could recruit better players. Taking its by now customary middle-of-the-road approach, the LTA, with support from leading sponsors Wills and Rothmans, created a "sinking fund" to help clubs struggling to obtain tournament sponsorship, and also enforced a cap on the amount of tournament sponsorship a club could obtain. The cap was deemed unfeasible upon closer examination, however, while the allocation of financial assistance was policed unfairly; 'completely amateur' tournaments received full reimbursement, while arguably the most resourceful clubs that sought, but failed, to attract top players by offering inflated expenses were given far less. For example, only 44 per cent of Hurlingham Club's £655 loss in 1968 was reimbursed by the LTA (*Guardian* 7 March 1969:21). Tingay questioned the LTA's continued perception of commercial sponsorship as tainted and perhaps slightly unethical:

> Is there a danger of too much money being poured into the game? I doubt it. Sponsorship may well arrest the decline in British open tournaments. That, it seems to me, must be all to the good of lawn tennis.
>
> (*LT&B* 1 May 1965:226)

He added later: 'In my experience sponsors ask for astonishingly little in return for their money and I have yet to hear of any sponsor trying to influence the conduct of a tournament' (*LT&B* 15 November 1965:620). This might have been the LTA's initial fear but, with its back against the wall, it was forced to embrace some measure of commercial input after having legislated against it for almost eighty years.

The LTA's support for television broadcasting was even more lukewarm, though they reacted early enough to its potential. In 1950, Templewood announced television's growing influence with apparent trepidation, urging the LTA to take precautions to ensure that tennis was not 'exploited for money by outside organisations and individuals', given the possibilities of attempts made to 'extract large sums of money out of televising tennis tournaments'. He advised all British sports governing bodies to 'act together', and in response to this new threat, the LTA added a new clause to its constitution that gave them the right 'to control, sanction and where necessary promote television in all aspects' (*LT&B* 15 December 1950:719). The 1954 Championships made just £1,500 from BBC coverage, but after ITV emerged the following year to share Wimbledon broadcasting, even some BBC staff expressed anxiety over their comparatively sub-standard coverage (Whannel 1992). The competition lasted until 1963, when ITV realised the commercial impracticability of double coverage, especially given the BBC's plans to launch a second channel (Maskell 1974).

Televised sport grew slowly but steadily. The LTA experimented with the sale of rights for other events but made only modest profits, reporting just £384 in 1956 and £513 in 1958. Some LTA councillors expressed fear that television might have an 'adverse effect' on tournament 'gates', which presented a considerable risk given television income was 'extraordinarily low' (*LT&B* 1 January 1959:10). They were right to show concern; the final rounds of the 1958 Covered Court Championships at Queen's Club were arranged 'to suit the requirements of television', which brought 'mixed feelings' from some of the press and players who were inconvenienced. It was said: 'The gearing of a tournament to the needs of television rather than to the players was a distinct shift in the amateur administration of tournaments'. That said, 'the value of television in the further popularisation of lawn tennis cannot be gainsaid. ... Nor, of course, can the financial benefits be overlooked' (*LT&B* 1 April 1958:156). This was a confident declaration of faith, given the full commercial benefits of selling television rights were not yet fully appreciated. Still, television's influence on sports programming alongside its presentation, organisation, finance, competitive structure and even rules was becoming increasingly apparent by the early 1960s, just as public television ownership skyrocketed (Whannel 1992). At the beginning of the 1950s, a television set was considered a luxury item, with only 350,000 British households owning one, but by 1960, nearly three-quarters of the entire UK population owned one, and within ten years, ownership had jumped to nearly 95 per cent (Bédarida 1979).

Shortly after BBC2 was launched in 1964, programming space was made available to significantly extend Wimbledon coverage. Television's potential to transform its entire spectacle was being realised, despite claims that it desensitised audiences to its aura (Whannel 1992). Most correspondents agreed that on balance it promised more than it threatened, and this was likely a chief reason behind the push for "open tennis", which arrived in 1968. Up until then, from the mid-50s, Wimbledon profits had remained fairly constant from £46,000–62,000, and recovered very well after taking a slight dip to accommodate the offer of prize money. By the mid-70s, the AELTC committee negotiated television rights deals that allowed the Championships to gross profits over the next 20 years that grew exponentially: the Championships of 1973 recorded just over £58,000; eight years later, the £1,000,000 mark was broken and by 1997 had surpassed £30,000,000. Minus tax, all of this money went directly to the LTA.

While the greater economic stability of clubs and tournaments was welcomed alongside more scientific methods of play that helped improve standards, the pursuit of these outcomes that signalled greater acceptance of commercialism and professionalism brought consequences that some in the British amateur fraternity had been predicting for decades; namely, the escalation of what was considered "bad" on-court behaviour (Lake forthcoming). An increasing number of incidents occurred from the late 1940s onwards, which served to fuel an anti-commercial/anti-professional backlash. Bob Falkenburg's famous "delay tactics" at Wimbledon in 1948 – taking inordinate amounts of time to rise after his frequent tumbles – were widely condemned, as they undermined unwritten ethical codes (Brady 1959). Trower vented: 'Lawn tennis has a strong and healthy tradition of sportsmanship … A certain standard of conduct is taken for granted … The centre court is justly jealous of its dignity' (*LT&B* 15 August 1948:528). Other incidents followed, however, including Earl Cochell's ejection from the 1951 US Nationals for bad language, Chuck McKinley's USLTA suspension for losing his temper in the 1960 Davis Cup Inter-zone final against Italy, and the omission of Bob Mark, Bob Hewitt and Ken Fletcher from their Australian Davis Cup squad because of breaches of etiquette in their own national championships (Lake forthcoming). The British players from John Barrett's touring squad in 1967 were also lambasted for their behaviour by an 'angry hotelier' in the French Riviera, who complained: 'certainly the old tradition of good British sportsmanship was not enhanced' (*LT&B* May 1967:150).

The LTA began to exert their disciplinary powers against the incidence of bad behaviour by publishing rules of etiquette in *LT&B*. The first in 1947 listed bad habits to avoid, including a 'baleful glare at an umpire, the hands raised high to heaven when that wonderful winner is adjudged out, the disgusted throwing down of the racket' (*LT&B* 1 June 1947:853). This was followed by "do's and don'ts" for tournament players, which stressed overall that 'self-discipline' was imperative to earn 'the respect and goodwill of all those officiating and watching' (*LT&B* 15 March 1959:124). Juniors were advised on being a 'useful club member', which included exhibiting sportsmanship, showing willingness to "make up a four", looking after the grass courts, keeping the clubhouse tidy, and volunteering around the club (*LT&B* 1 May 1965:223). Other similar lists of supposedly "unwritten" rules appeared in 1966 and 67 (see *LT&B* 1 March 1966:101; *LT&B* March 1967:63). The USLTA also commissioned several experts to compile explicit "codes of conduct" that detailed points of etiquette ranging from the common, e.g. how to control your temper and how to dress properly, to the mundane, e.g. how to cross courts at changeovers and how long to allow for a toilet break (Blue 1982; Powel 1974; Shannon 1981). According to Baltzell (1995:388), the noticeable acceleration of such information was indicative of escalating bad behaviour and the general decline of 'traditional class authority'; 'unwritten class codes of honour, decency, and deference' were replaced by 'bureaucratic rules' written by administrators. Players, thus, were stripped of their ethical responsibilities as the "unwritten" code of conduct that demanded personal self-restraint and integrity was replaced by explicit duties, which denied players opportunities to demonstrate sportsmanship (Bodo 1995).

Broader societal changes were brought to bear within a specifically British context, impacting on general behavioural standards. Bédarida (1979:250–1) contended that Britain's historically rooted and 'unyielding framework of tradition and conformity' began to crumble because of declining religious influence, liberalising social norms and sexual freedoms, and enhanced levels of affluence among the young, which led to a 'collapse of standards', particularly with regard to 'ideas of duty, honesty, respectability, hard work [and] ... self-respect', alongside 'voluntary self-discipline which made adherence to the law, whether the law of the land or the social code, a matter of individual personal responsibility'. Barrett (1986:162) agreed, suggesting that Britain in the 1980s was a 'more violent and less law-abiding society. Sexual attitudes were more liberal, alcoholism and drug-taking among the young were no longer minor problems.' Broadly speaking, the British became reoriented to the new ideas of "individualism", where people increasingly confined themselves to narrow social relations, followed their own codes of conduct and ceased 'concerning themselves or interfering with the behaviour of others, or bothering about setting an example', and "consumerism", which found a new lease of life in post-war Britain, but took its toll on social relations, collective values and behaviour (Bédarida 1979:252). The 'spirit of thrift' had been 'eroded' by this 'limited and materialistic' philosophy, argued Bédarida (1979:254): 'Doing without was no longer a virtue, but a misfortune; instant enjoyment and conspicuous acquisition, egged on by advertising and the mass media, became the paramount consideration'.

Fields of leisure were not spared the effects of consumerism, particularly the loosening of ethics and behavioural standards and the endeavour for more instant forms of gratification. Bédarida (1979:257) contended:

> This neo-capitalist world, based on the maximisation of private profit, is suffused with a complex commercial ideology which taints all social and moral values. Neighbourly relations, family life, and in general every medium of social communication are indissolubly impregnated with it. This ideology ... is simply based on the philosophy of getting and having.

This shifting middle-class habitus found expression in tennis most likely as a consequence of its commercialisation and professionalisation, which brought discernible behavioural implications.

The American Davis Cup captain David Freed campaigned in 1960 for more lenience on crowd noise from umpires, undoubtedly recognising such behavioural prohibitions contrary to 'widespread attempts to make tennis more "popular" among all classes'. It was probably true that some spectators were offended by the strict expectations of self-restraint, but his expectations seemed naive in the context of the sport's historically rooted elitism. Indeed, correspondents responded to Freed's idea by suggesting it would 'cheapen the game, feeling that tennis is a historically dignified, well-ordered sport. ... Part of the game's charm ... is precisely this lack of a noisy, ill-mannered spectator backdrop' (*LT&B* 15 September 1960:464). From this, it was clear that behavioural codes served more than simple pragmatic functions. By helping to distinguish tennis from other sports, they also distinguished its participants. Amateur associations were torn between the mutually exclusive ideals of inclusivity and exclusivity. The former was considered commercially advantageous, but the latter, socially desirable. While the democratisation of tennis helped inject new spectator interest and raise playing standards, it also invited new professional attitudes and commercial interests, which were beginning to take over. For British administrators in particular, these conflicting ideals brought much soul-searching, as they attempted to justify their own self-proclaimed moral leadership amidst the sport's inevitable modernisation.

Bibliography

Bale, J. (1982). *Sport and Place*. London: C Hurst & Co.
Baltzell, E. D. (1995). *Sporting Gentlemen: Men's Tennis from the Age of Honor to the Cult of the Superstar*. New York: Free Press.
Barrett, J. (1986). *100 Wimbledon Championships: A Celebration*. London: Collins.
Bédarida, F. (1979). *A Social History of England 1851–1975*. London: Methuen.
Blue, C. (1982). *Tennis Disputes*. New Jersey: United States Tennis Association.
Bodo, P. (1995). *The Courts of Babylon: Tales of Greed and Glory in the Harsh New World of Professional Tennis*. New York: Scribner.
Brady, M. (1959). *The Centre Court Story*. London: Sportsman's Book Club.
Cannadine, D. (1990). *The Decline and Fall of the British Aristocracy*. New Haven: Yale University Press.

Clerici, G. (1975). *The Ultimate Tennis Book: 500 Years of the Sport*. Chicago, IL: Follett Publishing Company.
Cooper, M. (1959). *Cooper's Annual of Lawn Tennis, 1959/60*. Bournemouth.
Day, D. (2011). Craft Coaching and the 'Discerning Eye' of the Coach. *International Journal of Sport Science and Coaching*, 6(1), 179–196.
Fewster, K. (1985). Advantage Australia: Davis Cup Tennis 1950–1959. *Sporting Traditions*, 2(1), 47–68.
Frankenberg, R. (1966). *Communities in Britain*. London: Penguin.
Gare, T. (2000). *Bramhall Lane Lawn Tennis Club: A Story of More Than 90 Years of Tennis*. Stockport: Bramhall Lane LTC.
Green, M., and Houlihan, B. (2005). *Elite Sport Development: Policy Learning and Political Priorities*. London: Routledge.
Hendrick, H. (1997a). *Children, Childhood and English Society 1880–1990*. Cambridge: Cambridge University Press.
Hendrick, H. (1997b). Constructions and Reconstructions of British Childhood: An Interpretive Survey, 1800 to the Present. In A. James and A. Prout, *Constructing and Reconstructing Childhood: Contemporary Issues in the Sociological Study of Childhood* (pp. 33–62). London: Falmer Press.
Hill, M., and Tisdall, K. (1997). *Children and Society*. London: Routledge.
Hoad, L. (1959). *My Story*. London: Sportsmans Book Club.
Houlihan, B. (1991). *The Government and Politics of Sport*. London: Routledge.
Kirk, D., and Gorely, T. (2000). Challenging Thinking about the Relationship between School Physical Education and Sport Performance. *European Physical Education Review*, 6(2), 119–134.
Lake, R. J. (2014). Discourses of Social Exclusion in British Tennis: Historical Changes and Continuities. *International Journal of Sport and Society*, 4(2), 1–11.
Lake, R. J. (forthcoming). The 'Bad Boys' of Tennis: Shifting Gender and Social Class Relations in the Era of Nastase, Connors and McEnroe. *Journal of Sport History*.
Maskell, D. (1974). Television. In M. Robertson, *Encyclopedia of World Tennis* (pp. 188–192). New York: Viking Press.
Maskell, D. (1988). *From Where I Sit*. London: Willow.
McDonald, I. (2011). High-performance Sport Policy in the UK: An Outline and Critique. In B. Houlihan and M. Green, *Routledge Handbook of Sports Development* (pp. 371–385). London: Routledge.
McKibbin, R. (1998). *Classes and Cultures: England 1918–1951*. Oxford: Oxford University Press.
Meller, H. (1976). *Leisure and the Changing City, 1870–1914*. London: Routledge & Kegan Paul.
Menzies, R. G. (1972). The Great Game of Tennis. In A. Danzig and P. Schwed, *The Fireside Book of Tennis* (p. 3). New York: Simon and Schuster.
Mills, A. (2005). *Lifting the Covers: Allan Mills, the Autobiography*. London: Headline.
Murphy, J., and Smart, J. (1997). *The Forgotten Fifties: Aspects of Australian Society and Culture in the 1950s*. Melbourne: Melbourne University Press.
Noel, S. (1954). *Tennis in Our Time*. London: Sportsmans Book Club.
Phillips, M. G., and Hicks, F. (2000). Conflict, Tensions and Complexities: Athletic Training in Australia in the 1950s. *International Journal of the History of Sport*, 17(2–3), 206–224.

Phillpots, L. (2011). Sports Development and Young People in England. In B. Houlihan and M. Green, *Routledge Handbook of Sports Development* (pp. 131–142). London: Routledge.

Physick, R., and Holt, R. (2000). 'Big Money': The Tournament Player and the PGA, 1945–75. In A. Smith and D. Porter, *Amateurs and Professionals in Post-War British Sport* (pp. 60–80). London: Frank Cass.

Polley, M. (1998). *Moving the Goalposts: A History of Sport and Society Since 1945.* London: Routledge.

Polley, M. (2000). 'The Amateur Rules': Amateurism and Professionalism in Post-War British Athletics. In A. Smith and D. Porter, *Amateurs and Professionals in Post-War British Sport* (pp. 81–114). London: Frank Cass.

Porter, D., and Smith, A. (2000). Introduction. In A. Smith and D. Porter, *Amateurs and Professionals in Post-War British Sport* (pp. vii–xvi). London: Frank Cass.

Powel, N. (1974). *The Code of Tennis.* New Jersey: United States Tennis Association.

Shannon, B. (1981). *U.S. Tennis Association's Official Encyclopedia of Tennis.* New Jersey: Harper Collins.

Smart, B. (2007). Not Playing Around: Global Capitalism, Modern Sport and Consumer Culture. *Global Networks,* 7(2), 113–134.

Stacey, M. (1960). *Tradition and Change: A Study of Banbury.* Oxford: Oxford University Press.

Vamplew, W. (2013). Theories and Typologies: A Historical Exploration of the Sports Club in Britain. *International Journal of the History of Sport,* 30(14), 1569–1585.

van Someren, J. (2010). *Women's Sporting Lives: A Biographical Study of Elite Amateur Tennis Players at Wimbledon.* Unpublished PhD dissertation, University of Southampton.

Whannel, G. (1986). The Unholy Alliance: Notes on Television and the Remaking of British Sport 1965–85. *Leisure Studies,* 5, 129–145.

Whannel, G. (1992). *Fields in Vision: Television Sport and Cultural Transformation.* London: Routledge.

Williams, W. M. (1956). *The Sociology of an English Village: Gosforth.* London: Routledge & Kegan Paul.

Wolfenden Committee. (1960). *Sport and the Community: The Report of the Wolfenden Committee on Sport.* London: Central Council of Physical Recreation.

14 The enduring amateur–professional dichotomy and the new struggle for authority in world tennis

The impression of elite-level pre-open-era tennis is a skewed and confusing one. Almost as soon as many of the top males won Wimbledon or the US Nationals, which was often in their early twenties, they signed professional contracts and were removed from the public spotlight. Pauline Betz recalled, after signing in 1947, that professionals remained a profoundly stigmatised group: 'I was guilty of the blackest, foulest deed in the USLTA history. I was a criminal, a leper, a pariah' (Betz 1949:145). Given the growing threat that professional tours represented to the social prestige and economic viability of amateur competitions, alongside the oft-repeated suggestion that professional tennis was played at a noticeably higher standard, it is unsurprising that amateur officials ceased encouraging professional tours. Working often outside the mainstream press and amateur-run tennis magazines, the movements and achievements of professional players were left to rogue journalists to report; *Lawn Tennis & Badminton*, *American Lawn Tennis* and *World Tennis* simply ceased devoting space to them. Kramer (1979:53) recalled: 'Pro tournaments were never part of the records. We were like the old Negro baseball leagues. We played and we kept score, but somehow it wasn't considered worth remembering'.

Such deliberate censorship of professional tennis news did not necessarily help the amateur game, however, which subsequently was subject to even greater scrutiny of its practices. Misdemeanours involving under-the-table expenses offered by tournament organisers, secret deals with sporting-goods manufacturers, and even illicit gambling, became public knowledge, yet amateur officials continued to turn a blind eye. They appeared unashamedly deceitful and hypocritical, yet at times naive to the social conditions of post-war tennis and of post-war tennis players. In their efforts to promote and develop elite-level amateur tennis, ironically, they had helped professionalise it. According to Baltzell (1995:309), players like Don McNeill, Ted Schroeder and Joe Hunt, who 'played the game as an avocation, graduated from college and sought careers outside sport', were gradually replaced by those who were more aspirational and individualistic in their motivations and pursuits, and considered that tangible rewards for effort and expertise were just and right within a meritocratic system. Players like Bobby Riggs,

Frank Parker, Jack Kramer and Pancho Gonzáles considered tennis a viable career choice and 'saw the game as a way up in the world and spent their whole lives in the sport'. These players, according to Richard Boeth from *Sports Illustrated* (*SI*) (19 December 1960), demanded 'more than a pat on the back' to make their training and development worthwhile: 'More and more they are making it plain that they want not only kudos but cash for all their years of hard work.' Gonzáles (1959:169) described what characterised amateur stars as full-time professionals in all but official status:

> Day after day he runs countless miles. ... Physically, the game exerts its toll. He's dehydrated as a squeezed sponge. His feet take a terrific pounding. ... His heart and body are taxed to the limits of physical endurance. While he may not realise it – he's in business. And he's putting as much into it as the business man carrying the brief case under his arm. Sometimes much more.

To complement their efforts and further fuel their motivations, increasingly lucrative opportunities were made available for amateurs to live as full-time players. While amateur associations decreed that players should not capitalise on their tennis talents, they, themselves, capitalised on the enhanced image and organisational prestige that their players' efforts afforded. Ultimately, the lure of wealth and prestige that tennis offered was sufficiently strong to pull the sport from its amateur roots, as the quest to retain amateurism in the face of social change was considered 'a losing battle'. According to Forbes (1978:277):

> Tennis was entertainment and the players were entertainers, and entertainers in this modern world were accustomed to being paid for their skills. ... The money gods took a long look at it, voted in favour and began moving in; and with the money came an entirely new status quo.

This period therefore represents the last great effort of amateur administrators to cling disingenuously and ultimately hopelessly to their power.

The main aim of this chapter is to discuss the opportunities and challenges associated with the decline of amateurism and the rise of professionalism in international tennis, as it related to British-specific issues. After initially examining the post-war professional tour, three key periods are discussed: first, from the late 1940s until the late 1950s, when the LTA and its partner associations seemed ignorant of continuing practices of "shamateurism", and sought chiefly to sustain exploitative and corrupt amateur traditions at the expense of integrity; second, from 1960–68 when, after a shift in perspective, the AELTC and LTA in combination successfully galvanised their global partners to sanction "open" competition; and, third, the early open era, from 1968 until the 1980s, when the ILTF's failure to remove entirely the amateur–professional distinction allowed professional promoters to thrive at their expense and intensify rather than quell the power struggle between them. One related outcome was the emergence of the players' union, the Association of Tennis Professionals (ATP), which almost instantly transformed the entire structure and governance of men's elite-level tennis.

The momentum that professional tours had generated in the mid–late 1930s was stemmed by WWII (Bowers 2005). Bobby Riggs and Frank Kovacs attempted to tour with Perry and Budge in late 1941, but America's declaration of war against Japan in December precipitated a drop in public enthusiasm, and the tour was terminated prematurely (Bowers 2007a). Immediately after the war, quite naturally, amateur competitions were prioritised for recovery efforts, while the professional tour initially floundered. It needed an overhaul; specifically, it required new leadership from a dynamic and confident figure who knew the game, was popular among the players and the press, and was stubborn enough to ensure professionals were justly rewarded.

The Californian Jack Kramer proved just the person. Twice US Nationals singles champion in 1946 and 47 and Wimbledon singles champion in 1947, Kramer's game was aggressive and dominant, much like his personality. He signed a professional contract with Jack Harris late in 1947 and toured North America with Budge and Riggs. Handsomely defeating them both, as well as tour newcomers Pancho Gonzáles, Frank Sedgman and Pancho Segura, he helped the professional competitions recover well and generate substantial public interest. Comparisons between the relative playing standards of amateurs and professionals made for compelling debates, and helped "sell" the tour. Initially, Kramer's successes dispelled the myth of professional dominance, but from when he took the helm as tour promoter in 1951, the physically demanding schedule of events he devised helped propel the professionals to even greater fitness levels. Also, early signings meant many players reached their relative playing peaks – usually considered the late twenties – when playing as a professional. Even those who dominated at Wimbledon and Forest Hills struggled as tour newcomers, such as 23-year-old Australian Ken Rosewall. Signing in 1957 after winning four major championship singles titles and reaching four other major finals, he failed to dominate 36-year-old Pancho Segura, a player who had never won a major singles championship. One commentator remarked that since turning pro 'most of Rosewall's strokes had become remodelled' by Kramer, which gave the impression 'that Rosewall had really only started to learn the game of lawn tennis since he turned professional'. Similarly, when his Davis Cup teammate Lew Hoad signed the following year, it was reported that 'he has yet only shown very in-and-out form in his new environment' (*LT&B* 15 October 1957:527). One correspondent complained, subsequently: 'It is impossible, even ridiculous, to consider Wimbledon a world championship as things stand at present' (*LT&B* 1 November 1957:559). When Rod Laver signed in 1962, fresh from his first "Grand Slam", he lost ten of his first 12 matches against Hoad and Rosewall, which implied, albeit crudely, that professionals were stronger (Clerici 1975). In truth, the vastly different structures of competition made hypothetical comparisons difficult to make; the professionals concentrated their skill-set to compete among a handful of players. Still, the perception that professional-level tennis was better mattered more than whatever the reality was. To many, Wimbledon and other major amateur tournaments became in effect qualifying competitions for the professional tour.

Winning a major championship was the key to receiving a large offer to turn professional, as promoters relied upon the latest star leaving the amateur ranks with a certain cachet. Pancho Segura was exceptional in making a name for himself in the professional game alone, yet while the diminutive Ecuadorian held his own on court against Kramer and Gonzáles, he struggled at the box office. 'As entertaining as Segura could be', Kramer (1979:93) recalled, 'that wouldn't do us any good coming into a town, because he didn't come in with a lot of amateur publicity – no Forest Hills or Wimbledon title, no Davis Cup play'. Amateur competitions were crucial for showcasing the next top stars, so from their administrators' perspectives, the entire professional set-up was parasitic. In total, of the 15 players achieving number-one ranking from 1946–67, ten turned professional.

Problems associated with professional tours were particularly acute for the USLTA and LTAA. America lost more players to early signings than any other nation, while attendances at Australia's amateur competitions suffered if there was a clash with a professional match. The Hoad–Gonzáles tour of 1958, for example, broke attendance records in ten of the 13 dates in Australia and New Zealand, and created an attendance vacuum within amateur competitions. This prompted the LTAA to ban Kramer's professional troupe from using courts in affiliated clubs (Kramer 1979), which apparently cost Kramer $25,000 annually in lost revenues, but cost LTAA-affiliated clubs twice that amount in court rentals (*SI* 19 December 1960). While amateur administrators were content to "bite off their nose to spite their face" by attempting to prohibit the growth of professional tours, the players themselves considered them often a necessary evil to ensure they were justly rewarded for their efforts and talents.

Professional tours were anything but glamorous; the circus-like features of tour life remained from the interwar period, which demanded an exhausting schedule of matches, huge travel commitments and constant pressure to fill arenas in small towns and avoid getting ripped off by sales-figure-fiddling local promoters (Kramer 1979). Nervous breakdowns were not uncommon. Kramer (1979:192) recalled that toward the end of his 123-match tour with Gonzáles, he 'cracked' on court, started 'belting balls over the fence' and repeatedly screamed: 'I'm losing my mind!'. Lew Hoad also found the repetitive grind to be overwhelming, transforming him into a 'worried, hurt, moody figure, entirely lacking in confidence'. Invitations came thick and fast for product endorsements, sports-writing opportunities and radio and TV interviews, however: 'Overnight I became a one-man band, a combination of salesman, press relations expert, huckster, newsprint celebrity, sporting hero for pay', but all of this 'unsettled my poise and my tennis' (Hoad 1958, cited in Phillips 1999:97–8).

Depictions of professional tennis from amateur outlets were often less than balanced. An *LT&B* correspondent warned amateur players of its perils; touring was described as a 'deadly dull and dreary' display of 'anything more than a polished display of the strokes of the game' (1 July 1946:160). L.H.J. Dorey wrote that while he did not blame players for turning professional, he did not envy them, 'for play turned into work must in the end spell weariness of the flesh as of the spirit'. He asked:

> Can anyone imagine a more mournful performance than two players touring twenty or thirty towns, playing each other by day and by night, sometimes winning, sometimes losing, the boredom of it with nothing but a pay-packet to look forward to? The bare idea makes one want to scream.
>
> (*LT&B* 15 February 1947:635)

Amateur accounts of tour life overlooked the possibility that professionals might have enjoyed their tennis; in descriptions, they toiled and they were exploited and alienated from their bodies and their work. USLTA President Holcombe Ward declared:

> Tennis loses something intangible, but very real, when played for money. When the profit motive enters play, a fundamental change takes place; the game becomes a business, recreation becomes a vocation, and play becomes work; the spirit which animates the competition undergoes a subtle transformation, for love and money will not mix.
>
> (*LT&B* 15 February 1947:646)

The accounts from players themselves suggest that, while tour life was undoubtedly tough, they took their tennis seriously, built close relationships and were largely financially successful (Budge 1969; Gonzáles 1959; Hoad 1958; Kramer 1979).

The system of remuneration was never equitable, however, as only the best players turned a considerable profit. The vast majority played without guarantees and subsequently only got by with leftover "scraps" of money. Still, they were probably more secure financially than if they had remained amateur, the system of which Kramer (1979:63–4) described as 'rotten'. He pulled no punches in highlighting the hypocrisy of amateur officials, who through their own 'selfish personal motives ... thought of hanging onto their petty power, not of the game'. Forbes (1978:280) described amateur officials as both controlling and self-interested; 'they enjoyed their powers far too much. They developed grandiose notions and became carried away by their own importance'. Kramer was keen to wrest power away from these officious types. He contended that hundreds of young men were exploited as false ideals of amateurism were perpetuated for public consumption; they 'had their lives seriously damaged by the arrangement' (Kramer 1979:64). Players over 30 years of age nearing the end of their playing days were particularly vulnerable, as Pancho Gonzáles (1959:171) stated:

> To regress to the business world and try to carve a niche for himself is a mammoth undertaking. He's already lost ten productive years. He's too old to start at the bottom, too inexperienced to hold down a top position. All he's got to show for his efforts is a scrapbook, blistered feet, and tarnished trophies.

The acuteness of such problems was country dependent. Australian amateur officials openly worked alongside sporting-goods firms like Dunlop to arrange part-time employment so players like Frank Sedgman and Lew Hoad could remain amateur (Clerici 1975; Fewster 1985), but such opportunities in Britain were scarce. Angela Buxton worked part-time at Lillywhites, but was offered the paltry weekly wage of just £5. Most of her female contemporaries, having spurned university or early career opportunities to concentrate on tennis, retired in their late twenties with little money and very few employment prospects outside of tennis coaching (Schoenfeld 2004).

In response to accusations that the LTA were not sufficiently assisting players with finding employment to combine with their tennis, Templewood considered introducing a fund to help players 'qualify for a permanent career, instead of drifting into a blind alley that would leave them stranded' (*LT&B* 15 December 1952:532). Offering no details, he merely speculated that 'a world champion may well be a real asset to a particular business'. This was not only unsubstantiated, but downright laughable with respect to the top male players, when considering Kramer's five-figure offers that employers would have to match. Moreover, after years of public adoration, it is inconceivable that a world champion might find fulfilment in a lowly full-time desk job. Only those below the top rank might consider this a viable option, but it is likely they would be considered more a burden than an "asset". Still, the LTA continued to peddle their hollow statements about helping young players 'find a compromise between the demands of a normal career and the specialised effort needed for world class lawn tennis', but Lance Tingay remarked: 'So far the will in this seems to have been stronger than the deed' (*Telegraph* 20 June 1955). Alfred Knight wondered aloud at the 1958 LTA AGM: 'Who is going to employ a man or woman for three months of the year and let them go away and play tennis when they want to? Would anyone here have an employee under the same circumstances?' (*LT&B* 1 January 1959:11).

Players began to demand more of the available spoils for their efforts, but what events transpired to bring "open" competition to fruition? At stake was the future of tennis: who would play it and what rewards would be available for doing so? How would the game be played and with what effect on the sport's ethical foundations? And, most crucially, who would run it administratively?

After the debacle in 1938 when the LTA succeeded in rejecting the "eight-weeks rule", the Council returned after the war to vote it in by a large majority. A.K. Trower predicted its adoption 'would be quickly followed by a raising of the standard at the top, which might even be transmitted to the lower levels' (*LT&B* 1 December 1947:1238). The episode demonstrated yet again that LTA support for amateur ideals was contingent upon their competitive success, as councillors seemed willing to ignore its underlying implications toward professionalism and overlook reported abuses so long as British players could be better assisted in international competition. Mr Stowe remarked sympathetically:

> The cost of lawn tennis generally has become so great that we feel some help should be given to those who are striving their best to make England once again a great playing nation. We feel it is not too much to give these players some help towards the attainment of something we all desire to see.
>
> (*LT&B* 1 January 1948:20)

This was the first indication during the post-war period of shifting attitudes toward professionalism, but was based on confused thinking and inconsistent prioritising of chief objectives. Both the LTA and ILTF went back and forth repeatedly with their rulings on expenses, which served only to undermine amateur authority.

In 1951, the eight-weeks expense allowance was extended to an entire year, but seven years later they backtracked after numerous reported abuses. The LTA's first attempted solution was to insist upon written statements of intention from players seeking expenses from overseas tournaments, but the predictions that such demands would be 'impossible to enforce' and likely to make the LTA 'look silly' by only 'pretending to control' amateur players were proved accurate (*LT&B* 1 January 1957:13). In 1958, the ILTF reduced the expense allowance to 150 days abroad, excluding the Davis Cup, and 90 days at home, but within two years, the allowance abroad was extended to 210, after the South African and Canadian associations complained that their late-season national championships were being skipped by top players who had already exhausted their expenses allocation.

These repeated adjustments in the expense allowance proved how little control the amateur authorities had over their players. Not only were players and tournament officials in cahoots over under-the-table payments, but national associations were culpable by 'making little or no effort to enforce [the rules]' according to an official ILTF report (*LT&B* 1 September 1959:387). Desperate to repair their damaged image after further reported abuses, in 1963 the ILTF again removed all expenses restrictions, which returned them to the situation that existed from 1951–58. Interestingly, the LTA continued to enforce the 210-days rule, and actually threatened to suspend one up-and-coming player for exceeding her allowance. Throughout this period, they also offered lower per diem expenses than other nations; most gave the maximum £5, while the LTA initially gave just £3. Such actions communicated to other associations that British players were not only sufficiently rewarded but also above such potential abuses, but some correspondents were less than convinced. *Guardian* journalist David Gray suspected the LTA were 'punishing the minor offender [but] winking at breaches of the rules by major players', which made them look 'ridiculous' (12 November 1963:11). His cynicism was shared by many, as it was plainly evident that the "honour system" upon which the regulation of expenses was based had proved ineffective in Britain, as elsewhere. In this environment of greater rewards for success, there was simply no way of preventing officials slipping wads of extra cash into players' coat pockets. Admitting this, however, meant admitting fundamental flaws in the amateur ethos that was based on honesty, personal integrity and the self-regulation of behaviour. Given how deeply entrenched the amateur ideology had become within British sporting cultures and policy, this would be a bitter pill to swallow by any stretch.

A change in attitude among the national associations was necessary if tennis was to pull itself out of the "shamateur" quagmire, and the first to champion the cause was the FFT. Its president, Guy de Bazillac, admitted at the 1959 ILTF AGM that "amateurism" was in a 'turbid situation'. In a sympathetic report written and prepared by Jean Borotra, he called to attention players' 'living conditions' and stressed the importance of earning one's living honourably, 'in the full light of day' (*LT&B* 1 September 1959:387). Players, he contended, were victims of an unjust system that compelled them 'to violate the rules of amateur status in order to live', and allowed associations to renege on duties of care toward them (*LT&B* 15 May 1960:239–41). Players desirous of full-time tennis careers, the FFT argued, were forced to take handouts to survive in the absence of proper financial support. Claiming the ILTF's failures to effectively deal with shamateurism had become embarrassing, the FFT proposed creating a category of "authorised players", who would be allowed to receive full and limitless expenses and remain eligible for the Davis Cup and other amateur events. Somewhere between "amateurs", whose expenses were still limited, and "professionals", who were ineligible for amateur events, this third category set the best players apart by effectively legalising what was commonly occurring within the shamateur system.

The proposal was prudent, well thought-out and timely. In efforts to curb professional tours and protect legitimate coaching professionals, it stipulated that authorised players could not play exhibitions against professionals, compete for a wager or teach the game. Alongside a second proposal to approve eight "open" tournaments the following year, which were to be run by amateur rather than professional promoters, the FFT's suggestions allowed amateur administrators to retain control over their two most important assets, the top players and the leading tournaments. From this standpoint alone, the proposals were logical and ostensibly in the best interests of amateur tennis at this time. Both were put to the ILTF for discussion and vote at the 1960 AGM.

Hindsight would suggest that the notion of a "authorised player" would likely have done little to prevent the very best amateurs from turning professional, given Kramer's unmatchable inducements, but the extra leniency would have afforded most players the realistic option *not* to turn professional, rather than making it an absolute economic necessity for many. Stronger fields in amateur competitions would have resulted, and promoters would have had fewer client-players and thus exerted less control. However, in this environment, long characterised by fear, mistrust and suspicion of anything associated with professionalism, the adoption of this perspective represented a leap of faith for associations like the USLTA and LTAA. However, in the run-up to the AGM, representatives from both declared their support, which led Lance Tingay among others to presume, ultimately naively, that "open tennis" was assured:

> The chances are that ... many will be looking back to 1960 with nostalgic feelings. Certainly as far as the big championships are concerned it will presumably rank as the year that saw the last of the amateurs. ... The advent of open championships ... have now become an extremely likely proposition.
>
> (*LT&B* 15 March 1960:123)

Roger Williams from *LT&B* (15 June 1960:299) called it 'a certainty': 'For the first time since it was formally proposed a quarter-century ago, open tennis seems assured of acceptance.' The stage was set for an epic upset.

The 1960 ILTF AGM was recorded as 'one of the best attendances ever', with 48 nations represented (*LT&B* 15 August 1960:419). Despite early signs of promise, the proposal for "registered players" failed to receive American or Australian support. The second proposal to support eight open tournaments in 1961 received unanimous support from the four leading tennis nations, but, with an overall vote of 134 to 75, it was still 5 short of the necessary two-thirds majority. The British were confused and dismayed by what initially appeared as hypocritical voting. Barrett (1974:73) condemned the delegates 'who held their hands on their hearts ... and swore that their nations ... were not making illegal payments, [who] would return home and pay players at their own tournaments out of sheer expediency'. Tingay singled out the Irish representative Mr Walsh as a chief culprit; earlier, he made an 'impassioned speech' to the ILTF promoting the 'retention of strict amateurism', yet Ireland apparently was 'well known' for 'conducting its major and official championship with illegal payments to leading players' (*LT&B* December 1966/January 1967:4).

Kramer took the defeat to heart and speculated that personal resentment against him had brought it about, a verdict the LTA Chairman, W.E. Ramsden, concurred with; he cited 'the fear ... that Jack Kramer might assert a subversive influence over some of the "open" championships' (*LT&B* 1 January 1961:11). In actuality, Kramer had always declared himself an avid supporter of open competition given its potential to 'arouse new interest generally and bring more youngsters into the game' (*SI* 3 March 1957), but was vocal in his disappointment at having not been consulted about the proposals beforehand or been told how the amateur authorities intended professionals to be represented within their organisation. That his perceived doggedness was the chief cause of the defeated vote is unlikely, however, given that his professional tours were played in some of the very nations that supported the proposal. Instead, it seems economic concerns were paramount. While Australia and America would likely sustain the greatest risk with open tournaments, they were also best placed to secure compensatory forms of income. Conversely, the smaller nations worked to a tighter budget and likely considered the risk to their own tournaments too great. Would they have been able to continue recruiting star players if they could not offer comparable prize money? While morally justifiable, open tennis might have proved financially ruinous (Reay 1974).

Feeling victimised after the shock result, a frustrated Kramer took matters into his own hands and created the Kramer Cup, a team competition between nations like the Davis Cup, but played only by professionals. The move backfired spectacularly. Jean Borotra considered the proposition antagonistic to amateur tennis and counterproductive to fostering good relations; in fact, he believed Kramer was being deliberately hostile. The LTA and LTAA were equally peeved; both responded by banning Kramer and all Kramer Cup matches from their courts. LTAA President Norman Strange fumed: 'These hostile manoeuvres on Kramer's part are most unfortunate, particularly at a time when he is seeking our cooperation' (*SI* 19 December 1960). After failing to galvanise public support, the Kramer Cup was abolished in 1963. Thus, it achieved little as a tennis competition or as an instrument of diplomacy, and instead of smoothing the path towards open tennis, Kramer managed to alienate himself still further from the amateur establishment. While once the champion of open tennis, he was soon considered its impediment but, graciously and astutely, he admitted as much by announcing his departure in 1962:

> I suddenly realised that my presence ... is actually retarding the development not only of professional tennis but of tennis as a whole. As long as I'm around, amateur officials all over the world can use me as their excuse for not going ahead with open tennis. ... My affection for tennis is so great that I want it to prosper – with or without me.
> (*SI* 28 May 1962)

Kramer remained an active advocate of open tennis, but for the next six years his involvement was limited to that of an occasional advisor for his newly formed player's union, the International Professional Tennis Players' Association. Still, Kramer's understanding and respect for tennis, and his vision of just rewards for players, counted greatly. Perhaps more than anyone else, he had the most significant impact on curbing some of the exploitative actions of amateur administrators and prompting the removal of the hypocritical amateur–professional distinction. The period from the 1960 ILTF AGM until the summer of 1968 represents another crucial phase in this story when the British led the global push for open tennis.

For Britain, the post-war period had unfolded in ways that threatened its sense of being a "chosen nation", and its connected ideologies of insularity and isolationism. 'Since the calamitous setback of Suez in 1956', argued Bédarida (1979:274), when Britain's expectations of political deference and global superiority were shaken, they 'had been troubled with a painful sense of lost identity. ... The vision of the "new Elizabethan age" that everyone had hoped for at the Queen's coronation had vanished, and cries of "decadence" were heard instead'. Despite the proverbial furore, the "Swinging Sixties" represented an embarrassing period of British resignation, neurotic self-questioning and 'national introspection' (Bédarida 1979:274). The "Suez syndrome", according to Margaret Thatcher, had crippled the nation's sense of collective confidence for decades, and was only "cured" after the Falklands War in 1982 (*Economist* 26 July 2006). Widespread despondency came as a consequence of numerous interrelated developments: the decline of empire through decolonisation throughout the Indian subcontinent, then later throughout Asia and Africa; their lack of nuclear power in the burgeoning Cold War; and the mounting evidence of economic weakness and stagnant growth in comparison to Germany and other European rivals. Suddenly, Bédarida (1979:275) claimed, Britain 'no longer knew her position in the world pecking-order'. The European Common Market offered a means to stimulate Britain's flagging economy, if not signal future dependencies, yet its first membership application in 1961 was vetoed because of fears about their self-proclaimed "special relationship" with America, during a period of raging Cold War-induced anti-Americanism on the Continent (Golsan 2006).[1] Britain's new-found global position was a far cry from earlier times, acting less as a leader and more as a chief ally to America – some even stooped to call Britain a "US satellite" – and a cog, though not even the largest one, in the European wheel.

In this broader context, the events that transpired during the mid-1960s in the corridors of British tennis administration seem all the more impressive. The poise, leadership, assertiveness and strength of conviction demonstrated by some LTA and AELTC officials was commendable, as both institutions gambled with their respective positions of authority without any guarantees of international support. Their combined actions were exceptional as far as broader political developments were concerned, displaying the nation at its diplomatic best, striding confidently through a morass of corruption, hypocrisy and ineffective ILTF leadership, and remaining steadfast in their efforts to alter the organisational structure of elite-level tennis on a massive global scale. That these officials sought this course of action not for economic reasons, but for the sport's sake, was truly commendable.

Taking the FFT's lead, the LTA responded to the 1960 vote defeat by championing the push for open competition. Despite wavering USLTA and LTAA support as a consequence of Kramer's Cup, the British proposed at the next ILTF AGM an open Wimbledon for 1962, alongside the reassurance that all non-amateurs would be banned from administrative positions. While this was warmly welcomed, again it seemed economic issues took centrestage in the voting, even for Australia and America. The LTAA remained concerned with losing their own players to tournaments abroad and of declining attendance figures at home, while the USLTA, along with the German and Italian associations, foresaw their loss of significant tax breaks associated with "amateur" sport. At this time, television revenue and commercial sponsorship offered only limited possibilities for recouping losses. Consequently, Britain's proposal was firmly rejected, as were three more introduced in 1962 that, respectively: recommended removing entirely the amateur–professional distinction; called for greater powers to police amateur infringements; and, suggested delegating responsibility for defining and enforcing laws of amateurism to individual member nations. J. Eaton Griffith fumed at the apparent stalemate: 'To go on ... doing nothing was bringing everyone into disrepute. ... The ILTF should lead the game, but year after year they delayed giving definite opinions' (*LT&B* 15 September 1961:469). Tingay called the situation: 'a triumph for the status quo and a sad and big defeat for those who have worked hard and long to remedy the problems and abuses that bedevil lawn tennis today' (*LT&B* 1 September 1962:456).

By the time two more British proposals, for open lawn tennis in general and for an open Wimbledon in particular, were rejected in 1964, the forces for radical action had strengthened among the more progressive member nations, which Britain was now leading. For Forbes (1978:277), it was clear that 'the venerable old [amateur] system was falling apart. But so steeped were the players, officials and spectators in the traditions of amateurism that it died hard'. Until Wimbledon changed, he argued, 'the other major tournaments would hold their ground'. So, in 1964, the AELTC took the stand that many feared but few foresaw, proposing at that year's LTA AGM for the 1965 Championships to be open to all players regardless of amateur/ professional status. In justification, Herman David, Chairman of both the AELTC and the Championships Management Committee, argued the ILTF had 'lost sight completely of the reason for its existence', and had 'wilfully blinded itself' to players' financial concerns. He agreed with the American position that called for limited ILTF jurisdiction, so member nations could control their own players and run their own tournaments as they wished. Frustrated at the ILTF's inability to achieve 'anything constructive' and the apparent fact that tennis had become 'the laughing stock of other sports', David and the AELTC considered themselves duty-bound to lead 'the rest of the lawn tennis world' (Macauley and Smyth 1965:294). Tingay asked: 'Is the tyranny of the ILTF great enough to justify an armed insurrection?' (*LT&B* 1 August 1965:446). Forty LTA councillors out of the 128 present believed so and voted accordingly, but generally, while it was agreed that 'the ultimate aims of the Council and the Club are identical … [i.e.] to press for "open" tennis in some form at Wimbledon and elsewhere', this ultimatum came too soon for the LTA. If accepted, they would be forced to resign or face expulsion from the ILTF; Wimbledon would cease as an affiliated competition, meaning that its competitors would risk their amateur statuses; and, Britain would be denied entry to international cups. The move was high risk given the lack of assured support from abroad.

Following the spectacular World Cup victory for the English football team in 1966, which fielded professional players entirely, the diehard amateur stalwarts within the LTA had to concede that nobody seemed to mind as long as they won. After a succession of fairly drab Championship meetings that brought declining television figures, the AELTC decided in 1967 to pilot an end-of-the-season professional tournament at Wimbledon. Laver joined Hoad, Rosewall, Gonzáles and other stars for a large money prize supported by £35,000 BBC sponsorship. This was Wimbledon's first outside broadcast on colour television, and the event drew huge and receptive crowds. For Tingay, it 'proved beyond all doubt that professionals at Wimbledon are acceptable to the public' (*LT&B* October 1967:349). Barrett (1986:138) confirmed that the 'quality of play contrasted sharply' with what had been seen during that summer's Championships. More than just a symbolic gesture to support open tennis, this move proved it could be commercially viable and popular.

A reading of the minutes from the momentous 1967 LTA AGM revealed that, with a whopping 295–5 majority vote, the Council supported the motion that: 'all reference to amateurs and professionals be deleted from the rules of the LTA' (*LT&B* November 1967:385). Along with Herman David, the crusade was led by Derek Hardwick, recently elected Chairman of the LTA Council, and Derek Penman, Chairman of the LTA Rules and International Committee. Despite the probable likelihood of ILTF expulsion and subsequent financial implications, to which they gave full consideration, they championed the cause for open tennis as a matter of institutional integrity and moral duty. These were gentlemen of assertiveness, courage and guile; they were true leaders, but internal disagreements within the LTA forced some to question whether this move was supported comprehensively. Gerald Williams, a *Daily Mail* correspondent before becoming LTA Promotions Officer, suggested most of his LTA colleagues played 'lip-service' to open tennis because of ulterior motives. Most of them

> had just gone along with it in '68 because Herman David had given them an ultimatum and they knew Wimbledon held the purse strings. … Most of them were loath to do anything to upset Wimbledon because

they all harboured the hope that one day they might get invited to be a member of the club.

(cited in Evans 1993:67)

If this assessment holds truth, their sustained line-toeing is testament to the LTA's resolve, but equally worrying given the momentous changes afoot.

Managing to silence their conservative and diffident colleagues, the charismatic "two Dereks" travelled to Australia and America seeking support as LTA envoys, while a good amount of public correspondence threw weight behind their moral position. The *Sunday Times* produced a two-page spread detailing financial misdemeanours, and the open negotiations that often occurred in the players' tea-room at Wimbledon as tournament directors bartered for their services (Evans 1993). A ranking list was provided of weekly fees for players' appearances, ranging from $300 for players like Mike Sangster to over $1,000 for Wimbledon champions like Manolo Santana. Such reports helped fuel the LTA's moral convictions, which the Australian Davis Cup player Ken McGregor commended: 'I think the British LTA are the only people in the world who have the best interests of tennis at heart.' Then, digging at his own LTAA's decision to decide upon open tennis according to relative financial implications, he continued: '[The LTA] did not need extra gate money in order to induce them to vote in favour of open tennis' (*Times* 30 January 1968:10). Linda Timms from *World Tennis* (January 1968:20) similarly commended their courage for 'the enviable certainty that we have done the right thing. The worst we can accuse ourselves of is rashness but, win or lose, this action is on the side of honesty, reason and common sense.' Revealing some amount of surprise, she then concluded, tongue-in-cheek: 'It is a rare and delightful sensation to find oneself wholeheartedly in support of the LTA. So often one has castigated the men of Barons Court for being stuffy, backward-looking or obtuse.' In fact, beyond Hardwick and Penman, her assessment might still have held true.

Under the leadership of Giorgio de Stefani, the ILTF announced its plans to suspend the LTA from 22nd April, considering their position "undemocratic" and likely to have devastating consequences. Both *Tennis Pictorial International* (*TPI*) and *World Tennis* featured commentary on the LTA/AELTC decision from leading tennis personnel. Numerous amateur players spoke out in defiance of ILTF rules in support of open competition. Arthur Ashe remarked: 'I will play at Wimbledon if I can get [Army] leave, no matter whether the USLTA backs them or not. I'm sticking my neck out' (*WT* March 1968:12). He was joined by other high-profile Americans like Billie Jean King, Charlie Pasarell, Cliff Richey, Allen Fox and Gene Scott. Notable administrators also weighed in, some even asking for ILTF resignations, though a minority were less supportive. Harry Hopman, a long-time opponent of open tennis, joined others in considering the move 'tragic' for Wimbledon, which would likely lose its premier status (*TPI* February 1968:23).

It was the Swedish LTA that officially proposed to abolish the amateur–professional distinction and institute open competition, and called for an emergency ILTF meeting. They were soon joined by Switzerland and South Africa, while Australia and America were teetering. Under immense pressure to respond, the ILTF Committee on Amateurism reluctantly produced a report that indicated what open tennis might look like in 1968, with a compromise that allowed an open Wimbledon but sustained the amateur–professional distinction, by way of Borotra's original 'authorised player' idea from 1959. Hardwick immediately rubbished this suggestion and, on the LTA's behalf, released a statement condemning the "authorised player" as 'the quintessence of hypocrisy – it is no cure for shamateurism, as we shall still get players who are not authorized but are still receiving money above legitimate expenses under the table'. He strongly criticised the report's implied suggestion that 'professionals shall be a breed apart' (cited in *Times* 22 February 1968:15), but Ireland's stipulation shortly after, that 'any individual who plays the game for no pecuniary gain has the right to demand that he or she shall be called an amateur', strongly implied the sustained "professional" stigma (*Times* 28 February 1968:14). Throughout the public deliberations, De Stefani maintained: 'It [is] better to keep ... hypocrisy in the case of some 50 players, rather than taking a decision which negatively affects 20 million ILTF members' (*WT* March 1968:12). His personal credibility was undermined by a publicised scandal two months earlier, however. As head of the Italian Federation in the early 1960s, he was implicated in under-the-table payments made to Nicola Pietrangeli to ensure his participation for Italy in the Davis Cup (Evans 1993). Rex Bellamy stated the obvious consequence: 'The "floating voters" of the world may now be thinking that Dr. de Stefani should put his own house in order before making holier-than-thou statements to other people' (*Times* 16 January 1968:11).

The unanimous agreement among the 47 participating member nations to institute open competition at the emergency ILTF meeting in late March demonstrated just how successful Hardwick and Penman's efforts had been. Allowing the LTA to retain full ILTF membership, they agreed to four open tournaments in Britain (Bournemouth, Queen's, Beckenham and Wimbledon) among a dozen internationally. However, crucially, they declined to yield to the LTA's pivotal recommendation to dispense with amateur–professional distinctions (Barrett 1974). Individual national associations were granted the freedom of self-determination with respect to dividing players into four distinct categories. Three catered to those who accepted the authority of their respective national association: registered players, who accepted payment and were eligible for Davis Cup play; coaching professionals, who accepted payment for teaching but were ineligible for Davis Cup play; and amateurs, who received no money. The fourth category was contract-professionals, who did not acknowledge the authority of their national association and therefore were ineligible for Davis Cup selection (Barrett 1974).

228 The amateur-professional dichotomy

The ILTF's decision to maintain these distinctions had important and far-reaching consequences.

The first "open" tournament at the British Hard Court Championships in Bournemouth was, by Tingay's account, 'conspicuously, resoundingly successful', and saw the professional Ken Rosewall crowned as champion (*TPI* June 1968:26), but the main story was Englishman Mark Cox's five-set second-round win over Pancho Gonzáles, which was the first victory by an amateur over a professional in championship history. Clarence M. Jones, in *Sports Illustrated* (6 May 1968), called his victory a 'triumph' for tennis. The British public proved its thirst for open competition by allowing the West Hants Club to register record attendance levels and gross gates of almost three times their recent averages.

Despite these positive signals, it soon became apparent just how fundamentally flawed the ILTF's rulings were. By initially limiting the amount of open tournaments, Rex Bellamy warned:

> They have missed a chance of bringing contract-professionals fully within their orbit. ... The sooner the ILTF lift their limit on open tournaments – and give the contract-professionals a voice in their deliberations – the better it will be for the game.
>
> (*Times* 5 April 1968)

After Bournemouth, the ILTF were persuaded to increase their sanction of open tournaments to 30 in 1969, spread across 16 countries, but by then the professional promoters had established themselves. By failing to entirely remove the amateur–professional distinction, the ILTF provided little more than "window-dressing" for those who considered the retention of amateur control the key priority. Some weeks before the result, Hardwick shrewdly predicted that by setting professionals apart, it '[plays] into the promoters' pockets and at the same time [drives] them away from control and [asks] them to form their own association' (*Times* 22 February 1968:15). While Britain removed its amateur–professional distinction, other important nations like Australia and America did not, which allowed professional promoters to retain a stronger foothold within them. Thus, the ILTF's compromising but imprudent measures designed to protect amateur interests ultimately served to harm them, bringing administrative turbulence and instability over the following years.

The economic conditions of tennis, its players and associations, and of the wider world itself, were markedly different in 1968 compared to 1959 when Borotra first proposed his authorised-player idea. The professional tour structure had made notable advances, becoming better established and more profitable. Increasing revenues from television and sponsorship allowed new entrepreneurial professional promoters to offer more money to up-and-coming amateurs, to travel to more locations and play more tournaments. In 1959, player distinctions would not have facilitated greater control for professional promoters; in fact, had Kramer been properly consulted before the 1960 meeting, an affirmative vote likely would have led to the establishment of stronger relations between amateur and professional interests in the following years. Moreover, the promoters who replaced Kramer proved a far more self-interested and power-hungry bunch. Indeed, they weren't successful former players with dedication to and passion for tennis, but ruthless, profit-motivated businessmen. By sustaining amateur–professional distinctions, these new promoters were able to drive the wedge still deeper between the amateur and professional establishments, with the players used as political pawns. Instead of being strongly constrained, they grew in wealth and stature to the extent that they controlled the majority of the top players alongside a growing proportion of the tournament calendar and main stadiums. Barrett (1974:76) reflected:

> In the euphoria [of open tennis] … the ILTF believed that the promoters would conveniently disappear as open tournaments rewarded the players with prize money honestly earned. They could not believe that professional tournaments could succeed; they were now unnecessary.

However, through careful negotiations bolstered by the promises of lucrative signing bonuses, George MacCall and Lamar Hunt successfully signed the best young players with National Tennis League (NTL) or World Championship Tennis (WCT) respectively, instead of them remaining independent and playing for their national associations.

Forced into a corner after a large number of contract-professionals skipped the 1970 Australian and French Opens, the ILTF commissioned Jack Kramer to design and institute their own "Grand Prix" circuit, which had the blatant intention to draw talent from WCT, which under Hunt's leadership eventually absorbed NTL to become the leading professional organisation (Tingay 1973). To his credit, Hunt (1982) recognised the importance of raising the profile of professional tennis, so the best players could appear on television and compete in the world's major stadiums on a regular basis. He responded to the Grand Prix by expanding his own circuit through lucrative sponsorship deals, which put WCT in an increasingly powerful position to negotiate high "corporate fees" to ensure their players competed in ILTF events. While Hunt managed to broker deals in America, in Britain he was apparently snubbed and 'treated with appalling rudeness' by AELTC members and the press, 'who were determined to portray the quiet, courteous Hunt as a power-crazed Texan who was hell-bent on taking over the game and buying up Wimbledon in the process' (Evans 1993:49). Such blatant commercialism was most unwelcome; 'hypocrisy still had too strong a hold on people's attitudes for anyone to admit that a British sporting institution would lower itself to such behaviour', argued Evans (1993:48).

All agreed that a unified tour and high-quality fields for tournaments made for more exciting and more profitable tennis, but capitalist-driven greed and power-hunger had come increasingly to replace amateur ideals, and in this period of growing mutual mistrust, a long-term deal between WCT and the ILTF was difficult to broker. The first of numerous attempts was in early 1972, when secret talks were arranged under the direction of Dereks Penman and Hardwick. The ILTF's new president Allan Heyman was against the idea of negotiations with WCT, however; he preferred instead to try to force Hunt out of the game by continuing the recent ban imposed on contract-professionals playing in ILTF tournaments. In one of his first press conferences, Heyman memorably stated that Hunt 'did not have anything to give to the game', leading Evans (1993:70) to speculate whether Heyman was 'totally unaware of the unprecedented standards of professionalism WCT had set' in their tournaments or was merely revealing his 'pig-headed nature'. Unable to broker a deal before Wimbledon, the Championships of 1972 proceeded without the reigning champion John Newcombe, nor stars Rod Laver, Ken Rosewall and Arthur Ashe. The whole episode revealed international tennis administration in shambles, leading Barrett (1974:80) to state: 'After four years of open tennis, during which the game had boomed as never before in its history, the prospect loomed of a return to the dark ages of split worlds'.

Another attempt at a negotiation was made in 1973, when Hunt and Heyman agreed to split the season in half between WCT and Grand Prix events, but the experiment failed, given Hunt's tendencies toward dominating negotiations and filing law-suits against those that defied him. In 1978, after severe cutbacks, WCT and the Grand Prix merged again, but the marriage only lasted four years, by which time Hunt's reputation as a 'bully on the block with no concern for the game' began to precede him (Kramer 1979:279). Hunt (1982:6) personally defended the split on the grounds that the ILTF sought to impose new 'onerous' conditions when they attempted to renew their contract. The two organisations merged for good in 1985 but, by the end of the decade, the ATP Tour had taken over the Grand Prix.

Such power struggles also impacted the Davis Cup, which since 1968 had rather counterintuitively prohibited all contract-professionals from competing, despite the event's dwindling public interest. Sir Carl Aarvold predicted astutely in his 1969 LTA Presidential address: 'We have no doubt that the [Davis Cup] Competition will not fulfil its hold on the public imagination and interest if for any reason of contractual control the finest players are excluded from participation' (LTA 1969). In 1970, nine of the top nations, including America, Australia, Britain and France, were 'not permitted to select their strongest teams' (*Times* 4 March 1970:9), and not until 1973 were contract-professionals invited to participate, only after the newly formed ATP made negotiating their inclusion a primary objective. The years of decline had brought irreparable damage as, by then, argued Evans (1993:168), 'it was becoming unfashionable for the big stars to play'. The competition took from six to eight weeks to complete and offered paltry financial guarantees. According to Evans (1993) and Feinstein (1991), the Davis Cup was saved only by John McEnroe's unfaltering dedication to it onwards from his debut in 1978, helping to attract spectators, television, and sponsorship from the global electronics company NEC in 1981.

Two decades of mutual suspicion and ruthless back-biting had left the men's game in a terrible state administratively, and it showed most clearly in the ILTF's faltering position amidst growing "player power". Describing the troubles of the early open era, Evans (1993:70) wrote: 'the players were the great beneficiaries of a divided game. With two powerful elements in a tug-of-war for their services the only certain outcome was that the prices would go up'. The shifting long-term economic conditions of tennis on a global scale had a somewhat negative impact on British tournaments and the LTA itself. In 1971, John Dewar, sponsor of the prestigious Dewar Cup, demanded an end to the inflation of prize money, to protect tournaments from huge financial losses: 'The game has gone mad in the higher echelons', he claimed; 'fundamentally, no player is worth more than the amount he will draw at the gate. By taking more than that, they are in danger of killing the goose that lays the golden egg' (*Times* 12 March 1971:14).

Throughout the 1970s, the ILTF had failed to properly regulate player guarantees and prize-money offerings or stem the escalating number of tournaments during the busy summer season, leaving those events without sufficient backing to decline because they failed to recruit enough top players to draw satisfactory gates. British tournaments were hit particularly hard, as they struggled to afford the players' appearance fees to compete with their European counterparts. Their long-standing sponsorship relationship with tobacco companies also hampered them, given the growing anti-smoking lobby and new government restrictions on tobacco advertising, which was banned on television in 1965. Still, in the early 1970s, one-third of all sponsorship derived from tobacco companies (Whannel 1992). Nevertheless, some of the most prestigious British tournaments suffered. Cuts in Wills sponsorship in 1973 were followed by Dewar, Rothmans and Green Shield the following year, and by Commercial Union in 1976, which negatively impacted, among others, the British Covered Court and Hard Court Championships, the Welsh and Kent Championships in Newport and Beckenham respectively, the North of England Championships at Hoylake, the "Northern" at Didsbury, and popular tournaments in Ilkley, Cardiff, Billingham, Surbiton and Newcastle. Another casualty was the Bristol Open, which had, by 1973, become 'the principal British pre-Wimbledon grass court tournament', but the ascent of big-money events in Hamburg and Brussels forced the LTA to withdraw its support, because the ILTF stipulated that only three Grand Prix events could be staged during the same calendar week (*Guardian* 19 January 1973:25). Forced to choose between Bristol and Nottingham for the third spot, the LTA went with the latter, leading Wills to withdraw their sponsorship. After a fall to just £5,000 prize money, Bristol drew a weakened field. Subsequently, the committee decided to cease operations and the tournament was not staged again until 1981.

232 *The amateur-professional dichotomy*

Whilst tournaments and associations were getting squeezed, the players were enjoying ever greater prosperity, but by the early 1970s, the perceived necessity for unionisation was stronger than ever. From the interwar period onwards, all previous efforts to create an independent organisation for professionals had failed, because they lacked vision and struggled to galvanise sufficient player support. Various developments throughout the 1960s, however, signalled that action was needed by the players to prevent what they perceived as exploitation and arbitrary control over their livelihoods. The LTA's motion in 1960 to make participation in its County Week tournament mandatory for all selected players reeked of 'unseemly dictatorial powers', according to Tingay (*LT&B* 1 January 1960:12). The outgoing USLTA President, George Barnes, warned his European contemporaries of a "Player's Union", which he implied might turn players into employees with a consequence to sport's fundamental essence (*LT&B* 1 March 1962:101). It seemed that tennis players were expected to behave like employees when it suited their associations, but not always when it suited themselves.

Cliff Drysdale, the articulate South African, helped raise awareness of the growing plight for players, as they 'were constantly being told what to do and where to play by their national associations'. He reminded the Australians and Americans 'how their immediate predecessors had been forced to ask permission before they could even leave the country to play abroad' (cited in Evans 1993:85). He was referring to the LTAA's motion in 1964 that forbade its players from leaving Australia before April each year. Regardless of how badly Australian tournaments were suffering or how much players "owed" to the LTAA, it was clear they would not stand for such dogmatic measures, which in one instance denied a player's departure even though she was not intending to play tennis. Tingay called the LTAA's action 'like something out of Alice in Wonderland' and further remarked: 'One pictures a triple series of barriers to pass before getting out of the country, first customs, then immigration and then a sporting association' (*LT&B* 1 August 1964:420).

Despite the LTA's momentous move to sanction open competition for 1968 being made with the players' interests at heart, they failed to consult them on the finer details. Tingay was sufficiently moved to advocate for an 'authoritative professional organisation, free from financial motives ... to liaise with the amateur bodies and with the ILTF on the fairest way to conduct open tournaments' (*TPI* June 1968:27). It took four years, but at the US Open in September 1972, the ATP was duly formed, bringing nearly all the world's leading players, including ex-contract-professionals and "independents", within one organisation. Fittingly, Kramer and Drysdale were unanimously elected as their first Executive Director and President, respectively.

Within its very first calendar year, the events surrounding the Yugoslav Nikki Pilic threatened to stunt the ATP's growth by forcing a test of strength against the forceful, if somewhat authoritarian and belligerent, ILTF. It was alleged that Pilic was suspended by his national association for not playing in a Davis Cup tie against New Zealand, despite him writing to the Yugoslav association promising to play 'on certain conditions' (*Guardian* 13 June 1973:27). Not only were these conditions not met, but also the match in Zagreb clashed with the finals of a lucrative doubles tournament that he had qualified for, and withdrawing would be to renege on contractual agreements and mean that neither he nor his partner could collect their prize money. Believing that Pilic had chosen to compete for money over representing his country, the ILTF threatened suspension. For Evans (1993:85), 'money had nothing to do with it'; professionals resented amateur officials 'who thought they could run a professional athlete's career as a part-time hobby'.

As a show of support, the ATP threatened to withdraw all of its players from the forthcoming French Open if Pilic was disqualified from playing there, but as a compromise, the ILTF allowed Pilic to play (he ended up reaching the final) and reduced his proposed suspension from nine months to just one. Given this particular month included the Italian Open, Queen's and, most importantly, Wimbledon, the ILTF felt they had the upper hand. It was Evans' (1993) opinion that ILTF President Allan Heyman had chosen Wimbledon deliberately to force a "showdown". Kramer, among others, despised the arrogant officials who deemed Wimbledon unmissable, but claimed, diplomatically: 'The ATP players do not want to boycott tournaments – they only want to play in them. But we exist to see that our members get fair treatment' (cited in *Guardian* 13 June 1973:27). In their refusal to agree to an independent inquiry, which meant they 'acted as both prosecutors and judges in the matter', the ILTF seemed intent on 'gunboat diplomacy' with the ATP 'as an attempt to break their union' (*Guardian* 13 June 1973:27). Kramer and Evans agreed; the latter remarked: 'The game's hierarchy had treated the players like workers for too long. Now the players were acting like workers and implementing their right to strike' (Evans 1993:90). Seventy-nine ATP-registered players called the ILTF's bluff and withdrew from the 1973 Championships, including 13 of the top 16 seeds. Despite the demonstration, Wimbledon drew record crowds; no doubt, the public were fascinated by the novel possibility of unearthing unknown talents, as seeded for the first time were none other than Bjorn Borg and Jimmy Connors.

The ultimate effects of the boycott were far-reaching as far as tennis governance was concerned. By demonstrating the scope and potential clout of collective action, the ATP justified its existence and ensured its future presence as an administrative force in men's tennis. The episode revealed how far power relations had shifted in world tennis, 'stressing that professional [sportspeople] had rights over their own careers that their employers had not been allowing them' (Polley 1998:121). The ILTF were damaged irrevocably, as from the ashes of the 1973 boycott grew the idea of forming the Men's International Professional Tennis Council (MIPTC) to administer the sport. Heyman initially objected to the Council's nine-man structure, which gave equal representation to tournament officials and the ATP alongside the ILTF, yet the ultimate irony was that, two weeks earlier, Heyman's ILTF sought cooperation from Herman David's AELTC committee to manipulate Wimbledon in his power struggle with the ATP, but was now suggesting that tournament directors were undeserving of direct representation. Heyman preferred his part-time officials to retain arbitrary control over professional tennis players instead (Evans 1993). The MIPTC administered the sport from 1974 until 1988 when the ATP Tour was instituted.

As another consequence of the ILTF's somewhat soured reputation, support was more readily obtainable for alternative tennis competitions that offered cash incentives, like World Team Tennis (WTT). Spread over three months of the season, the mixed-gender team-tennis league that flourished from 1974–78 not only drew players and fans away from some of the smaller ILTF events, but also clashed with the French Open, which had suffered in recent years from declining television fees, corporate support and spectator interest because of crumbling facilities and frequent star-player absenteeism (Feinstein 1991). Philippe Chatrier, FFT president from 1972–92, took measures to curtail its development, including a ban on WTT players. 'Those were desperate times. We took desperate measures', Chatrier reflected (cited in Feinstein 1991:218). In the late 70s, Roland Garros resurged after the terrestrial French-government television network, TF1, agreed to copy the BBC's model for Wimbledon and televise the event solidly throughout the tournament. The choice of greater exposure over money helped turn the tournament into a national event and thus a matter of national pride, and Bjorn Borg's six singles titles from 1974–81 led the event to surpass even the US Open in prestige and popularity (Feinstein 1991). In the open era, the precariousness of even the leading tournaments was fully appreciated by tennis officials.

Throughout the 1960s and 70s, international tennis administration was markedly transformed from its original amateur-run, ILTF-dominated structure to incorporate business interests, in the form of television networks and corporate sponsors, and growing player power, emphasised through the ATP's emergence and the rise to prominence of agencies and management groups. The ILTF survived, but short-sightedness with regard to sustaining the amateur–professional distinction, alongside the formation of the ATP and the MIPTC, forced a reduction of their overall power. In the early open era, the Davis Cup suffered greatly, and the four major championships under the ILTF's authority merely stumbled through, at times losing ground to strictly professional tournaments or competitions like WTT. Moves toward professionalisation and commercialisation were seldom made voluntarily; "modernisation" for national associations and the ILTF was necessary for survival.

After their commendable stand against the ILTF to usher in open tennis, the LTA entered the post-1968 era full of confidence, but, like other associations, they realised fairly quickly they were being outmuscled by profit-driven corporations and promoters. Outside of Wimbledon and a small handful of pre-Wimbledon events, their tournaments had declined in prestige relative to their Continental and American rivals, their players and talent-development schemes were comparatively poorly funded, and their facilities needed updating. Partly in consequence, relative playing standards reached an all-time low, particularly among the elite British men. Enhanced funding came eventually, but against the backdrop of inveterate prejudices against women, the working classes and ethnic and religious minorities, access to talent-development opportunities continued to be limited. It was evident that post-war growth in tennis occurred in the context of white, male, upper-middle-class dominance, yet the civil rights and feminist movements abroad helped reveal the relative extents that the needs and desires of marginalised people were discounted. The revolutionary mindset that found expression through demonstrations, international conflicts and decolonisation campaigns shook the foundations of traditional conservative Britain. In tennis, as in other spheres of society, the opportunities for ethnic and religious minorities and women to reap the rewards and opportunities their white, male, Protestant counterparts obtained remained scant, yet their achievements were notable. The following chapter attempts to position their personal challenges and achievements in the broader contexts of social change.

Note

1. Their granted entry in 1973 was ratified after a referendum two years later.

Bibliography

Baltzell, E. D. (1995). *Sporting Gentlemen: Men's Tennis from the Age of Honor to the Cult of the Superstar*. New York: Free Press.
Barrett, J. (1974). Open Tennis. In M. Robertson, *The Encyclopeda of Tennis*. New York: Viking Press.
Barrett, J. (1986). *100 Wimbledon Championships: A Celebration* (pp. 72–84). London: Collins.
Bédarida, F. (1979). *A Social History of England 1851–1975*. London: Methuen.
Betz, P. (1949). *Wings on my Tennis Shoes*. London: Sampson Low, Marston & Co.
Bowers, R. (2005, 22 November). *History of the Pro Tennis Wars 1926–1945, Chapter X: Budge's Great Pro Year, 1939*. Retrieved April 11, 2014, from Between the Lines: An Analytical and Sometimes Controversial Look at the Pro Tennis Tour: http://www.tennisserver.com/lines/lines_05_11_22.html
Bowers, R. (2007a, 19 March). *Between the Lines: Forgotten Victories: A History Pro Tennis 1926–1945, Chapter XII: America 1942*. Retrieved April 11, 2014, from A History of Pro Tennis 1926–1945, Chapter XIII – The High War Years 1943–45. Retrieved April 11, 2014, from Between the Lines: An Analytical and Sometimes Controversial Look at the Pro Tennis Tour: http://www.tennisserver.com/lines/lines_07_03_19.html
Budge, D. (1969). *A Tennis Memoire*. New York: Viking Press.

Clerici, G. (1975). *The Ultimate Tennis Book: 500 Years of the Sport.* Chicago, IL: Follett Publishing Company.
Evans, R. (1993). *Open Tennis: 25 Years of Seriously Defiant Success On and Off the Court.* London: Bloomsbury.
Feinstein, J. (1991). *Hard Courts: Real Life on the Professional Tennis Tours.* New York: Villard Books.
Fewster, K. (1985). Advantage Australia: Davis Cup Tennis 1950–1959. *Sporting Traditions*, 2(1), 47–68.
Forbes, G. (1978). *A Handful of Summers.* London: Heinemann.
Golsan, R. J. (2006). From French Anti-Americanism and Americanization to the 'American Enemy'? In A. Stephan, *The Americanization of Europe: Culture, Diplomacy and Anti-Americanism after 1945* (pp. 44–68). New York: Berghahn Books.
Gonzáles, P. (1959). *Man with a Racket: The Autobiography of Pancho González.* New York: A.S. Barnes and Company.
Hoad, L. (1958). *The Lew Hoad Story.* Englewood Cliffs, NJ: Prentice Hall.
Hunt, L. (1982). World Championship Tennis ... A Reflection. In R. Humphries and T. Meredith, *1982 Guide to World Championship Tennis* (pp. 3–6). Texas: World Championship Tennis.
Kramer, J. (1979). *The Game: My 40 Years in Tennis.* London: Andre Deutsch.
Lawn Tennis Association. (1969). *Lawn Tennis Association Annual General Meeting Presidential Address.* London: Lawn Tennis Association.
Macauley, D., and Smyth, J. (1965). *Behind the Scenes at Wimbledon.* London: Collins.
Phillips, C. (1999). *The Right Set: The Faber Book of Tennis.* London: Faber & Faber.
Polley, M. (1998). *Moving the Goalposts: A History of Sport and Society Since 1945.* London: Routledge.
Reay, B. (1974). Administration of the World Game. In M. Robertson, *The Encyclopedia of Tennis* (pp. 87–94). London: George Allen and Unwin.
Schoenfeld, B. (2004). *The Match: Althea Gibson and Angela Buxton.* New York: Harper Collins.
Tingay, L. (1973). *A History of Lawn Tennis in Pictures.* London: Tom Stacey.
Whannel, G. (1992). *Fields in Vision: Television Sport and Cultural Transformation.* London: Routledge.

15 "All whites" at Wimbledon?
The achievements of Gibson, Ashe and Buxton amidst shifting race relations in Britain

Since before the Cold War had commenced, the power of propaganda to influence both domestic and foreign opinion was well understood. In the 1950s, America and the Soviet Union both embarked on international tours, hosted events and manipulated media broadcasts principally to enhance their image and spoil the opposition's. In this context, the post-war civil rights issues in America achieved global relevance and provided the impetus to expedite the process of desegregation to convey publicly a narrative of progress (Thomas 2012). In the 1950s, British and American foreign policies were tied together closely, so progress for the civil rights movement and African-American athletes more specifically were matters of some relevance. This was especially so, given the subtle but pivotal roles indigenous athletes played in fostering anti-imperialist sentiments that featured in widespread decolonisation movements from the 1950s onwards.

As the first African-American tennis player to succeed at the highest level, Althea Gibson's achievements resonated in Britain. Despite winning five major championships, however, embarrassingly little has been written of her in the context of developing race relations; in sports historiography, she has often been overlooked in favour of male athletes, particularly those from boxing, athletics and the leading North American team sports (Lansbury 2001). Her achievements have also remained shamefully under-celebrated in tennis circles, according to Harris and Kyle-DeBose (2007:74):

> The tennis establishment has done virtually nothing to keep alive Althea's legacy. The WTA ... has no award for her, no tournament named for her, no championship trophy named for her. The US Open, played in New York City where she was reared, has no court or any section of the National Tennis Centre named for its first-ever African-American champion.

In Britain, Gibson was greeted with an often indifferent reception. Some considered her an inspirational symbol of perseverance, while others, in subtle racism characteristic of this period, discussed her in the context of subversive black physicality as arrogant and mannish. Her unique partnership with

British Jew Angela Buxton, which culminated in victory at Wimbledon's 1956 Doubles Championship, has been accorded some recognition in hindsight, but its significance at the time was largely underappreciated. At face value, their achievements point to the ways in which developments in sport reflect those in broader society; they have been mythologised as sporting heroines (Schoenfeld 2004). However, setting their achievements (and failures) in a wider socio-historical context reveals the active rather than passive role that sport played. Polley (1998:5) recommended considering 'how sport is shaped and constrained by wider forces, and how it interacts with them and reproduces them; ... how sport works as part of British society, not just how sport reflects demographic trends'. From this vantage point, one can more readily identify the ways that tennis was both a catalyst for change within an increasingly multi-cultural and multi-ethnic Britain, but also a useful platform to rearticulate and reinforce structures of social inequality. This was particularly the case with Arthur Ashe, whose rise to tennis prominence coincided with a period of burgeoning anti-racism campaigns, but against a backdrop of working-class resistance to racial assimilation in the context of Britain's economic decline. The aims of this chapter are to position the relative successes of Gibson, Ashe and Buxton in the context of shifting race relations in Britain.

The rise of Althea Gibson from the farm-town of Silver, South Carolina, to victory on Wimbledon's Centre Court was nothing short of meteoric. Born and raised when Jim Crow laws dictated the types of restaurants, stores, cinemas, schools and sports clubs black people in particular southern American states could frequent, Gibson's experiences reflected simultaneously the progress and limits of the civil rights movement. Previous to her emergence, the only opportunity for high-level competitive tennis for African-Americans was through the American Tennis Association (ATA). Formed in 1916, this body represented chiefly the interests of black players, despite being officially open to all, irrespective of race. Throughout the interwar period, they organised tournaments and galvanised financial support from African-American elites, which helped lend legitimacy to their association that, by 1941, catered for over 1,000 players from 145 affiliated clubs (Harris and Kyle-DeBose 2007). That virtually none of their champions aside from Gibson became household names is indicative of the strict policy of racial exclusion the USLTA had in force. When the ATA lobbied for Gibson to compete in the US Nationals in the late 1940s, her application was rejected because 'she had not participated in enough USLTA tournaments', which was an inevitable outcome of being denied such opportunities by the (white-dominant) affiliated clubs themselves (Harris and Kyle-DeBose 2007:54). Alice Marble wrote an eloquent open letter to the USLTA, published by *ALT* (July 1950:14), urging Gibson's inclusion:

> It's time we acted a little more like gentlepeople and less like sanctimonious hypocrites. ... The entrance of Negroes into national tennis is as

inevitable as it has proven to be in baseball, in football, or in boxing; there is no denying so much talent.

The USLTA relented under public pressure, but facing the three-time defending Wimbledon champion and 1947 US Nationals champion Louise Brough in the second round, she was perpetually harangued with shouts of 'Beat the nigger, beat the nigger' and eventually succumbed 9–7 in the third set (Harris and Kyle-DeBose 2007:57). After a poor performance at Wimbledon she contemplated quitting, but was soon invited on a goodwill tennis tour to Southeast Asia. Organised by the US State Department, Gibson's inclusion alongside several white players was, according to her, entirely based upon her being black (Schoenfeld 2004). The tour's purpose was propaganda, to defuse Soviet charges of racial inequality by helping to portray America as 'colour-blind and democratic' (Alamillo 2009:948). It also served the purpose of helping to reignite Gibson's passion for tennis, as within weeks she began accumulating tournament victories. Her first major singles championship at Roland Garros in 1956 was followed by the US Open and Wimbledon in 1957 and 58, but comments about her physical appearance and skin colour had become ubiquitous in the media. Many women found her physicality and playing style intimidating; even her future doubles teammate and lifelong friend Angela Buxton recalled her first sight of Gibson practising: 'She didn't look like a young woman playing. ... She played with a vest and shorts. I thought it was a young man out there' (cited in Harris and Kyle-DeBose 2007:61). Correspondents made reference to her supposed lack of on-court femininity. Gibson's serve and overhead at the 1956 Surrey Championships were described as 'man-like' and 'fierce', respectively (*LT&B* 15 June 1956:288). The *New York Times* (7 July 1957:4) noted Gibson's 'mannish style of play', while the *Atlanta Constitution* (5 July 1958:10) described her 'manlike power' when hitting the ball. Gibson's physicality alongside her indefatigable competitiveness, ruthless killer instinct and ubiquitous "blackness" combined in media representations to caricature her as "different" in the context of her gender and race, which helped to marginalise further her athletic achievements (Lansbury 2001). Hughson (2009:95) contended the exhibition of tough play and competitiveness was 'more problematic for a female sport hero than for a male sport hero'.

Gibson's qualities did not win many white, middle-class admirers in either America or Britain. In 1956, the *Sunday Graphic* correspondent Scottie Hall criticised the British crowds after her semi-final loss to Shirley Fry: 'Shame on the Centre Court. I accuse the Wimbledon crowd of showing bias against Miss Gibson. ... It wasn't anything that was whispered ... [or] shouted. ... It was just an atmosphere, tight-lipped, cold' (1 July 1956). When she and Buxton triumphed in the women's doubles, which represented the first Wimbledon Championship title ever won by a black person, the British press were reticent; Buxton recalled: 'It was as if the press felt, "Maybe she'll go away." When we won the doubles title, there was in one of our major papers in England a small column in thin type, "Minorities Win." That was it' (cited in Harris and Kyle-DeBose 2007:62). The following summer, it was reported that the Wimbledon crowd 'turned against her' because of a strong 'colour feeling' (*Sunday Graphic* 7 July 1957).

That the British public did not immediately warm to Gibson is unsurprising, given the context of race relations at this time. The docking of SS *Empire Windrush* at Tilbury port in 1948 that brought 492 West Indians to Britain launched an open immigration movement that lasted until the 1960s. Initiated to help in post-war recovery efforts by providing the relatively cheap and mobile labour needed in the booming industrial areas, the new Commonwealth immigration policy extended invitations also to those from the Indian subcontinent, but unfortunately coincided with a severe housing shortage (Rich 1986). Into the mid-50s, the influx of West Indian immigrants ran at around 3,000 per year, and brought fears among the major government ministries of social and political problems associated with racial tensions, segregation and the creation of black urban "ghettos". These fears were realised at least partly with the rise of patterned black immigration in Camden Town, Paddington and North Kensington. Their "seedy" image and association with organised crime and prostitution only deepened racial tensions (Rich 1986).

Hostilities in Britain did not reach the levels of violence or outright discrimination experienced in the southern USA, but Britain's self-proclaimed bold and high-principled liberal attitude toward ethnic minorities was at times found wanting, particularly in working-class areas where competition for housing and employment exacerbated racial tensions (Rich 1986). The Nottingham and Notting Hill race riots of 1958 serve as examples. Moreover, the embarrassing Suez crisis in 1956 and ongoing decolonisation campaigns did little to assuage fears of imperial decline (Bédarida 1979; Polley 1998). Race relations were uncontrovertibly bound within these broader political issues (Rich 1986).

Among the more restrained white British middle classes, reactions to new immigrants were often initially characterised by passive awe and curiosity rather than open aggression. Gibson's Wimbledon victory in 1957 was described according to, and contextualised by, her ethnicity; writers fell into the "trap of reductionism", treating 'a sportsman or woman's colour and cultural heritage as if they [were] the only things that [mattered] about them' (Polley 1998:140). Indeed, not a single mainstream newspaper report of her achievement failed to mention her race. *LT&B* correspondent Geoffrey Green contextualised the moment when Gibson received her trophy from the Queen: 'Here in a small way was a pointer to the shifting forces of the mid-twentieth century. That, indeed, was an historic moment, a fitting climax to the whole colourful fortnight' (15 August 1957:446). Correspondents were keen to illustrate a rags-to-riches narrative, which helped to frame Gibson's achievements in the context of her race (Lansbury

2001). Stanley Doust (*Daily Mail* 7 July 1957) emphasised her impoverished upbringing:

> Althea Gibson, the 29-year old coloured American who learned her tennis with a wooden bat in the dank, dusty play streets of Harlem, graduated to glittering stardom. ... For her, Wimbledon was a personal crusade to achieve something for her race that had never been done before.

Despite her successes, she was vilified by the "black" press for 'refusing to assume a more outspoken role as race hero' that was expected (Lansbury 2001:244). In some southern states, African-Americans continued to be lynched, schools remained segregated despite the Brown vs. Board of Education decision in 1954, and black voting rights were routinely obstructed (Thomas 2012). Her way of "getting involved" was to win tennis tournaments; she refused to take a public stand on civil rights issues (Schoenfeld 2004). Her sporting success was thus a double-edged sword, and her case study highlights the combined pressures of being forced to actively and simultaneously represent three marginalised groups: women, black people and working-class people (Lansbury 2001).

Given that her participation was in a white-dominated, upper-middle-class sport, expectations of behavioural restraint and high standards of sportsmanship and personal appearance were sustained. These expectations were especially crucial for blacks, where disgust and resentment were felt toward 'the dregs who debased themselves and their race' (Schultz 2014:57). Gibson (1958:29) remarked that black elites

> had rigid ideas about what was socially acceptable behaviour. They were undoubtedly more strict than white people of similar position, for the obvious reason that they felt they had to be doubly careful in order to overcome the prejudiced attitude that all Negroes lived eight to a room in dirty houses and drank gin all day and settled their arguments with knives.

Common also for black players was their appropriation of conservative "white" styles of dress, and generally, most socially aspirational African-Americans were keen to distance themselves from degrading stereotypical images associated with being black (Schultz 2014). Therefore, it is likely for this reason that Gibson's perceived 'aloofness', 'arrogance', and lack of 'poise' and 'grace' when among reporters and players hurt fellow African-Americans, who considered high standards of deportment a duty to their race (Lansbury 2001:245).

While Gibson often rejected such behavioural expectations, Arthur Ashe considered them at times subversive but a legitimate means to further his cause for racial equality. The "black conservatism" he endorsed represented a means to articulate his upper-middle-class background within a liberal integrationist programme of reform. His reasoned, eloquent, mild-mannered personality contrasted with the brash, aggressive posturing of other black male activist-athletes, like Muhammad Ali (Thomas 2010). His key achievements as a tennis player, winning the 1968 US Open, 1970 Australian Open and 1975 Wimbledon Championships, propelled him to international fame and provided a platform to advocate for stronger African-American leadership. The personal values of piety, respectability and humility that he projected publicly, both on- and off-court, did much to warm Ashe to the white middle-class audiences in America and Britain. Exhibiting self-restraint, honesty and respect to all opponents and officials, regardless of how they treated him, his exemplary manners contrasted with the wild and ill-disciplined conduct of white counterparts like Jimmy Connors and Ilie Năstase. His successes did not fundamentally challenge the power structures of amateur tennis administration, but to some extent they certainly contested dominant stereotypes of black athletes as arrogant and disobedient. For some among the African-American community, however, Ashe's enduring politeness and courtesy toward the white establishment attracted accusations of him being a subservient "sell-out". Like Gibson, he was vilified among the "black" press for his seemingly contradictory behaviours in the face of broader race integration issues (Thomas 2010), but he reasoned:

> For the first seventeen years of my life, white people in Virginia had told me what I could do, where I could go to church, in which taxi I could ride, where I had to sit on the bus, in which stores I could try on a coat. Then, in my second seventeen years, militant black people were trying to tell me, once again, exactly what to think and do.
> (Ashe 1993:155)

The "black man's burden", as Ashe himself put it, consisted of two forms of racial oppression: first, that a black man should become a spokesman for black issues when he succeeds in a white world; and second, that social and political conservatism and being black are incongruous for black men and allied to being a traitor to his race (Bodo 1995).

In Britain, at a time when middle-class black-British men and women were gaining much greater access to tennis club memberships, the tennis public were more willing to embrace him. Particularly given his less sophisticated public exposure, he was not presented critically as a contradictory figure. Thus, Ashe became an important model and spokesperson for racial equality in Britain, but, unlike Gibson, he was acutely aware that his tennis achievements translated to opportunities to win support for larger racial objectives. The British Centre Court crowd reacted to Ashe's stylish, calculated and 'masterly' dismantling of the brash and irritable Connors in the 1975 Wimbledon final with great enthusiasm (Barrett 1986:152). They gave 'lustful applause', according to Harris and Kyle-DeBose (2007:92), which 'made it sound as if they had temporarily adopted the lean, graceful black man from Richmond, Virginia' as their own. Frank Rostron from *The Express* recalled the 'most emotional, almost hysterical, ovation' he received (7 July 1975). British newspapers described his warm personality, restrained behaviour and refined background that were appreciated by the middle-class public. The *Daily Mail* (7 July 1975) referred to his 'cool dignity and intense tactical concentration', while Michael Davie from the *Sunday Observer* (6 July 1975) witnessed his 'intelligence and sanity ... [not] a showcase black'. He was able to galvanise the white British tennis-playing public in ways that Gibson never could, despite his success occurring during a period of even greater racial unrest in Britain.

The 1968 and 1971 Immigration Acts attempted to institute stronger controls on Commonwealth immigration, but by then the escalating problems of urban unrest were well documented; Britain's non-white population had reached a sizeable 1.5 million – 2.5 per cent of the total population (Bédarida 1979). The 1970s was characterised by a tumultuous period of political rule, which saw no fewer than five prime ministers in office, from Harold Wilson to Margaret Thatcher, and marked economic instabilities: high inflation, reaching a peak of around 25 per cent in 1975; the devaluing of Pound Sterling in 1967; rising unemployment, which moved upwards from 1 million in 1970 to over 3 million by the mid-1980s; and stagnant economic growth compared with its European counterparts, in part due to trade union unrest and miners' strikes (Bédarida 1979). In such an unstable environment, racist right-wing groups galvanised the disenchanted and partook in systematic violence against blacks. Years of racist discrimination in job and housing allocations and police brutality were presumed a chief cause of inner-city race riots in Toxteth and Brixton throughout the 1980s. Around the time of Ashe's win, bad feelings endemic particularly among working-class blacks and whites were simmering, and this was also in the wake of controversial anti-Apartheid sporting boycotts against South Africa. Michael Herd from *The Standard* (26 June 1974) recalled the irony of seeing a 'vicious and insulting' painted slogan on the wall outside Southfields tube station that read 'Negro out' at precisely the time when Ashe had just been elected president of the ATP; as both a successful black sportsman and administrative leader, it was inevitable he would be singled out as a political voice for black people wherever he went.

If Gibson's and Ashe's triumphs were considered part of a larger movement toward racial/ethnic emancipation, Angela Buxton's were not. As a British Jew, she remains a single brush-stroke on the canvas of post-war British-Jewish sports history. She did not pave the way for a swathe of elite-level British-Jewish tennis players, and nor were her accomplishments given much weight in the wider context of combating anti-Semitism in Britain (Dee 2011).

Historically, sporting participation has been a contentious subject for Jews, despite considerable efforts to challenge stereotypes of Jewish men as weak, effeminate and more concerned with intellectual than physical pursuits (Meyer 2011). Dee (2011) discussed the anti-Semitic sport propaganda that emerged in the 1930s among right-wing organisations like the British Union of Fascists, which derided the Jews' lack of sportsmanship, misunderstanding of the "fair play" ethos and over-concern with money-making, and condemned Jewish managerial control over sport generally. These ideas reinforced notions of Jews as "the other", "different" or "un-British", which remained pervasive even after WWII. Middle-class clubs for golf and tennis continued to discriminate against Jews, enacting subtle but pervasive exclusionary measures that bordered on systematic, and forced many Jews to form their own "parallel institutions" (Dee 2011). Some assembled under the Maccabi World Union umbrella, for example the Manchester Maccabi and Liverpool Maccabi tennis clubs, while others developed substantial Jewish memberships more organically, like Chandos LTC in Golders Green, a principally Jewish north London neighbourhood.

Buxton's interests and ultimate achievements in tennis marked her out from the beginning of her playing career as different and unusual. Her shameless and open ambitions to excel contrasted somewhat with expected middle-class reserve (Dee 2011). 'Those who were raised properly were taught never to let that ambition show, at least to the point where it could cause someone else discomfort', argued Schoenfeld (2004:90). Alongside the propensity to ostentatiously display her material wealth, her pushiness and individualism – all common Jewish stereotypes at the time – offended some in the British tennis establishment (Dee 2011). After being denied membership at the prestigious Cumberland Club in north London and later at the Los Angeles TC in California, in both cases because she was Jewish, Buxton's application for membership was accepted at Chandos LTC. She was also granted membership at Queen's Club, which had become especially liberal with membership given its post-war financial struggles. Buxton made Queen's her chief training facility for her brief but notable playing career from 1953–56.

Various injuries among other British players precipitated her selection for the 1954 Wightman Cup squad, and she went on to represent Britain twice more. Alongside Angela Mortimer and Shirley Bloomer in the 1955 Cup, however, journalists contended that cultural/religious differences produced a 'certain amount of coolness' between them; Mortimer and Bloomer travelled and roomed together, leaving Buxton on her own, and apparently 'it never occurred to them to ask Angela to join them' (Schoenfeld 2004:134). Despite feeling excluded, she achieved her first taste of public recognition in the 1956 Championships, when she became the first British player since Kay Stammers in 1939 to reach the singles final. Also winning both the French and Wimbledon doubles Championships with Gibson, she reached a world ranking of five.

Her successes failed to translate into public honours as one might have expected, however. The Lawn Tennis Writers' Association, which gives an annual award to the individual they consider made the greatest contribution to British tennis, preferred to leave the 1956 award vacant than give it to Buxton. The AELTC were equally reluctant to honour one of their most successful post-war players. While winning the Wimbledon singles Championship was the only way to guarantee automatic membership to the club, the offer of honorary membership had become an established custom for British players who achieved notable success. Buxton's achievements more than qualified her, but she believed, and still believes 50 years later, than inveterate anti-Semitism among the club committee prevented her membership application ever being accepted. In a recent interview with *The New York Post* (13 June 2004), she remarked being on the waiting-list since the 1950s and stated: 'The mere fact that I'm not a member is a full sentence that speaks for itself'. While other British players, some of whom never entered the world's top 100 let alone reached two Wimbledon finals, continue to be added to the AELTC membership list, Buxton remains a most notable omission for reasons that are likely never to be disclosed.[1]

In numerous subtle but persuasive ways, the achievements of Gibson, Ashe and Buxton are as telling of existing class structures and patriarchy as they are of racial intolerance. In her assertive playing style and unrelentingly competitive demeanour, Gibson epitomised a new brand of womanliness. While dancing and singing off court, she looked a picture of dominant heterosexual femininity, but on court she defied conventions in her aggressive playing style and unwillingness to lose graciously. Much like Alice Marble, she was a quintessential tomboy, but her ubiquitous "blackness" made her a subversive figure. Thus, elements of her race and gender combined to marginalise her sporting achievements. Buxton's problems were primarily religious, but often applied in the context of her gender. While her uncompromisingly stylish appearance complemented feminine ideals, she was considered brazen with it. Ashe's case study confirmed that pressures to conform to behavioural conventions were even greater for minorities, though perhaps were less important for men who were successful. Where both Gibson and Buxton failed to live up to exalted virtues, Ashe most definitely succeeded, through exhibiting a full repertoire of textbook qualities befitting a British sporting hero that resonated with the public: modesty, sportsmanship, pluck, coolness under pressure, an ostensibly effortless playing style and "underdog" success. While being white, male or home-grown certainly might have eased acceptance into the bosom of the British tennis fraternity, the exhibition of "class", in both rigid socio-economics and in a behavioural-ethos sense, continued to prove more important. The subtle but nonetheless ostensible public rejection of Gibson, Buxton and even Fred Perry, yet the celebration of Crawford, Drobny and Ashe suggested that attitude, style and grace remain of greater relevance to the middle-class public celebration of sporting heroes than race or nationality.

The fact that this analysis of race/ethnicity focused heavily on female athletes also points to the progress made and the challenges faced by women during this period, in the context of broader shifts in societal gender relations. It was evident for both Gibson and Buxton that pejorative attitudes toward their race/ethnicity or religion worked alongside norms and values accorded to their gender; they were thus doubly constrained, or triply constrained in the case of Gibson's working-class background. The following chapter considers developments for female players in the context of the second-wave feminist movement, which highlights areas of notable progress alongside other spheres where important discrepancies remain.

Note

1. Other Jews have since been admitted as AELTC members.

Bibliography

Alamillo, J. M. (2009). Richard 'Pancho' Gonzalez, Race and the Print Media in Postwar Tennis America. *International Journal of the History of Sport*, 26(7), 947–965.

Ashe, A. (1993). *Days of Grace*. London: Mandarin.

Barrett, J. (1986). *100 Wimbledon Championships: A Celebration*. London: Collins.

Bédarida, F. (1979). *A Social History of England 1851–1975*. London: Methuen.

Bodo, P. (1995). *The Courts of Babylon: Tales of Greed and Glory in the Harsh New World of Professional Tennis*. New York: Scribner.

Dee, D. (2011). *Jews and British Sport: Integration, Ethnicity and Anti-Semitism, c.1880–1960*. Leicester: Unpublished PhD dissertation, De Montfort University.

Gibson, A. (1958). *I Always Wanted to Be Somebody*. New York: Harper Collins.

Harris, C., and Kyle-DeBose, L. (2007). *Charging the Net: The History of Blacks in Tennis from Althea Gibson and Arthur Ashe to the Williams Sisters*. Chicago, IL: Ivan R. Dee.

Hughson, J. (2009). *The Making of Sporting Cultures*. London: Routledge.

Lansbury, J. H. (2001). 'The Tuskegee Flash' and 'the Slender Harlem Stroker': Black Women Athletes on the Margin. *Journal of Sport History*, 28(2), 233–253.

Meyer, A. R. (2011). Jewish and Christian Movements and Sport. In B. Houlihan and M. Green, *Routledge Handbook of Sport Development* (pp. 20–30). London: Routledge.

Polley, M. (1998). *Moving the Goalposts: A History of Sport and Society Since 1945*. London: Routledge.

Rich, P. (1986, January). Black People in Britain: Response and Reaction, 1945–62. *History Today*, 36(1). Retrieved from History Today.

Schoenfeld, B. (2004). *The Match: Althea Gibson and Angela Buxton*. New York: Harper Collins.

Schultz, J. (2014). *Qualifying Times: Points of Change in US Women's Sport*. Champaign, IL: University of Illinois Press.

Thomas, D. L. (2010). 'Don't Tell Me How to Think': Arthur Ashe and the Burden of 'Being Black'. *International Journal of the History of Sport*, 27(8), 1313–1329.

Thomas, D. L. (2012). *Globetrotting: African-American Athletes and Cold War Politics*. Champaign, IL: University of Illinois Press.

16 'Particularly concentrated upon the boys'

Persistent struggles for women in post-war tennis

Developments for women in the early post-war period were tinged with contradiction. The "nuclear family" was put forward as the clichéd model of middle-class suburbia, but the promise of higher standards of living as a consequence of low unemployment and a booming economy were juxtaposed with the return of women to their domestic duties. In tennis, women remained largely absent from club and association committees; their responsibilities were reduced to serving refreshments, catering for visiting teams, organising social events and fund-raising activities. American women, in particular, made notable advances in playing styles and training methods, but this did not immediately translate into progress in other areas, as they compensated for their increasing aggression on court by both dressing and behaving in accordance with traditional gender roles. As the second-wave feminist movement took hold, women demanded greater economic freedom and educational opportunities, equal pay and reproductive rights. In several key areas, tennis was significant in the physical emancipation of women, joining in both liberal and radical movements at certain moments, particularly in the post-1968 era.

When tennis went "open" the new opportunities for legitimate income both from prize money and product endorsements went disproportionately toward the men. Actions from some of the leading females to stake claims for legitimacy and contend with their marginalisation brought forth challenges to the inveterate patriarchal structures of tennis administration. The fruits of their labours included the creation of the highly successful Virginia Slims tour, the formation of the Women's Tennis Association (WTA), the victory of Billie Jean King over Bobby Riggs in the much-publicised "Battle of the Sexes" match, and the marked escalation of prize money and endorsement opportunities for female players. In accordance with social, cultural and political trends toward equal rights and opportunities in Britain, advances were also noticeable for homosexuals and people with disabilities. Both were outcomes of a shifting discourse of the body (Polley 1998), which played an important role in the context of broader shifts in gender relations and the "commercialisation of sexuality" that occurred throughout the mid–late twentieth century (Hargreaves 1994). The aims of this chapter are to position key developments for women's tennis in the broader context of shifting gender relations. Developments in America proved particularly influential in Britain, helping to contextualise similar problems and experiences there, at a time when American cultural influences were coming increasingly to bear upon British lifestyles.

When the all-male LTA Executive Committee met at the first post-war AGM in 1946, their discussions were narrowly focused on two key issues, namely how to restore British on-court prowess and how to deal with the problems related to amateurism/professionalism. Essentially, both were primarily concerned with men's tennis. Davis Cup success and having a male singles champion at Wimbledon were widely agreed as the key achievements that defined Britain's overall standing, so these goals received a disproportionate amount of LTA resources. Males were targeted more than females for subsequent talent-development and coach-education schemes and LTA-sponsored tours. For example, a special fund to provide financial assistance for promising youngsters initiated in 1952 was to be 'particularly concentrated upon the boys', argued Templewood, 'for the obvious reason that [their] standard … is at present higher' (*LT&B* 15 December 1952:532). This is debatable, as even during their mid-50s to mid-70s heyday, women's tennis was allocated inequitable resources. Also, the problems that "open tennis" sought to overcome chiefly implicated male players; indeed, outside of some exceptional cases, elite men received the lion's share of under-the-table expense payments and also dominated the professional tours. Kramer as a promoter considered women a weaker draw and any contracts offered were usually as sideshow acts for the showcase matches involving men.

Despite tennis offering greater opportunities for women to participate, excel and gain public admiration for their talents than most other sports, women remained limited in other qualitative ways. Female players were marginalised, their performances were often trivialised and deemed less important than those of male players; their identities were constructed as wives and mothers first rather than athletes, and in media representations they were subject to infantilisation, often referred to as "girls" rather than "women"; their bodies were sexually objectified; and, they were often forced into segregated sporting spaces, including separate tournaments or clubhouse rooms (Hargreaves 1994; Messner, Duncan and Jensen 1993). Tennis was not unique in obstructing the progress of, and discriminating against, sportswomen in terms of their social position, roles and behavioural expectations.

A key contributing factor was the lack of female presence in key decision-making positions within sports associations (White and Brackenridge 1985). From a photograph in *LT&B* it appears as if Mme Gerke from Czechoslovakia might have been the first female ILTF Council member in 1946, but her name failed to reappear on published lists. Onto the LTA Council, only three women were elected during the entire interwar period, and after the war, their representation improved only marginally. In 1960 just five of the LTA's 99 council members were female, and in 1970 just three from 79, representing a mere 3.8 per cent. Likely as a result of wider societal developments shortly thereafter, including the passing of the 1975 Sex Discrimination Act, the proportion increased to 12.5 per cent in 1980 and to 21 per cent in 1990. This was still far from equitable in a sport that enjoyed near equal participation among the sexes at a recreational level. However, the position and rights of women in clubs was not necessarily assisted by the Sex Discrimination Act, given that "private and single-sex clubs and voluntary associations" were exempt from the law (Hargreaves 1994).

Their lack of presence in associations' boardrooms was reflected in media production, as all key aspects of this process continued to be male-dominated and male-focused (Hargreaves 1994; Markula 1995). The vast majority of regular correspondents and writers in the major British tennis magazines remained men until well into the open era. Mary Hardwick became a regular news correspondent and feature writer in *LT&B* from the late 1940s, and was possibly the first female to hold such a position. An assertive character, she did not exclusively focus on issues pertinent to women's tennis, possibly in a conscious effort to garner greater credibility among male colleagues. Gladys Heldman also created and chief-edited *World Tennis* in 1953, yet these remain exceptional cases. When women did voice a particular grievance, they often complained about a specific circumstance rather than the broader system of patriarchy. For example, in 1953, E.A. Rodacanachi, the Honorary Ladies Match Secretary for Sussex, grumbled about the difficult task of securing teams for inter-county matches during the winter, principally because they were scheduled on weekdays when an increasing number of young women were in full-time work. As a solution, she proposed playing instead on weekends, as the men did, but wondered how clubs 'would feel about lending their courts' (*LT&B* 15 November 1953:572). Despite making no explicit reference to them, Rodacanachi's comments spoke to deeply embedded structural inequalities that favoured men's work over women's and, in this instance, men's tennis over women's. Such was the norm; most differences noted in gendered experiences were often considered situational rather than structural. It was some time later that women more assertively connected individual experiences like these with broader social-structural inequalities, and began collectively championing the cause for fundamental change.

The war effort brought British women more centrally into industry, as they worked in engineering, munitions, mechanics, shipbuilding, aircraft production and metal-work, alongside their roles as administrators, clerks and telephonists. From being actively recruited and later, through conscription, forced to learn skills and trades traditionally reserved for men, after the war, with stable families recognised as the most important institution in the reconstruction of British society, many women seemed content to settle back into traditional family roles, subordinated by the demands of domesticity and child-rearing (Bruley 1999). Into the 1950s, any rumblings of discontent because of unequal pay or reduced hours were dismissed, as economic prosperity led to improved middle-class standards of living. In many respects, women colluded with men with regard to setting standards of behaviour and appearance, and they continued to vote for male leaders. Feminine ideals for sport remained similarly conventional. The preservation of homophobic beliefs during this period of general conservatism played an important role in the process of narrowing and more strictly defining the models of feminine appearance and behaviour that sportswomen were expected to conform to. The cropped-haired, muscular, tomboy image of athletes like Mildred "Babe" Didrikson became incompatible with post-war ideals, which were reinforced as much from female athletes themselves as from male administrators and social commentators (Cahn 1994). The potential for sport to masculinise its female participants was considered an increasingly problematic issue from an educational and moral perspective. Widespread efforts were made not necessarily to curtail women's participation opportunities per se but to more closely regulate them. It was well known, for example, that Didrikson was both cautioned on and ridiculed for her unfeminine appearance, compelling journalists to "remedy" her unfeminine appearance by referring to her abilities in sewing, cooking and curtain-making (Cahn 1994).

The particular codes to which female tennis players were expected to adhere were multifaceted, stretching to how women should play, how they should appear on and off court, what attitude toward training and the pursuit of sporting success they should adopt, and what overall role sport should play in their lives. In 1947, an *LT&B* correspondent hinted at these expectations:

> Despite our present-day coupon and laundry troubles our British lady players manage to look wonderfully well-turned out on the courts. It's a miracle to me how they manage to do it and also in many cases to run a house and a family as well.
>
> (1 June 1947:853)

Media representations reinforced the notion that sport participation for women was more of a hobby than a sustainable career; sport was not to encroach on a woman's chief maternal and marital duties (Tolvhed 2012). Many women viewed work as a stopgap between education and marriage, but female tennis players used their sport participation as a substitute for work (van Someren 2010), and there was a well-established and more-or-less taken-for-granted expectation that getting married and starting a family meant the end of a competitive sports career (Hargreaves 1994). When American player Beverly Fleitz discovered she was two months pregnant during the 1956 Wimbledon Championships, she immediately withdrew, despite having reached the semi-final; she and her husband agreed it would be 'terribly irresponsible' of her to continue. There was little indication that

Fleitz objected to her withdrawal; 'tennis was an ephemeral pursuit, while a family meant forever', argued Schoenfeld (2004:199). The Newsome Report from 1963 gave explicit state-level support for the clear-cut sexual division of labour within the workplace and family home, stressing the woman's 'main social function ... is to make for themselves, their children and their husbands a secure and suitable home and to be mothers' (cited in Beddoe 1983:61). In 1979, a BBC Wightman Cup commentator stated: 'Since Chris [Evert] married, tennis hasn't been quite at the top of her priorities – which is quite natural' (BBC 2 November 1979). After all, he added, why should a highly successful career impede a woman's main duty and calling? Evert reflected some years later: 'All my life, I've been asked the same two questions. When I was single, it was always, "Who are you dating?" When I'm married, it's always, "When are you going to have a baby?"' (cited in Feinstein 1991:452). Female players, compared to male players, were more frequently defined and described according to their marital or maternal statuses well into the twenty-first century, and the persistent reinforcement of emphasised gender differences rooted in biological determinism has made it difficult for them to justify their achievements in sport as equal to those of men (Hargreaves 1994).

Alongside the expectation that they approach tennis with less seriousness, their game was also held on a higher pedestal of morality. While men often avoided persecution for minor behavioural transgressions, any questioning of calls, glares at an umpire, unpleasant reactions to crowd noise, emotional outbursts, gamesmanship and ostensible arrogance were considered more seriously when executed by women, who were, according to Bodo (1995:310), 'more sensitive about and to such things'. Indeed, one of the many reasons why Althea Gibson failed to win public admiration was her refusal to be obsequious, though some would say courteous, toward her more experienced opponents. The public were not quite ready for her ruthless and unashamed competitiveness, which could also be said for Serena Williams over 50 years later. Billie Jean King reflected on a verbal outburst against a line-judge at the 2009 US Open:

> You see all those [male] players go absolutely ape, and people move on with them. They don't want to seem to move on with Serena. They think it's kind of funny sometimes with the guys. They *never* think it's funny with women.
>
> (cited in Baird and Major 2012)

Most post-war female players successfully masked their uncompromising intensity and fierce devotion to tennis through their cheerful demeanours and feminine appearances. Despite the impression of carefree disinterest, for many, tennis was anything but inconsequential, even as children when they learned to play with vigour, resourcefulness and assertiveness (Kay 2010; van Someren 2010). Christine Truman (1961:8), for example, reflected: 'I wanted to be really good. I could never see any point in just playing for a hit and a giggle'. Virginia Wade (1978:45) said similarly: 'From the beginning I had an unrestrained competitiveness in tennis. ... I cared more about it than others did. If devotion was any measure, then I should be the best'.

Evidently, the popularity and long-term viability of the women's game was predicated upon a combination of factors, all of which created a challenging context for females to succeed in. While the demonstration of their athletic talents was acceptable, they were expected to hide their competitiveness under the veil of "playing for fun", while also managing their appearance in line with predetermined feminine ideals. Struggles related to the proposed liberalisation of tennis attire in the 1950s underlined the importance of appearing appropriately "feminine". Numerous high-profile figures, including Hazel Wightman, objected to the advancement of tennis fashions that conveyed immodesty or were ostensibly "masculine" in style (Tinling 1983). Perry Jones, a leading official in Southern California, embarrassed some of the leading players who chose to wear t-shirt and shorts combinations: he offered money to Maureen Connolly's mother for her to purchase a replacement outfit; he excluded a young Billie Jean Moffitt from the group photograph at the Southern California Junior Championships; and, argued publicly with Angela Mortimer at the Pacific Southwest Championships (Lumpkin 1981).

British officials were similarly constrained by tradition, as the case of Gertrude "Gorgeous Gussy" Moran's outfit at the 1949 Championships proved. At the pre-Wimbledon event at Hurlingham, she appeared in a tennis outfit that revealed lace panties underneath, prompting rows of photographers to line the court on their stomachs to catch a glimpse (Tinling 1983). After she appeared in the same outfit at Wimbledon, the outfit's designer, Ted Tinling, was verbally attacked by an AELTC committee member: 'How could you do something so tasteless? ... You have put sin and vulgarity into tennis' (Tinling 1983:131). After serving for 23 years as official call-boy at Wimbledon, the episode resulted in Tinling's subsequent split from the AELTC, but created a media backlash. Apparently, the public enjoyed the fashion transgression; its 'explosive' public reaction provided a springboard for widespread changes in tennis fashions, and exposed the subconscious urge to 'return to femininity and sexual attraction in clothing' (Tinling 1983:119). Tinling said later: 'People were bored out of their skulls after the war. It was the same old, same old. They needed cheering up, they needed and wanted some kind of change. They were ready for sex' (cited in Bodo 1995:188). The masculinised uniform appearance of early post-war female players was soon replaced by shorter and more figure-hugging costumes that accentuated rather than hid the curvaceous female form, and into the 1960s, tennis dresses became even shorter and tighter and exposed more flesh than was customary.

Moran's fashion transgression shot her to international fame, but when she signed for a professional tour at just seventh in the US rankings in 1951, she could not contain the on-court dominance of Pauline Betz. Crowds flocked to see Moran perform, but her good looks did not translate into good tennis or any long-term financial success, leading Kramer (1979:94) to state: 'If ever I had any doubts, I learned from this experience that tennis fans come out to see tennis. ... The lace-panty publicity was worthless. All that mattered was that ... Pauline was routing Gussy'. It proved that male audiences in particular *did* care to watch good competitive tennis, particularly once the novelties of new fashion trends and statements had worn off. Thus, while the increasingly sexualised public presentations of the female sporting body in the 1950s and 60s helped to raise the popularity of women's tennis, changes in appearance alone would not have sustained spectatorship on a long-term basis. Some important structural and institutional changes played an important role.

The first major change came in 1962, when, after a prolonged campaign led by Helen Jacobs and Mary Hardwick, the ILTF agreed to organise a women's international team-tennis competition (Lumpkin 1981). Finance was an issue, though, as the ILTF refused to provide funding for travel expenses as it did for the Davis Cup; to make it economical, the competition had to be strategically timetabled to coincide with a country's own national championships. The first "Federation Cup" played at Queen's Club alongside the London Grass Court Championships was said to have been 'an outstanding additional fixture', but cost the LTA over £1,700 (*LT&B* 15 December 1963:643). For the Cup to survive, ultimately it had to open itself up to large-scale commercial sponsorship, which was at this point largely underexplored. Despite an inauspicious start, the Cup managed to position itself fairly well after agreeing a sponsorship deal with Colgate in 1976 and NEC from 1981–94. The British squad were supported by a £4,000 deal from Green Shield Trading Stamp Company from 1970. Such sponsorship facilitated marked growth; in 1963, just 16 nations were represented, but in 1994 there were 73.

Slowly but steadily, women were making inroads. The drain of talent from the men's amateur ranks increased notably after the 1960 ILTF vote on open competition, leading Tingay to remark that men's tennis had become too standardised and homogenised: 'When you have seen one [male player] you have seen the lot'. Despite his personal preference 'to concern himself with men's matches in preference to those of women', he could not contain his feeling that the latter had become more compelling to watch, concluding: 'Women play classic lawn tennis and it is very nice to see' (*LT&B* 15 May 1962:240). The influx of new captivating personalities into the women's game, including Maria Bueno, Margaret Court and Billie Jean Moffitt, helped boost popularity in the women's game considerably, and their improved standards of play and physical fitness added credibility and greater excitement. The *LT&B* editor admitted: 'It is a fact that women's matches arouse very much the same interest as the men's in the top-class play in this country'; the men's game was centred on 'the big service, big volley and big smash', whereas women's matches were '[campaigns] of well-directed and well-planned groundshots involving absorbing rallies and more flexible tactical manoeuvres' (*LT&B* 15 December 1963:642). Problems for men's tennis continued in 1964, when the Scandinavian Covered Court Championships reduced all matches but the final from best-of-five to best-of-three sets, after complaints: 'spectators were tired of long serve and volley duels' (*LT&B* 15 February 1964:76). Wimbledon in 1965 was described as 'not a great vintage year', because of a depleted men's draw, which contained no Europeans in the last eight, and the champion Roy Emerson's unmemorable play. 'Had it not been for the women', Tingay admitted, 'the tournament would have been no more than just a good one'. The final between Bueno and Smith was particularly commended, when 'superb play and the arts of the aggressive women's game can rarely have been revealed to such a high degree' (*LT&B* 1 August 1965:446).

The top female players lived a heady, leisured lifestyle, including an abundance of international jet-travel, first-class accommodation and other luxuries, which was the envy of other sportswomen (van Someren 2010). While more radical feminists would have been sceptical of these developments, given they occurred in the context of male dominance, and because their achievements failed to challenge inveterate patriarchal structures, liberal feminists would argue pragmatically that they managed to manipulate sport for their own interests, and were active to some extent in the (re)construction of their own identities. That their achievements occurred in the context of male dominance and in accordance with often male-defined notions of appropriate femininity, however, made these women's suggestions for change less threatening and more palatable for male administrators. Subtle improvements in the social status of female players certainly assisted the cause of women's liberation and helped pave the way for more radical developments that occurred after 1968.

The second-wave feminist movement of the 1960s and 70s concerned itself with a wide range of issues, including equal opportunities in education and equal pay and self-determination through the right to abortion (Hattery 2010). In the UK, various legislative reforms signalled such progress, including the 1967 UK Abortion Act, the 1970 Equal Pay Act, the 1974 Women's Educational Equity Act, and the 1975 Sex Discrimination Act. There is little evidence to suggest that feminists recognised sport's full potential as a vehicle for change, however. Hargreaves (1994:25) argued: the women's movement 'tended to focus on questions of legal, political and ideological importance, rather than on cultural issues such as sports and leisure'. Even if it was not entirely appreciated, however, the central role of "the female body" as contested terrain lent sport real significance, particularly in tennis, where women and their bodies were highly visible objects subject to intense and constant scrutiny.

The creation of open tennis, with its clearly set-out prize-money allocations, helped make visible the differential levels of compensation for male and female players, when previously the financial deals were arranged in secret (Spencer 1997). Understandably, male players sought to sustain the higher payments they had enjoyed for years, initially as expenses and now as legitimate prize money. Even Arthur Ashe stated: 'Men are playing tennis for a living now. They don't want to give up money just for girls to play. ... Why should we have to split our money with them?' (cited in Howard 2005:38). The first open Wimbledon Championships in 1968 offered £2,000 for the male champion, but just £750 for the female champion, while other tournaments offered even greater disparities (Collins 1974). The British player Ann Haydon-Jones was notably the first to voice her objections in 1968, threatening to withdraw from the open tournament in Bournemouth as a protest against the women's winner offered just £300 compared to £1,000 for the men, but ultimately compromised her position by stating: 'We are not asking for equal prize money, but it should be at least half of the men's amount, not a third as they are offering now' (*WT* April 1968:34). The talented Americans Billie Jean King and Rosie Casals were less easily placated, and commenced their campaign for *equal* prize money at the Pacific Southwest Championships in 1970, which offered $12,500 to the men's singles winner, versus $1,500 for the women's champion (Evans 1993). Kramer, as tournament organiser, justified this disparity by rearticulating his opinion that most female players drew insufficient crowds to warrant comparable prize money. The 1953 US National Championships final between Maureen Connolly and Doris Hart, for example, attracted less than three thousand spectators (Tinling 1983). While a disparity undoubtedly existed, it was also true that tournament committees tended to privilege men's matches with better courts and facilities. Shortly after winning Wimbledon in 1969, Ann Haydon-Jones played the final of a tournament in Aix-en-Provence, France, on a back court, and recalled there were 'no linemen, no ballboys, no spectators and not even a glass of water to drink' (Jones 1971:165). Even LTA officials, after travelling over to Paris for the French Open final in 1961, were 'more concerned with their lunch as none of them watched my match. At about 4:30pm one or two did enquire how I got on!' (Jones 1971:84). In fact, she had won the tournament.

By 1970, arguably, the global appeal of women's tennis had improved significantly, but seemingly the attitudes of some tennis officials remained conservative. After Kramer refused to amend the discrepancy, the reaction from the leading female players was immediate, decisive and enduring. King and Casals organised a boycott of his tournament, and appointed *WT* editor Gladys Heldman to secure sponsorship for an alternative event in Houston. Virginia Slims cigarettes were approached; they tapped into the feminist movement as part of its advertising campaign, with their slogan 'You've come a long way, baby'. In time, this would become a fitting slogan for the new Virginia Slims (VS) tour, which launched after nine of the top players, including King and Casals, signed $1 contracts in defiance of the male-dominated USLTA (Tinling 1979). Facing the possibility of suspensions, but buoyed by their initial success, a further dozen tournaments were negotiated and staged over the coming months. All were fully backed by VS and outside of USLTA/ILTF jurisdiction; all offered at least $10,000 prize money, and all but two made a profit (Bodo 1995; Lumpkin 1981). Collins (1974:69) remarked:

> The women's rebellion caught fire but no one was really sure if the public would come out to watch. To their great surprise and delight, the public adored the women and enjoyed the slower pace, greater variation and top consistency of women's matches as compared with the men.

A protracted power struggle ensued between the VS tour and the USLTA/ILTF. The latter attempted to penalise VS professionals by removing their eligibility for many USLTA events, outside of the US Open. However, the lure of greater prize money was enough to create a mutiny, and the rebellious tour continued to grow. From the original nine – seven Americans and two Australians – by 1972, there were 55 players, and by 1978 there were 84, when still over half (43) were American. Given the involvement of American-based corporations in sponsorship and the relative dominance of American players, it was unsurprising that the uprising against unequal rights, pay, recognition, and status would spring from America. Under King's stewardship, they unionised under the Women's International Tennis Foundation (WITF), which was the precursor to the WTA that officially formed at Wimbledon in 1973.

The USLTA responded with their own tour, enlisting newcomers Chris Evert, Martina Navratilova and Evonne Goolagong, but their lighter schedule and lower prize money compared unfavourably with VS. As a last-ditch compromise, the USLTA/ILTF proposed equal prize money for men and women at the 1973 US Open, in return for an amalgamated circuit under USLTA jurisdiction, but with Heldman remaining tour promoter and VS a key event sponsor (Lumpkin 1981). Bolstered by broadcasting agreements with CBS and further sponsorship by Avon and Colgate, the WTA increased its stature, and, as an unintended outcome, tournament prize money and opportunities for supplementary income from product endorsements exploded for female players (Collins 1974). In 1975, Chris Evert earned $300,000, which was more that year than Arthur Ashe and even the first-ranked golfer Jack Nicklaus (Koster 1976). Two years later, she was the first female athlete to earn $1 million.

Alongside the VS tour and the creation of players' unions, arguably the most significant event for women's tennis globally was Billie Jean King's exhibition match against Bobby Riggs in September 1973. Labelled the "Battle of the Sexes", King's comprehensive straight-sets win against the 55-year-old outspoken chauvinist was attended by a record-setting crowd of 30,472 and an estimated 37 million American television viewers

(Lichtenstein 1974). King's vision and courage to champion the campaign for women's rights in tennis as part of the broader feminist struggle helped to galvanise the non-tennis-playing public and propel tennis to greater heights and public attention (Lumpkin 1981). Moreover, the UN spokesperson for sport, Richard Lapchick, suggested that King's victory translated into 'victories for women in the board room, in higher education and in other areas of life'; the leading American activist, Gloria Steinem, felt the outcome helped legitimise the cause of feminism (cited in Hahn 1998:25). Spencer (2000) posits that King's efforts were adopted within a radical feminist framework, despite important aspects of her accomplishments incorporating liberal approaches that only touched underlying patriarchal structures. For instance, while the VS tour was managed by Heldman, it was backed by male tobacco industry executives. More pertinently, the players agreed to dress more provocatively to attract bigger crowds. Ellen Merlo, from the VS parent company Philip Morris, remarked: 'We figured that to be important, women's tennis had to look important, so we hired ... Tinling to make the girls look glamorous when they were normally playing in T-shirts' (cited in Tinling 1979:308). The players also made special efforts to convey femininity, and compensated for the exhibition of athleticism through their demeanour and off-court interests. The media helped reinforce this "feminine apologetic" to reassure audiences of the athletes' femininity and heterosexuality (Cahn, 1994; Hargreaves 2000; Kane 1996).

Given King's tomboy image and perceived association with the feminist movement, she appreciated the importance of appearing "feminine" for the tour and especially for her match against Riggs. She prepared in true 'showbiz' style by getting a 'terrific tan' (Taylor-Fleming 1998:131), and appeared on court in a glamorous Tinling creation, short in length and studded with sequins (Tinling 1983). When she entered the arena "Cleopatra style" on a raised chair carried by four muscular, bare-chested men, ABC's Howard Cosell described King as 'a very attractive young lady' and announced: 'sometimes you get the feeling that if she ever let her hair grow down to her shoulders and took her glasses off, you'd have somebody vying for a Hollywood screen test' (Arledge 1973). Her efforts to cultivate her appearance, however, reflected the dominance of heteronormative ideologies and practices, which implicitly condoned both heterosexism and homophobia (Hargreaves 2000).

King's victory against Riggs made tennis 'an instrument of world communication', according to Tinling (1983:185), but subsequently put the spotlight even brighter on its female players to conform to accepted measures of femininity. Female athletes in general not only came to be 'treated with condescension', but were also 'derided as mannish freaks, arrested tomboys, or some exaggerated horde of closeted lesbians' (Howard 2005:46). Tennis players faced 'pronounced bigotry', summarised here by Stan Smith's expressed fears:

These tennis girls would be much happier if they settled down, got married and had a family. Tennis is a tough life and it really isn't good for them. It de-feminizes them. ... [They become] too independent ... They want to take charge, not only on the courts but at home.

(cited in Howard 2005:38)

While lesbians suffered the indignant criticism of masculinising women's tennis, heterosexual female players were labelled as lesbians if they displayed characteristics like aggression, independence and competitiveness; 'the notion of a sexy woman athlete was a contradiction' (Howard 2005:46). However, Horne and Bentley (1989:4) contended that the late 70s represented a turning point in dominant sporting femininity, as 'the "worked on" female body [became] not only permissible, but presented as desirable'. "America's Sweetheart" Chris Evert epitomised this new more palatable form of sporting athleticism with her "girl-next-door" good looks, in the process of winning 18 major singles championships throughout her illustrious career. Her brief romance with Jimmy Connors was billed by the *Sunday Telegraph* (7 July 1974) a "love match", and later her wedding to the handsome British number one John Lloyd ranked just behind the Charles and Diana royal wedding in showbiz glamour (Feinstein 1991). Beneath her ultra-feminine veneer, however, was a finely-tuned athlete, who considered her actions crucial in countering assumptions of rampant lesbianism on the women's tour: 'I don't think there's any doubt that one of the reasons I became the girl-next-door to the public was my sexuality. People could relate to the fact that I was always dating men' (cited in Feinstein 1991:455).

The British tabloid press in the late 70s, around the time of Evert's peak, were particularly prone to trivialise the performances of her colleagues through sexual objectification. A revealing photograph capturing the instant when one of Linda Seigel's breasts fell out of her outfit at Wimbledon in 1979 brought the headline 'Linda Serves a Smasher' in *The Sun* (28 June 1978); the article mentioned how 'she bounced out of her low-cut dress', before featuring a comment supposedly from Seigel admitting that she tends not to wear a bra while playing. That same year, Betty Ann Stuart received tabloid attention for her revealing outfits. Accompanying numerous photos were articles describing her as "gorgeous" and "lovely". John Jackson from *The Mirror* (5 July 1979) joked: 'Betty Ann Stuart reaching for a low return is still one of the best sights at Wimbledon. ... Oh yes, her tennis is reasonable, too'.

At least Evert's successes forced some attention upon her tennis. Her ascendancy came at an opportune time to boost the glamour and spectacle of women's tennis, which was still reeling from various scandals involving questionable sexes and sexual orientations of its players (Lake forthcoming). In 1976, the arrival of a male-to-female transsexual tennis player by the name of Renée Richards (born Richard Raskind) exposed the difficulties that beset female players across the entire gender spectrum, and also out the spotlight on the inability of sports associations to legislate effectively, fairly and respectfully in cases of perceived anomalies. After Richards' decision to compete in the 1976 US Open, the USTA and WTA followed the IOC in requiring a chromosome test to "confirm" her gender (Howard 2005). Chromosome testing had been officially sanctioned from the mid-60s, but Pieper (2012:679) contends that it was used for the first time in 1976 specifically 'as a way to remove Richards from competition'. The basic notion of gender testing supports the idea of polar distinctions between male and female athletes; 'a binary predicated upon the patriarchal assertion of male biological advantage' (Pieper 2012:678). Men were not asked to undergo the test, as it was assumed that being born "female" was not an advantage on the men's tour. Despite "failing" the test and being barred from that competition, a Supreme Court ruling in 1977 declared the USTA/WTA decision in violation of civil rights. Her right to compete on the women's tour was reinstated, yet caused widespread controversy and protest, from male administrators alongside other female players (Birrell and Cole 1990). The international sports authorities demonstrated a preference for clearcut dichotomous characterisations of gender – either male or female – and these broad divides in "the West" were heightened in the Cold War context, when images of butch, muscular and likely steroid-enhanced Soviet or East-German female athletes provoked fear over the loss of femininity in sport and the possibility that gender distinctions between men's and women's sports were blurring (Pieper 2012; Ritchie 2003). Moreover, as political and ideological differences intensified, the female body was politicised in ways that reflected and represented national identities, which provided the impetus to exaggerate differences between women of competing nations still further (Cahn 1994; Tolvhed 2012).

In what Birrell and McDonald (2012:354) argued was a 'shifting cultural landscape', the 1970s and 80s were characterised by 'feminist challenges to conventional sexual arrangements and advocacy for greater sexual autonomy for women' and 'burgeoning gay urban cultures' that 'forged the social support and resources necessary to challenge homophobic legislation and attitudes'. Despite the broader liberalisation of gender/sexual norms stemming from various legislative victories for gays in both Britain and America, homosexuality in women's tennis continued to be viewed as "different" and therefore abnormal. Ted Tinling recalled an incident in the 1970s at his favourite Eastbourne tournament when a spectator, possibly intoxicated, stood up during a changeover for a match involving two known lesbians, and shouted: 'That's it. That's *it*, I'm not watching these bloody dykes for one more second! I've had it!' Pointing his finger then at Ted, also a known homosexual, he shouted: 'And you, Tinling, you fucking homosexual you, you shouldn't be watching them play either!' (cited in Feinstein 1991:85). Parents began travelling more frequently with their daughters on tour principally, according to Feinstein (1991), because of exaggerated stories about players being "recruited" into lesbian relationships.

The public "outings" of both King and Navratilova in 1981 brought the sport further to the forefront of public judgement and fuelled a climate of fear and homophobic backlash. Papers like the *National Enquirer* incited in effect a "lesbian witch-hunt" by offering money to players in exchange for details about other lesbians on tour (Birrell and McDonald 2012; Festle 1996). Moreover, King's admittance to bisexuality and Navratilova's to lesbianism led them to receive homophobic abuse and hate-mail and cost them both millions in lost endorsement earnings (Cahn 1994; Hargreaves 2000; Howard 2005; King 1982; Mewshaw 1993). Navratilova reflected on a 'very good endorsement possibility' that emerged in 1984, for example, but was rejected by the company's president; it was reported: 'he said no, because she's gay' (*Guardian* 21 November 1991). That same year Navratilova was criticised for her "sexless" appearance at Wimbledon:

> With her sleeveless pullover and open-neck shirt, Czech Martina Navratilova is the epitome of today's sexless look. Except for the fact she is wearing a skirt, her clothes are completely uni-sex. I believe in tennis as ballet and I accept that women should dress to enhance their femininity.
>
> (*Daily Mirror* 6 July 1984)

Comparing endorsement deals with Monica Seles, who at that time had only won one major championship compared to Navratilova's 18, Navratilova remarked: 'Seles is making more money from Yonex than I am. If I said that doesn't bother me, I'd be lying. ... It isn't a matter of needing the money; it's other people putting some kind of value on you' (cited in Feinstein 1991:390). These discrepancies reflected the dominant narrative of heterosexuality as the ideal, and while Evert's rise certainly encouraged greater spectatorship and corporate sponsorship, which helped the women's tour survive and flourish, her often exaggerated femininity that was normalised and privileged, impeded efforts to oppose homophobia.

It is plausible that these developments in women's tennis also had an impact on how men displayed physical dominance toward each other, judged by the introduction of more extreme forms of behaviour and a general down-trend in on-court manners from the mid-70s onwards (Lake forthcoming). Players like Ilie Năstase, Jimmy Connors and John McEnroe built reputations on their "bad-boy" images: Năstase was known to swear at crowds and "pull tricks" as gamesmanship tactics; Connors was 'pugnacious and cocky and nearly as unpopular as he was talented' (Clerici 1975:320); and McEnroe alienated some fans through his verbal tantrums at referees, line judges and opponents. It appears they seemed to relish their hyper-masculinised public portrayals, not only because they enhanced the sport's entertainment value, but also because they helped to dignify men's tennis as more than an upper-class, "sissy sport". Examples are numerous of open-era players defending tennis as a masculine endeavour. Cliff Richey (2010:144) reflected: 'I didn't like all [the] prim and proper bullshit. ... I was always proud of the fact that I brought a little more manliness to the game'. Connors (2013:11) agreed with Andre Agassi's (2009) likening of tennis to a form of boxing, 'throwing blows at each other until there's only one man left standing'. The media had played on this analogy, replete with abrasive language, since the 1970s. As a BBC radio commentator, Fred Perry remarked of Connors' comprehensive defeat of Vitas Gerulaitis in the 1978 Wimbledon Championships: 'Today Connors became a man. He got the guy on the floor and tore him apart' (*Mirror Sport* 7 July 1978).

The emergence of such discourses of masculinity in the men's game reflected another trend toward the overt commercialisation and commodification of the body, which had long been present in women's tennis. The sportswear and accessories that adorned the female sporting body, the make-up worn, the styles of hair and overall "look" were invested with cultural meaning and valued according to crude market principles (Hargreaves 1994). They became effectively moving manikins, displaying the latest clothing lines to be worn over the coming season in clubs across Britain. This ostentatious display was particularly visible at Wimbledon, where fashions, styles and appearance showed no sign of diminishing as popular public conversations.

Countless female players in the open era supplemented their incomes with modelling pursuits or product endorsements that obliged the sexual objectification of their bodies, including Gabriela Sabatini, Steffi Graf, Jennifer Capriati, Martina Hingis, Anna Kournikova, Maria Sharapova, Serena Williams and Caroline Wozniacki. British players like Sue Barker and Annabel Croft became commodities in a different sense, exploiting earning potential from their fame through the expansion of opportunities for women in television commentary (Polley 1998). From a liberal feminist perspective, Spencer (1997) believed such actions helped reverse the negative media attention that earlier players had received; no longer were they ignored or automatically labelled as tomboys or lesbians, but their raised profiles gave them a stronger platform from which to re-create their own identities as independent women. Apologetic actions did little to challenge the distinct male/female binary, however, as women conformed largely to male-defined notions of femininity that marginalised non-conformists as "deviant". Consequently, eating disorders like anorexia and bulimia were not uncommon – Carling Bassett-Seguso and Zina Garrison admitted to suffering from both – yet the WTA, alongside players' agents and corporate sponsors, continued to pressure female players to look pretty and slender, which was the only entirely acceptable form of female athleticism allowed (Feinstein 1991). Raised profiles came at a price.

Tolvhed (2012) noted that the characteristics of the female body were used to both explain and justify the social exclusion of women in sport, and in many ways, people with disabilities faced similar myths, as their bodies were objectified and defined according to predetermined notions of appropriate behaviour. Wheelchair tennis emerged from California in the late 1970s and quickly spread internationally under the International Wheelchair Tennis Federation (Bunting 2001). Britain began as one of the eight founding members, where the ideology of wheelchair tennis fitted in well with growing discourse around "Sport for All". This became a key government policy objective in the late 70s/early 80s that specifically targeted "disabled people" alongside women, the elderly, school-leavers, the unemployed, inner-city youth, and ethnic minorities (Gratton and Taylor 2000; McIntosh and Carlton 1985; Tomlinson 1987). The LTA's involvement in wheelchair tennis commenced around 1988, when the LTA Trust was formed as a registered charity to cater for grass-roots tennis initiatives. Sue Wolstenholme, who was formerly Chairman of the LTA's Development, Coaching and Schools Committee for able-bodied tennis, was appointed its first Director, and her aims to raise the sport's profile culminated in the inaugural British Open staged at Bishops Park, London, in 1990. She was also instrumental in spearheading efforts to create the British Open Deaf Tennis Championships and tennis events for players with learning disabilities.[1] In these ways, the increasing opportunities for wheelchair tennis players and others with special needs is indicative of broader shifts in welfare-state provisions and attitudes toward the body, which reflected a more inclusive view of ability.

The phase of development that tennis underwent in the open era was characterised not only by commercialisation and politicisation, whereby the sport was increasingly driven by capitalist forces and imbued with pseudo-political messages linked to inclusion, equal rights and opportunities legislation, but also by increasing government interest. The rising economic and political importance of tennis facilitated its manipulation as a vehicle for nationalism, particularly in the open era. This is the subject of the following chapter.

Note

1. Wolstenholme was awarded an OBE in 2007 for her Services to Disabled Sport.

Bibliography

Agassi, A. (2009). *Open: An Autobiography*. New York: Vintage.
Arledge, R. (Producer) (1973). *Battle of the Sexes* [Motion Picture]. New York: American Broadcasting Corporation.
Baird, M., and Major, M. (Directors) (2012). *Venus and Serena* [Motion Picture].
BBC (2 November 1979). Wightman Cup, Great Britain v. USA. London.
Beddoe, D. (1983). *Discovering Women's History*. London: Pandora Books.
Birrell, S., and Cole, C. (1990). Double Fault: Renee Richards and the Construction and Naturalization of Difference. *Sociology of Sport Journal*, 7(1), 1–21.
Birrell, S., and McDonald, M. G. (2012). Break Points: Narrative Interruption in the Life of Billie Jean King. *Journal of Sport and Social Issues*, 36(4), 343–360.

Bodo, P. (1995). *The Courts of Babylon: Tales of Greed and Glory in the Harsh New World of Professional Tennis*. New York: Scribner.
Bruley, S. (1999). *Women in Britain since 1990*. Hampshire: Macmillan.
Bunting, S. (2001). *More Than Tennis: The First 25 Years of Wheelchair Tennis*. London: International Tennis Federation.
Cahn, S. (1994). *Coming on Strong: Gender and Sexuality in Twentieth-Century Women's Sport*. Boston, MA: Harvard University Press.
Clerici, G. (1975). *The Ultimate Tennis Book: 500 Years of the Sport*. Chicago, IL: Follett Publishing Company.
Collins, B. (1974). The Postwar Pro Game. In M. Robertson, *The Encyclopedia of Sport* (pp. 63–71). New York: Viking Press.
Connors, J. (2013). *The Outsider: My Autobiography*. London: Bantam Press.
Evans, R. (1993). *Open Tennis: 25 Years of Seriously Defiant Success On and Off the Court*. London: Bloomsbury.
Feinstein, J. (1991). *Hard Courts: Real Life on the Professional Tennis Tours*. New York: Villard Books.
Festle, M. (1996). *Playing Nice: Politics and Apologies in Women's Sports*. New York: Columbia University Press.
Gratton, C., and Taylor, P. (2000). *Economics of Sport and Recreation*. London: Spon.
Hahn, L. (1998, August). The Shots Heard Round the World. *Tennis*, 34(4), 22–25.
Hargreaves, J. (1994). *Sporting Females: Critical Issues in the History and Sociology of Women's Sport*. London: Routledge.
Hargreaves, J. (2000). *Heroines of Sport: The Politics of Difference and Identity*. London: Routledge.
Hattery, A. (2010). Feminist Theory and the Study of Sport. In E. Smith, *Sociology of Sport and Social Theory*. Champaign, IL: Human Kinetics.
Horne, J., and Bentley, C. (1989). Women's Magazines, 'Fitness Chic' and the Construction of Lifestyles. *'Leisure and Health Wellbeing': Leisure Studies Association Annual Conference*. Leeds.
Howard, J. (2005). *The Rivals: Chris Evert Versus Martina Navratilova: Their Epic Duels and Extraordinary Friendship*. London: Yellow Jersey Press.
Jones, A. (1971). *A Game to Love*. London: Stanley Paul.
Kane, M. (1996). Media Coverage of the Post Title IX Female Athlete: A Feminist Analysis of Sport, Gender, and Power. *Duke Journal of Gender Law and Policy*, 3, 95–127.
Kay, J. (2010). A Window of Opportunity? Preliminary Thoughts on Women's Sport in Post-War Britain. *Sport in History*, 30(2), 196–217.
King, B. J. (1982). *Billie Jean*. New York: Viking Books.
Koster, R. (1976). *The Tennis Bubble: Big-Money Tennis, How it Grew and Where It's Going*. New York: Quadrangle.
Kramer, J. (1979). *The Game: My 40 Years in Tennis*. London: Andre Deutsch.
Lake, R. J. (forthcoming). The 'Bad Boys' of Tennis: Shifting Gender and Social Class Relations in the Era of Nastase, Connors and McEnroe. *Journal of Sport History*.
Lichtenstein, G. (1974). *A Long Way Baby: Behind the Scenes in Women's Pro Tennis*. New York: Morrow.
Lumpkin, A. (1981). *Women's Tennis: A Historical Documentary of the Players and Their Game*. New York: Whitston.

Markula, P. (1995). Firm but Shapely, Fit but Sexy, Strong but Thin: The Postmodern Aerobicizing Female Bodies. *Sociology of Sport Journal*, 12, 424–452.

McIntosh, P., and Carlton, V. (1985). *The Impact of Sport for All Policy, 1966–1984, and a Way Forward*. London: Sports Council.

Messner, M. A., Duncan, M. C., and Jensen, K. (1993). Separating the Men from the Girls: The Gendered Language of Televised Sports. *Gender & Society*, 7, 121–137.

Mewshaw, M. (1993). *Ladies of the Court: Grace and Disgrace of the Women's Tennis Circuit*. New York: Crown.

Pieper, L. P. (2012). Gender Regulation: Renee Richards Revisited. *International Journal of the History of Sport*, 29(5), 675–690.

Polley, M. (1998). *Moving the Goalposts: A History of Sport and Society Since 1945*. London: Routledge.

Richey, C. (2010). *Acing Depression: A Tennis Champion's Toughest Match*. New York: New Chapter Press.

Ritchie, I. (2003). Sex Tested, Gender Verified: Controlling Female Sexuality in the Age of Containment. *Sport History Review*, 34(1), 80–98.

Schoenfeld, B. (2004). *The Match: Althea Gibson and Angela Buxton*. New York: Harper Collins.

Spencer, N. E. (1997). Once Upon a Subculture: Professional Women's Tennis and the Meaning of Style, 1970–1974. *Journal of Sport and Social Issues*, 21(4), 363–378.

Spencer, N. E. (2000). Reading Between the Lines: A Discursive Analysis of the Billie Jean King vs. Bobby Riggs 'Battle of the Sexes'. *Sociology of Sport Journal*, 17, 386–402.

Taylor-Fleming, A. (1998, September/October). The Battles of Billie Jean King. *Women's Sports & Fitness*, 130–135, 168, 171.

Tinling, T. (1979). *Love and Faults*. New York: Crown Publishers, Inc.

Tinling, T. (1983). *Tinling: Sixty Years in Tennis*. London: Sidgwick & Jackson.

Tolvhed, H. (2012). The Sports Woman as a Cultural Challenge: Swedish Popular Press Coverage of the Olympic Games during the 1950s and 60s. *International Journal of the History of Sport*, 29(2), 302–317.

Tomlinson, M. (1987). State Intervention in Voluntary Sport: The Inner City Policy Context. *Leisure Studies*, 6, 329–345.

Truman, C. (1961). *Tennis Today*. London: C. Tinling & Co.

van Someren, J. (2010). *Women's Sporting Lives: A Biographical Study of Elite Amateur Tennis Players at Wimbledon*. Unpublished PhD dissertation, University of Southampton.

Wade, V. (1978). *Courting Triumph*. London: Hodder & Stoughton.

White, A., and Brackenridge, C. (1985). Who Rules Sport? Gender Divisions in the Power Structure of British Sport from 1960. *International Review for the Sociology of Sport*, 20(1/2), 95–107.

17 'A sporting event as much as a social phenomenon'

Nationalism, commercialism and cultural change at Wimbledon

Throughout the post-war period, the Championships grew to sustain itself as Britain's tennis monolith, a social institution invested with immense cultural significance. John Lloyd (cited in Bodo 1995:246) stated:

> The premier event isn't really about athletics; it's about England and about being British. It isn't a sporting event as much as a social phenomenon, a quirky, ritualized, national event that has more in common with the American celebration with the Fourth of July than it does with the World Series.

In *The English Season*, Geoffrey Smith (1987) included the Championships alongside the Epsom Derby, Royal Ascot, cricket at Lord's and the Henley Regatta as a key "London season" event for the social elite. It is a ubiquitous symbol of Britain's deep-rooted obsession with leisure and sport, and, through ostentatious displays of wealth and status, its class-laden social history.

Over time, as opportunities to commercially exploit Wimbledon became more readily available, particularly since the 1980s, the AELTC committee exercised increasing care to avoid trading on its unique social position. Wimbledon's distinct marketing strategy played on its "Victorian garden-party" Englishness, and helped to rearticulate national identities, particularly at times of home success. Domestically, Virginia Wade's triumph in the Queen's presence during her silver-jubilee year of 1977 sparked a media frenzy of euphoric national celebration. One aim of this chapter is to consider this event through various media narratives related to ideas about British/English national identity.

The downward spiral of Britain's on-court fortunes that followed Wade's victory was matched by Wimbledon's growing stature, which presented an interesting paradox in how British tennis came to define success. The globalisation of tennis, coupled with its professionalisation and commercialisation, injected new blood into the competition, but brought what some considered subversive elements. The downward trend in the court manners of male players, witnessed from the mid-70s to the early 90s, afforded the

British press and public opportunities for national introspection. Particularly John's McEnroe's presence at Wimbledon and, moreover, his playing success and notoriously unapologetic competitiveness came at the expense of arguably more staid and restrained British players at the time, which signalled for some the necessity for cultural change within British tennis in order to more successfully develop talent. Accordingly, another aim of this chapter is to position changing behavioural etiquette among male players in the 1980s in a broader context.

As Wimbledon entered the 1980s, its prominent position was challenged by the ensuing commercial takeover of elite-level spectator sport. The AELTC navigated this period cleverly by limiting Wimbledon's corporate exploitation yet simultaneously maximising its exclusive value. As its chief beneficiary, the LTA were afforded greater opportunities to fulfil their increasingly ambitious objectives, as its economic value exploded. However, more money brought more problems, as the extra accountability to invest responsibly brought increased expectations for success. This chapter's final aim is to critically assess the LTA's key endeavours from the 1980s onwards that sought to instigate widespread "cultural" change in British tennis.

Into the post-war era, it became clear that tennis, as a widely followed international sport, had the capacity to both unite and divide populations. Bairner (2011) argued that nationalism became more deeply embedded in the processes of sport being developed in particular societies, and this is clear in the British context. Sport was more than an opiate for the masses; it was a symbolic means for groups to identify and define themselves in relation to a particular team or individual seen to represent them and share their goals and values. Television helped bring sports stars from disparate British communities into people's living rooms, which in turn blurred class distinctions and strengthened bonds of nationhood. Post-war commercialisation and professionalisation of sport provided the basis from which corporate sponsors and the media exploited nationalism to sell their products and services.

From the interwar period onwards, the LTA's official magazines tapped into populist sentiments by making special mention of, and attempting to establish connections with, important national events and movements. Despite King George V's involvement in tennis being limited to AELTC and LTA patronage, occasional Wimbledon attendances and a telegram sent to the victorious 1933 British Davis Cup team, the *LT&B* editor still thought it reasonable to make the extraordinary claim, during the week of his silver jubilee: 'The interest our King is pleased to take in the game of lawn tennis is indeed a prime factor in its ever-increasing popularity' (4 May 1935:7). His death a year later offered another opportunity to celebrate his involvement in tennis, which was at best superficial (see *LT&B* 25 January 1936:1069). Enthusiasts sought to make it a prominent feature during the 1951 Festival of Britain, which was organised by the government to showcase the nation's contributions to science, technology and the arts, and to provide closure on the gloom and austerity of WWII. Visitors to London's South Bank were treated to tennis playing and coaching demonstrations from Dan Maskell and an exhibit of old tennis artefacts and trophies, while *LT&B* contributed a special "Festival of Britain Edition". Running from May to September 1951, it contained numerous features, historical accounts and recollections from prominent officials and former players, with the obvious objective of aligning itself with British popular consciousness by celebrating the sport's rich history. When Queen Mary, a Wimbledon regular, passed away in 1953, the AELTC gave commemorative coronation ashtrays to each competitor that year (Barrett 1986). In these instances, tennis was reaffirmed as essentially British.

Alongside these events, periodic British successes provided opportunities for modest national celebrations, but arguably Virginia Wade's Wimbledon triumph in 1977 trumped all others in galvanising the nation. Bairner (2011:32) argued that, historically, 'there has been little sense that female athletes carry with them the hopes and ambitions of the nation', but an exception must be made for Wade, who achieved her ultimate ambition at 31 years of age in uniquely fitting circumstances. Britain was 'subjected to a huge collective ecstasy' as a consequence of 'the divine intervention of mellow gods', as Wade's victory coincided with the Championships' centenary and the Queen's silver jubilee (Forbes 1978:326–7).

After Mark Cox, the last-remaining British male, lost in the fourth round, public attention was directed more intimately upon Wade and Sue Barker, both of whom reached the semi-finals. With the prospect of an all-British final, journalists constructed the story in the strong nationalistic narrative; a British victory would be a fitting acknowledgement of the Championships' exalted position in British society, and a symbolic gesture or "gift" to the Queen in her special year. The *Mirror Sport* headline from 28th June read: 'Rule Britannia! Wimbledon can this week crown a British champion in a glorious final to its centenary'; Geoffrey Green's article in *The Times* that same day began: "The British can still keep their jubilee flags flying", while Colin Myler from *The Sun* wrote: 'Britain's golden tennis girls Virginia Wade and Sue Barker yesterday promised the Queen a real Silver Jubilee treat.'

Despite Barker's loss to the Dutchwoman Betty Stöve, Wade's exquisite performance against the top seed and favourite Chris Evert was described as a victory that united a nation. Patrick Clancy from *The Telegraph* (30 June 1977) constructed a narrative of togetherness that crossed class, gender and geographical lines:

> The world stopped somewhere around two o'clock yesterday afternoon as the length and breadth of Britain sat itself down, held its breath and willed Virginia Wade into the Wimbledon final. If moral support was any help out there on … Centre Court, Virginia Wade had a reservoir stretching from Land's End to John O'Groats. Offices and factories turned a blind eye as workers followed her every move via radio commentaries

and portable TVs. ... Housewives deserted the high streets for the television. ... The whole nation is behind her.

The mention of 'offices and factories' and 'housewives', alongside the idea that 'moral support' stretched deep into the Scottish highlands, implies that *all* of Britain was united behind Wade as *their* representative, despite her being born in Bournemouth and brought up in Durban, South Africa, until she was 15. This narrative overlooks the possibility that fans in Scotland, Wales and the north of England might not have identified with her so comfortably, and neither might ethnic minorities or the working class.

Wade's success was also constructed as an offering to the Queen. Colin Myler and Harrison Edwards wrote in *The Sun* (30 June 1977): 'Virginia Wade kept her jubilee promise to the Queen yesterday by storming through to the Wimbledon singles final'. Tabloids and broadsheets alike constructed the event as historically significant for Britain, as did the Queen herself, who changed her plans and toured through the streets of Wimbledon the day before the women's final, undoubtedly in response to the mediated symbolism of Wade's potential victory.

Despite being willed by 15,000 Centre Court spectators and millions more watching on televisions, Wade's victory was anything but straightforward. Under the combined pressures of being expected to beat a weaker opponent and of performing in front of the Queen and on behalf of an entire nation, she lost the first set; only after a double-fault from Stöve in the third game of the second set did she recognise a momentum shift, and came through 4–6, 6–3, 6–1 (Wade 1978). Regardless of her performance, what mattered was the end result. 'Queen Ginny!' ran one headline in *The Sun* (2 July 1977); Peter Wilson (*The Sun*) called it 'a fairy tale'. John Barrett preferred to contextualise her victory in patriotic terms; 'hundreds of Union Jacks were waved', in what amounted to a public outpouring that never failed to live up to expectations (*Financial Times* 2 July 1977). The Queen, well aware of how her victory was being constructed, invited Wade to a private tea party shortly afterwards, where she was quoted as saying: 'Wasn't it marvellous for Virginia, especially in Jubilee year?' (cited in *Sun* 2 July 1977).

In time-honoured *Daily Mail* style, Brian James sought a more contentious line by describing how Wade 'upstaged' the Queen, and also used the victory over Stöve to amplify national differences with the Dutch.

> A crowd was singing For She's a Jolly Good Fellow and cameramen heaved and jostled like a mob of pickets when, with exquisite tact, the Queen backed gently out of the scene; she knew this time the singing and the clicking shutters were not for her. ... It was [Wade's] reward for winning a 96-minute session of Dutch roulette... About 2.40 yesterday a couple of million mums about the country were in the mood to hurl the Edam into the dustbin, throw the Delft at the TV, and send the kids

out to dig up and trample on the tulips. ... [We witnessed] the momentary eclipse of a real queen by a canon's daughter.

(2 July 1977)

The utilisation of sport for nationalistic purposes was nothing new in 1977, but the cultural significance of Wade's victory was enhanced in the context of her gender, class, upbringing and age, and the specific historical moment in which it occurred. Others also remarked of her apparently temperamental and tempestuous personality as significant. Tinling (1983:200) suggested ironically that it was perhaps her atypical and "un-British" personality that ultimately made her a crowd favourite, despite her tendencies to 'bristle when annoyed', adopt 'haughty airs' and give off 'an aura of high-level indignation emanating from every pore' when losing. In these ways, she was different in style and personality from the more staid and conventional Angela Mortimer and Ann Haydon-Jones before her. Wade's dominant personality and enduring self-confidence, notwithstanding so many previous disappointments, propelled her into the nation's bosom. In previous Wimbledons, when she had 'contrived to lose to all sorts of players who were not fit to tie the ribbon in her hair', her plucky performances and never-say-die attitude endeared her to the British crowds (Tinling 1983:198). Evans (1993:154) contextualised the occasion in the context of her previous 'catalogue of disasters' at Wimbledon:

> Since her victory at Forest Hills nine years before, the cry of 'Oh, Virginia, not again!' had become an annual wail of lament at Wimbledon as the British No. 1 managed to present some less talented rival with a victory that should have been hers for the taking.

Likely, it was because she was not instantly successful at Wimbledon that her ultimate success in 1977 was so widely heralded. Thus, in a strangely perverse but uniquely British collective mentality, Wade became more popular over the years as she repeatedly failed to achieve her ultimate ambition, and any failings or flaws in her personality that might have previously irked or offended became endearing. Wade embodied the collective frustrations of an entire nation year after year, and her ultimate success at the highest level and on the most profound occasion lifted the nation, and was undoubtedly influential in restoring pride to the beleaguered and long-suffering British tennis public.

Wade's achievements represented the swansong of British success for women in the twentieth century. Britain's 1978 Wightman Cup victory was to prove their last one ever, as the event was disbanded 11 years later because of indisputable American domination, which negatively impacted spectator interest. Britain's loss to America in the 1981 Fed Cup final was also to prove their last major run of the century.

The men struggled in equal measure. Some put this down to inhibitive cultural mores and practices that retained elements of an outdated amateur ethos. It was certainly the case that the rampant professionalisation and commercialisation of post-war tennis left Britain behind, both ideologically and materially, but it is difficult to ascertain the extent that British players felt at ease with the ultra-competitive, single-minded, win-at-all-costs mentality that was seemingly expected for success. John Lloyd's testimony provides some insight. Following in Buster Mottram's footsteps to achieve the British number-one ranking in the mid-70s, Lloyd was heralded as a talented player capable of great success, yet he 'lacked that fire' to become a champion, according to Bodo (1995:215), apparently as a consequence of his affluence:

> He came from a thoroughly middle-class British family of tennis nuts for whom Wimbledon represented the perfect world. But a typically British concept of his own place in the grand scheme of things – a by-product of Britain's class system – inhibited him.

Ultimately, his highest world ranking in singles was a respectable but hardly awe-inspiring 21, winning just one career title and reaching no further than Wimbledon's third round. His run to the final of the 1977 Australian Open and his quarter-final appearance at the 1984 US Open reminded the British public of his potential, but he openly admitted his comfortable upbringing was a hindrance:

> If I had been born in the States, where it's so much more competitive, where success alone is so much more the be-all and end-all, I might have been forced to work harder and maybe I would have become a better player. ... Born in England ... I was among the top two or three players at every level. I was handed things on a plate.
> (cited in Bodo 1995:215)

With this last statement Lloyd might have been referring to a number of "things": media attention, free equipment and perks, endorsements from British businesses, fan adulation, free club memberships, or tournament wildcards. Indeed, from 1977 when Wimbledon wildcards were first issued to eight male and six female players, almost all were British.[1] Not once from 1977–2006 did fewer than six British male players receive one of the eight available. Some were aging stalwarts: John Lloyd received four wildcards from 1980–83. Others were supposedly budding young talents: Andrew Jarrett received seven wildcards from 1977–83, but never once reached the third round. Jeremy Bates received six wildcards between 1983 and 91, only managing to raise his ranking sufficiently high enough to gain automatic entry on three occasions. His best performances were fourth-round defeats in 1992 and 94. In their wake, most notably, were Chris Bailey (six wildcards from 1988–94; Wimbledon best: 2nd round 1993), Mark Petchey (eight wildcards from 1988–97; Wimbledon best: 3rd round 1997), Chris

Wilkinson (wildcards for nine straight years 1990–9; Wimbledon best: 3rd round 1993–95, 98), Danny Sapsford (six wildcards from 1990–8; Wimbledon best: 3rd round 1999), and Alex Bogdanovic (eight wildcards from 2002–9; Wimbledon best: never progressed beyond the 1st round). Of these, only Petchey broke into the world's top 100 ranking. When another British wildcard entry, Nick Brown, sensationally beat the 10th seed Goran Ivanisevic in the second round in 1991, he was the second best player in Britain, but with a world ranking of just 591. His higher-ranked compatriot, Jeremy Bates, was also outside of the world's top 200 at the time.

Almost all of these players achieved greater success in doubles. Lloyd reached the quarter-finals of three major doubles championships, and won three major mixed-doubles titles (French Open, 1982; Wimbledon, 1983 and 1984); Jarrett reached the Australian Open semi-final in 1978 with British partner Jonathan Smith; Bates reached the Australian Open final in 1988 and two Wimbledon quarter-finals in 1990 and 93, while winning two major mixed-doubles majors at Wimbledon (1987) and the Australian Open (1991); Petchey won his only career title in doubles, the pre-Wimbledon grass-court tournament in Nottingham with Sapsford in 1996; Wilkinson reached the Wimbledon quarter-final in 1993 with British partner Paul Hand. Bodo (1995:246) explained this phenomenon by commenting that 'the English are essentially team players', preferring to subordinate personal goals to team objectives.

The AELTC committee cannot be criticised for wanting to offer wildcards to those players likely to be most appealing to home spectators, yet it is evident the wildcard's function was shifting markedly as players came to expect it as a reward for a high British ranking. Bogdanovic admitted the existence of a culture of abuse with wildcards, when interviewed in 2004 (26 October): '[In Britain] it is like ... when Wimbledon comes along, "Oh, maybe I can get a wildcard". Sometimes people could have got spoiled with that ... they think everything gets easy. ... Sometimes you can get carried away' (cited in Lake 2010b:484). It is suspected that this sense of entitlement was fuelled by the media. Bodo (1995: 77) remarked that top-ranked British female and male players, Jo Durie and Jeremy Bates, received more press coverage than some top-10 performers from other nations, despite struggling to stay in the world's top 100, but 'the key word here is coverage – not respect or encouragement or even sympathy'. Indeed, despite being harangued for its often negative coverage of home players, British newspapers have also been quick to place unrealistic expectations upon young players, which has afforded them countless opportunities to criticise British methods when they fail. These sentiments were so pervasive that some players seemed to internalise them. Indeed, John Lloyd considered his own failures from a British cultural perspective:

> In our tradition we learn to settle for a good effort. We're not supposed to get all carried away and obsessed with winning. And deep down we

still believe that you're missing the point if winning is all-important. We *say* we admire winners, but we don't really mean it. So we end up focusing on the controversial winners and use their behaviour to justify our suspicion of total commitment to winning.

(cited in Bodo 1995:245)

As the LTA grew in size, stature and wealth from the 1980s onwards, chiefly as a result of increasing Wimbledon profits, the British media and public became ever more expectant of Wimbledon success, but concomitantly impatient with the lack of it. Even the eminently more successful British player Tim Henman, who *The Times* correspondent Simon Barnes called 'the best we've had for 70 years', was often derided as "a typical British loser" in reference to his lack of major championship titles. Barnes (2006:24) discussed this curious phenomenon:

> It is Henman's sad fate to be regarded as a loser – as something rather pathetic and hapless and hopeless; as something rather despicable and spineless and useless. We have absurdly high expectations of Henman; and still more absurdly, feel that his failure to fulfil our expectations makes him something to be despised, reviled and spat upon.

His less successful compatriot Greg Rusedski largely escaped such personal lambasting, perhaps because of his Canadian upbringing, which begs the question of whether seemingly national "traits" hold much meaning at all or are merely suggested to explain defeat when more plausible reasons connected with coaching/training methods or tactics are too complex to articulate. Overall, it demonstrates the extent that behavioural expectations form part of how players are seen to represent their nation. For Henman, the unmistakable "Englishness" in his playing style and appearance tended to attract the most simplistic and uncritical examinations of his overall performances as being tied unequivocally but certainly unfairly to his English, white, middle-class identity.

The story of John McEnroe's increasing popularity at Wimbledon represents the other side of this British tendency. His behavioural transgressions went from being strongly abhorred and publicly rejected at the start of his career to curiously embraced and hotly anticipated toward the end. This process occurred at a time when Britain's collective sense of self was being redefined in political and economic terms, which gave it added weight. As Britain rebounded from economic recession to rediscover its potential for creativity, dynamism and guile, the shifting norms of middle-class behavioural etiquette in industry and commerce were reflected in tennis, as players like McEnroe who embodied a more determined, aggressive and proactive attitude were more warmly welcomed. It has been argued that the continued downturn in the overall manners and behavioural etiquette at this time reflected not only the democratisation of tennis and blurring of gender lines but also Britain's entry into a new consumer-oriented, neo-liberal age where individual ambition was seen to take greater precedence over collective duties (Lake forthcoming). Particularly when examining McEnroe as the embodiment of a shared inclination toward narcissism, it is likely that the process of redefining appropriate on-court behavioural etiquette to suit requirements of modern elite-level tennis had an indirect influence on the broader social fabric of British society more generally. Moreover, Thatcher's attempts to reduce the "dependency culture" and instil individualism and a sense of personal responsibility for prosperity were influential in, and influenced by, the USA, which had its own complementary version: "Reaganomics" (Pugh and Flint 1997).

Thatcher was ultimately successful in boosting Britain's economy and its people's collective confidence, but by the early 1990s the class of ruthlessly ambitious, upwardly mobile "Yuppies" who exemplified Britain's transformation toward a thriving modern post-industrial society became also an embarrassing blot on polite civility and human decency. The new cultural manifestation of greed, individualism and ostensible lack of public concern for others – to look after "number one" – was criticised as the worst outcome of Thatcherism. Leading papers spoke of "vulgarism" and Britain's decline as a "nation of decency"; Robin Leigh-Pemberton, Governor of the Bank of England, told the *Sunday Times* (17 June 1990): 'Old style thrift has gone out of fashion. The attitude is, "I want it, and I want it now"'. Douglas Hurd, Tory Home Secretary, described in similar disparaging terms what he saw in middle-Britain:

> You do not find much poverty or social deprivation there. What you do find are too many young people with too much money in their pockets ... but too little notion of the care and responsibility they owe to others.
>
> (cited in Pugh and Flint 1997:127)

They both could have easily been describing the newest generation of professional tennis players.

The growing focus on individual achievement, personal ambition and materialism not only led, as Baltzell (1995) and Bodo (1995) claimed, to a saddening decline of meaningful friendships between players on tour, but also attracted criticism about players behaving like unreliable, greedy and petulant children. It had become common for players to skip tournaments they were contractually obligated to participate in, "tank" matches so they could depart to their next destination early, and demand inflated guarantees from tournament directors (Feinstein 1991). The British media were contemptuous of this behaviour, reflected both on and off court, and at Wimbledon, the presence of the fiery and tempestuous McEnroe and the brash, arrogant and sometimes vulgar Jimmy Connors did little to curtail public fears of negative American influences. The AELTC Chairman, Air Chief Marshall Sir Brian Burnett, was one of many establishment figures who considered that tennis 'was *not* the most important thing in the world; and that tennis players, accordingly, should know their place' (emphasis added), according to McEnroe's biographer, Tim Adams (2003:24). Furthermore, Burnett's committee

> entertained fears when the tournament became open [in 1968] that something of its spirit would be diluted. With the course aggression of Connors, the intimidating gamesmanship of Năstase, and the scowling torments of McEnroe, many of their worst fears were being realised.
> (Adams 2003:25)

Wimbledon's love affair with McEnroe was erratic and turbulent. His loss to Borg in the 1980 final, by way of an epic 34-point fourth-set tie-break, was heralded by commentators as one of the finest displays of tennis ever seen, yet after his poor conduct the following year, he became the first player to be refused automatic club membership after winning the singles title.[2] The press had a field day that year, as 'McEnroe displayed an adolescent sense of injustice un-tempered by any sense of adult civility' (Baltzell 1995:368). After his 'petulant' behaviour against Tom Gullikson in his opening-round match, *The Sun* blasted "The Brat is Back", while the *Daily Mail* headline read: "The Shame of John McEnroe; Disgrace of Super Brat" (23 June 1981). Barrett and Little (2006:135) reflected on McEnroe's frequent tantrums and four-letter outbursts:

> Never in the history of the sport was there so public a display of bad court manners when his temperament caused him to behave beyond acceptability. ... His offensiveness to the official – including the phrase 'You're the pits of the world' as a term of abuse – was established as an example of what sportsmanship should not be.

Calls for McEnroe's disqualification were made repeatedly but, as was proved on numerous occasions previously and subsequently, his celebrity status made that option difficult to rationalise. Bodo (1995:441) explained:

> The very same promoters and officials who sat around condemning McEnroe for his behaviour put up with everything that he dished out when their own self-interest was at stake. Furthermore, the burgeoning administration of the professional establishment elevated the survival and success of the bureaucracy and the tour itself above all other things. The administration of the game knew that adopting a clear and swift concept of justice was not in everyone's best interest, least of all their own.

Wimbledon referee Alan Mills (2005:4) reflected on the 1983 Championships, when pressures from numerous quarters compelled him *not* to disqualify their chief drawing-card:

> It's very difficult to feel at peace when you are standing surrounded by 14,000 people with the eyes of tens of millions of others around the world looking on to see how you might tame [McEnroe] ... I also knew that those in charge at the All England Club would be watching my performance intently. I was on a one-year contract and was effectively on trial. The reputation of their Championships, the oldest and most august tournament in tennis, to a large extent depended on how the officials, with me as their chief, would cope.

Suffice to say, McEnroe was not disqualified from this particular Wimbledon, nor any other in his career. Moreover, contrary to how his seemingly wild behaviour might have appeared, McEnroe exhibited self-control when in the final throes; he could 'push a disciplinary situation right to the wire before reining himself in. He was clever like that. He always knew exactly how far he could push it' (Mills 2005:7).

Over the years, the British press depicted McEnroe in numerous ways that reflected broader changing perceptions of how his personality, attitudes and overall accomplishments might influence the sport. He went from being depicted as a nasty pest and a threat to the events' traditions to a supremely talented one-of-a-kind athlete, and then to a beloved legend who fought for cultural change and modernisation, to open up tennis to new-found competitiveness. McEnroe railed against arbitrary rules, behavioural restrictions and poor officiating at tournaments, which came to appear increasingly outdated. Invariably, his targets for abuse were officials and line judges who he deemed incompetent, rather than his opponents. He recalled his first trip to Wimbledon in 1977:

> When I saw those dozing linesmen, I thought, *This isn't what Wimbledon should look like.* ... The whole atmosphere was totally set in its ways and self-important beyond belief. I couldn't help resenting how badly the organizers treated the lesser players and how they genuflected to the stars. I was incredulous at all that bowing and curtsying to royalty and lesser royalty. It felt like the class system at its worst.
>
> (McEnroe 2002:66)

Most certainly, McEnroe challenged some of the conservative traditions that sustained the sport's exclusivity. There was perhaps some connection with McEnroe's second Wimbledon singles title coinciding with the AELTC's decision to elect the progressive and broad-minded former Slazenger boss, R.E.H. "Buzzer" Hadingham, as Chairman and Alan Mills as Wimbledon referee. Both made it their personal missions to improve access to, and relations with, the players. Mills (2005:5) reflected:

> My door was always open, especially to the players. I didn't want to come across as a sort of headmaster figure from a bygone era, hidden

away in my study. I wanted to foster a closer relationship with the players, to encourage them to give vent to any frustrations or concerns they might have.

Feinstein (1991:313) felt the committee's efforts to subtly realign Wimbledon's image with more liberal "modern" values, and to 'separate traditional from silly rules', were imperative. Adams (2003:34–5) considered them necessary in the context of growing 'cynicism' toward and declining 'faith' in the relevance of elitist British institutions in general; the problems of football violence and urban race-rioting made 'the gentle England of Thermos flasks and "Oh, I say"' appear like 'something of a museum piece'.

Tabloid newspapers like *The Sun* excused McEnroe's behaviour as a manifestation of working-class frustrations. Despite his affluent middle-class American upbringing, his "anti-establishment" attitude was comprehensively 'exploited' (Adams 2003:36). Moreover, to the dismay of Wimbledon's officials, the British public seemed to enjoy and identify with McEnroe's behaviour: 'He voiced some of the nation's own frustration and anger at the way [their] institutions were run – often amateurishly – by the same old boys' club of peers and grandees' (Adams 2003:38). Even middle-class broadsheets conceded to McEnroe's broadening appeal. In 1980, *The Telegraph* ran an editorial about his behaviour but were forced to print nearly a full page of responses from those in support. One correspondent wrote: 'I feel very sad when I contemplate what is happening to young McEnroe. ... He is a very rare, indeed a unique talent, amounting to genius, which I fear is to be crushed out of existence by a small-minded, rigid tennis establishment'. Another wrote: 'I find all his matches on television vastly entertaining, which is more than I can say for some of his predecessors, who used to make me drop off in front of the box' (cited in Adams 2003:39). According to Adams (2003:58), the British public found something cathartic in McEnroe's outbursts, as if he embodied 'a similar kind of relief' through the self-expression of 'bottled-up feelings'. Thus, it could be that McEnroe's on-court behaviour not only reflected and expressed, but also inspired a broad psycho-social behavioural shift among middle-class Brits throughout the 1980s, who seemed galvanised by his embodied narcissistic perfectionism. Bemoaning McEnroe's absence from the 1987 Championships, *The Times* (26 June 1987:16) stated: 'The greatest entertainer in living memory ... will be sadly missed this summer', before asking 'Will there be nothing to relive the serve-return-and-volley tedium of the centre court?'. Identifying Britain's love affair with the tempestuous red-head, the correspondent wondered whether Britain should try and breed 'another Superbrat', but confessed:

> The odds must be against it. ... The trouble is that our philosophy needs updating. As a nation we are obsessed with being good losers, taking our defeats gallantly on the chin. Next time, instead of shrugging our shoulders with a rueful grin, on being told that their service was out, the

Brits should shout "you cannot be serious" at the umpire, throw a racket or two at the crowd and aim their next shot at the photographers.

History has written of McEnroe as an iconic figure, who perhaps given his natural talent should have won more than his three Wimbledon and four US Open singles titles, but probably his most significant achievements were socio-cultural: expediting the institution of more competent and open-minded match and tournament officiating at Wimbledon and other tournaments; helping to popularise and appropriate more expressive forms of on-court behaviour; and, in the process, altering the sport's conservative image and possibly its prospective fan base.

Despite the vast changes that had beset tennis globally in the post-war period, Wimbledon stayed true to many of its structural/organisational conventions and traditional values. It has managed also to remain relevant, presenting itself as an impressively modern tournament with a certain prestige unmatched by any other major championship. The Australian Open experimented with different court surfaces and tournament and match timetables; the French Open was forced to attract a title sponsor and make numerous concessions to television in the late 1970s, which included playing night matches; and the US Open experimented with three different court surfaces in the midst of relocating from Forest Hills to Flushing Meadow in 1978. The move satisfied sponsors and television, improved access to greater numbers of spectators, and allowed the USTA to gross higher profits.[3]

That same year, the *Sunday Express* (10 September 1978) lauded America's newest tennis complex, before urging Wimbledon to embrace its own commercial potential:

> Many think Wimbledon can do a lot more for the public in making the place more comfortable and better equipped to serve the spectators. ... It is up to Wimbledon to jerk itself into action with the same urgency that the Americans have put into building their new showplace.

Praise for Flushing Meadow was fleeting, however. Remarking on its 'night playing' and 'the need to please the television networks', the 'concrete bowl' with an interior 'splashed with advertisements', the 'cheap, carnival-midway milieu', and its 'frantic [and] crass materialism', Baltzell (1995:358–61) joined numerous others (e.g. Bodo 1995; Cash 2002; Evans 1993; Feinstein 1991) in criticising its vulgarity, unattractiveness and shameless "selling out" to commercialism. Comparing it to Wimbledon, he also remarked:

> Flushing Meadow, having cast off any mannerly restraints which might have still remained at ... Forest Hills, is surely a fitting symbol of the egalitarian and moneyed values of modern American tennis. While Wimbledon is doing its best to retain some semblance of the manners of

the amateur game ... the Flushing Meadow establishment has frankly recognised that the modern game is played for green [and] ... the moneyed values of the Fourth Estate, especially television.

(Baltzell 1995:357)

The AELTC committee's stubborn refusal to allow commercialism to dictate how the Championships were run or how its players behaved likely seemed counterintuitive to ensuring profitability, if not downright petty. In 1969, for example, Ann Jones was asked by the tournament referee to cover the Pepsi logo on her holdall, and all soft-drinks labels by the umpire's chair were replaced by clear containers, in part, David Gray argued, because the BBC tightened their rules on 'giving free advertisements to commercial firms' (*Guardian* 29 July 1969:14). The AELTC committee also intervened on several occasions when players breached the club's all-whites rule; both Rosie Casals and Martina Navratilova were asked to change outfits before going on court because their shirt "patch" advertisements were too large (Barrett 1986). As an experiment, the AELTC erected a William Hill betting tent inside the club grounds during the 1975 Championships, but this was soon removed 'because of the obvious temptations [of players placing bets] and the potential danger of matches being fixed' (Barrett 1986:149).

Despite them appearing backward or snobbish, arguably the committee's clear sense of purpose brought them long-term public credibility. Their refusal to part ways with the BBC, their unwillingness to maximise the utilisation of their club grounds for concerts or other events, and their commitment to only allow subtle "product placement" advertising rather than ostentatious billboards, has brought lower profits, but endeared them to tennis crowds, players and the media, who appreciate their efforts to retain the sport's charm over the pursuit of profit.[4] Over time, the "mystique" of Wimbledon and its exalted position as the world's premier tournament has increased its commodity value, which has allowed them subtly to raise ticket and merchandise prices for spectators, alongside (mostly international) television rights and sponsorship opportunities for its small number of exclusive brands like Rolex, HSBC, IBM, Hertz, Lanson champagne and Polo Ralph Lauren. Their long-standing commitment to the comparatively small-scale British brands of Robinsons and Slazenger has allowed the AELTC to position Wimbledon as a highly respectable and visibly English brand in itself, but their desires to avoid saturating the market with cheap mass-produced products of little exclusive value meant they limited the sale of Wimbledon merchandise to a small number of chosen outlets external to the club grounds.

These decisions did increase profits somewhat but helped sustain its somewhat elitist image that remains incompatible with the LTA's own liberal and progressive goals of fostering inclusivity and removing barriers to participation (Lake 2014). Colin Richardson, in *The Guardian* (21 June 2003), criticised tennis as 'one of the last remaining bastions of class privilege' in Britain, meanwhile:

> Tennis clubs such as… The All England Club – exclusive, expensive and… royally patronised – have ruined the image of the game. No amount of initiatives in primary schools will attract large numbers of children to the game so long as it is seen as the preserve of the rich. … The exclusive, upper-middle-class image of the game in this country is a disincentive and a barrier to opportunity.

Repeatedly, the AELTC was forced to defend its decision to retain its all-whites clothing rule, despite it appearing outdated, and its grass courts, despite most tennis now being played on clay or hard courts, and the international grass-court season now just four or five weeks long. In truth, the AELTC's public image, often depicted as antiquated and conservative, has come quite unfortunately (though some would say cleverly) to mask the club's enduring commitment to embrace structural change to maximise spectator and player enjoyment, alongside advances in telecommunications and media that adopt the most cutting-edge technologies. Moreover, their underlying commitment to develop children's talent was revealed in 2001, when the Wimbledon Junior Tennis Initiative was launched, which afforded local schoolchildren opportunities to receive coaching at the club. These efforts were enhanced in 2002, when Road to Wimbledon was launched: a nationwide 14-and-under tournament with the final rounds played at the club. Given imbalanced media reporting, however, the AELTC's efforts in these domains have often been overlooked.

For their part, the LTA made notable efforts to modernise in the face of growing public criticism in the years following their bold stand for open tennis, when they exhibited a lacklustre commitment to developing playing standards. Evans (1993:18) reflected:

> How an organisation that had taken such a dynamic stand in 1967 should fall back into a state of apathy in the 1970s as far as the development of British Tennis is concerned remains one of the game's saddest mysteries.

Derek Penman's replacement as LTA Chairman in 1970 likely facilitated a decline in momentum for change. The burgeoning markets for corporate sponsorship and television rights in British sport provided opportunities for exploitation, yet the LTA retreated in its commitment to such partnerships.

In 1986, the LTA (1986a:8) admitted: 'In the dramatic growth of sport and leisure in recent years, British tennis has not kept pace with its competitors. … It is clearly the LTA's responsibility to try to reverse these trends'. By then, they had taken measures to transform themselves into a more professional association, including creating a Board of Management, reducing retirement age from 75 to 70 and imposing of an upper-age limit of 55 for new members. In 1982, the offices of Chairman and President were combined and a maximum three-year term was introduced. In 1985, the LTA headquarters relocated to Queen's Club, and within three years had founded the LTA Trust as a registered charity for grass-roots initiatives.[5] In terms of talent development, the LTA's efforts focused chiefly on short tennis, tennis academies, and improvements in coaching and facilities (Houlihan and White 2002). However, progress in each of these areas was stifled by inadequate planning.

Short tennis was an ingenious Swedish concept: a child-friendly version of tennis with softer, slower and bouncier balls and smaller rackets, played on reduced-size courts with lower nets. Despite it developing into a fully fledged sport in itself, many of its best players failed to make the important transition to proper tennis. Tennis academies like Bisham Abbey, opened in 1982, had as their sole aim the development of professional players, but 'the idea of removing children from their home environment to live at a national centre is now considered unwise' underpinned assumptions made about progress that ignored the specific emotional and developmental needs of the children (Houlihan and White 2002:199). Eventually, the LTA moved toward regional tennis centres, which fulfilled the same function, the merits of which are still debatable, but nevertheless did not require children to be resident. The LTA's efforts to expand coaching opportunities involved hiring County Development and Coaching Officers, but their efforts extended only as far as identifying and developing talent and remained disconnected from schools and local authorities and an 'overall national development plan' (Houlihan and White 2002:199). Their efforts to improve facilities were successful in galvanising local authority support, particularly once the National Lottery injected funds from 1994. The Indoor Tennis Initiative, which sprang from a partnership with the Sports Council and AELTC, registered an impressive increase from 67 indoor courts in 1987 to 910 in 1999 (LTA 1999) but, as many were located in the private rather than public sector, the LTA had little control over matters of access and inclusion (Lake 2008).

These outcomes were undesirable and unintended, and ostensibly at least brought Britain no closer to achieving its goal of another Wimbledon champion. Criticism of the LTA's efforts in the context of their swelling coffers became perennial, particularly during the Wimbledon fortnight, when 'a spate of articles [appear] in the national press analysing reasons for Britain's lack of top-class players' (Houlihan and White 2002:97). There was little room for complacency. In 1993, the LTA Marketing Department was constructed with aims to raise the profile of tennis and its related programmes and schemes, and also to critically review the LTA's own corporate identity. Thus, and not without controversy, resources were allocated for the LTA to alter its image, which was deemed an important investment given the growing competition between British sports governing bodies for sponsorship, government funding, television time, media space, and the commitment of young players (LTA 1994). In their endeavours to "modernise", however, the LTA was held back: first, in its plans for talent development that underestimated the need for long-term planning and infrastructure development (Lake 2008, 2011b; Maskell 1988); and, second, with Britain's tennis club culture that tended to resist change and interference from outside organisations, including the LTA (Lake 2008).

Based on consultation with key partners in sport development, the LTA published its first ever national development strategy in 1995 entitled: *The Development of Tennis in Great Britain 1996–2001*. This seminal text stressed children as a talent-development priority and privileged elite-level development and "performance" ahead of mass participation (LTA 1995). Their explicit shift was undoubtedly inspired by the Conservative government's changing agenda. In 1994, the Minister of Sport, Iain Sproat, announced that Sports Council activity would 'withdraw from the promotion of mass participation ... instead shifting its focus to services in support of excellence' (McDonald 1995:72). For Oakley and Green (2001:81), this policy statement represented 'the end of a broad definition of sports development to a more focused, achievement-orientated provision'. *Sport: Raising the Game*, published in 1995, reaffirmed the push toward performance through developing elite performers and academies, creating higher-education institutions for fostering elite athletes, and allocating funds to supportive associations (Houlihan, 1997). The overall outcome was to push the LTA to define most of its aims in accordance with elite-level objectives. Even the success of short tennis or its rebranded version Mini Tennis was measured by how much it widened the "base of the pyramid", with the implicit assumption that increasing the pool of young talent would lead inevitably to production of champions (Lake 2008). In 1997, the LTA hired John Crowther as CEO, a gentleman whose tennis knowledge failed to stretch beyond his own low-level recreational experiences, but who, as a high-flying entrepreneur, promised to bring business acumen to the Association. He was quick to "modernise" the LTA in accordance with New Labour-inspired business practices, by establishing accountability and responsibility through "key performance indicators" and "deliverables".

Of all Crowther's different efforts, his attempts to change "club culture" undoubtedly presented the most disheartening results. The LTA's frustration with clubs stemmed from the results of a survey from 1985 entitled: *The Juniors in Britain's Tennis Clubs*. All 2,495 LTA-affiliated tennis clubs in Britain were sent two letters asking for responses to various proposals designed to 'encourage clubs throughout the country to provide more help to young players... to raise standards of the game at individual, club and national levels' (LTA 1985:3). These included removing restrictions on court use, facilitating junior–senior play, encouraging junior representation on club teams, fostering voluntarism among junior club members, and hiring a coach to establish junior programmes and school-club facility sharing. Only 112 clubs responded, a meagre 4.4 per cent of the total, which indicated reluctance among clubs even to engage with these matters, let alone adopt some of the proposals. While many that did respond offered encouraging views, the overwhelming attitude of clubs to change was 'disappointing'. An honorary secretary of an anonymous county LTA wrote:

> I am sure that the proposals you make are very sensible, but my own experience tends to make me think that it is going to be very difficult if not impossible to persuade many, if not a majority of affiliated clubs to provide a better service for their junior members.
>
> (LTA 1985:5)

Even high-ranking officials struggled to hold back their frustration. Paul Hutchins, Britain's Men's National Team Manager at the LTA, stated forcefully in 1984:

> Clubs must get off their backsides and start encouraging juniors. They must stop treating juniors like second-class citizens: make sure that there are courts for them at decent times of the day, play them in senior matches if they are good enough etc. They should remember that they are the senior members of the future.
>
> (cited in LTA 1985:5)

The LTA recognised the absurdity of financially supporting clubs that remained resistant to developing talent, promising in 1991 to 'tighten up' on the criteria for clubs to qualify for funding, given that 'many' are 'playing lip-service' to junior development: 'Amongst a number of requirements clubs must have a five-year plan and charge realistic levels of subscriptions. There must also exist an acceptable junior programme' (LTA 1991:2). Defining a "realistic" subscription level or an "acceptable" junior programme was open to interpretation, but clarification soon came. The 1998 facilities strategy specified that only those clubs that 'promote programmes in line with LTA policies and which have the structure in place to prove themselves viable for development' were eligible for LTA loans (LTA 1998b:8). The gradual formalisation of such stipulations led to Club Vision, a "modernisation" strategy introduced in 2000 to bring about cultural change in clubs (LTA 2000). This involved encouraging clubs to remove clothing restrictions, membership restrictions based on ability (e.g. playing-in tests), and inequitable playing times and opportunities for children, and to hire a coach, institute children's talent-development programmes like Mini Tennis, and foster facility-share partnerships with local schools. At considerable expense, the LTA also went about improving their affiliation benefits, to ensure that as many clubs as possible were under their jurisdiction (LTA 1998a; 1999).

In numerous pieces of LTA correspondence, the necessity of transforming "club culture", breaking down barriers to access, making them more welcoming, inclusive, vibrant, child-friendly, and performance-oriented was repeatedly highlighted (LTA 1995, 1998a, 1998b, 2001, 2002, 2003; Sandilands 1996). There was a very clear sense that the LTA's vision for how clubs should look and operate was rooted in "consensus bias". This functionalist-underpinned notion, in this case, implied that *all* clubs *ought* to agree on how best to organise tennis and deliver the LTA's objectives (Lake 2011b). Not only did this overall approach overlook the divergent or oppositional interests of clubs – i.e. that clubs did not care about producing British champions – but also implied that "club culture" was something malleable that the LTA could consciously manage with intended outcomes (Lake 2011b).

Given the challenging socio-economic developments the LTA were fighting against, progress within clubs in accordance with their requirements was unlikely. Throughout the 1980s, 90s and into the 2000s, clubs were continuously faced with escalating costs. New "commercial" clubs like David Lloyd emerged to intensify competition for members, forcing the traditional voluntary-run clubs to be more proactive (LTA 1995). Many replaced their grass courts with all-weather surfaces or invested in floodlighting or indoor facilities in order to survive. The LTA registered a decline in affiliation numbers from around 2,700 in 1985 to an unprecedented low of 2,341 in 1996 (LTA 1996). Forming a club, attracting and retaining members, and remaining financially solvent were simpler for all types of sports clubs in previous decades, and a declining spirit of voluntarism intensified difficulties still further (Nichols, Gratton, Shibli and Taylor 1998). Alongside the secularisation of society, declining welfarist ideals and the stand against "collectivism" experienced during Thatcher's reign, the growth of consumerism helped to change gradually what being a member of a club entailed and how a "club" was defined (Heinemann 1999; Koski 1999). Time constraints, rising income levels and expanding middle-class leisure opportunities fostered a decline in voluntarism, as willingness to undertake the increasingly demanding administrative work and club maintenance declined (Gratton and Taylor 2000; Stamm and Lamprecht 1999). Lusis (1998:67) remarked: 'With people indoctrinated in the ways of consumerism, many expect their leisure pre-packaged and off the shelf. They do not want to spend time painting clubhouses or mending fences before they can play tennis'.

These influences, which made clubs needier for financial assistance, actually afforded the LTA better opportunities to intervene in club matters, but their forceful and, at times, bullish attitude brought numerous unintended consequences, hurting relations with clubs and ultimately hindering their ability to meet their stringent development targets (Lake 2010b). Possibly the most damaging consequence was to push exclusive practices out of view, imperceptible to county LTA inspectors but no less powerful, as evident in one particular ethnographic case study (Lake 2013). The LTA's efforts to 'prioritise [their] resources, focusing on a smaller number of clubs that offer a full range of performance programmes from Mini Tennis right through to a high performance player programme' (LTA 2006:11), effectively isolated and marginalised those clubs with divergent interests. Since its formation, the LTA has always considered itself responsible for sustaining or helping to restore Britain's tennis prowess, but only since its funding escalated did it become deliberately selective in who it sought to establish partnerships with, oftentimes turning against those clubs, businesses and even charities with slightly divergent but nonetheless relevant interests (Lake 2008).

As the LTA entered the twenty-first century, it reinforced its intentions to crown another British Wimbledon singles champion. But Murray's cathartic triumph in 2013 revealed if anything the irrationality of measuring an entire institution's strength on the performance of a single individual, particularly when that individual did not claim to fully represent that institution. Murray was famously critical of the LTA after his elder brother Jamie blamed his Cambridge academy for 'wrecking' his game, stating:

> I was forced to change my forehand, which messed it up so completely that it's still my main weakness. Before I went to Cambridge it was my best shot, but how could a 12-year-old argue that they were wrong? I couldn't take it anymore, went home to Scotland and didn't pick up a racket for three months. It was a bad experience and I took a long time to get over it.
>
> (*Independent* 1 April 2007)

Andy, conversely, registered his preference for the Sanchez-Casal academy in Barcelona during his formative years. His rejection of the British system did not seem to detract from the occasion of his victory, however, and neither did Virginia Wade's seminal talent development in South Africa detract from the nationalistic significance of her victory, or the LTA's desires to celebrate these victories as their own.

History has revealed that during periods of poor home performances, Britain's fans, media and tennis institutions have clung to outsiders with greater frequency or celebrated foreign victors with greater enthusiasm, particularly when they were seen to represent an important national movement or Britain's collective consciousness more generally. Fittingly, it was McEnroe who commentated Murray's final, a man vilified 30 years earlier for audaciously questioning officials and criticising the club for its snobbish treatment of players. As he progressed through his career, he enjoyed greater Wimbledon support, both among spectators, who came to appreciate his ardent determination and asked why British players could not seem to match it, and institutionally, as the AELTC welcomed McEnroe's commodity value, which helped sustain Wimbledon's profitability and prestige in the face of mounting pressures to commercialise the event.

The AELTC's subtle adjustments, particularly since the 1980s, complemented the LTA's efforts to modernise itself and approach British talent development with greater intent. However, the exaggerated emphasis on elite-level progress as a measure of the Association's general health, rather than, say, the playing standards and organisational strength of recreational, parks and schools tennis, present an illogical and potentially ruinous paradigm, particularly if individual performances that may or may not actually reflect the sport's general health are used to inform policy. In 1987, the LTA executive Phillip Sandilands considered it 'unfortunate' that his organisation was 'judged by our lack of Wimbledon success as a tennis nation' because it '[negates] a lot of good work that is being done… [through] short tennis… and various schemes run by local authorities', but reservedly claimed: 'We have to live with that type of publicity' (Sandilands 1987). Despite the LTA's attempts to define their own success differently, the British press and public expect not only on-court results but off-court accountability. In this regard, the tens of millions the LTA have to invest annually often seems as much a burden as a privilege.

Notes

1. From 1983, Wimbledon issued women eight wildcards.
2. McEnroe found the member's tie in his locker the following year, but claimed he was not officially accepted until his second Wimbledon victory in 1983 (McEnroe 2002).
3. Arguably, the USTA's commercial intentions were established in 1970 when they first adopted the tie-break. Devised in 1965 by an American, Jimmy Van Alen, the tie-break was a clever means to satisfy television's requirements for exciting, climactic and unpredictable outcomes, alongside making match finishing-times easier to calculate (Cooper 1995; Whannel 1986).
4. In 1988, the AELTC's Committee of Management Chairman admitted that an extra £5 million could be raised by using a sponsor's name or allowing perimeter advertisements (Wilson 1988).
5. The LTA Trust was renamed the British Tennis Foundation in 1996.

Bibliography

Adams, T. (2003). *On Being John McEnroe*. London: Yellow Jersey Press.
Bairner, A. (2011). Sports Development, Nations and Nationalism. In B. Houlihan and M. Green, *Routledge Handbook of Sports Development* (pp. 31–41). London: Routledge.
Baltzell, E. D. (1995). *Sporting Gentlemen: Men's Tennis from the Age of Honor to the Cult of the Superstar*. New York: Free Press.
Barnes, S. (2006). *The Meaning of Sport*. London: Short Books.
Barrett, J. (1986). *100 Wimbledon Championships: A Celebration*. London: Collins.
Barrett, J., and Little, A. (2006). *Wimbledon Gentlemen's Singles Champions 1877–2005*. London: Wimbledon Lawn Tennis Museum.
Bodo, P. (1995). *The Courts of Babylon: Tales of Greed and Glory in the Harsh New World of Professional Tennis*. New York: Scribner.
Cash, P. (2002). *Uncovered: The Autobiography of Pat Cash*. Exeter: Greenwater.
Cooper, I. (1995). *Game, Set & Match: A Developmental Study of Tennis, with Particular Reference to Lawn Tennis*. Leicester: Unpublished MA dissertation, University of Leicester.
Evans, R. (1993). *Open Tennis: 25 Years of Seriously Defiant Success On and Off the Court*. London: Bloomsbury.

Feinstein, J. (1991). *Hard Courts: Real Life on the Professional Tennis Tours*. New York: Villard Books.
Forbes, G. (1978). *A Handful of Summers*. London: Heinemann.
Gratton, C., and Taylor, P. (2000). *Economics of Sport and Recreation*. London: Spon.
Heinemann, K. (1999). Sport Clubs in Europe. In K. Heinemann, *Sports Clubs in Various European Countries*. Schorndorf: Hofmann.
Houlihan, B. (1997). *Sport, Policy and Politics: A Comparative Analysis*. London: Routledge.
Houlihan, B., and White, A. (2002). *The Politics of Sports Development*. London: Routledge.
Koski, P. (1999). Characteristics and Contemporary Trends of Sports Clubs in the Finnish Context. In K. Heinemann, *Sports Clubs in Various European Countries*. Schorndorf: Hofmann.
Lake, R. J. (2008). *Social Exclusion in British Tennis: A History of Privilege and Prejudice*. London: Unpublished PhD Dissertation, Brunel University.
Lake, R. J. (2010b). 'Managing Change' in British Tennis 1990–2006: Unintended Outcomes of LTA Talent Development Policies. *International Review for the Sociology of Sport*, 45(4), 474–490.
Lake, R. J. (2011b). A Critique of Functionalist Values within Recent British Tennis Policy. *International Sports Studies*, 32(2), 47–59.
Lake, R. J. (2013). 'They Treat Me like I'm Scum': Social Exclusion and Established-Outsider Relations in a British Tennis Club. *International Review for the Sociology of Sport*, 48(1), 112–128.
Lake, R. J. (2014). Discourses of Social Exclusion in British Tennis: Historical Changes and Continuities. *International Journal of Sport and Society*, 4(2), 1–11.
Lake, R. J. (forthcoming). The 'Bad Boys' of Tennis: Shifting Gender and Social Class Relations in the Era of Nastase, Connors and McEnroe. *Journal of Sport History*.
Lawn Tennis Association (1985). *The Juniors in Britain's Tennis Clubs*. London: Lawn Tennis Association.
Lawn Tennis Association (1986a). *Annual Report*. London: Lawn Tennis Association.
Lawn Tennis Association (1991). *Annual General Meeting: Report of the Council*. London: Lawn Tennis Association.
Lawn Tennis Association (1994). *Annual Report*. London: Lawn Tennis Association.
Lawn Tennis Association (1995). *The Development of Tennis in Great Britain 1996–2001*. London: Lawn Tennis Association.
Lawn Tennis Association (1996). *Annual Report*. London: Lawn Tennis Association.
Lawn Tennis Association (1998a). *Annual Report*. London: Lawn Tennis Association.
Lawn Tennis Association (1998b). *National Tennis Facilities Strategy 1998–2002*. London: Lawn Tennis Association.
Lawn Tennis Association (1999). *British Tennis and You: A Strategy for the New Millennium*. London: Lawn Tennis Association.
Lawn Tennis Association (2000). *Annual Report*. London: Lawn Tennis Association.
Lawn Tennis Association (2001). *Annual Report*. London: Lawn Tennis Association.
Lawn Tennis Association (2002). *Annual Report*. London: Lawn Tennis Association.
Lawn Tennis Association (2003). *Annual Report*. London: Lawn Tennis Association.
Lawn Tennis Association (2006). *Blueprint for British Tennis*. London: Lawn Tennis Association.

Lusis, A. (1998). *Tennis in Robin Hood's County: The Story of Tennis Clubs in Nottinghamshire*. Nottingham: the Author.
Maskell, D. (1988). *From Where I Sit*. London: Willow.
McDonald, I. (1995). Sport for All – 'RIP': A Political Critique of the Relationship Between National Sport Policy and Local Authority Sports Development in London. In S. Fleming, M. Talbot and A. Tomlinson, *Policy and Politics in Sport, Physical Education and Leisure* (pp. 71–94). Eastbourne: Leisure Studies Association.
McEnroe, J. (2002). *Serious*. London: Time Warner Paperbacks.
Mills, A. (2005). *Lifting the Covers: Alan Mills, the Autobiography*. London: Headline.
Nichols, G., Gratton, C., Shibli, S., and Taylor, P. (1998). Local Authority Support to Volunteers in Sports Clubs. *Managing Leisure*, 119–127.
Oakley, B., and Green, M. (2001). Still Playing the Game at Arm's Length? The Selective Re-investment in British Sport, 1995–2000. *Managing Leisure*, 6, 74–94.
Pugh, P., and Flint, C. (1997). *Thatcher for Beginners*. Cambridge: Icon Books.
Sandilands, P. (1987). The Indoor Tennis Initiative. In S. Council, *Indoor Tennis Initiative: Making It Work* (pp. 4–11). London: Sports Council.
Sandilands, P. (1996). Court Report. *Tennis Facility News*, 23, 2–3.
Smith, G. (1987). *The English Season*. London: Pavilion Books.
Stamm, H., and Lamprecht, M. (1999). Sports Organisations in Switzerland. In K. Heinemann, *Sports Clubs in Various European Countries*. Schorndorf: Hofmann.
Tinling, T. (1983). *Tinling: Sixty Years in Tennis*. London: Sidgwick & Jackson.
Wade, V. (1978). *Courting Triumph*. London: Hodder & Stoughton.
Whannel, G. (1986). The Unholy Alliance: Notes on Television and the Remaking of British Sport 1965–85. *Leisure Studies*, 5, 129–145.
Wilson, N. (1988). *The Sports Business: The Men and the Money*. London: Piatkus.

Conclusion
Continuity and change in the social history of tennis in Britain and future directives for the LTA

The aims of this book have been far-reaching in attempting to describe and explain how tennis emerged, developed and changed within the context of broader social historical processes in Britain from the mid to late nineteenth century to the present day. While much of this work has concentrated on important elite-level developments among top players and coaches and within leading clubs and associations, an attempt has been made to capture the mundane in British tennis social history, considering the challenges and opportunities that ordinary people dealt with in and through tennis, and how they expressed aspects of their identity in their playing styles and patterns, on-court appearances, off-court behaviours, club memberships, talent-development efforts, and other areas of involvement. This book has attempted to show: how tennis has been a site for struggles in relation to gender, social class, race/ethnicity and nationalism, and an engine to help drive important societal changes in these areas; how tennis served to help in the recovery from two world wars as an arena for returning to and maintaining British values that helped the British to recover their sense of self; and, how, while being a site for success in issues of inclusion and equality, it has also, paradoxically, remained at least administratively a white male-dominated elitist sport.

Indeed, conversely, this book has aimed to expose areas of continuity, to demonstrate how tennis in Britain is so closely connected with its past both in ostensible, plainly visible ways – many of them positive – but also in how it sustains age-old and arguably antiquated ideas, values and practices to forcibly exclude, alienate, show prejudice or discriminate against particular social groups. This concluding chapter aims to summarise these main areas before highlighting some avenues for future exploration, to consider the ways that tennis may continue to fascinate the British and provide a lens through which we can critically and meaningfully view ourselves in relation to broader social structures.

Bar none, tennis on an international scale has led all other sports in several key determinants of female equality. In terms of numbers of recreational players, the participation of women has been near equal to men. While once noticeably different, average earnings for the top male and female players have evened out, meaning tennis players are among the highest earning female athletes in the world. Many elite-level female players enjoy near equitable corporate-sponsorship/product-endorsement opportunities and similar amounts of media coverage. Spencer (2000:399) was right, though, to question the overall extent that improvement for elite-level women can be identified within the broader feminist movement: 'Even if [they] earn equal pay at Grand Slam events, that does not address issues that affect the majority of women. Nor do the endorsement contracts of a select few translate into widespread opportunities for sportswomen.'

In Britain, tennis has played a significant role in shifting public attitudes toward women's physical capabilities, and over the years has also afforded middle-class women in particular greater spatial and social freedoms and helped accelerate dress reform. Recently, it has helped address inequalities in status and public recognition. That said, key features like its rules and etiquette, how it is played and organised in clubs and administered in governing bodies, and the ways in which it is sold and packaged for consumers and reported on, continue to marginalise and objectify women and trivialise their performances. Women continue to be presented as inferior to men in several important areas: (i) the provocative and "feminine" ways women are encouraged to dress on court, and their – often complicit – sexualised presentation in television commercials and product endorsements, which serves to disempower women by reducing them to objects for men's sexual satisfaction; (ii) the biased media reports that continue to portray female players as psychologically frail and undermine their play by focusing on their private lives, seeking gossip about heterosexual relationships and other players (Vincent 2004); (iii) the more restrained and "ladylike" on- and off-court behavioural expectations of female players and, concomitantly, the greater leniency shown to male players over transgressions; (iv) the silencing of homosexuality as an issue, which ignores how lesbians are socially excluded or denied endorsements and other opportunities; (v) the rule whereby women's championship matches are played over best-of-three sets instead of best-of-five, which reinforces the anachronistic ideas about women's physical incapacities upon which the rule was originally based; (vi) and, crucially, their lack of presence in high-level administrative positions, as exemplified by the fact that in 2008, the last year the LTA published its Official Handbook, it listed 122 council members, but only 24 (19.7 per cent) were female.

Despite tennis being heralded as a leader among sports in various aspects of gender equality, it still privileges patriarchal ideologies that celebrate hegemonic masculinities and exclude and/or marginalise homosexuals. The efforts of some leading male players throughout the post-war period to legitimise men's tennis by countering its image as an effeminate sport have actually helped to sustain homosexuality as a taboo subject on both the men's and women's tours, and worked against broader liberalising movements in society. Martina Navratilova recently opined to the *Daily Mail*

(24 June 2013) that many gay male players remain fearful of revealing their homosexuality: 'We know they are there, but they are so far in the closet I don't know who they are'. The only known post-war elite-level player to "come out" was the low-ranked Paraguayan Francisco Rodriquez in 2008, who waited until he had retired for fear of becoming 'an outcast'. The lack of elite-level role models for gay male players, however, is countered by the establishment, in recent years, of several "gay" or "gay-friendly" tennis clubs in England. The Gay and Lesbian Tennis Alliance that formed in North America in 1991 established a British affiliate, Tennis London International, and shortly afterwards clubs formed in Brighton (Brighton Lesbian and Gay Sports Society) and Manchester (Northern Aces Tennis Group). Arguably, tennis is ideally placed to join the anti-homophobia campaigns that have commenced in football and other sports, and with its largely university-educated middle-class following in Britain would likely receive considerable public support. Dominic Bliss, a sports writer and former editor of *Ace*, the leading British tennis magazine, which is commercially sponsored by the LTA, recently revealed, however:

> The one subject they wouldn't tolerate was any mention of lesbians in tennis. This LTA policy was a weird one. Basically, at that time, those in charge believed that if parents thought the sport had lesbians in it they would discourage their daughters from playing. How stone age was that?
>
> (personal communication 10 April 2012)

The LTA's inclination to ignore rather than confront this issue would imply their inadvertent support for the status quo.

Tennis in Britain has remained a sport riddled with subtle class distinctions, expressed in behaviour, dress, playing style and attitude, which, when combined with explicit restrictions through club memberships, availability of coaching opportunities and prohibitive equipment costs, has limited tennis participation to people of sufficient wealth and status. The working classes, when employed as groundsmen or coaching professionals, were invariably banished from clubhouses, but often accepted their marginalisation by internalising class relations as an immutable feature of British society. In the interwar and post-war periods, democratisation was witnessed not only through greater working-class participation, but also by the growing acceptance of lower-middle or working-class sporting values, or those associated with competitiveness, money-making and professionalism. Fred Perry is often considered to personify this change, but the extent that his success sparked a frenzy of working-class interest is unclear, given that war severely hampered talent-development efforts. Moreover, while the LTA sought to claim him as their own product, in reality their involvement came fairly late in his formative development. Also, if the response his first Wimbledon victory garnered from the AELTC committee was an indication of how the establishment in general treated him, his success should be considered an outcome *despite*, rather than because of, the system of development in place. In fact, Perry's story reveals the extent that personal qualities and ambitions were fundamental in determining future success and likely were equally if not more influential than any talent-development system.

Accounting for patterns of foreign success witnessed from the 1970s–90s, Bodo (1995:45) contended that broader societal conditions were of most consequence: the availability of tennis courts in Sweden by means of municipal investment; the 'energetic, increasingly prosperous, bourgeois society' in Germany that afforded investment for talent development; the considerable private-sector investment in American tennis talent; and the widespread desires among Eastern European children to use tennis to escape their 'environment of scarcity'. Conversely, Australia's explicit efforts to identify and develop tennis champions through the Australian Institute of Sport (AIS), opened in 1981, produced 'dismal' results, in Bodo's (1995:43) words. Despite their previous successes, which occurred organically, 'the Aussies somehow came to the conclusion that the development of a tennis player could be institutionalised'. Even Pat Cash, Australia's top-ranked male player in the 1980s explicitly avoided AIS involvement, despite the financial implications. Still, British followers of the idea that talent can be purposefully "produced" remain devout, despite a lack of compelling evidence and a track record that suggests most of Britain's recent star players developed outside of their system. Given this fact, it certainly remains a key challenge for the LTA to produce a genuinely British/LTA developed champion.

Only recently have the LTA showed willingness toward more flexibility and open-mindedness in their approaches (LTA 2006), but arguably they are still far from fully appreciating the depth and relevance of social-class structures that influence take-up and player development. Public parks' tennis remains woefully underfunded and, despite published rhetoric that suggests a renewed enthusiasm for identifying talent among low-income families in inner cities (e.g. through the City Tennis Clubs scheme), such programmes continue to represent a small proportion of the LTA's annual operating budget. Moreover, given that Andy Murray developed largely outside of the British system, it is still questionable whether his successes have justified the huge amounts spent by the LTA on elite-level development over the last decade, which included paying Murray's coach, Brad Gilbert, £1 million for 16 months of work in 2006–7, and constructing a £40-million National Tennis Centre in Roehampton. Some might have reason to argue that the LTA's main priority should be grass-roots development instead of elite-level success.

Clubs remain a curious target for investment. Given their relative autonomy from external interference, many have remained bastions of elitism, by privileging behavioural etiquette, rule observance, self-restraint, chivalry, and the display of deference toward higher-status members (Lake 2013). Much as they function in settings of education and employment, such behaviours as bred through the socialisation processes of young members help demarcate club members and players according to social rank and also distinguish clubs from one another, as they compete for prestige. Far from being removed as an outcome of increasingly blurred lines of class demarcation, status distinctions are now just articulated in different ways, more subtle but still potent. Thus, many clubs have retained class patterns in tennis participation and continue to exclude those without the necessary cultural capital.

The other perspective on this issue, which is just as valid but less fashionable, recognises the importance of social exclusivity in sustaining the participation of the core middle-class tennis-playing demographic. Historically speaking, the sport's elitist image played a crucial role in ensuring its survival amidst a proliferation of alternative leisure pursuits. But our contemporary left-of-centre, liberal-minded approach to sport development conveniently overlooks the potential benefits of exclusivity for those who are fortunate enough to be "included". Rather than leaping to the automatic conclusion that exclusivity is the cause of Britain's national decline in tennis – hence the huge investment in children's programmes, particularly in clubs, with the aim of improving participation opportunities for new groups – perhaps the LTA might benefit from a more dispassionate reading of the sport's history. It is possible that pulling investment from one specific avenue that has a consistent track record of producing good players in order to spread funding thinly to service all social classes, might actually produce worse results. It is worth considering that it is not, and likely never will be, the FA's goal to attract more middle- or upper-class children to football, so why should the LTA attempt the opposite goal, as if working-class children are somehow a richer source of potential talent. A quick study of Rafael Nadal, Roger Federer, Novak Djokovic and many of the world's leading players in the early twenty-first century, including Andy Murray, shows them to be disproportionately "middle class", as judged by their family background. The Williams sisters' story, used often by the LTA anecdotally to justify their efforts to broaden participation, remains and likely always will remain exceptional. Moreover, their success stemmed almost entirely from their father's dedicated efforts rather than from any specific USTA endeavours to identify and develop talent in inner-city areas. Therefore, some might perceive the LTA's efforts to replicate their unique success story an unsound investment that is unlikely to bear much fruit.

Perhaps the LTA might see better results if their most promising players were not comprehensively supported and, instead, forced to fight for "scraps" of funding, international tour opportunities, Wimbledon wildcards, and access to world-class facilities and coaching, which some have argued are given out too readily and too early in the players' careers. While the swathes of talented youngsters emerging from low-income families in Eastern Europe might inspire the LTA to delve more deeply into British working-class communities to find the next Andy Murray, it is impossible to replicate the societal conditions that function to inspire the players themselves to pursue tennis careers, particularly when the LTA are so much wealthier than other associations. Like wealthy parents trying not to spoil their children so they learn the value of money, it remains a challenge for the LTA to ensure promising players develop the necessary psychological toughness, will-to-win and "hunger" required to compete successfully.

In terms of race and ethnicity, tennis remains undoubtedly a "white preserve", which is a feature inarguably connected to its early development and popularisation by white, Protestant, middle-class Europeans, North Americans and Australasians, for the purpose of showcasing culturally defined norms of physical prowess in accordance with amateur values. Thus, its written and unwritten rules were broadly defined in accordance with its dominant light-skinned playing demographic. There was little room for cultural diversity early in the sport's history, as ethnic minorities were looked upon with curiosity as exotic and "different". Even as it spread internationally, its arbiters remained happily indoctrinated into the dominant colonial-British amateur sporting ideology, which demanded play in accordance with traditional behavioural standards.

In the decades after WWII, Britain and Wimbledon were introduced to their first "black" tennis players, and while the majority among the British public and press could not be accused of anything more than subtle racial marking, the dominant narratives of their successes were always put in the context of their race. For the most part, their on-court self-restraint and off-court grace and deference to authority ensured some measure of politeness from British crowds. Particularly for Arthur Ashe, this cultural capital was accrued through years of playing a predominantly white sport, in white clubs, at tournaments organised by white people in front of predominantly white spectators. Often, motives to express culturally divergent behaviours or customs were suppressed by deep-rooted desires to "fit in" rather than accentuate racial and cultural differences, as the Williams sisters have shown more willingness to do (Schultz 2005). In Britain, the successes of Arvind Parmar, Anne Keothavong and, more recently, Heather Watson, who broke into the top 40, remain exceptions in a sport that, despite the LTA's valid attempts to foster greater accessibility, has remained dominated by white players and governed internally by predominantly white executives. As the City Tennis Development Officer and later as the Equality and Diversity Manager for the LTA until 2009, Funke Awoderu came to understand basic poverty as a key issue, alongside a lack of suitable role models in performance, coaching and administration/governance positions (Gabriel 2005). While Baltzell (1995) brought to attention American tennis clubs that were known to be racially exclusive and inaccessible to Jews, blacks and other distinguishable ethnic minorities, there is a noticeable gap in our understanding of racial prejudice in tennis clubs, and also of those clubs like Chandos LTC, which formed with a distinctive minority racial/ethnic or religious following, as an avenue of cultural resistance. While other sports have enjoyed far more comprehensive analyses of racial/ethnic/religious segregation and exclusion, the full story in British tennis remains untold.

From its incipient development, lawn tennis reflected national culture and reinforced ideas about Britain's global position. British players invested national significance in their playing styles, most notably through efforts to adhere to amateur ethics and sportsmanship: the quintessential traits of British sportsmen. Playing styles were perceived to reflect shared national temperaments, which were significant from the earliest days of international competition. Before WWI, Britain's (and the LTA's) claims to unequivocal global administrative dominance were reinforced often, while Wimbledon's prestige was considered to reflect Britain's national prowess more generally. The Championships were invested with cultural significance and used often to convey important messages about England and Britain more generally. The ILTF's marked expansion in the interwar and post-war periods also harboured British desires to sustain their prestige and status in the allocation of votes, which reflected Euro-centrism and conveyed an implicit administrative hierarchy. The Davis Cup, particularly in the "amateur" era, was invested with political significance and used repeatedly in the sanctions imposed against the participation of certain nations because of external political conflicts and wars.

In the open era, tennis remained an important medium to transmit messages about English/British national identity. Greg Rusedski's controversial adoption of British citizenship in 1995 was somewhat downplayed by the press, given his performances on the international stage brought much-desired positive attention at a time of consistently poor results. In many ways, his relatively smooth path to public acceptance reflected an age-old process of the British making claims upon particular outsiders to represent them. The key differences were that Rusedski did not seem to represent the British ideologically, like Drobny did, for example, through his playing style and demeanour, and also Rusedski chose Britain rather than the other way round. Certainly, the events surrounding his changing nationality remain conspicuously under-researched. Louis Cayer, Canada's Davis Cup captain at the time, believed he departed 'for financial reasons', which left a lot of people 'bitter'. The journalist Bruce Wallace agreed, noting Rusedski's discouragingly unsuccessful attempts to generate corporate sponsorship in Canada and the likelihood of better endorsement opportunities in Britain (*Macleans* 26 June 1995). Regardless of whether there is any truth in this accusation, Rusedski's determination to switch his nationality, reducing him to "persona non grata" in Canada, reflects the perceived rewards associated with tennis and, concomitantly, the shifting motives of some players to achieve them, by whatever means necessary.

Pat Cash went on to describe Rusedski's relationship with Henman as tumultuous, connected to the circumstances of his arrival:

Negotiations for the switch of nationalities had been going on for some years – but Greg hadn't bargained for a really top flight, home-grown player bursting through at just the time of his arrival: namely Tim Henman. The result was, that all the best deals went to Henman, and some of Rusedski's were cheap by comparison.

(Cash 2002:301)

Henman's persona as quintessentially "English" was reflected in his southern, middle-class accent; his respectable, dependable and clean image; his abiding self-restraint, magnanimity, and sportsmanship; and, even in his modest chip-and-charge playing style that appeared almost old-fashioned against the aggressive, big-serve, top-spin attacking styles of Pete Sampras and others. Henman's years of near misses at Wimbledon, which included four semi-finals and four other quarter-finals appearances, had a flavour of Virginia Wade about them, as he toyed with the nation's hopes on countless occasions, but, unlike Wade, ultimately he never came good. Nevertheless, and perhaps contentiously, he will likely be remembered as the most celebrated British tennis player of all time, even more than Perry, Wade or Murray. 'Henman's annual tilt at the dragon of SW19 was part of the rhythm of national life' stated Simon Barnes (2006:24), but 'so is the dragon's ultimate inevitable victory'. Despite his ability to make us 'despise ourselves for the hope that we guarded within us' that he would win Wimbledon, his often agonising annual defeats were a memorable, 'defining point of the summer'. Perhaps therein lies Henman's cultural significance. 'There is real nobility in that: in the not giving up, in the belief that his destiny lies in his annual tryst with the dragon' (Barnes 2006:27).

Likely due to Henman's enduring legacy as the quintessential English male tennis player – plucky, supremely talented, intelligent, sportsmanlike, restrained, modest – early efforts to rename Henman Hill as Murray Mount, made soon after Henman retired, were doomed to failure (*Reuters* 25 June 2009; *Guardian* 1 July 2009). Despite Murray's greater success, his uncompromising determination and unapologetic ruthlessness, not to mention his perceived separatist views, which were undoubtedly taken out of context in 2006, nevertheless likely alienated him among the southern, middle-class English who make up the bulk of Wimbledon's regular crowds.[1] Time will tell how Murray's place within British tennis history will be written, which might be of significance in the context of Scotland's movement toward political independence. For now, he remains a shining beacon of tennis prowess, in a nation whose clubs are still rooted chiefly in amateur ideals but whose governing body, media and tennis-playing public demand and expect professionalism and success from their leading players.

The attitudes of Britain's leading tennis officials in the areas of gender, social class, race/ethnicity and nationalism influenced their views on amateurism/professionalism, coaching, talent development and commercialism. Their collective desires to avoid working-class influences underpinned their safe, reserved conservatism and resistance to change. The notable shift from the determined and at times dogmatic British leadership of the pre-WWI era, toward middle-ground, compromised, "wait-and-see-what-others-do" policies, reflected growing fears of Wimbledon's demise in the context of the sport's globalisation and commercialisation, and of imperial decline more generally. The LTA's lukewarm support for coaches, shown through their reluctance to afford them complete independence, and their heavily compromised talent-development initiatives reflected a general disinclination to encourage professionalism. British tennis officials were a close-knit and deeply established group of like-minded and similarly socially positioned gentlemen, who each enjoyed the prestige that their position afforded and were reluctant to instigate changes that might challenge their authority or compromise their privileges. As the institution of tennis grew, with expanding networks of relations and ties of interdependence, their ability to foresee how single changes might unfold was increasingly limited. Unintended consequences were more numerous and harder to envisage; an outcome clearly highlighted in the LTA's pursuit of removing the amateur–professional distinction. In this moment, their vision of negative consequences was proved to be insightful, yet their unwillingness to fully commit to commercialism undermined all but their premier tournament. If British tennis prowess could be measured by Wimbledon's rank among other tournaments, instead of by the performances of its own players in it, Murray aside, the nation could proudly boast at being world-leading. However, in such a proud and expectant nation, with a press ruthless and unwilling to allow complacency to set in, such an easy "get-out" is unlikely.

Alternatively, perhaps Britain should measure itself on the health of tennis as a sport in itself, which its noble citizens duly (re)invented, developed, popularised and codified in its formative years, before leading in its early international administration and governance. British leadership administratively remains a key area of pride, expressed not only through Wimbledon's ability to sustain its pre-eminent status and the AELTC's competence in running a hugely successful, modern tournament, but also through British direction within the ITF, which retains its headquarters in west London, adjacent to the LTA. While the British have overseen or helped oversee the development of tennis into one of the most economically successful, popularly followed, widely played international sports, their challenges in relation to fostering greater equality and inclusion in participation remain daunting, particularly in clubs which have received so much of their funding attention. Their propensity to rely on quantitative measures of performance in ignorance of deep-rooted structures of inequality that qualitatively impact club members' experiences certainly needs addressing, as does their tendency toward short-term goal-setting and an overall lack of knowledge of historical processes (Lake 2010b, 2011b, 2013). The greater accountability that others have demanded, and that the LTA have come to demand of themselves, has certainly pushed them to become more structured and business-like in their methods, and in this sense they are world-leading, though it remains to be seen whether they can overcome some of the challenges presented by Britain's dominant sporting ideology that remains in key areas tied to its amateur roots.

Note

1. See http://news.bbc.co.uk/2/hi/5128028.stm (29 June 2006).

Bibliography

Baltzell, E. D. (1995). *Sporting Gentlemen: Men's Tennis from the Age of Honor to the Cult of the Superstar*. New York: Free Press.

Barnes, S. (2006). *The Meaning of Sport*. London: Short Books.

Bodo, P. (1995). *The Courts of Babylon: Tales of Greed and Glory in the Harsh New World of Professional Tennis*. New York: Scribner.

Cash, P. (2002). *Uncovered: The Autobiography of Pat Cash*. Exeter: Greenwater.

Gabriel, D. (2005, 23 June). *Why Black British Tennis Players Are Missing from Wimbledon*. Retrieved February 20, 2014, from I Am Colourful: www.deborahgabriel.com/wp-content/uploads/2010/05/Why-black-British-tennis-players-are-missing-from-Wimbledon-June-2005.pdf

Lake, R. J. (2010b). 'Managing Change' in British Tennis 1990–2006: Unintended Outcomes of LTA Talent Development Policies. *International Review for the Sociology of Sport*, 45(4), 474–490.

Lake, R. J. (2011b). A Critique of Functionalist Values within Recent British Tennis Policy. *International Sports Studies*, 32(2), 47–59.

Lake, R. J. (2013). 'They Treat Me like I'm Scum': Social Exclusion and Established-Outsider Relations in a British Tennis Club. *International Review for the Sociology of Sport*, 48(1), 112–128.

Lawn Tennis Association (2006). *Blueprint for British Tennis*. London: Lawn Tennis Association.

Schultz, J. (2005). Reading the Catsuit: Serena Williams and the Production of Blackness at the 202 U.S. Open. *Journal of Sport and Social Issues*, 29(3), 338–357.

Spencer, N. E. (2000). Reading Between the Lines: A Discursive Analysis of the Billie Jean King vs. Bobby Riggs 'Battle of the Sexes'. *Sociology of Sport Journal*, 17, 386–402.

Vincent, J. (2004). Game, Set and Match: The Construction of Gender in British Newspaper Coverage of the 2000 Wimbledon Championships. *Sociology of Sport Journal*, 21(4), 435–456.

Index

advertising *see* sponsorship
AELTC 2, 28, 42, 48, 70, 106, 173; anti-commercialism stance 84, 229, 277–8, 285; branding 278–9; coaching 152, 157; commercialism 103–4, 278, 284; during World War II 178–9; early administrative dominance 17, 25, 57–60; elitism 68, 278–9; female representation 108; interwar developments 102–4; ladies events 28, 49; modernisation 275–9, 284; media 134; membership 200, 245, 246, 274, 285; player relations 275–6; post-war recovery 179–80; public criticisms 59–60, 276; push for open tennis 208, 223–6; relations with the LTA 63, 83–4, 179–81; relocation 102; talent development 279; television 208; vs. Fred Perry 166–7; Sunday play 42; vs. Ted Tinling 252
AELTCC 16
agents *see* management groups
all-whites clothing rule 32–3, 278, 279
amateurism 3, 9, 20, 24–5, 65, 297; anti-professionalism 137–8, 168–9, 208, 228; coaching/training 9, 24, 65; early definitions 85–6, 139–40; effortlessness 9, 27, 76; exploitation 145, 172, 214, 217–8, 223, 232; journalistic endeavours 139–41; playing for intrinsic/extrinsic motives 9, 24, 38, 52–5, 66, 132, 205; post-1968 amateur-professional distinctions 227–30, 234; restrictions against ex-amateurs 147; self-restraint 9, 24–5, 209; shifting ideals 65–6, 119, 144–5; specialisation 9, 65; sportsmanship 9, 24, 100, 208–9, 294; white attire 32–3; *see also* behavioural etiquette; *see also* ILTF, amateur rules; *see also* LTA, amateur rules; *see also* shamateurism
American Tennis Association 238
Americanisation 102, 134, 223
anti-commercialism 21, 66, 83–6, 132, 136–9, 142–3, 170, 205–8; *see also* LTA, anti-commercialism
anti-Semitism *see* Jewish tennis players
Ashe, Arthur 226, 230, 238, 245, 255, 256, 293; at Wimbledon 242–3; racism 241–3
athletics 2, 66, 98, 115, 157, 206, 237; British decline 83, 94, 187; match-fixing 53
ATP 215, 232, 234, 243; ATP Tour 230, 234; Pilic affair 232–4
Austin, Henry "Bunny" 111, 160, 162, 165, 169
Australia 81, 94, 100, 101, 171, 188, 202; AIS 291; amateur rules 232; early tennis development 71–3, 78; nationalism 78; open tennis controversy 222, 224, 226–8; professional tours in 216; sanctioned amateur tours to 186, 201; social inclusion/exclusion 72, 202; successes 72, 200–2; training methods 200–1; women's tennis playing opportunities 71, 73; *see also* LTAA
Australian Open/Australian Championships 160, 186, 208, 242, 270, 271, 277

badminton 13, 25, 70
Barker, Sue 186, 261, 267
Barrett, John 201, 204, 208, 268
Bates, Jeremy 1, 270, 271

Batley, Arthur 95, 115–16
BBC 1, 208, 225, 234, 278; early development 134; selling television rights 207; tennis commentary 251, 261; tennis coverage 1, 134–5
Beckenham tournament 227, 231
behavioural etiquette 14, 17, 38, 124, 128, 130, 289; breaches 208, 266–7, 272–7; coaching 153, 157; in clubs 128–9, 291; published rules 208–9; reflection of gender 24–5, 28, 34; reflection of social class 14, 20, 26, 54, 128–30; 210, 276, 290; spectators 129, 210
Betz, Pauline 213, 253
Birmingham 15, 37, 84, 106, 119; parks tennis 61, 125, 126
Bloomer, Shirley 186, 244
BOA 45, 78, 97, 99, 100, 123
Boar War 33, 77, 82
Bogdanovic, Alex 271
Borotra, Jean 117, 220, 222, 227, 228
Bournemouth 19, 51, 203, 268; tournament 179, 227–8, 255
Bristol 37, 43, 61, 172, 195, 231
Britain: 1951 Festival of Britain 266–7; critique of training methods 81–2, 187; empire/national decline 82–3, 87–9, 96, 124, 223, 240, 296; gender relations 31–2, 106, 111, 247, 254; moral leadership 100, 189, 240, 294; nationalism 4, 9, 45, 58, 196, 266–9; race relations 237–43, 244; sense of racial/social superiority 78, 80–1, 88, 96; sporting decline 78–9, 87–8, 185–7, 235; sporting mentality 270–2, 276–7, 284; sporting success 1–2, 3, 160, 165, 186, 225, 267–9, 284
Brookes, Norman 72, 78, 79, 92
Budge, Donald 126, 171, 172, 215
Buxton, Angela 204, 218; at Wimbledon 186, 238, 239; racism 243–6; *see also* Jewish tennis players
Buxton Gardens tournament 18, 48, 49, 60, 61

Cambridge University 8, 10, 43, 60, 74, 78, 93, 157, 169; LTA representation 63; lawn tennis club 50; women's tennis 30
Canada 73, 81, 101, 219, 294; Greg Rusedski's defection 272
Cardiff 61, 231

Casals, Rosie 255, 278
CCPR 197, 202, 203; Wolfenden Report 203
Chambers, Dorothea Lambert 32, 33, 93, 107, 109, 110, 114
Chatrier, Philippe 234
children: advances for 117–18, 132, 163, 191–2, 197, 202–5, 279–82; coaching 157–8; discrimination in clubs 118–19, 132, 151, 158, 191–3, 281–2
coaches: associations/unions 150, 157–60, 199–200; competitive playing opportunities 65, 153–4; complaints about 158–9, 200–2; distinctions between ex-amateur touring professionals 150, 154; improving status/position 64–5, 151–3, 197, 199, 201, 280; LTA paternalism 65, 157, 160; prejudice toward 63–4, 150–1, 153, 160, 165, 199–200, 290, 296; qualifications 153, 159, 200; war shortage 178
Cochet, Henri 117, 170
Cold War 223, 237, 259
Connors, Jimmy 233, 242, 258, 260–1, 273, 274
Conservative Party 7, 70, 83, 122, 123, 132, 177, 281
consumerism 209–10, 270, 283; commercialising the body 253, 258–9, 261
counties: Bedfordshire 118, 157; Cheshire 61, 62, 119; Derbyshire 18, 125; Kent 62, 131; Lancashire 61, 198, 203; Middlesex 62, 84, 125, 158; Nottinghamshire 61, 108, 118, 124–5, 127, 131, 179; Staffordshire 61, 107, 110, 179, 203; Surrey 62, 118, 124, 130, 131, 158, 239; Yorkshire 37, 61
Cox, Mark 204, 228, 267
Crawford, Jack 166–7, 245
Cricket 3, 48, 60, 70, 94, 141, 163, 206; British decline 83, 94, 187; comparisons with lawn tennis 2, 9, 12, 18; gatekeeper for lawn tennis global development 71–5; professionals 64, 66, 151, 257; public schools 67, 123; relationship/rivalry with tennis 18, 20, 32–3, 49, 50; women 34, 37; *see also* Lords Cricket Ground

Croft, Annabel 261
croquet 13, 16, 18, 50
Crowther, John 281
Cumberland Club 178, 183, 244
cycling 30, 31, 53, 83

David, Herman 224, 225, 234
Davies, Mike 186, 198, 201
Davis Cup 66, 137, 162, 188, 200–1; amateur rulings 219–20, 227, 230; political tool 97–8, 294; British defeats 75–7, 114–17, 171; British successes 77, 156, 160, 165–6, 171; criticisms 168; declining reputation 230–4; early development 76–8
David Lloyd tennis clubs 283
Davis, Dwight 76, 166
decolonisation 196, 223, 235, 237, 240
Desborough, 1st Baron William Grenfell 45, 70, 98, 123
Didrikson, Mildred "Babe" 250
Djokovic, Novak 1, 292
Dod, Charlotte "Lottie" 32–4, 36
Doherty, Hugh Lawrence "Laurie" 52, 65, 66, 71, 77, 169
Doherty, Reginald Frank "Reggie" 52, 65, 66, 71, 77
doubles tennis 27, 46, 49, 101, 146, 154, 173; All England Championships 60; British successes 271; Buxton/Gibson team 239–40; gender distinctions 28, 30, 35; sportsmanship 25; *see also* mixed doubles
Drobny, Jaroslav 188, 189, 204, 245, 294
Dublin University 48, 63
Durie, Jo 271

Eastbourne 19, 49, 53, 61, 154, 179, 259
Eaton Griffith, J. 202, 224
Edgbaston 15, 42, 50, 54, 61, 63
Edinburgh 37, 63, 119, 125
Evert, Christine Marie "Chris" 251, 256, 258–60, 267
England: competitions against Ireland 71; Englishness/Britishness 4, 265–7, 272, 294; geographical spread of tennis 61–3; north vs. south enmity 58–63, 95–6, 125, 197–203, 268; *see also* Britain
Eugenics 31, 81

Federation "Fed" Cup 253, 269
FFT 117, 140, 144, 171, 220, 224, 234; de Bazillac, Guy 220
First World War 92–6; anti-German sentiments 96–8; class relations 93; gender relations 106
Fitzwilliam Cub 44, 48, 58, 64, 69–71
football 70, 172, 292; anti-homophobia campaigns 290; British decline 3, 83, 163, 187; coach migration 65; FIFA 99, 100; gender 34, 123; Olympics 98–9; professionalism 53, 66, 206; public schools 67, 123; social comparisons to lawn tennis 12, 34; sportsmanship 25; violence 276; World Cup 3, 98, 225
France 65, 71, 94, 100, 101, 117, 140, 173, 230; Davis Cup vs. Britain 160, 165; Four Musketeers 117; French Riviera 65, 71, 75, 85, 94, 110, 155, 208; shamateurism 135–6
French National Championships/French Open/Roland Garros 94, 140, 160, 186, 229, 233–4, 255, 277

gambling 21, 53, 65, 71, 206, 213, 278
gamesmanship 130, 167, 251, 260, 274; Bill Tilden 140–1; Fred Perry 167; *see also* Jimmy Connors; *see also* John McEnroe; *see also* Ilie Năstase
Gem, Major Harry 11, 15–6
gender: administrative/leadership 13, 37–8, 107–8, 109, 247, 248–9, 289; artwork 19–20, 29, 111–12; decline in men's tennis 253–4; early tennis for women 12–13, 28–9, 33, 49, 62; eating disorders 261; feminism 31, 106–7, 247, 251, 254–61, 289; gender testing 258–9; gentlemanly conduct 8–10, 16, 20, 24–5, 27, 96; inter-war developments for women 106–9, 113; men's fashions 33, 112; modified rules for women 26, 28, 289; paternalism 36–7; patriarchal ideologies 29–31, 113, 248, 259, 289; playing styles/behaviour 24–5, 28, 34–6, 112–13, 251–4, 289; post-war disparities in talent development 248; prize money 247, 254–6, 289; social advances for women 30–3; suffrage movement 106; Suzanne Lenglen's influences 109–14; women's domesticity 30, 107–8, 249–51; women's appearance/sexual

objectification 30–4, 112, 250–3, 257–9, 261, 289; women's preference for doubles play 30–1; women's fashions 29, 31–4, 110–12, 252–3, 260–1, 289; *see also* homosexuality; *see also* Wightman Cup
Germany 82, 83, 153, 186, 259; anti-German racism 97; early tennis development 81; First World War 95–8; industrial advances 87, 223; Second World War 174; tennis governance 224; tennis successes 114, 291
Gibson, Althea 186, 251; racism 237–46
Glasgow 19, 125, 203
globalisation 74, 100, 135, 162, 189, 265, 296
golf 17, 48, 109, 141, 256; anti-Semitism 80, 244; British decline 94; professionalism 66, 151–2, 206; rivalry with lawn tennis 50; social similarities to lawn tennis 2, 10, 19, 20, 70; women's participation 30, 34
Gonzales, Pancho 214, 215, 216, 218, 225, 228
Gore, Spencer 10, 16, 25
Great Depression 124, 132, 163

Hardwick, Derek 225–8, 230
Hardwick, Mary 187, 201, 249, 253
Henman, Tim 1, 272, 294, 295; Henman Hill 295
Heyman, Allan 230, 233, 234
Hierons, Charles 64, 115, 153, 157
Hoad, Lew 202, 215–17, 218, 225
hockey 30, 31
homosexuality *147*, 247, 259, 289–90; gay/lesbian tennis clubs/associations 290; homophobia 257–60, 289–90
Hopman, Harry 201, 226
Hunt. Lamar 229–30
Hurlingham Club 183, 206, 252

ILTF: affiliation 98, 100–1; amateur rules 138, 142, 170, 172–3, 214, 219–21, 227–8, 233; British leadership 87, 294; early formation 87; Grand Prix 132, 229–30; lack of female representation 10–109, 248, 253, 256; open tournaments 154–6, 214, 219–34; public criticism 87, 98, 224–5; vs. IOC 98–100

India 13, 79, 96, 156; subcontinent 101, 223, 240
industrialisation 7, 21, 82, 87, 95, 177
Ireland 27, 28, 48, 58, 64, 96; development of tennis 69–71; GAA 70; ILTF matters 221, 227
Italy 82, 171, 186, 208; de Stefani, Giorgio 226, 227; early tennis development 71; Italian Championships 184, 186, 233; tennis governance 274, 277; tennis successes 114
ITF *see* ILTF

Japan 82, 100–1, 215
Jarrett, Andrew 270, 271
Jewish tennis players 80, 174, 238, 243–5, *246*, 293; Prenn, Daniel 174
Johnston, William "Little Bill" 94, 126, 139, 172
Jones (née Haydon), Ann 186, 255, 269, 278

Kasiri, Miles 2
King (née Moffitt), Billie Jean 226, 247, 251, 252, 255–7, 260
Knight, William "Billy" 186, 201
Kramer, Jack 214, 229; Kramer Cup 222; on women's tennis 248, 253, 255; professional player/promoter 215–18, 221; vs. amateur establishment 217, 222–3, 229; working with ATP 232–3; working with ILTF 229

Labour Party 7, 122, 167, 177; New Labour 281
Lacoste, René 117, 140, 159
Laver, Rod 201, 215, 225, 230
Lavery, John 19, 29, 112
Lawford, Herbert 27, 74
lawn tennis *see* tennis
Lawn Tennis Foundation 192, 203–4
Leamington LTC 15
Leeds 125, 127, 154, 202
Lenglen, Suzanne 34, 94, 114, 135; fashions 109–10; playing style 110, 112, 113; professional tour 143–6
Liberal Party 7, 21, 70, 83, 123, *132*
Liverpool 48, 58, 172; Liverpool Maccabi tennis club 244; parks tennis 61, 125
Lloyd, John 1, 258, 265, 270, 271
Lohden, Fred 123, 146, 162

London: centrism 57, 60, 61, 96; high season 48, 265; ILTF headquarters 87, 296; LTA headquarters 62, 70, 96; parks 61, 125; tennis clubs 42, 44, 46, 64, 119, 125, 155, 244, 290; tennis competitions 63, 253, 262

Lords Cricket Ground 2, 48, 265

LTA: affiliation of overseas clubs/associations 83, 86, 97; amateur rules 137–8, 142–3, 170, 172–4, 219–20; anti-commercialism 84–5, 132, 136–7; anti-professionalism 137–8, 144, 199–200, 218, 296; Conservative led 70; county associations 61–2; defining success 2, 284–5, 296; early formation 17, 57–68, 83; elitism 198–9; finances 100, 180–1, 272, 282; funding of players 219; global leadership 69, 83, 162, 296; imperialism 69, 78, 101; modernisation 279–82, 284; National Tennis Centre 3, 291; partnerships 132, 158, 197, 204–5, 279–84; public criticisms 62–3, 65–6, 174, 280, 284, 292; push for open tennis 223–7; relationship with AELTC/Wimbledon 83–4, 179–81, 205, 223–7; relationship with clubs 132, 181, 184–5, 281–3; relationship with coaches 63–5, 150–60, 296; sanctioned international tours 66–7, 104, 162, 165, 168, 179–81, 186, 201, 208; white-dominated 294; *see also* talent development

LTA Trust 262, 280, *285*

LTAA 201, 216, 221, 222, 224, 226, 232

McEnroe, John 231, 266, 284, *285*; at Wimbledon 260, 272–7

McKane (née Godfree), Kathleen "Kitty" 114

Mahony, Harold S. 26, *68*, 69, 76

management groups 205, 234, 261

Manchester 48, 58, 84, 115, 154, 244, 290; Manchester Maccabi tennis club 244; parks tennis 61, 62, 125, 202

Marble, Alice 111, 238, 245

Marshall, Julian 16, 57–60

Maskell, Dan 146, 157, 159, 160, 199–201, 267; at Queen's Club 152; at the AELTC 153; Davis Cup coach 165; publicly celebrated 152–3; working with Fred Perry 197–8

MCC 15–19, 45, 57, 58

media 5, 59, 102, 132, 266, 277, 280, 284; American players 135, 273; British players 271–2; developments 134–6; femininity 114, 239, 248–50, 252, 257, 261, 289; gender disparities 249–50, 257, 289; masculinity 260–1; narratives of Virginia Wade 267–9; political propaganda 237; professional tennis 64, 141, 147, 155–7, 213, 217; race/ethnicity 239–40, 243; relationship with AELTC 278–9; tennis celebrities 135, 139, 144

middle class: anti-commercialism 21, 84; behavioural etiquette 97, 128–30; factions 10–11, 20, 50; historical emergence 8–9; homophobia 290; race/ethnicity 239–45; sporting philosophy 8–9, 55, 270, 276–7, 292–3; social aspirations 16–17, 21, 41, 44–5; societal shifts 119, 124, 182, 196, 209–10, 250, 272, 276; tennis crowds 166, 210, 242–3, 293, 295; tennis dominance 4, 15, 20, 41–2, 57, 66, 68, 198, 235, 279, 292; values 10, 65, 209–10, 245; women's sport 31–3, 106, 112–13, 289; working-class sympathies 21, 61, 122–3, 195; *see also* tennis clubs, social exclusivity

Mills, Alan, 2, 198, 200, 274, 275

MIPTC 233–4

mixed doubles tennis 29, 60, 271; gender relations 19, 29, 34–6, 112–14

Monckton, H.H. 141, 142, 147, 154, 173

Moran, Gertrude "Gussy" 252–3

Mortimer, Angela 186, 244, 252, 269

Mottram, A.J. "Tony" 183

Mottram, Christopher "Buster" 1, 270

Murray, Andy 1, 2, 284, 291–2, 295–6

Murray, Jamie 284

muscular Christianity 9

Năstase, Ilie 242, 260, 274

nationalism 4, 45, 97, 262, 266–9, 288, 294–5; *see also* Britain; *see also* LTA, imperialism

Navratilova, Martina 256, 260, 278, 289
New Zealand 78, 81, 83, 101, 216, 233; early tennis development 71–2
Northern LTA 13, 45, 48, 58, 60
Northern LTC 48, 193, 231
National Tennis League 229
Nuttall, Betty 114

Olympics: 1908 London Games 82; 1912 Stockholm Games 83, 85, 86; 1952 Helsinki Games 187; 2012 London Games 2; IOC 86, 95, 97, 142, 206, 259; IOC vs. ILTF 98–100
open tennis 3, 155–6, 175, 220–7, 255; early sanctioned open events 65, 153–5, 225; *see also* ILTF, open tournaments
Osterberg, Madame Bergman 31
Oxford University 8, 31, 43, 45, 49, 60, 74, 93, 157; LTA representation 63; lawn tennis club 50

Palmer, Archdale 84, 92
Penman, Derek 225–7, 230, 279
Perera, Juan Batista Augurio 15, 16
Perry, Fred 1, 3, 88, 145, 153, 162; BBC commentator 261; British tennis hero 295; LTA employment 197; poor treatment by British tennis establishment 166–7, 245, 290–1; professional tour 171–2, 215; social background 162, 167–8, 197; successes 160, 162, 165–6; turning professional 156, 162, 169, 170–1; vs. LTA 143; working-class role model 158, 290
Petchey, Mark 270, 271
Pilic, Nikki 232–4
Pim, Joshua 27, 69, 75, 76
polo 17, 18
pot-hunting 52–5, 66, 132
professional tours: amateur defections 138–9, 147, 216; in Britain 146, 172; inter-war 143–7, 150, 155, 162, 169, 171–2; post-war 213, 215–8; promoters 141, 143, 155, 214–6; 220–1, 228–9, 248, 256; public stigma 213, 217, 227
Protestantism 9, 70, 96, 235
public schools 8, 9, 18, 43, 115, 158, 195, 197; Eton 10, 60, 67; for girls 31; Harrow 10, 45, 60, 123; interest in tennis 88, 123, 196; old-boys 123, 199; rejection of tennis 10, 67, 123; Westminster 10

Queen's Club 64, 115, 244, 253; children's membership 191; coaches 64, 152–3; Covered Court Championships 205, 207; during World War II 178; exclusion of women 13; grass-court tournament 233; LTA headquarters 279–80; open tennis 227; professional competitions 154–5

racquets 13–17
race and ethnicity: American civil rights movement 237–43; links with gender 237, 239–40, 244–5; links with social class 81, 240–1, 242; racism toward non-whites 4, 79–81, 237–46, 293–4; whiteness 79; *see also* Britain; *see also* Jewish tennis players; *see also* South Africa, racism
Real Tennis 13–17
Renshaw, Ernest 10, 17, 26, 27, 33, 45, 53, 54, 57, 71, 74
Renshaw, William 10, 17, 26, 27, 33, 45, 53, 54, 57, 71, 74
Richards, Renée 258–9
Richards, Vincent 94, 154, 178; professional tours 143–7, 155
Riggs, Bobby 213, 215, 247, 256, 257
Roper Barrett, Herbert 75, 77, 126, 152, 169
Rosewall, Ken 188, 215, 225, 228, 230
Round, Dorothy 111, 160, 186
rowing 2, 30, 53, 83, 94, 137, 163; Henley Regatta 48, 265
Royal Ascot 46, 48, 265
royalty/nobility 4, 8, 17, 45–6, 128, 275, 279; King Edward VII 45, 46; King George V 46, 93, 174; Queen Elizabeth II 240, 265, 267–9; Queen Mary 46, 178, 267; Queen Victoria 12, 45, 71
rugby union 9, 13, 67, 123; British decline 83, 94; development abroad 73, 74; GAA restrictions 70; gender distinctions 34; professionalism 53; social comparisons to lawn tennis 2, 12, 34; sportsmanship 25
Rusedski, Greg 272, 294–5

Sabelli, H.A. 107, 158, 200
Sangster, Mike 1, 197, 201, 226

Sapsford, Danny 271
Scotland 58, 67, 125, 197, 268; children's tennis 118; early rivalry with golf 50; early tennis development 46, 62, 69; LTA administrative matters 96; Murray brothers 284, 295; *see also* Britain
Scrivener, Harry S. 60, 141
Scrivener, Margaret "Peggie" 160
Second World War 175, 177–9; gender relations 249; professional tennis 215
Segura, Pancho 215–16
shamateurism 135–6, 155, 172–3, 183–4; early development 54–5; LTA culpability 66–7, 85, 136, 165; post-war escalation 213–4, 219–21, 226–7, 248
Sheffield 61, 118, 125, 202
Slazenger 33, 84–5, 275, 278
social class: club member hierarchy 10, 72, 128, 151–3, 193–5; democratisation of tennis 51, 88, 93, 119, 122–3, 127–8, 182, 196–8, 210, 272, 290; social exclusivity 10, 14–21, 71, 180, 210, 275, 278–9, 283, 292; tennis as a status symbol 12–15, 20, 41, 128–9, 194–5, 265, 294–5; *see also* middle class; *see also* upper class; *see also* working class
Social Darwinism 31, 37, 81
South Africa 101, 168, 183, 219, 227, 268, 284; racism 73, 81, 243
Sphairistiké 13, 16; *see also* Major Walter Clopton Wingfield; *see also* tennis
sponsorship 65, 216, 225, 277–8, 285, 294; British tournaments 204–7, 231, 253, 278; women's tennis 247, 253, 255–6, 260–1, 289
sport development 203, 281; club developments 281–3; government alignment 203–4; National Lottery funding 280; UK Sports Council 203, 281
Stammers, Kay 160, 186, 244
Sweden 71, 227, 280, 291
Switzerland 83, 100, 227

talent development 4, 137, 158, 197, 204, 280; academies 202, 280; clubs 118–19, 132, 191–2, 196, 279, 282–4; criticisms of British methods 77, 88, 115–18, 123, 196, 198–9, 280, 291–3; early post-war efforts 178–81, 185, 189, 191; geographical variations 61; increasing role of coaches 63–5, 150–4, 196; parks 126; schools 67–8, 123, 158, 189, 196, 204
Taylor, Roger 1, 197
technology 52, 196; for Britain 52, 87, 96, 118, 124, 196; for tennis 14–15, 279
television 205–8, 225, 234, 277–80; *see also* BBC
Templewood, 1st Viscount Samuel Hoare 169, 170, 175, 180, 186, 188, 197, 200, 207, 218, 248
tennis: artwork 19–20, 29, 131–2; diplomatic/political tool 73–4, 163; garden parties 2, 12, 19, 20, 29, 30; inter-club competitions 62, 63, 129, 131; invention 13–16; noble heritage 14, 17; parks 61–2, 123–7, 198, 202–3, 291; player associations/unions 215, 223, 232–4, 256; recreational vs. competitive 131–2, 193–4; scoring 14, 16, 17; Sunday play 42, 124, 126; weather 18–20
tennis clubs: amateurism 42; coaches 63–5, 151–3, 200; dress codes 130, 282; early development 41–51; etiquette 128–9; facilities 127, 192, 283; finances 163–4, 181–5, 203, 282–3; gender discrimination 28–9, 37–8, 249; in workplaces 125, 127; inter-club matches 62–3, 108, 123, 129, 130–1, 179; LTA affiliation 41, 62, 124–5, 179, 182, 185, 189, 196, 281–3; patronage 14, 17, 20, 37, 44–7, 128, 194–5, 266; playing-in tests 129, 193, 282; post-war recovery 178; racism 73, 80, 81, 238–9, 244, 293; resistance to LTA 132, 184–5, 281–2, 291; social exclusivity 43–4, 51–2, 69, 72, 127–30, 192–5, 283, 291–3; status distinctions 46–51, 125, 130–1, 136, 193–4, 202–3, 292
Thatcher, Margaret 223, 243, 273, 283
Tilden, William "Big Bill" 94, 135, 178; amateurism issues 138–43; professional tours 146, 169, 171–2
Tingay, Lance: LTA contribution scheme 185; open tennis 221, 224–5, 228, 253, 254; player restrictions 232; sponsorship 204, 206; talent development 218; tennis clubs 192, 193; tournaments 182–4, 205
Tinling, Ted 252, 257, 259

Torquay 19, 54
tournaments: commercialism 52–3, 65, 135–6, 141, 145, 164, 182–4, 204–7; early growth 47–9, 52–5; European development 71, 86, 94, 183–4, 205, 219, 231; financial struggles 50–1, 164, 178–9, 181–4, 204–6, 231; post-war recovery 178, 182; shamateurism 85, 135–6, 183–4, 213, 219, 226
Truman, Christine 186, 251

upper class: early influences 14–17, 20, 27, 44–6, 57; historical decline 7–9, 83, 195; middle-class relations 8; patronage 20, 37, 42, 44–7, 128, 170–1, 194–5, 266, 279; sporting philosophy 9–10, 27, 44, 54, 74
US 2, 37, 154, 168, 171, 237; administrative/political relations with Britain 101–2, 221–9, 273; developments for women 247–8, 255–7; early sporting competitions vs. Britain 74–7, 81–3, 114; nationalism 83; parks 126, 202; racial discrimination 237–9, 241–2, 293; sports media/reporting 135; successes 76–7, 81–3, 94, 139, 185–6, 269; talent development 67, 81, 88, 95, 115, 117, 187, 201
US National Championships/US Open 76, 147, 172, 179, 213, 234, 237, 256; British avoidance 75; fashions 111–12; Forest Hills 99, 155, 215, 269, 277; Flushing Meadows 277–8; rule changes 103
USLTA 76, 147, 216, 232; amateur rules 85, 138–41, 155; anti-commercialism 155; anti-professionalism 155; early formation 74; ILTF member 87, 95, 101–2; open tennis 155–6, 170, 224; player behaviour 208–9; playing through 103; racism 238–9; shamateurism 136; talent development 117; vs. Bill Tilden 139–41; vs. touring professionals 213, 217, 221; women's tennis 28, 255, 256
USTA *see* USLTA

Vines, Ellsworth 126, 146, 171, 172
Virginia Slims tour 247, 255–7

voluntarism 4, 94, 281; associations/clubs 41–5, 192, 194–5, 283

Wade, Virginia 108, 186, 252, 284, 295; Wimbledon success 265, 267–9
Wales 58, 194, 204, 231, 268; early tennis development 62, 69
Wallis Myers, A. 33, 54, 79, 139, 141, 142, 169
Walsh, J.H. 16, 141
Watson, Maud 33
World Championship Tennis 229–30
welfarism 177, 181, 191, 195, 196, 262, 283; vs. individualism 209, 273
Wembley stadium 2, 146, 172
wheelchair tennis 261–2
Wightman, Hazel 108, 186, 252
Wightman Cup 107–9, 114, 185, 196, 244; British defeats 185–6; British successes 114, 186, 269; male captains 107
Wilding, Anthony 64, 72, 78, 79, 92, 103
Wilkinson, Chris 270–1
Williams, Serena 251, 261, 292
Wills, Helen 111, 114, 129, 135–6, 145
Wilson, Robert "Bobby" 186, 201
Wimbledon 2, 36, 44, 51, 87, 147, 171, 235, 295; a British institution 266–7, 294; amateur rules 173–4; boycotts 3, 230, 232–4; branding 265, 277–9; British decline 114–15, 269–72; British success 160, 165–6, 186, 267–9; commercialism 84, 103–4, 163, 179, 208, 266, 277–8, 296; early foreign competitors 52, 75, 77, 78, 92, 94; fashions 110–11, 252, 258, 260, 261; finances 3, 51, 83, 102, 163, 179–80, 201, 205, 207–8, 272; funding players 136, 173–4; international prestige 3, 17, 48, 123, 162, 189, 294, 296; inter-war developments 102–4; media 134–5, 207–8, 225, 234; of 1877 16; of 1895 51; of 1948 208; of 1954 188–9; of 1965 254; of 1968 3, 255; of 1972 230; of 1973 3, 232–4; of 1975 242–3; of 1977 267–9; of 1983 274–5, 285; of 2013 1, 284; open tennis 224–7; playing through 102–3; public criticisms 59–61, 280; qualification 103; racism 239–41; relations with the LTA 83, 205; royal patronage 45–6, 266, 279;

Wimbledon (*cont.*)
  seeding 103; shamateurism 136; sponsorship 278; ticket allocation 48, 103, 125, 181–2, 199, 278; ticket prices 180; vs. professional tour 215–6; wildcards 270–1, *285*, 292; *see also* AELTC
Wingfield, Major Walter Clopton 11, 13–17
WITF 256

working class: coaches 64, 151–3, 157; enhanced access to tennis 122–4, 235, 290; exclusion 43, 290; narratives of Fred Perry 158, 168, 290; narratives of John McEnroe 276; poverty 18; racism 238, 240, 243; sporting philosophy 54, 296; talent development 202, 292–3
World Team Tennis 234
WTA 237, 247, 256, 259, 261